D1713884

The Border That Joins

Maryland Studies in
Public Philosophy

Edited by the Director of
The Center for Philosophy and Public Policy

The Border That Joins

MEXICAN MIGRANTS AND U. S. RESPONSIBILITY

Edited by
Peter G. Brown
and
Henry Shue

Rowman & Allanheld
PUBLISHERS

325.272
B728b

ROWMAN & ALLANHELD PUBLISHERS

Copyright © 1983 in this collection by Rowman and Littlefield

First published in the United States 1983 by Rowman and Littlefield, 81 Adams Drive, Totowa, New Jersey 07512.

Library of Congress Cataloging in Publication Data
Main entry under title:

The Border that joins.

(Maryland studies in public philosophy)
Includes bibliographical references and index.
1. United States—Emigration and immigration —Addresses, essays, lectures. 2. Mexico— Emigration and immigration—Addresses, essays, lectures. 3. Alien labor, Mexican—United States—Addresses, essays, lectures.
4. Mexicans—Employment—United States— Addresses, essays, lectures. I. Brown, Peter G. II. Shue, Henry. III. Series.
JV6794.B67   325'.272'0973   82-7526
ISBN 0-8476-7072-4   AACR2
ISBN 0-8476-7206-9 (pbk.)

84 85 86 87 10 9 8 7 6 5 4 3 2

Printed in the United States of America

Contents

Tables and Figures

Preface

The Center for Philosophy and Public Policy, an interdisciplinary research program on the Washington metropolitan area campus of the University of Maryland at College Park, was founded in 1976 to focus on the values and concepts that underlie public policy. Most other research into public policy is empirical: it assesses costs, describes constituencies, and makes predictions. The Center's research is conceptual and normative: it investigates the structure of arguments and the nature of values relevant to the formation, justification, and criticism of public policy. The Center explores these questions through its research and publications, including its quarterly newsletter, QQ, and in its development of teaching materials, most recently in a series of model syllabi available as Maryland Courses in Public Philosophy.

This is the third volume of Maryland Studies in Public Philosophy. The first, *Income Support: Conceptual and Policy Issues*, edited by Peter G. Brown, Conrad Johnson, and Paul Vernier, dealt with issues that arise in the design of the welfare system. *Boundaries: National Autonomy and Its Limits*, edited by Peter G. Brown and Henry Shue, considered differences between the individual's responsibilities to fellow citizens and to noncitizens, including questions that underlie some of the discussions in this book. The fourth volume of Maryland Studies will be *Energy and the Future*, to be edited by Douglas MacLean and Peter G. Brown, which will examine issues about the effects of current energy policies on the quality of life available for future generations. Each volume of Maryland Studies in Public Philosophy is designed to allow the discussion of concrete policy choices and the discussion of general philosophical issues to enrich each other.

This volume evolved from discussions sponsored by the Center for Philosophy and Public Policy, primarily in the form of sessions of a Center Working Group on Mexican Migrants and U.S. Responsibility. Financial support for the working group was provided by the International Relations Division of the Rockefeller Foundation and the Mexico City office of the Ford Foundation. General support for the Center is provided by the University of Maryland and the Rockefeller Brothers Fund. Each chapter was written specifically for this volume. The views expressed are those of the individual contributors and do not represent the views of other contributors, the Center, or the sources of the Center's funds.

ix

These chapters and the arrangements for the sessions of the working group from which they grew benefited as well from the work and thought of many hands and heads at the Center. We would like to thank Elizabeth Cahoon, Louise Collins, Carroll Linkins, Rachel Sailer, Robin Sheets, and Virginia Smith, each of whom left her mark on the quality of both process and outcome. Special thanks go to the Center's editor, Claudia Mills, who prepared both the introduction and the index, and guided the entire manuscript through all its stages.

P. G. B.

H. S.

Introduction

Hundreds of thousands of Mexican citizens now travel illegally back and forth across the 1,945–mile border stretching from the Pacific Ocean to the Gulf of Mexico, leaving home to seek work. The U.S. response to these workers is taking on increasing importance for both national governments and, of course, for the Mexican workers themselves and those elements of American society that may resist or welcome their coming.

One of the most prominent suggestions for a U.S. response to the current illegal flow is to legalize and regulate it through the creation of a new temporary worker program. The Reagan administration's immigration proposals include establishment of an experimental foreign worker program, and such a program has historic precedents. From 1942 to 1964 the United States and Mexico maintained a formal temporary worker program, which brought millions of Mexicans to work in American industry and agriculture, and Western Europe has had extensive experience with guestworker programs that many observers believe to be a successful solution to international labor problems. The creation of any temporary worker program, however, raises controversial and complicated questions, both factual and philosophical, which this volume is designed to address.

Are temporary worker programs desirable or feasible? How many workers should be permitted to come, and for how long? What benefits and protections should temporary workers be granted? What corresponding obligations should they incur?

These questions can be answered only against the background of a careful look at conditions in the United States and Mexico to determine what policy is indeed in the interests of each country. Also required is a look at the more conceptual and theoretical issues of how to weigh one national interest against another, in cases where the two conflict, and indeed how to weigh and aggregate different elements of each national interest. What are the extents and limits of international obligation? What role do human rights play in setting foreign and domestic policy? The answers to these questions determine in large part our assessment of any proposed immigration program.

The National Interest

When U.S. policymakers debate the merits and demerits of a temporary foreign worker program, should they look beyond what course of action would best

1

further American interests, the interests of their own fellow-citizens and constituents? What reasons could they have for actively pursuing policies that would work to the advantage of some other nation?

It is indeed a widespread view that U.S. policymakers are charged only with protecting the interests of U.S. citizens, that they would in fact violate their mandate by designing policies advantageous to foreign interests. Nations, it is thought, at best owe to other nations duties of noninterference, i.e., respect for their territorial sovereignty and national autonomy. These duties fulfilled, they may pursue their own national interest unchecked.

CONSTRAINTS FROM INTERDEPENDENCE

In her chapter, Judith Lichtenberg disputes the standard view that nations have such limited international duties. In her view, nations also have positive duties to promote each other's interests, duties to offer help as well as to refrain from harm. These obligations arise historically, growing out of a wide range of past relationships. A owes something to B if A does harm to B, but A also owes something to B if A and B are friends, neighbors, or economic partners.

The standard view that Lichtenberg criticizes rests on an "obsolete picture . . . of nations as virtually closed systems in which what goes on inside has no significant ramifications outside—where effects of actions stop at the border." This picture profoundly misrepresents today's increasingly interdependent world, in which a vast web of political, economic, and technological links mean that "what happens within national boundaries has morally relevant consequences for those outside."

Even less does such a picture describe the close relations binding the United States and Mexico: geographical contiguity, a long shared history, and a host of intricate economic relations, including the legacy of bilateral government-sponsored migration programs. Furthermore, insofar as Mexican migration is caused by U.S. fostered and encouraged policies of agricultural and industrial development, the United States bears responsibility on those grounds alone to consider Mexico's interests in formulating immigration strategy. Interdependence constrains the pursuit of national interest.

In any case, Lichtenberg makes clear that the national interest is far less straightforward than it might seem. "In most cases there is not a single interest common to all a nation's members, but instead a diversity and often a conflict of interests." Temporary foreign worker programs may be in the interests of American business and consumers, but against the interests of America's least-advantaged workers. They may serve the interests of those who migrate, but thwart the interests of those who stay behind. Are such programs in the national interest of either country?

Lichtenberg suggests that the national interest overall can be determined by a weighted aggregation of all the different and perhaps competing interests of relevant groups and individuals—weighted, because not all interests are equally important or worthy of consideration. In particular, those interests that involve claims of *rights* are especially weighty. Thus, if American workers have a *right* to some decent means of livelihood, then their interest in keeping their jobs would weigh more heavily than the interest, say, of American consumers in paying a few cents less for a head of lettuce picked at lower wages by migrant labor. In their chapters, Edwin Reubens and Vernon Briggs debate the impact of imported labor on the welfare of domestic workers.

RIGHTS AS CONSTRAINTS

Lichtenberg argues that pursuit of the national interest must be constrained by duties arising out of international interdependence. If choosing to have a temporary worker program has ramifications for Mexico, the United States must consider those ramifications in making its choice. In his chapter, James Nickel appeals to a different kind of constraint: international human rights. Any temporary worker program must be designed to respect and uphold the human rights of those participating in it. These rights include rights to due process, rights to personal security and autonomy, rights to political participation, rights to equality, and economic and social rights.

Human rights, by their very nature, are not mere goals or aspirations—they generate obligations on the part of individuals and governments to respect and uphold them. Nickel argues against the view that governments have obligations to respect and uphold only the rights of their own citizens, obligations that grow out of a special contract or agreement between citizens and their state. Such contractarian positions would lead to the implausible conclusion that a government would do no wrong in killing an alien in its territory, or refusing to prevent such a killing.

On Nickel's view, "Human rights flow from one's humanity, not from one's citizenship status." Thus "states have the same prima facie obligations to respect and uphold the human rights of aliens in their territories that they have to uphold the rights of their citizens." Such rights might be overridden during dire threats to national security, but it is the mark of human rights that they may not be set aside lightly. If the United States admits foreign nationals to work in its farms and factories, it must do so in full willingness to take responsibility for their rights as human beings.

Nickel considers two controversial kinds of rights that governments might not be willing to accord temporary workers: rights to political participation and to economic welfare. He agrees that it may be permissible to deny some political rights to aliens of brief residence—for example, the right to vote on international issues on which their native country's interest is pitted against the host country's. But governments may not refuse to grant economic rights to alien workers. Given that "rights to the minimal requirements of survival and a decent life are grounded, like other rights, in considerations of human dignity, autonomy, and welfare, then these rights are possessed independently of whether one is a native or an alien." Any temporary worker program, on Nickel's view, must see that such rights are duly protected.

Learning From the Past

In trying to formulate an immigration policy to serve the interests of both the United States and Mexico, current policymakers have ample experience to draw from. Each nation has struggled to achieve a mutually beneficial immigration policy for the better part of this century, and highly acclaimed guestworker exchanges have been worked out in considerable detail in Western Europe. Most policies now proposed for regulating and legalizing migration have been tried to some extent earlier or elsewhere, with varying degrees of success.

THE BRACERO PROGRAM

The chapter by Manuel García y Griego traces a close chronological history of Mexican-American labor and migration policies through this century, with special attention to the *bracero,* or Mexican contract labor, program, under which Mexicans were sent to work in certain agricultural areas of the United States during the 1940s and 1950s as a result of bilateral agreements between the two governments. Created in 1942 to meet perceived wartime labor shortages, the program remained in operation for 22 years; at its peak in the late 1950s, over 400,000 Mexicans were employed in U.S. agriculture and industry.

The story of the bracero program is the story of a continual tug-of-war between changing U.S. and Mexican interests. At some points, when demand for inexpensive labor was keen, the United States strongly supported a temporary worker agreement, while Mexico expressed serious reservations about the exploitation of its workers and the draining of its domestic labor supply. At other points, Mexico sought to continue the program as a safety valve for skyrocketing unemployment and a curb on illegal immigration, while adversely affected U.S. workers fought for its demise. This see-saw of interests continued for the duration of the program, with the shifting interests of both governments seldom coinciding. At the height of tensions in 1954, an alert newsman photographed a bracero being pulled in a literal tug-of-war between a Mexican and a U.S. border official.

Although Mexico held the upper hand in negotiations to initiate the bracero program in the early 1940s, Mexican dominance proved short-lived. From García's history emerges a portrait of the United States manipulating Mexico for its own interests—actively recruiting Mexican labor during times of boom, and rounding up and deporting Mexican labor in times of bust—usually with little regard to the effects of such recruitment and deportation on the Mexican workers or the economy they left behind. If Lichtenberg's arguments are correct, any new proposed temporary worker program will have to arise out of a genuine regard for the shared interests of both nations. And if Nickel's arguments are correct, programs will have to be designed to avoid many of the abuses to Mexican workers chronicled in García's account—abuses that hastened the earlier program's termination.

THE EUROPEAN GUESTWORKER EXPERIENCE

W. R. Böhning, in his chapter, examines Western Europe's experience with guestworker programs to uncover possible lessons for the United States and Mexico; for France, Switzerland, and the Federal Republic of Germany have for many years formally recruited temporary labor from their poorer neighbors. He notes, however, that the hallmark of the European experience is guestworker, rather than temporary worker, programs: temporary worker programs recruit workers for a stated, limited period of time and imply voluntary or coerced exit when that time is up: guestworkers, while subject to some occupational restrictions, are allowed to stay as long as they wish; they are not forced out at the close of a specified period. Guestworker programs, in Böhning's view, are politically and morally preferable, but they carry with them the danger that guests will overstay their welcome.

In comparing the Western European experience to the American one, Böhning analyzes the causes of migration and dismisses the assumption that migration in Europe is determined by labor demand, while here it is determined by labor supply. Both factors play a crucial role. On his analogy, in today's world the pipe is full of potential migrants, who migrate in fact when host countries turn the tap, thereby ensuring the flow. Thus, migration between the United States and Mexico must be understood in terms of both push and pull factors: rural unemployment in Mexico and the lure of higher wages across the border.

Böhning devotes much of his discussion to a careful examination of factors that cause migrants to return home or to stay on in the host country, for presumably the United States is genuinely interested in importing temporary labor. (In his chapter, Reubens compares the advantages of temporary worker programs with enlarged quotas for permanent immigration.) His conclusions are not encouraging. It is extremely difficult to predict "temporariness": neither migrants' stated intentions, nor the presence or absence of accompanying family members, nor such factors as marital status and rural origin explain the propensity to leave or stay. Nationality correlates more positively (nine out of ten Italians return home from Germany, but only three out of ten Turks do), but the implications of this correlation for Mexican migration to the United States are not clear. Böhning's cautious lesson: "The United States should accept high or low temporariness rather than try to manipulate it." If truly temporary programs are in the Mexican and U.S. interest, there is little guarantee that this interest can be safeguarded.

The Mexican Interest

García's and Böhning's chapters highlight some of the difficulties in negotiating immigration and labor programs that steer between competing and conflicting national interests, or national interests whose fulfillment is highly doubtful. We must now look more closely at the relevant national interests in the debate over temporary worker programs between the United States and Mexico.

Why do Mexican workers by the hundreds of thousands stream across the border? What macro- and micro-level push factors on the Mexican side of the border encourage Mexican migration? Is it indeed in the Mexican national interest that Mexican workers continue to migrate?

THE CRISIS OF RURAL DEVELOPMENT

August Schumacher's chapter surveys the devastating effects of postwar agricultural development policies in Mexico, policies largely responsible for the current Mexican exodus. Following the Cárdenas presidency (1934–1940), Mexico embarked on a bi-modal agricultural policy of making heavy government investment in irrigated, commercial agriculture, while providing minimum support to the majority of Mexico's farmers in rain-fed areas. This bi-modal policy achieved a high rate of agricultural output, but at the cost of extensive levels of rural unemployment: 81 percent of Mexico's food was produced by only 3.3 percent of its farmers. By the mid-1960s, 35 to 45 percent of the total workforce in rural Mexico was underemployed. Thus Lichtenberg's disection of "the national interest" again becomes relevant, for development strategies in the interests of large commercial growers may not be in the interests of smallholding farmers and their families.

Since 1973, however, substantial federal funding has been directed toward creating a large, geographically dispersed, labor-intensive rural works program, redirecting government attention and resources toward rain-fed, smallholding agriculture. Schumacher outlines several of the principal programs and agencies created under this new uni-modal strategy, including PIDER (Integrated Rural Development Program, designed to channel federal funds to small projects in villages in the poorest regions of the country); CUC (Coordinated Development Agreement, designed as a form of revenue sharing for small public works); COPLAMAR (Coordinating Program for Marginal Zones, designed to coordinate the many agencies involved in improving living conditions in the most marginal areas of Mexico); the Rainfed Districts Program (designed to promote rainfed agriculture); and SAM (the Mexican Food System, designed to work toward self-sufficiency in maize and beans and to reverse declining nutritional standards for poor Mexicans).

Schumacher is encouraged by the success of these programs as a stop-gap measure until small-scale agriculture in Mexico can be revitalized and made self-sufficient. But he notes that uni-modal development policies require a heavy outlay of funds and a time span of decades to achieve relatively modest results. A federal investment allocation of even 25 percent of the total investment budget may not be sufficient for even a moderate impact on food output and permanent job creation. Thus, even such a dramatic reversal in development policy will do little in this century to decrease the surplus supply of Mexican labor.

RURAL DEVELOPMENT AND MIGRATION

Lourdes Arizpe analyzes the evolving pattern and cycles of Mexican migration as they have been influenced by the crisis of smallholding, rain-fed agriculture over the past decades. She argues, however, that migration must be understood at two levels of analysis. It is not enough to explain the processes of urbanization and industrialization that transform a peasant economy into a market economy. It is necessary as well to examine the social structure of rural towns and villages, to look at the consequences of macro-agricultural policies on families and communities, on the passing of a rural way of life. Only at this second level of analysis can one explain why some rural inhabitants stay on while others migrate, and why some migrate internally to Mexican cities while others cross the border to seek work in the United States.

Arizpe's own fieldwork shows that "the social and political structure of a town or community will soften or sharpen the negative aspects of integration into the market economy." In some villages, a cash-crop encourages migration, by centralizing land and capital. In others, a cash-crop deters migration, by enabling peasant families to obtain much-needed cash locally and by stabilizing seasonal fluctuations of employment. Communities that have found ways to diversify their sources of income through crafts, cottage industries, and local wage labor have been able to maintain a viable economy based on rain-fed agriculture. But communities in which local sources of income have disappeared contribute many migrants to swell the tide.

The bulk of Mexican migrants coming to the United States, Arizpe finds, are small landholders from rain-fed regions that have no longer been able to maintain economic viability. The poorest, landless people tend to stay on in rural areas or to migrate within Mexico. American-bound migrants are principally adult men attracted by the higher wages across the border. In determining which migrants actually cross the border, pull factors override push factors.

This means, for Arizpe, that the United States "is not bearing the brunt of the rural crisis in Mexico," since it is receiving the most able-bodied and enterprising migrants, migrants who have been fed, clothed, and educated by already weakened Mexican communities. She deplores the current unequal exchange of benefits between the two nations: "It is unacceptable that Mexican rural households should provide nursery, social security, and unemployment services for workers in U.S. jobs—workers who can be sent back in periods of economic recession, overburdening an already burdened Mexican rural economy." The movement of migrants between Mexico and the United States can benefit both partners—but only under a policy "that gives proper acknowledgment to both partners' needs and benefits."

The American Interest

Would a temporary foreign worker program be in the American interest? Clearly, legal and illegal Mexican migrants would not continue to come if they were not responding to some strong demand, but in what segments of society is this demand felt? Foreign labor is attractive to American business and industry for any number of alleged reasons: because foreign workers are cheaper, more reliable and industrious, harder to unionize, easier to exploit. Foreign labor is attractive to American consumers who are battered by losing battles against spiraling costs for goods and services. But are American workers—and particularly America's lowest-paid and least-skilled workers—victims of corporate and consumer interests they do not share? The chapters by Briggs and Reubens debate the impact of Mexican workers on American domestic labor. Reubens argues that any effects are negligible or positive; Briggs argues that proposed temporary foreign worker programs can only cause the position of American workers to deteriorate.

Reubens argues that alien workers to a marked degree do not compete with American workers. Aliens are concentrated in unskilled or semi-skilled occupations, with wages at the bottom of the American payscale. Such jobs have proved unattractive to American workers, who had been abandoning them in great haste long before illegal migrants came to take their places. Reubens quotes a New York Department of Agriculture official as stating: "It's a fact of life that New Yorkers don't want to pick apples!" Low-skilled, low-paid jobs have few attractions even to unemployed American workers, who frequently turn to other means of support, such as unemployment compensation or food stamps. Claims Reubens, "Insofar as alien workers seek jobs of the low-level kind that native workers despise and avoid, the former are not competing with the latter and do not displace them."

On Reubens's view, alien workers make a positive contribution to the American economy that benefits all segments of the population. Many small-scale, low-profit industries and businesses rely on alien labor for financial survival, and thus alien workers may actually create jobs for other Americans. In the South and Southwest, where huge inflows of illegal workers are concentrated, employment is booming vigorously. Legal immigrants, and many illegal immigrants as well, pay taxes, while making few demands on social services. Reubens dismisses much antagonism to alien workers as grounded in myth and xenophobia.

Briggs disagrees. Citing American unemployment figures that are among the highest for any Western industrialized country, he protests that there is no demonstrated need for foreign workers in the American economy: "There is no evidence at all that citizen workers will not do the work that illegal immigrants now do." It is not any given type of work that citizen workers shun, but the prevailing wage rates and associated working conditions.

On Briggs's view, the adverse effects of illegal and legal aliens is disproportionately felt in the low-wage labor markets of the United States. The unskilled and semi-skilled occupations taken by aliens are precisely those in which our most disadvantaged workers are found. Briggs points to employment curves that show considerable overlap in occupational patterns between Chicano citizens and Mexican aliens. A temporary worker program "would adversely affect job and income opportunities for many Americans who have the least capability for defending themselves from their competition. . . . It is because it is a program that may benefit the privileged, but will adversely affect opportunities for the less fortunate in American society, that such proposals are put forth."

Reubens proposes his own temporary foreign worker program, with the following features: several hundred thousand foreign workers would be admitted annually, on limited-time visas (mostly for three years); the visa would specify authorized occupations and locations, by broad category of occupation and by region of the US; workers' dependents would not be authorized for admission; the number of visas issued could be put on a sliding scale for greater sensitivity to changing economic conditions in both countries. Reubens believes that his program could largely replace the current volume of illegal immigration. Briggs replies that such a program would only increase illegal immigration by exposing still more foreign workers to the economic attractions of the American labor market. (In his chapter, García shows that the bracero program alternately stimulated and substituted for the illegal flow.)

It is clear that any temporary worker program must be evaluated against the kind of historical background García and Böhning provide, against the Mexican needs and interests discussed by Schumacher and Arizpe, against Nickel's human rights standards, and against Briggs's charge of adverse labor market impact. Throughout all eight chapters in this book runs a common theme: the need for Mexico and the United States to sit down together to determine the best policy for regulating the flow of persons across the border that joins them.

PART I

Philosophical Frameworks

1

Mexican Migration and U.S. Policy: A Guide for the Perplexed

JUDITH LICHTENBERG

I

What kind of policy should the United States adopt concerning Mexican workers in its territory? Let us ascend to the next level and ask: What kind of question is this? What does one need to know to answer this question adequately? What do philosophers have to contribute to such an inquiry?

Our initial question is a practical one. An answer depends on assumptions about a complex array of issues: some normative (both moral and other evaluative issues), some empirical. The empirical issues are themselves of various kinds, not only because they belong to traditionally different disciplines but also because they occur at different levels. There are first-order questions about "how the world works": the causal mechanisms and "push-pull" factors involved in migration and related processes. Why do Mexicans migrate to the United States? How do they affect the wages, working conditions, and patterns of employment of U.S. workers? What are their aims with respect to permanent settlement? In addition, there are what might be called second-order empirical questions about the feasibility of various policy proposals—their political acceptability to the American people and to their decision-makers. First- and second-order questions are related, but there is, unfortunately, no correlation of the sort one might hope for: what is politically acceptable may or may not be so in light of an accurate perception of the first-order issues. But a realistic attempt to formulate policy cannot ignore these second-order issues, whether their foundation is rational or not.

Once one recognizes how subtle and complicated the relations among these—moral and other evaluative issues, first- and second-order empirical questions—can be, one can better appreciate the somewhat confusing spectacle confronting the student of this problem. The migration issue makes strange bedfellows. In contrast to other public policy issues such as abortion and capital punishment, where liberals and conservatives line up predictably on one side or the other, here we find a great diversity of positions advanced by people proclaiming similar political principles, while those who share no other common political ground find themselves aligned.[1] The lack of consensus among those who commonly agree, and unusual alignments between those who do not, occurs because of the diversity of questions relevant to arriving at a policy decision, and because of the absence of agreement about answers to even the seemingly most straightforward of these questions.

By the straightforward questions I mean, of course, the empirical ones. The modern Western intellectual climate is imbued with the idea that "facts" are objective, true, and incontrovertible, while "value judgments" are subjective, unprovable, and "up to the individual." Such a view obscures the extent to which disagreement about policy, about what ought to be done, results from disagreement about the facts. But anyone who has spent time with social scientists and policymakers concerned with this issue soon realizes that the facts are as much in dispute as are the value questions.[2]

The reasons for this are various. For one thing, the term "fact" is often used indiscriminately to mean everything from simple, albeit difficult to establish, statistics (the number of illegal aliens residing in the United States) to sophisticated claims about complex social or economic phenomena (the underlying causes of migration). In addition, many of what are sometimes called facts are themselves complex admixtures of empirical and normative claims. And a better understanding of the nature of scientific theory and its relation to fact undermines the assumption that there are "hard facts" independent of their role in theories and without normative presuppositions.

There are also more mundane reasons for the lack of consensus about what happens and why. In many cases we simply lack the relevant information. This is partly because undocumented workers are undocumented, and gathering information about them is like writing a history of the prehistoric era. But it is also because much of what we need to know is difficult if not impossible to measure: the phenomena are large-scale and not easily susceptible to the usual techniques of policy analysis. Even when available, isolated bits of information have little meaning except in larger contexts, in conjunction with many other assumptions—assumptions that are likely to be controversial.

This brings us to the role philosophers can play in resolving these issues. It is often thought that the philosopher aims to be the conscience of policymakers, advising what they ought, morally speaking, to do, and perhaps explaining how this might figure in the tough, pragmatic world of politics. This puts the matter badly. First, it suggests that there is such a thing as "what one ought, morally speaking, to do" that is determinable in advance of a problem's practical aspects—some ideal that better creatures than we could attain and from which compromise might be sought; and second, it portrays the philosopher as one with some special moral gift to impart to those who lack it.

But the moral is not an aspect separable in the way this view suggests from the world's practical or other aspects. Ethics is not a species unto itself—the department of altruistic affairs; it is practical reasoning. As such it embraces whatever is relevant to decision-making, not just some high-minded realm called morality. Thus the philosopher is one who provides structure to arguments for practical conclusions, situating whatever is relevant, including what are commonly thought of as the moral or evaluative aspects of a problem—but not only these. What happens, what must happen, what is efficient, what is necessary for survival and growth—without understanding and incorporating these, all argument about what ought to be done is idle.

Of course, the philosopher is not an expert on all or even most of the issues relevant to enlightened decision-making. But then who is? It is an inevitable feature of most current public policy issues that no single person can be an expert, i.e., a specialist, in all the relevant issues. This is the result of increasing specialization, on the one hand, and of the increasingly complex and interdisciplinary nature of practical problems, on the other. For this reason there must be those who, although not experts on every issue, can evaluate the data and findings of others and can situate them in a larger context and explain to which conclusions they are relevant. Philosophers have a role here. They can also perform an essential task by saying where expertise ends and value judgments begin. (The debate in the abortion controversy about when life begins is a good example.) Values cannot be wholly eliminated, but they can and should be revealed. They need not be arbitrary. Again philosophers can contribute their expertise, which consists not in a unique moral vision but rather in knowing how and to what extent value judgments can be supported.

So far I have, in characteristic philosophical fashion, approached our original policy question by posing further questions about it, in the hope of learning more about its nature and ultimately its answer. We can now approach the original question somewhat more directly, though piece by piece. What are the constituent questions from which the makings of an answer must come? I suggest the following: What policy is in the U.S. interest? To what extent, if any, and on what grounds does the United States have an obligation in making policy to consider Mexican interests? Where do Mexico's interests lie? How are U.S. and Mexican interests related?

These questions are still too large to be answered whole, and will require further analysis. Nor, of course, can they all be exhaustively treated here. But they will provide the structure within which to understand the problem and the means to its resolution.

II

A prevailing view, often expressed in the popular media, is that the growing influx of Mexican workers to the United States may be good for Mexico, but is not good for America. Undocumented Mexican workers, it is said, who are desperate for employment unavailable at home and fearful of discovery and deportation by the American authorities, are prime targets for exploitation by employers. This, in addition to their sheer numbers, results in the displacement of American workers and depression of their wages and working conditions. Thus a more restrictive policy is needed to protect American interests.

Even assuming, as we shall for the present, that our concern is only for the U.S. interest, several questions need answers to evaluate this interpretation of the problem. First, what evidence is there that Mexicans have a negative effect on U.S. workers? Second, does it follow that Mexican workers are harmful to U.S. interests; if so, on what view of U.S. interests? And third, is a restrictive policy the only or even the best solution?

The view that Mexican workers displace Americans and depress their wages and working conditions possesses intuitive plausibility, primarily because of its fit with the logic of supply and demand. It is, however, an empirical thesis and as such warrants empirical support. But little if any hard evidence has been produced, and the claim is disputed among economists.[3] Only near the border itself does it seem undeniable that there is a problem. Admittedly, hard evidence for such a claim is difficult to produce. But there are reasons for thinking that the logic of supply and demand may be misleading.

In the first place, the areas of highest unemployment in the United States, the cities of the Northeast, do not have high concentrations of Mexicans.[4] Second, it does not follow that more foreign workers mean fewer jobs for Americans. Employment is not a zero-sum game: workers are also consumers and may create jobs as well as fill them. But since, in general, Mexicans send some part of their income back to Mexico, it is not clear how much force this argument has here. The most important point is that whatever displacement and depression of U.S. workers occurs can be explained as much by the illegal status of Mexican workers as by their presence.[5] Because Mexicans are illegal they fear discovery and so are vulnerable to exploitation by employers. Americans are therefore less attractive to employers because they are more expensive. Nevertheless, improving the situation of American workers does not necessarily mean stopping the flow of Mexicans; the same goal could be served by legalizing their status, without sacrificing whatever advantages Mexican workers bring.[6]

But arguing about the truth and extent of the displacement/depression thesis obscures the normative issues implicit in the concern about the U.S. interest. (At the same time, it reveals the extent to which such concerns turn on empirical rather than normative matters.) Even supposing the presence of Mexican workers does have a depressive effect on the market for U.S. workers, it does not follow that, all things considered, Mexicans' participation in the U.S. labor force is not in the best interests of the United States. To draw this conclusion one needs, first, knowledge of the extent of displacement and depression and of the benefits Mexican labor brings to other Americans or to the American economy as a whole, and, second, a means of weighing such benefits against the costs.

These issues raise questions about the concept of national interest around which much of the debate takes place. The term suggests that there is such a thing as the national interest—a good that is distributed among the entire population. There may be such goods; in these cases the concept of national interest may be unproblematic. But in the case before us, different segments of society have different and often competing interests. The Mexican workers who may be detrimental to unskilled American workers are beneficial to at least one group: those businesses that employ Mexicans and whose operating costs would increase without them. Americans qua consumers are also therefore probable beneficiaries.

How then can one assess the claims of these competing groups? The most obvious way would be to multiply the benefits by the number of individuals benefited, the costs by the number harmed, and let the numbers decide. In the absence of more precise information than is currently available and more refined analytic techniques, such a proposal is hopelessly unfeasible. But it is open to serious criticism on other grounds as well, for it treats all costs (conceived as units of some external thing, e.g., dollars) as on a par, without distinguishing costs (or benefits) borne at different levels of welfare. This conflicts with the reasonable belief that the "same" costs exact greater tolls on those who have less—the economists' assumption of diminishing marginal utility. If costs were conceived as some kind of psychological stuff (e.g., Bentham's hedons), the (as it were) greater costs of costs borne at lower levels of welfare would be figured in. The suggestion is not that we revert to the psychological formulation, which encounters well-known problems, but that some way be found to incorporate the constraints implied by diminishing marginal utility.

One way to ensure the priority of claims at lower levels of welfare is to express them in terms of rights, for rights by their nature carry a special urgency.[7] Thus we could argue that a person has a right to subsistence—to "have available for consumption what is needed for a decent chance at a reasonably healthy and active life"[8]—that takes precedence over mere aggregates of costs or benefits above the basic level. But rights to subsistence are highly controversial. Why? Not because anyone denies the evils of starvation and malnutrition, but primarily because rights must be tied to duties of other people to fulfill these rights; once we invoke duties, claims are made on people who themselves have interests and rights that may be jeopardized if any purported subsistence rights are satisfied.

Those who are skeptical along these lines of subsistence rights are not, it should be noted, rejecting the notion of rights altogether.[9] They agree that people have certain rights, such as rights to physical security (to others' nonaggression) and civil rights. But, they believe, these can be fulfilled at relatively little cost to others, whereas subsistence rights make stringent demands, economically and otherwise, on those who would have to satisfy them.

The skeptic's objection has at least one virtue: it keeps promoters of rights honest. In recent years, claims of rights have proliferated beyond all reason; rights are used to express every kind of desideratum. Here a kind of Gresham's law operates, and the currency of rights is made worthless. The skeptic may remind us that to admit something into the pantheon of rights—and it is and must remain a pantheon—at least two things need to be demonstrated: first, that from the point of view of the would-be rights-holder, what is claimed as a right is of some importance; and second, that from the point of view of those who would be put upon by acknowledgment of the right, they would not be unreasonably put upon. It is obvious that what is and is not reasonable depends on the particular case, especially on the necessitousness of the claim, and is rarely an open-and-shut matter. The claim that rights always concern what is important also needs qualification. In the first place, the concrete substance of a right need not always be important. If I have a right to dispose of some portion of my income as I please, then I have a right to buy a pair of lilac suede cowboy boots, and my having a pair of lilac suede cowboy boots is (probably) not important.[10] To dissolve this puzzle would require a foray into the problem of describing rights; we shall simply assume the problem can be handled without too much difficulty. Second, even though all talk of rights must be reserved for what is of some significance, still there are distinctions in importance among rights. Some are essential to the enjoyment of all other rights and more generally to the possibility of a decent life.[11] Where there are conflicts between rights, such rights have priority over less fundamental rights. If, alternatively, all rights were treated as absolute and always inviolable, rights would become worthless by being worth too much—we could never afford to invoke them.

Returning to the main line of argument, the question is whether rights to subsistence meet the conditions of rights just outlined. The first criterion—that what is claimed as a right is important—is obviously met. In fact, the controversy about subsistence rights hardly touches this point, for no one seriously disputes the importance of subsistence. The sticking point is the second condition: Does the acknowledgment of a right to subsistence impose an unreasonable burden on others? More specifically, is there a sufficient difference between this burden and that imposed by uncontroversial rights, such as the right to physical security, that justifies granting the status of rights to one but not to the other?

The traditional argument is that while security rights make only "negative" demands (that people refrain from doing certain things), subsistence rights make "positive" demands (that people *do* something, indeed that they do a great deal). The positive/negative distinction is questionable on both conceptual and moral grounds, but we shall not pursue these issues here.[12] The important point for our purposes is that the distinction cuts across both subsistence and security rights, since the fulfillment of both requires (positive) action as well as (negative) forbearance. As Henry Shue has forcefully argued, even if the core of a right is in some sense negative (requiring forbearance), if rights are to mean anything it is essential that they be protected, and this always requires social institutions whose installation and functioning demand substantial positive measures.[13] And given such protection, even the apparently positive core of subsistence rights may be deceptive, for with proper protection one may be able to "subsist for oneself," without the aid of others.

This is not to say that the acknowledgment of subsistence rights would require no sacrifices. It would. But if, as Shue has argued, ensuring subsistence of the world's population would require not an absolute reduction of present levels of consumption by the affluent but only a slower rate of growth,[14] the case is even stronger for ensuring subsistence within the nation, which is what concerns us now. It seems clear that no interests or rights as basic as subsistence are jeopardized by its fulfillment. For subsistence rights, along with rights to physical security, are the most basic: their enjoyment is essential to the enjoyment of any other rights and to life itself.[15] Only the subsistence rights or security rights of others can compete, and there is no reason to think these are endangered.

How do these arguments apply to the case before us? It is clear that if American workers are displaced by Mexicans, they lose their means of livelihood. Since these workers are among the least skilled and are already at the bottom of the labor market, they will not merely be forced to poorer jobs but will be expelled from employment altogether. But we cannot conclude that their subsistence rights are threatened, since they are presumably eligible for income transfer payments—"welfare" or the like. What is clear is that if policies are adopted that have the effect of displacing American workers, the latter are entitled to such payments, which do not in any sense constitute charity. Rights, by their nature, one may demand; charity, by its nature, one may not.

The distinction between subsistence as a right and subsistence as charity is, however, difficult for many people to grasp. The sentiment against so-called welfare runs deep; it may be as hard for recipients to maintain self-respect as it is for others not to believe they "could work if they really wanted to." To the extent that this is so, self-respect and dignity may be impossible without the ability to work, at least in American society. Since a decent life is impossible without self-respect and dignity, the right to work would seem to be a right of very high priority (although not as basic as subsistence and security rights, since, unlike these, it is not essential to the enjoyment of all other rights). In any case, most would agree that, other things being equal, it is preferable that people work in exchange for income. The question is, what are the costs to other Americans of protecting these jobs? (We will consider costs to Mexicans in section IV.) Some American businesses will have increased operating costs, so consumers will also pay more. At the same time, costs to the welfare system, and so to the citizen qua taxpayer, would presumably be lower. What would the net economic effect be? I have seen no serious estimates of these increases, but most commentators speak of paying "a few cents more for a head of lettuce." It seems clear that such costs, especially when spread among all those who would bear them, do not compete successfully against the interests of American workers threatened with loss of their livelihood. Thus, to the extent labor market depression is caused not by the illegal status of Mexican workers (which is remediable by legalizing them in some manner and so protecting them under U.S. law and labor standards)—but by their participation in the work force per se, benefits of their labor to some Americans do not outweigh costs to affected American workers, whose interests, amounting to rights of high priority, take precedence. But this is not the end of the matter.

III

We have been considering the claim that Mexican migration threatens the U.S. national interest. Two suggestions implicit in this view need to be questioned. One is that in formulating national policy only the U.S. interest is relevant and Mexico's interest need not be considered. The other is that the U.S. interest can be neatly isolated from that of others (e.g., Mexico's) in the way the analysis of section II suggests.

The idea that in formulating U.S. policy only what is in the U.S. interest is relevant is in keeping with the standard view of international relations, according to which nations must refrain (except in special circumstances) from interference in the affairs of other nations but need not positively promote the latter's interests. In the absence of agreements, treaties, and the like, nations have only negative obligations to other nations or to extranationals, not positive ones.[16]

Two kinds of arguments may underlie this view: a set of empirical premises about the way the world is, and certain ethical views about the ground of obligation. An important element in the underlying ethical view is the idea that one owes only noninterference to another unless he has incurred an obligation by some prior action, undertaking, agreement, or the like.[17] On this view, if I am walking by a lake and notice a perfect stranger drowning, I have no obligation to help the stranger, though it would doubtless be desirable if I did; and no one may force me to help. In the absence of relevant antecedent action, I am obligated to refrain from harm, but not to help, not to be a Good Samaritan.

One way to undermine the standard view of the obligations of nations is to impugn this view, by undermining the distinction between negative and positive obligations. This has been argued at length elsewhere.[18] The conclusion regarding nations is that they may have positive duties to other nations or to extranationals even in the absence of any prior relationship.

Here, however, I shall focus on a different route to defeating the standard view. Instead of trying to show how A owes x to B irrespective of what has happened (or not happened) between them—on what we may call *purely moral* grounds—I shall rely crucially on what has happened, arguing that A owes x to B in virtue of something A has done, or something B has done, or something that has occurred between A and B. Let us call all such arguments, and the relationships they presuppose, *historical*, to be contrasted with purely moral arguments.

What sorts of antecedent happenings, actions, and relationships are to be included? The genus of historical arguments is wide-ranging; their force and persuasiveness vary depending on the nature of the antecedent appealed to. Among the clearest cases are those where it is argued that A owes something to B because A has acted in a way that has harmed B and is therefore causally implicated in B's plight. But harm is not the only ground on which a positive obligation can rest. In addition to contracts and agreements, which are theoretically unproblematic, many kinds of relationships, characterized by friendship, shared history, interdependence, and other ties, are ordinarily thought to give rise to obligations.

In all such arguments for an obligation there is room for disagreement of two different kinds. One may question the meaning of a crucial term or the underlying principle (What constitutes harm? Does friendship bind in the way asserted?), or one may question the concomitant empirical assumptions (Did so-and-so do what is alleged?). In arguments from the harm principle, what is likely to be disputed is not the principle's validity but its meaning—in addition, of course, to the truth of the history assumed or asserted. It is not controversial that doing harm creates at least presumptive obligations to restore or compensate, but the lines around the boundaries of harm are drawn by different people at different places. What is central to harm is the idea of impinging on someone in a way that makes him worse off. The significance of harm depends on how badly off one is made—both relative to where one would have been in the absence of the harm and absolutely. Our judgment also depends on what refraining from acting would cost the agent. But in general it can be said at least that actions which seriously undermine a person's prospects for a decent life create strong presumptions of prohibition or compensation.

The question, then, is whether the United States owes anything to Mexico (e.g., regard to its interests in formulating a policy concerning Mexican workers) in virtue of its past or present actions toward, or relationship with, Mexico. Support for an affirmative answer comes both from some very general facts about the contemporary world as well as more particular ones about U.S.–Mexican relations.

The standard view of international relations, which sanctions the pursuit of national interest constrained only by nonintervention in other nations' affairs, rests on a view of nations and their activities that may once have been roughly accurate but is no longer. The obsolete picture is of nations as virtually closed systems in which what goes on inside has no significant ramifications outside—where effects of actions stop at the border. Were this view accurate, historical arguments would not ordinarily generate extranational obligations. For historical obligations depend on prior relationships and interactions, and on the old picture these are typical within nations but not between them.

It is clear that the old model never truly depicted the world; interaction among societies is not new. Still, the extent to which international interdependence (the somewhat misleading term in popular use) or interconnectedness has increased can hardly be exaggerated. As a result of the combined growth of technology, population, and knowledge, the world has changed so profoundly as to require a new model for understanding relationships among its inhabitants.

Worldwide interconnectedness has increased most obviously as a result of technological progress in such fields as communications, transportation, and medicine, as well as concomitant economic developments. Beneficial developments, such as the virtual eradication of infectious diseases, may have disastrous consequences in terms of population growth. New technologies result in pollution and environmental damage that respect no boundaries. The mass media not only reflect the world's events; increasingly they determine them. The affluent cannot claim ignorance of the plight of the world's poor, and the attractions of life in the developed countries are both more obvious and more accessible to those without opportunities in their homeland.[19] These are dramatic instances of what is a pervasive and irreversible feature of the contemporary world. The shrinking of the world, the disappearance of frontiers, and the resulting increase in interconnectedness are heightened by growing understanding of the causal mechanisms at work in the world. In consequence, an "ecological" model reflecting the delicate balance among living things and the way even subtle changes ramify through the whole system is appropriate to our world. Such a view has crucial consequences not only for beliefs about what is owed to others—as it becomes more and more difficult, whether on the individual or the national level, to isolate purely self-regarding actions—but also, as I suggest in section IV, for a conception of self-interest and its collective analogue, national interest. Here, however, we are concerned with the former.

To generalize: the standard view of international obligation is at best naive, for increasingly what happens within national boundaries has morally relevant consequences outside them. Given the enormity and complexity of these matters (not to mention our ignorance), however, it would be equally naive to suppose the new model cranks out precise determinations of duty. Rather it shifts the burden of proof toward those who would deny responsibility beyond borders. To do more requires a closer analysis of particular cases.

In the case of the United States and Mexico, several issues are relevant. First is geographical contiguity. Other things being equal, physical proximity heightens interconnectedness (although mass communications defy this rule). For this reason alone, the US and Mexico are more closely related than a random pair of nations. But contiguity cannot be disentangled from the political and economic ties that have long bound and continue to bind the two nations together.

One relevant fact is that what was once Mexico is now the United States, since Mexico ceded between a third and a half of its territory to the United States after the Mexican-American War. But it is not at all clear what practical implications this has for US responsibility today. Even if it is acknowledged that the original annexation was not wholly legitimate, the question of what, if anything, the US owes, and to whom, is highly controversial. In the first place, neither those wronged nor those who did the wrongs are alive, so responsibility must be ascribed elsewhere. Second, it is not clear if what is owed is, e.g., the difference between where victims of injustice are now and where they would have been without the injustice, or something short of this.[20] Even if these moral and philosophical problems could be resolved, our ignorance of the relevant counterfactuals—where so-and-so would have been if such-and-such had not happened—would greatly limit any practical conclusions. In this case, an appreciation of the history of U.S.–Mexican territorial relations leaves one with a sense of the contingency and artificiality of the border and its irrelevance to much of the life and culture of those who have lived with it rather than with any clear prescriptions for action.

What is less indeterminate and ultimately more important for establishing that moral ties bind the United States and Mexico are the intricate economic relations that connect them, and have done so for many years. Mexicans have been migrating to the US for many generations, a process especially encouraged by the US when, as in World War II, it was short of labor.[21] Mexicans today migrate primarily from the same areas from which they came generations ago. To the extent that the US encouraged this flow, such as by the *bracero* program, it bears some responsibility for the current situation. The United States has contributed to the creation of expectations and, more important, has helped set into motion the patterns now thought problematic. It is therefore not morally at liberty to do just as it pleases.

But the significance of migration goes much deeper than these facts alone suggest. Migration is a crucial element in economic development and in the relationship between the economies of developing and developed countries. "All industrial nations recruited the bulk of their industrial workforce from surplus agricultural labor";[22] industrialization requires the release of agricultural labor. In itself this process need not be problematic; it becomes so when the capacity of the industrial sector to absorb labor is outstripped by the amount of labor released. Whether this happens depends in turn on a variety of factors. Lourdes Arizpe and others have shown how the traditional rural economy and culture of Mexico have been eroded by processes characteristic of development, especially in the contemporary era, through "monetization of the economy, the destruction of local industries, and changes in the patterns of consumption."[23] As a result, rural Mexico cannot sustain its population unless large numbers of people migrate for employment to Mexico's cities, the United States, or elsewhere.

Thus it seems clear that agents of development bear significant responsibility for the situation that makes migration necessary. This does not mean, in general, that individuals ought to be blamed or villains isolated; this would misinterpret what is a very large-scale process resulting from the largely uncoordinated behavior of many individuals and groups over time. It does mean, however, that the flow of Mexicans cannot be treated solely as a variable to be manipulated as American interests demand, for the conduct of U.S. nationals has been a significant factor in bringing about the present situation.[24]

At this point one may well ask: Even if the foregoing account is accepted as description, how does it bear on the obligations of the United States as a nation? These "agents of development," as we have called them, are not identical with the nation "the United States," so why should the nation bear responsibility for their behavior? This question raises difficult moral and philosophical problems: What exactly is a nation and what relation does it bear to the individuals that constitute it? More specifically, how are the actions and responsibilities of nations related to those of their constituent members? We cannot pursue these questions adequately here, but shall suggest the outlines of an answer.

The view that it behooves the United States as a nation to consider Mexican interests rests on several assumptions. First is the philosophically unproblematic claim that in fact national policy has been partly responsible for the present situation—both directly, as through the bracero program, and probably more important, indirectly through laws and regulations that encourage or discourage relevant activities and their consequences. But developments have been affected more, let us assume, by nongovernmental activity.[25] Is the nation as a whole responsible for its members when they act (legally) as private persons or as agents of economic entities like corporations? Is it responsible for the behavior of corporations residing within its territory?

A nation is not to be identified with its government, although in the absence of tyranny the government is one of its elements. Nations survive the passing of governments and even forms of governments, as well as the entire transformation of their individual membership. Nations are bearers of cultures and of values. As such, they are accountable not only for acts done on behalf of the state but also for those carried out by members in the spirit of the culture, acts that embody the values of the nation. Thus, although much of what concerns us is not governmental action, it is action not simply consistent with but exemplary of American values and culture. (In ascribing responsibility, we do not imply that these values are inherently bad or have only bad consequences.) Just as individuals are partly responsible for the conduct of the larger groups to which they belong, so a nation is partly responsible for the conduct of its members when they act in a way expressive of the nation.[26]

It is, therefore, morally appropriate for the United States as a nation to bear some responsibility for the events that now make a policy regarding Mexican migration necessary. Given the nature of the underlying processes, it is also logistically appropriate. Where harm is the result of the largely uncoordinated activities of many individuals and groups who, except in rare cases, cannot (whether for pragmatic or moral reasons) be held individually accountable, the larger body to which they belong—in this case, the nation—is the natural locus of responsibility. Only the nation possesses the requisite power to alter the course of events—as all those now concerned to make policy on this issue are aware.

IV

I have argued that in formulating a policy concerning Mexican workers, the United States is obligated to consider not only its own but also Mexico's interests. It became clear above (if it was not already) that the concept of national interest is not as straightforward as its rhetorical uses suggest, for despite proclamations of *the* national interest, in most cases there is not a single interest common to all a nation's members, but instead a diversity and often a conflict of interests. In section II I argued for the priority of some of these interests over others; they were said to amount to rights, some of them fundamental rights. In light of this, it is not inappropriate to think of the national interest as the weighted sum of individual interests: accordingly, a policy may serve the national interest even if it conflicts with some individuals' interests, if the latter are outweighed by the more basic interests, amounting to rights, of others. I shall in what follows sometimes speak of "U.S.

interests" or "the Mexican interest" in this way. To say a policy serves U.S. interests in this sense means it serves them *all things considered*.

How then do alternative U.S. immigration policies serve U.S. and Mexican interests? Let us simplify the problem by considering only two broad policy types: a large flow of Mexicans to the United States, and a smaller flow, set by some kind of restrictive policy. These are admittedly vague categories, but they will serve present purposes.

In section II we examined the direct impact of the current de facto policy, which results in a large, unregulated, and illegal flow of Mexican workers into the U.S. labor market. The conclusion was that such a policy is significantly beneficial to those American businesses who employ Mexicans, slightly beneficial to consumers who pay lower prices than they otherwise would, and significantly harmful to American workers whose wages are depressed or who are forced out of work altogether. Since only the latter's basic interests are at stake, however, it seems that, on balance, the U.S. interest is not served by the current policy.

Nevertheless, because we do not know to what extent labor market depression results from the supply of Mexican labor and to what extent from its illegality, it is hard to draw conclusions about the possible effects on American workers of an explicit policy that was relatively unrestrictive as to entry but that protected Mexicans under U.S. law and labor standards, thereby removing what may be the primary cause of depression. Of course, Mexicans can be protected to a greater or lesser extent. Are they to be granted all the rights and privileges of Americans? According to the arguments of section III, the United States is not free to treat Mexicans just as it pleases, but we have not shown that it must treat them as U.S. citizens in every respect. This issue will remain unresolved here, since in any case we encounter the irony that, in the short run at least, Mexicans may fare worse as they are treated better: protecting them with the minimum wage, adequate fringe benefits, the right to join unions, etc. may have the effect of excluding them from employment altogether, by rendering American workers competitive. Thus, Mexican workers' most basic interests could be jeopardized by arming them with what are sincerely thought to be humane standards. This paradox can be resolved only by attention to the long(er) run, which we shall provide below. Here our concern is with U.S. citizens. The irony is compounded: the greater the protection given Mexicans, the better off, it seems, American workers will be. But this approach has its own costs and might defeat what many claim is the rationale of foreign labor: to keep prices down for businesses and consumers.

What would the effects of an unrestrictive U.S. policy be on Mexico? It is widely assumed that whatever the ill effects on the United States, as far as Mexico is concerned an open border is desirable—the more open the better. But this is plainly false. In the first place, those who migrate tend to be among the most enterprising and energetic of their society;[27] as the study of history confirms, the most downtrodden do not have the will to move. The continual exodus of the more vital is likely to constitute a serious drain of skill and energy from Mexico and hamper development. In addition, it has been persuasively argued that the "escape valve" provided by unlimited access to the US of otherwise unemployed or underemployed Mexicans, especially the most enterprising, serves to remove any incentive of the Mexican government to adopt policies that would relieve unemployment and improve the lot of vast numbers of Mexicans.[28] So the widening gap between rich and poor widens further.

Migration is in the immediate interests of those who migrate and their families, and it is in the interests of the ruling elites of Mexico. It is probably harmful to the very worst-off—those who are left behind. In the longer run, however, it is questionable whether migrants and their families benefit from migration. Whether one benefits from a policy depends on what its alternatives are. If the alternative to migration were the opportunity to earn a decent living at home, it is likely that those who migrate would choose to stay home. (Like most people, Mexicans move because opportunities are lacking where they are, not because of inherent dissatisfaction with their home or general *Wanderlust*.) In that case, not only the bottom 20 percent, for whom migration is plainly not beneficial, but perhaps the majority of Mexicans would be better off without massive migration.[29] And this is not just the majority, but those people whose most basic interests are at stake. But the crucial changes in the Mexican economy will not occur, many argue, as long as the escape valve of migration across the border remains open.

These considerations of the effects of migration on Mexico, together with an appreciation of U.S.–Mexican interconnectedness, force us to think more carefully about where U.S. interests really lie. Our earlier analysis operated within the narrow framework of the labor market alone; it assumed that U.S. interests were captured therein and could be neatly isolated from Mexico's. This assumption is useful up to a point, for we do want to know the labor market impact. But our conclusions must ultimately be incorporated into the larger picture that reflects the interconnections between the United States and Mexico. It seems certain that massive migration, whether legal or illegal, by undermining the Mexican government's incentive for developing programs to relieve unemployment, would perpetuate itself and indeed snowball: opportunities for employment in Mexico would become even scarcer as more people departed and local economies deteriorated even further.[30] Even if migration were not now a problem for the US, it would in time become one by force of sheer numbers. Whatever the short-term economic benefits of migration for the US, an open door will not serve its interests.

It is said that nowhere in the world do two more disparate and unequal societies share a border than at the Rio Grande. Such juxtapositions, even if less extreme than this one, may inevitably produce disequilibrium: the more-developed economy, open to cheap labor, acts as a magnet to attract those lacking opportunities in the less-developed one.[31] Only policies that redress the imbalance, rather than treating the symptoms, can bring genuine and lasting solutions.

This is not to say that the United States ought suddenly to adopt a severely restrictive immigration policy. Some claim that small businesses in the Southwest would be forced to close, because Americans are unavailable for the jobs now filled by Mexicans. There is reason to doubt this; more likely the result would be higher prices, which would be passed on to the public. A more compelling reason not to close the border (no doubt impossible in any case) is the impact such a policy would have on Mexico and indirectly on the US as well. An abrupt shutting off of the escape valve for Mexico's unemployed with no alternative measures would probably have disastrous consequences. Richard Fagen has described the unrest, consequent repression, and general destabilization of Mexico's political climate that would be the likely result. This would harm not only Mexico but also the United States, whose security and economic interests, including its need for Mexican oil, would be endangered by fighting and militarization at its doorstep and by the deterioration of the climate of confidence essential to the well-being of its economic interests.[32] Again it is apparent that the complex reverberations of events in the contemporary world make the narrow focus on national interest myopic.

Neither large-scale migration nor a sudden reversal of this trend, then, serves the long-term interests of the United States or Mexico. For the immediate future, it is clear that the two governments must together navigate the narrow channel between these to arrive at a reasonable and workable policy. In the long run, genuine solutions must address the structural features of the contemporary economic system that give rise to massive migration: to problems of rural development through labor-intensive programs, the role of the advanced economies in determining—for better and for worse—the course of the developing ones, and the widening gap between rich and poor so far associated with growth in the developing nations. I have argued that diverse motives converge to the search for solutions to these complex problems. Some may be moved by the pure desire to understand the world, others by a sense of duty, and some by the realization that, in any case, they will not remain untouched.

(

Notes

I am grateful to Henry Shue and Peter G. Brown for incisive criticisms of an earlier draft of this paper.

1. Cf. Teitelbaum's description: "Some conservatives have favored unrestrained immigration to cheapen labor and reduce the power of unions, while others have opposed it on xenophobic or racist grounds. It is easy to identify liberals who have supported unlimited immigration in the spirit of humanitarian concern for the poor of the world, and others who have opposed it in the spirit of humanitarian concern for the poor of the United States. The array of political forces favoring continued large-scale illegal immigration include such unlikely bedfellows as agribusiness and industrial interests seeking cheap and compliant labor, religious leaders promoting global egalitarianism, ethnic activists seeking supporters, liberal unions recruiting new members, and idealists desiring a world without borders. Opponents of illegal immigration include many members of disadvantaged minority groups, liberal labor unions, and racist groups such as the Ku Klux Klan." Michael S. Teitelbaum, "Right Versus Right: Immigration and Refugee Policy in the United States," *Foreign Affairs* 59 (Fall 1980): 58–59; also see pp. 32–33.

2. Some dispute even this, i.e., that the facts are in dispute. So there is disagreement about whether there is disagreement. But one finds that when pressed to specify just what is uncontroversial, few answers sufficiently precise to be useful are forthcoming.

3. For the view that Mexican and U.S. workers do not compete, see Edwin P. Reubens, "Immigration Problems, Limited-Visa Programs, and Other Options," Chapter 7, this volume, pp. 192–98; and Wayne A. Cornelius, "Legalizing the Flow of Temporary Migrant Workers from Mexico: A Policy Proposal," Working Papers in U.S.–Mexican Studies no. 7 (San Diego, Calif.: University of California, San Diego, Program in U.S.–Mexican Studies, July 1980). For the opposing view, see Vernon M. Briggs, Jr., "Foreign Labor Programs as an Alternative to Illegal Immigration: A Dissenting View," Chapter 8, this volume; and David North and Allen LeBel, *Manpower and Immigration Policies in the United States*, National Commission for Manpower Policy, Special Report no. 20 (Washington, D.C., 1978).

4. Reubens, "Immigration Problems," p. 195, this volume.

5. Cornelius, "Legalizing the Flow," p. 4.

6. Thus, even North and LeBel, whose work is widely cited in support of the displacement/depression thesis, assert that it is primarily the illegal status of aliens rather than their presence that is causally relevant: "The role of illegal aliens and nonimmigrants in the U.S. labor market is not due to the interplay of supply and demand considerations in the labor market, but to specific differences in the rights, equality under the law, and access to opportunity that aliens have in America" (*Manpower and Immigration Policies*, p. 148). But this crucial qualification is often forgotten; in fact it sometimes seems to be forgotten by the authors themselves.

7. See Ronald Dworkin, *Taking Rights Seriously* (Cambridge: Harvard University Press, 1977), pp. xi, 90–94; and Joel Feinberg, "The Nature and Value of Rights," in *Rights, Justice, and the Bounds of Liberty* (Princeton: Princeton University Press, 1980); and Mary Gibson, "Do Nations Have a Right to Exclude?" *The Border That Joins*, vol. 2 (forthcoming).

8. Henry Shue, *Basic Rights: Subsistence, Affluence, and U.S. Foreign Policy* (Princeton: Princeton University Press, 1980), p. 23.

9. One who did reject rights outright would have to be rejoined differently. Such a person might be denying that any claims are any more valid than any others, in which case discussions of the present sort would be beside the point. Or he or she might agree that some claims have priority, but reject expressing this in terms of rights for methodological or metaphysical reasons. What is said here could be acceptable to the latter sort of critic. Ultimately, everything that is expressed in terms of rights can be said without them—it just takes longer.

10. The "probably" is not facetious; we can imagine situations in which having a pair of lilac suede cowboy boots is vitally important—and if we can't, we know philosophers who can.

11. Here we extend Shue's usage. On his definition, rights are basic "only if enjoyment of them is essential to the enjoyment of all other rights" (*Basic Rights*, p. 19). The looser formulation suggests a continuum or hierarchy of rights from more basic or fundamental to less; and it covers rights that may be essential to the possibility of a decent life although not basic in Shue's sense, one of which we discuss below. None of this is to deny the rationale of an exclusive category of most fundamental rights—basic rights in the strict sense.

12. For criticism on moral grounds, see Judith Lichtenberg, "The Moral Equivalence of Action and Omission," *Canadian Journal of Philosophy* Supplementary Volume VIII, New Essays in Ethics and Public Policy (in press), and "On Being Obligated to Give Aid: Moral and Political Arguments" (Ph.D. dissertation, City University of New York, 1978), chap. 5. For a good collection of papers on the subject see Bonnie Steinbock, ed., *Killing and Letting Die* (Englewood Cliffs, N.J.: Prentice-Hall, 1980), part 3.

13. Shue, *Basic Rights*, pp. 36–40. Here subsistence-rights skeptics may object to what is implied in the phrase "if rights are to mean anything." They want to draw a sharper line between the content of a right and its value, claiming that correlative to a right is a direct duty not to violate it (e.g., a duty not to commit aggression correlative to a right to physical security), but not a duty to protect it against violation. I owe this point to Robert Fullinwider. By contrast, Shue argues for three kinds of duties correlative to every basic

right (*Basic Rights*, pp. 51–64). The disagreement parallels the one about liberty and the worth of liberty in the literature on Rawls and elsewhere. In Rawls's system, liberty is distributed equally, although its value is not equal to all. Hence the question: "Who cares about liberty if one can't use it?" For a persuasive argument against the meaningfulness of the distinction between liberty and the worth of liberty that is also relevant to the parallel issue about rights ("Who cares about rights that are unprotected?"), see Norman Daniels, "Equal Liberty and Unequal Worth of Liberty," in *Reading Rawls*, edited by Norman Daniels (New York: Basic Books, n.d.).

14. Shue, *Basic Rights*, pp. 104–10, especially p. 108.

15. Ibid., chap. 1.

16. For a discussion of this view see Charles Beitz, *Political Theory and International Relations* (Princeton: Princeton University Press, 1979), part 2; also relevant is Michael Walzer, *Just and Unjust Wars* (New York: Basic Books, 1977), part 2. For criticism of this view, see Judith Lichtenberg, "National Boundaries and Moral Boundaries: A Cosmopolitan View," in *Boundaries: National Autonomy and Its Limits*, Maryland Studies in Public Philosophy, edited by Peter G. Brown and Henry Shue (Totowa, N.J.: Rowman and Littlefield, 1981), where the general view outlined in the following pages is developed.

17. The purest form of this view is expressed by Robert Nozick, *Anarchy, State, and Utopia* (New York: Basic Books, 1974), especially p. ix and chaps. 3, 7. For the argument connecting the moral with the political theory, see Lichtenberg, "On Being Obligated to Give Aid," chap. 3.

18. See note 12.

19. "The smallest report of possible advantage dislodges the desperate people like stones before an avalanche" (Barbara Ward, *The Home of Man*, quoted in Otis L. Graham, Jr., "Illegal Immigration and the New Reform Movement," Immigration Paper 2 [Federation for American Immigration Reform, February 1980], pp. 10–11).

20. For a persuasive (although not wholly persuasive) argument that what is owed is something far short of the difference between where victims would have been without the original injustice and where they are with it, see George Sher, "Ancient Wrongs and Modern Rights," *Philosophy & Public Affairs* 10 (Winter 1981).

21. See Manuel García y Griego, Chapter 3, this volume.

22. Lourdes Arizpe, "The Rural Exodus in Mexico and Mexican Migration to the United States," Chapter 6, this volume, p. 161.

23. Ibid., p. 177. Eighty-three percent of all Mexican farmers were left at or below subsistence in 1960 as a result of their lack of participation in modernization programs. See Cynthia Hewitt de Alcantara, *Modernizing Mexican Agriculture: Socioeconomic Implications of Technological Change 1940–1970* (Geneva: United Nations Research Institute for Social Development, 1976), pp. 101–36, 305–22. Also relevant are Francisco Alba, "Mexico's International Migration as a Manifestation of Its Development Pattern," *International Migration Review* 12 (Winter 1978), and "World System and Labor Migration as Related Issues: A Proposal," in *The Border That Joins*, vol. 2, forthcoming. For a general discussion of these issues see Shue, *Basic Rights*, pp. 40–51.

24. From 1950 to 1966, direct U.S. investment in Mexico grew from $286 million to almost $1.2 billion. Several of the largest firms in Mexico are entirely owned by U.S. interests. See Judith Adler Hellman, *Mexico in Crisis* (New York: Holmes & Meier, 1978), pp. 59–64. Also see Richard S. Weinert, "Foreign Capital in Mexico," in *Mexico–United States Relations*, edited by Susan Kaufman Purcell (New York: Proceedings of the Academy of Political Science, vol. 34, no. 1, 1981); and Karl M. Schmitt, *Mexico and the United States, 1821–1973: Conflict and Coexistence* (New York: John Wiley, 1974), pp. 250–53. The latter contains detailed discussion of U.S.–Mexican relations since the late nineteenth century. For statistics on U.S. investment in Mexico, see Nicholas K. Bruck, "U.S. Direct Investment and Latin American Development," in *Latin American–U.S. Economic Interactions: Conflict, Accommodation, and Policies for the Future*, edited by Robert B. Williamson et al. (Washington, D.C.: American Enterprise Institute, 1974).

25. But the distinction will be hard to draw if, as claimed above, grounds are wanting for the distinction between negative and positive duties.

26. This doesn't mean that each individual is responsible for every exemplary (in the neutral sense) act done by a fellow national. It is the nation as a body that bears (some) responsibility. Individuals may for various reasons be exempted, for instance by having publicly opposed the acts in question. How their exemption can be affected is, however, difficult to say. For practical reasons, it may in the end amount to moral, though not material, exoneration.

For insight into some of the obscure issues raised in this paragraph and the metaphysical problems that surround them, see Roberto Mangabeira Unger, *Knowledge and Politics* (New York: Free Press, 1975), especially chap. 3.

27. Arizpe, "The Rural Exodus," Chapter 6, this volume, pp. 175–77.

28. See Graham, "Illegal Immigration," pp. 25–31; Teitelbaum, "Right Versus Right," p. 45; and George W. Grayson, *The Politics of Mexican Oil* (Pittsburgh: University of Pittsburgh Press, 1980), p. 231. All commentators seem to agree that the development of labor-intensive agriculture is a necessary condition for relieving pressures for migration.

29. These figures are of course very rough. They are suggested by the common estimate of 40 percent or more underemployment and unemployment; and by statistics showing that the richest 40 percent of Mexicans have 80 percent of the national income, while the poorest 60 percent have only 20 percent. For the latter see Martin M. McLaughlin et al., *The United States and World Development Agenda 1979* (New York: Praeger, for the Overseas Development Council, 1979), p. 182.

30. We assume here, again no doubt artificially, that all else remains the same and destabilizing crises do not result. The latter would have further harmful consequences for the United States.

31. For the argument that "migratory pressure is perpetual because it is inherent in technological inequality," see Kingsley Davis, "The Migrations of Human Populations," *Scientific American*, September 1974.

32. Richard R. Fagen, "The Realities of U.S.–Mexican Relations," *Foreign Affairs* 55 (July 1977): 689, 698–700. This essay makes a strong case for the substantial harmony of U.S. and Mexican interests, and closes with the assertion that "in the long run, allying with those who still wish to make real the bread and freedom promised to all Mexicans 60 years ago will surely prove to be in the interest of the majority of citizens, both north and south of the Rio Grande" (p. 700).

2

Human Rights and the Rights of Aliens

JAMES W. NICKEL

It is sometimes suggested that the United States, by admitting a large number of laborers from Mexico under a guestworker program, could reduce the number of Mexicans who enter or remain here illegally.[1] I doubt that a guestworker program would produce any such reduction, but such programs do appeal to many people. Advocates of such programs often propose substantial limits on the political and welfare rights of the people admitted; the guestworker plans put forward by both the Carter and Reagan administrations are examples of this. The 1977 Carter administration plan proposed creating a new legal status for foreign laborers, namely "temporary resident alien." Persons in this category would have the right to seek and enjoy employment, but unlike permanent resident aliens they would not be considered immigrants and would not qualify for naturalization. Neither could they vote, run for public office, serve on juries, nor be eligible for federal social services such as Medicaid and food stamps.[2] The recent Reagan administration proposals urge the creation of an "experimental temporary worker program for Mexican nationals" that provides regular wage and working standards for these people while denying them rights to bring along their families, unemployment insurance, welfare benefits, food stamps, and federally assisted housing. Similar restrictions would apply to those undocumented workers in the United States who were granted amnesty under the "renewable term temporary resident" program. Persons who held this temporary resident status for ten years would then be eligible to apply for permanent resident status, but they would have no welfare rights until then. The Reagan proposals do not mention rights to vote, run for public office, or serve on juries, but I assume that neither temporary workers nor renewable term temporary residents would be granted these rights.[3]

As these proposals illustrate, the idea of limiting the rights of alien workers is attractive to many Americans. My goal in this chapter is to develop a framework for evaluating such limits on the rights of aliens. I proceed on the not uncontroversial assumption that there are universal human rights of roughly the kinds declared in the *Universal Declaration of Human Rights*, and that these rights provide an important source of guidance in this matter.[4] I recognize that this is assuming a great deal, but I will not attempt to justify this assumption here.[5] It is worth noting, however, that an approach based on universal human rights has the advantage of appealing to internationally recognized standards rather than to American traditions or abstract philosophical arguments; thus it may provide a framework for thinking about this matter that is acceptable both to the United States and to Mexico.[6] Further, those who find my assumption of universal human rights unacceptable may nevertheless find interesting my attempt to trace and develop the implications of beliefs that many people hold.

I. The Contemporary Idea of Human Rights

The attractive but problematic idea of universal human rights has been carried into prominence in recent decades by the international human rights movement. That movement, which grew out of the horrors and rhetoric of World War II, has attempted to gain international recognition for minimal standards of decent conduct for states.

Human rights, as they are described in the documents of the human rights movement, have a number of characteristics. First, lest we miss the obvious, they are *rights*, not mere goals or aspirations. Briefly, a right is a high-priority prescription of a freedom or benefit that generates definite obligations for parties other than the rightholder.

Second, human rights are universal moral rights. This means that all people have them regardless of race, sex, religion, nationality, and social position, and independent of their being recognized in the legal system of the country in which a person resides. These rights may not be effective rights until they are recognized and implemented in a legal system, but they are alleged to exist independently as moral standards of argument and criticism.

Third, this conception implies that human rights impose duties on both governments and individuals. Governments have duties not to violate these rights by their own actions and to promote and protect their observance in their territories. Individuals have duties not to act in ways that violate these rights.

And fourth, these rights are alleged to be important enough to prevail in conflicts with contrary national norms and goals and to justify international action on their behalf. This importance is connected with the fact that human rights prescribe provision for people's most basic interests and freedoms.

The rights that are proclaimed by the human rights movement can be divided into five categories. These are (1) *rights to due process*, such as rights to a fair trial or freedom from torture; (2) *rights to personal security and autonomy*, such as rights to protection from crime, and rights to freedom of movement, privacy, and freedom of thought and religion; (3) *rights to political participation*, such as rights to vote and speak; (4) *rights to equality*, such as rights to freedom from discrimination and to equality before the law; and (5) *economic and social rights* (or welfare rights), such as rights to a decent standard of living, education, and medical care.

One goal of the international human rights movement is that people's rights as citizens come to include and implement all of their human rights, although their rights as citizens need not be limited to these. Universal human rights provide an international model for a basic set of civil rights.

Although the contemporary human rights movement presupposes a system of sovereign states, it attempts to guide the policies and actions of governments in humane directions—and a concern for the rights of aliens and refugees has been part of this. It is interesting that the concern of states with the treatment of their citizens abroad goes back to ancient times; states accepted international accountability for their treatment of foreign visitors and residents long before they accepted accountability for their treatment of their own people.[7] A number of provisions in contemporary human rights documents are directed to the treatment of aliens, travelers, and refugees. First, it is prescribed that persons should acquire a nationality at birth[8] and that people should not be arbitrarily deprived of their nationality.[9] Second, these documents assert rights to leave any country[10] and to return to one's own country.[11] And third, these documents assert a right to seek and enjoy asylum from persecution.[12] The *American Convention on Human Rights* is the most expansive in this area. In addition to the rights above, it asserts rights to be granted asylum,[13] to due process for aliens when a state seeks to expel them,[14] and against collective explusions.[15]

Nevertheless, these documents do permit states to restrict some rights to citizens. While most rights are ascribed to "everyone," some rights of political participation are ascribed instead to "every citizen."[16] This suggests that it is sometimes permissible to restrict the rights of aliens, but what makes this permissible is unclear. The economic and social rights that are proclaimed in most contemporary human rights manifestoes are not restricted to citizens; like most rights they are ascribed to "everyone."

Thus, a straightforward reading of contemporary human rights declarations suggests that a policy of denying some political rights to aliens is permissible, but that a policy of denying welfare services to them is not. It might be argued that denial of welfare services is also permissible on the grounds, recognized by the *International Covenant on Economic, Social and Cultural Rights*, that compliance with economic and social rights may not be immediately possible because of the high cost of making welfare and medical services available to all. Thus, the *Covenant* requires "progressive" rather than immediate implementation of these rights.[17] This loophole was intended, however, to apply to countries that were too poor to implement most welfare rights and not to the rich countries of Europe and North America.

In any case, the important issue here is not whether limits on the rights of aliens are compatible with the terms of contemporary rights declarations—which are obviously imperfect and open to controversy—but whether such limits are compatible with a philosophically adequate conception of human rights and the premises about human welfare, autonomy, and dignity that underlie such a conception. We must now begin to answer this question.

II. Contractarian Alternatives to Universal Rights

Most people believe that governments have duties to their own citizens that they do not extend to nonresident foreigners. The government of Canada, for example, is responsible for the Canadians residing in Argentina and how they are treated by the Argentinian government. The Japanese government does not have any comparable responsibility for how Argentina treats Canadians. Similarly, when Israeli athletes were taken captive in Munich by terrorists, the governments of Israel and West Germany had responsibilities and powers in regard to the safety and release of the hostages that the government of Australia, for example, did not.

One possible explanation of these special responsibilities of governments toward their citizens and of the absence of responsibilities of the same order to nonresident foreigners is found in a contractarian account of political authority and obligation. Citizens, unlike foreigners, stand in a special contractual relationship to their government; this contractual relationship is alleged to create governmental duties to citizens, and its absence is alleged to imply the absence of comparable duties to nonresident foreigners.

The strongest version of this kind of theory, which might be called Radical Contractarianism, asserts that no duties or obligations exist independent of agreements, except the "natural" duty to honor one's agreements—the only duty not deriving from an agreement. One who holds this view would assert that political authority—and the duties for citizens and governments that it involves—flows from explicit or tacit agreements. The state is viewed as a voluntary association. It may have duties to its members in virtue of the agreements that constitute it, but it need not have any duties to aliens. Privileges can be extended unilaterally to aliens on grounds of prudence (e.g., to generate trade or to promote good will), but these can be unilaterally revoked. Aliens can also be protected by reciprocal agreements between states or by special agreements between states and foreign entrants, agreed to at time of entry, concerning conditions of residence and treatment. But apart from such agreements governments have no obligations to people and aliens have no rights.

The most important objection to Radical Contractarianism in this context is that its implications are incompatible with some of our most basic moral convictions. On this view a state would do no wrong in killing, torturing, or enslaving a person not protected by agreements—e.g., a stateless refugee— because the absence of agreements would imply the absence of any duties. A closely related objection is that Radical Contractarianism cannot account for even the most basic human rights. A central characteristic of such rights is that they are held regardless of whether they are recognized or implemented by that state.

One might respond to these objections by allowing that substantive rights and duties exist independent of agreements and that states have negative duties to avoid violating these rights and duties. But a contractarian element could be preserved by alleging that states acquire duties to take positive steps to uphold and protect these rights only through agreements. Such Modest Contractarianism, as we might call it, differs from the radical version in roughly the same way that Locke's theory of political obligation differs from Hobbes's. The Lockean theory claims that the agreement making one a member of the polity generates a governmental duty to protect one's independently existing rights. A state could be obligated not to violate anyone's human rights independent of any agreement; but duties to take positive actions, such as protecting people against violations of their rights by other people or providing welfare benefits, would be incurred only by accepting someone for membership in the polity or by reciprocal agreements between states.

Even this account of the responsibilities of states to aliens would license morally objectionable policies, in my opinion, because it would permit a state to take no steps to prevent the murder or starvation of a stateless alien in its territory. If rights requiring protections or services from governments are viewed as special rights deriving from special agreements, it becomes impossible for any such rights to be universal. Further, both Radical and Modest Contractarianism are vulnerable to the traditional objections to explanations of political authority in terms of an original contract or tacit agreements.[18]

III. Human Rights and the Obligations of Governments

A theory of human rights is incomplete unless it contains an account of who is obligated to provide the freedoms and benefits that human rights prescribe. Since the human rights movement is internationally oriented, one might expect it to deny the relevance of national boundaries and to identify some international body, such as the United Nations, as the bearer of the main responsibility for protecting and upholding human rights. But given the weakness of international organizations in today's world and the insistence of states on self-determination, that position is very unrealistic.

The system of authority that we find on this planet at present is one that divides the earth into distinct territories, expects a government to emerge in each territory, and prescribes a high degree of autonomy for these governments. No genuine alternative to this system of sovereign states is currently available, and hence it should be taken as given at present in thinking about who should bear the main responsibility for the implementation of human rights.

If we focus on obligations to refrain from directly violating human rights, it is easy to answer the question of who has such obligations. The answer is "everyone." All people and all states have these negative obligations, and no reference need be made to national boundaries. Thus, the government of France would do as much wrong in having its agents kill an Egyptian in Cairo as in having them kill a Frenchman in Paris. Citizenship or nationality is irrelevant.

But not all the duties generated by human rights are negative; some require positive steps, not mere restraint from violating rights. To implement a right to legal counsel in criminal cases, lawyers must be educated and appropriate trials conducted; to uphold the right to life, people must be provided with protection against murderers; to implement the right to education, public schools must be made available. To distinguish between these two kinds of duties, we can say that negative duties generated by human rights are duties to *respect* human rights and that positive duties generated by human rights are duties to *uphold* human rights.[19]

Obligations to uphold human rights in a particular territory are seldom, if ever, duties of all persons. A Colombian peasant has a negative duty not to kill Venezuelans, but he or she does not have positive duties to bring it about that Venezuelans are provided with protection against crime or with other institutions to uphold their rights. This, it can reasonably be said, is the responsibility of the Venezuelan government. In accordance with this idea the human rights movement has assumed that each state has the primary responsibility for upholding the rights of people in the territory it governs. This does not rule out, of course, the existence of duties of states to assist in upholding rights in other territories through peaceful means; in fact, the United Nations takes as one of its goals "promoting and encouraging respect for human rights."[20]

There are at least two good reasons for assigning each state the primary responsibility for upholding human rights in the territories it governs. One is that to relegate primary responsibility for upholding rights in its territory to some other state or international organization would be incompatible with a state's autonomy and self-determination.[21] Protecting people's rights is such an essential role of governments that a "government" deprived of the responsibility for upholding the rights of its people would be no government at all. The second reason for this assignment of responsibility for upholding human rights is that only those who hold governmental power in a territory can effectively protect and implement people's rights there. The government of an alien's native land may be able to exert some influence to obtain decent treatment for that person in another country, but the primary responsibility must lie with those who have effective control. What other nations can do to protect the rights of their citizens within another sovereign state is likely to be little and late.

As high-priority and universal norms, human rights require implementation, even when this is inconvenient or expensive. Although human rights must be accommodated to and implemented within our existing international system, this should be done so as to provide fully for the upholding of everyone's rights. Thus, in determining the moral duties that flow from human rights, conceptions of those duties that provide for everyone's rights to be upheld are preferable to conceptions that leave some persons in a position where there is no agency obligated to uphold their rights.

If a state's duty to uphold a person's rights does not derive from an agreement, what can its source be? The answer, I believe, is that each person has human rights that obligate the person or agency that is best able to do so to uphold those rights—and the government of a state is normally in this position in regard to persons in its territories. Governments alone have the financial resources, administrative control, and police power that are requisite to upholding people's rights.

My suggestion, then, is that presence in a territory, rather than citizenship, determines whether the government of that territory has the primary responsibility for upholding a person's human rights. Human rights flow from one's humanity, not from one's citizenship status, and thus aliens have as much claim to provision for and protection of their rights as do natives. This conception of the obligations that flow from human rights is preferable to one that ties an obligation to uphold rights to citizenship, because it avoids leaving some people without protection for their rights. If a person is regularly resident in one country and is only temporarily resident in another, then the two governments might be said to share responsibility, but the primary administrative role must go to the host country. Whether in cases of this kind the host country must bear all the costs of upholding an alien's rights—or whether these costs can be transferred to the alien's native country—will depend, it seems to me, on whether reciprocal provision is made for each other's nationals, whether substantial taxes are collected from aliens, and whether the wealth of the two countries is roughly comparable.

The view that I have sketched here claims that states have the same prima facie duties to respect and uphold the human rights of aliens in their territories as they have to uphold the rights of their own citizens. Unlike Radical Contractarianism, my view presupposes rights that exist independent of agreements, and it breaks with Modest Contractarianism by denying that a government's duty to protect or satisfy someone's rights is dependent on citizenship. My view claims that people's human rights obligate governments to provide basic protections and services, independent of contribution, and that these obligations fall mainly on the government of the territory where a person is located. The grounds of human rights in considerations of human dignity, autonomy, and welfare are unrelated to alienage or citizenship and apply equally to aliens and natives.

One could allow that the human rights of aliens generate positive obligations for the governments of their host countries, and still deny that the existence of these rights and obligations settles the question of whether aliens should be given full civil rights with all of the concomitant protections and services. At least two arguments support this point of view. One is that human rights are not absolute (or at least some of them are not), and hence it is possible for competing considerations to overrride them and dictate restricted rights for aliens. The second argument claims that people waive some or all of their rights when they enter a foreign country and concludes that limits on the rights of aliens are therefore not objectionable.

The first argument recognizes that human rights are not absolute and concludes from this that more powerful, competing considerations can override human rights and dictate an inferior status for aliens. This is indeed a possibility, but in order to conclude that it is an important possibility we must identify some of the kinds of considerations that can override human rights. I am prepared to allow, for example, that bona fide considerations of national security during wartime might justify restrictions on the rights of aliens to travel within the country. But I doubt that such restrictions could be justified apart from emergency conditions. Attempts to provide such justification in other situations are likely to use false generalizations about the dangerous character of most aliens or to underestimate the weight of human rights. It is an essential part of the idea of human rights, and hence part of what one accepts in assuming the existence of universal human rights, that the prescriptions involved are weighty ones that are not easily overriden by considerations of national security, prosperity, or convenience. This weight makes human rights difficult to justify, but it is also part of their political appeal as firm guarantees of important freedoms and benefits. Although it is possible to override human rights in true emergencies, the expense or inconvenience of giving full civil rights to aliens is insufficient to override the duties that flow from these people's human rights. This issue will be dealt with in a concrete case when we discuss rights of political participation for aliens.

The second argument for the view that human rights sometimes fail to dictate how aliens should be treated involves the thesis that people waive all or some of their human rights when they enter a foreign country. It might be claimed, for example, that when one enters a country with the knowledge that the country restricts freedom of expression, one tacitly waives this right. There are many problems with this line of argument. First, many entrants know little of the legal practices of the countries they enter, and hence they either do not waive any rights or they do not know which rights they are waiving. Second, this kind of tacit consent to deprivation of one's rights seems to be just as mythical as the tacit consent that contractarian theories appeal to in order to justify political authority. To expect to endure the lack of freedom in a country that one enters is not the same as agreeing that there is nothing wrong with a system in which that freedom is unavailable. And third, the assumption that governments may require people to waive their human rights as conditions of receiving important benefits is incompatible with the effective implementation of human rights, since this assumption would allow repressive governments to argue that their people had waived their rights in exchange for food or other benefits.

IV. Two Controversial Kinds of Rights

RIGHTS TO POLITICAL PARTICIPATION

Human rights imply prescriptions for the creation of operative civil rights within the domestic legal system. In implementing human rights there are prima facie grounds for upholding the rights of both natives and aliens. Still, as the language of some human rights documents suggests, it may be justifiable to restrict to citizens some rights of political participation. If this is so, then there must be powerful considerations that override the general presumption in favor of respecting and upholding the human rights of aliens. I find two arguments persuasive in regard to the right to vote in national elections.

The first of these arguments notes that an important purpose of an electoral system is to allow people to remove from office those officials who act in ways contrary to their interests and rights. To satisfy this goal, those who vote must have some minimal degree of knowledge and maturity, so the right to vote in national elections is denied to young children. If aliens lack knowledge of a country's procedures and politicians—as may be the case for recently arrived aliens—this important goal of the electoral system would be less likely to be achieved. Thus one ground for the right to vote suggests some ways in which it should be qualified.

The second argument proceeds in a similar way. It notes that restrictions on the rights of aliens may serve to maintain the national sovereignty or self-determination that the international system takes as a fundamental norm. True self-determination requires that the people of a nation be able to shape their collective destiny as a group. If recently arrived aliens with little commitment to a country's culture, goals, and institutions were permitted to vote, their votes might swing a close election in a way that would frustrate the desires of a majority of permanent residents. For example, suppose that Turkish guestworkers in Germany were allowed to vote in national elections, that they happened to be greatly opposed to the German government's policies toward Greece, and that most of them knew or cared little about that government's other policies. If their votes were decisive in ousting the government, the interests of Turks would influence substantially the policies of West Germany. Thus, considerations of national self-determination may justify some restrictions on the voting rights of aliens.

Both arguments should be qualified by the following conditions: (1) these arguments would not justify denying voting rights to aliens who have resided in a country for a long time and have indicated a desire to become citizens; and (2) in areas where national loyalties are irrelevant and aliens have the requisite knowledge, there is no justification for exclusion. Participation in local elections may be justifiable, as may participation in workers' councils, unions, and other aspects of "industrial democracy."

A successful system of jury trials, like an effective electoral system, requires that participants have some degree of maturity and knowledge of the system. Since the impact of a single vote is likely to be much greater in a trial than in a general election, there are grounds for being selective in choosing jurors. It might be justifiable to exclude temporary resident aliens from jury service on the grounds that their knowledge of the host country's legal standards and practices is likely to be very limited. Nonetheless, this rationale would not be plausible for resident aliens who have resided in the country for, say, a decade or more.

Other rights of political participation seem to be largely unaffected by these kinds of arguments. Some countries limit the freedom of expression of aliens, for which I find no justification. Foreigners may come to a country in hope of delivering a message about that country's oppressive policies at home or abroad, and it is important to the defense of human rights that the delivery of such messages be possible. Further, this is a way of allowing the right of petition to operate across national boundaries. Suppose, for example, that African students in Switzerland wish to protest some aspect of Swiss policies toward South Africa. To claim that these students should be silenced or prevented from demonstrating peacefully so as to preserve the "autonomy" of Swiss political processes is to ignore John Stuart Mill's point that influence which uses words to persuade rational people to act in certain ways is not coercive influence.[22] The ability of Swiss voters and politicians to decide on the course that their country should take is not decreased by the presence of new and different voices; instead the voices provide additional perspectives. As Alexander Meiklejohn emphasized, self-government requires both freedom to express oneself and freedom to hear and question.[23] The effective exercise of rights of free expression and of petition requires freedom of association and peaceable assembly, and hence restrictions on these rights would also be unjustifiable.

RIGHTS TO WELFARE

One way in which the contemporary idea of human rights differs from its eighteenth-century antecedents is the addition of economic and social rights to the list of human rights. The idea that all people are entitled to the minimal conditions of a decent life is frequently challenged by those who believe that one is entitled only to the fruits of one's own labor.[24] One central argument to counter such a belief is that provision for people's essential material needs is as crucial to the maintenance of their dignity, autonomy, and welfare as is provision for their liberty or security.[25] If one is willing to allow that people are entitled, independent of contribution, to positive efforts by government to uphold their due process rights and rights of security and autonomy, it is but a small step to the view that people are also entitled to the minimal requirements of survival and to a decent life, regardless of their contributions. It should be noted, however, that a belief that people are entitled to the minimal economic requirements of a decent life does not necessarily commit one to the view that they are entitled, as a matter of human rights, to *all* the benefits available under a modern welfare state.

If I am correct in believing that rights to the minimal requirements of survival and a decent life are grounded, like other rights, in considerations of human dignity, autonomy, and welfare, then these rights are possessed whether or not one is a native or an alien. States have the same prima facie obligation to grant these rights to visiting aliens as to their own citizens. Of course, those countries unable at present to implement even a rudimentary welfare system will have to implement these rights progressively rather than immediately. But in countries where sufficient resources are available, economic and social rights impose obligations on governments to guarantee the availability of certain essential goods and services.

There are a number of additional arguments against extending welfare rights to aliens. One suggests that resident aliens are entitled to welfare benefits only if they have paid taxes to the host country. In fact, both legal and illegal aliens in the United States tend to pay taxes and make Social Security payments. Further, a legitimate concern that those who receive a share of a country's benefits should bear a fair share of its burdens need not be a prohibition of services in the absence of contribution. A duty to contribute is contingent on the ability to do so, and we do not cut off aid to those who, severely handicapped since birth, are unable to contribute. Similarly, resident aliens may be required to pay reasonable taxes, but if a guestworker is disabled in an industrial accident on his first day on the job (and thus before he pays any taxes), it would be grotesque to deny him aid on the grounds that no contribution had been made. A conception of the obligations flowing from human rights that made obligations to uphold a person's rights dependent on his having made a contribution to the host society would leave many people without effective provision for their human rights.

A second argument claims that since various provisions concerning responsibility for welfare benefits can be negotiated between countries sending and countries receiving guestworkers, no other standards have universal applicability. The most direct response to this is that diplomats lack the moral or legal power to waive the basic human rights of the people they represent, even while they may have considerable discretion in the kinds of arrangements they make for the implementation of those rights. Basic human rights are non-negotiable; the effective implementation of human rights is not compatible with requiring guestworkers to waive their rights as a condition of being allowed to participate in guestworker programs.

A third objection claims that providing aliens with welfare benefits unavailable in their native lands will give residents of less-developed countries even more reason to immigrate to rich countries like Switzerland and the United States. But the prospect of high wages, not the prospect of high welfare benefits, seems to be the main attraction in rich countries.[26] Further, the high priority of human rights implies that they cannot be superseded by such inconveniences as a slight rise in the number of persons wishing to enter a country.

V. The Rights of Undocumented Aliens

In many countries those who design immigration and guestworker policies must deal not only with aliens who are authorized to be in the country but also with those who lack such authorization—persons who have entered the country surreptitiously or who have overstayed residence permits. In the United States and Venezuela, for example, undocumented aliens are estimated to number in the millions.[27] Although I have no new proposals for dealing with this problem, the approach I have been developing does provide some guide-lines.

The most important point about undocumented aliens is that they too have human rights, rights which result from one's humanity, not from one's citizen-ship. In virtue of these rights, everyone is obligated to refrain from victimizing undocumented aliens, and at least one government should be obligated to protect and uphold these rights. I have argued that governments who have aliens in their territories are obligated to uphold the rights of these persons, and in my view the same is true of undocumented aliens. Police brutality would be no less troubling if it were mainly directed toward undocumented aliens, nor would malnutrition be more tolerable if it were only found among children of "illegals." Presence in a territory is sufficient to generate an obligation for the government of that territory to uphold a person's human rights—whether or not that person is documented. Presence generates this obligation, but it does not preclude deportation in accordance with due process of law.

Although I believe that rich states with room to spare have moral obligations to admit people fleeing persecution and poverty, I also believe that states have the right to limit immigration on the grounds (1) that the authority to control one's borders is an aspect of the national sovereignty that is granted to states under the current international system; (2) that establishment and mainte-nance of an effectively self-determining political community can be hindered by a large influx of people of a different culture and outlook, especially if these people come at a pace that makes economic and cultural integration impos-sible; and (3) that a state's ability to uphold rights within its own territory requires that it preserve its stability and resources. A corollary of the right to limit immigration is the right to deport those who enter or stay illegally. If I am right about this, then a state does not violate a person's human rights by refusing him or her entry (assuming that this is in accordance with a general immigration policy that is morally acceptable), even though the result is that the person remains in a country where his or her human rights are not fully respected or upheld.

One might object to my contention that governments are obligated to uphold the rights of aliens present in their territories by claiming that aliens forfeit their human rights when they illegally enter a country. To forfeit one's rights is to lose them for misconduct. Although some countries require those convicted of serious crimes to forfeit some of their civil rights, no civilized country strips criminals of all legal protections and guarantees. And since illegal entry or residence is a minor "crime," there is little basis for the view that aliens present in a country without authorization have forfeited all their human rights. Further, this view would have unacceptable consequences, I believe, since it would imply that a state would do no wrong in killing or torturing an illegal alien.

A more plausible version of this objection is that the undocumented alien loses, by his or her illegal presence in a country, not his or her human rights, but any claim upon the positive obligation to uphold those rights that a host government would normally have. Since he has not complied with a state's established immigration procedures, the undocumented alien cannot generate an obligation for the government of that territory to uphold his or her rights. Although the host government is obligated to *respect* an undocumented alien's rights, it is not obligated to *uphold* them.

This view may be attractive to one who wishes to minimize the costs of dealing with undocumented aliens, but it does not have much to recommend it as part of a theory of human rights. As discussed in section III, in choosing between alternative conceptions of the obligations generated by human rights, a conception that provides for the protection of everyone's rights in all places is preferable to one that sometimes leaves people without an agency to uphold their rights. Since the position that states have no obligations to uphold the rights of undocumented aliens has the result of leaving many people without an agency that is morally obligated to protect their rights, there is reason to reject this position in favor of a conception that postulates a prima facie obligation of each state to uphold the rights of all persons in its territory. Further, this view has unacceptable consequences, I believe, since it implies that a state would do no wrong if it refused to protect an illegal alien from an angry mob or to provide food for persons awaiting deportation.

If we allow that the human rights of undocumented aliens should be upheld and that governments may legitimately deport such persons when they are identified as undocumented in accordance with due process, how then can the human rights of undetected illegal aliens be implemented effectively? These people may benefit from general policies of respect and protection for human rights in a country, but more specialized protections and services cannot be sought without risk of detection. Undocumented aliens are often reluctant to seek legal remedies for wrongs done to them or to apply for welfare services, because to do so is to risk apprehension and deportation. As a result, unde-tected illegal aliens are in a position to be exploited, robbed, and blackmailed. It is impossible to uphold fully the rights of people who avoid all contact with government agencies, and this can lead to serious human rights problems in a country with millions of undocumented aliens. The "double bind" faced by illegal aliens seriously erodes their human rights.

This problem could be ameliorated if some important legal and welfare services could be obtained without proof of immigration status. The agencies providing these services might also be forbidden to release information about their clients to the immigration authorities. This might work as a short-term or compromise solution, but would result in less effective enforcement of immi-gration laws. A more adequate solution for the United States, it seems to me, would involve an amnesty for undocumented resident aliens, efforts to reduce illegal entrance, and a liberal immigration policy for people who wish to migrate to this country.

Notes

1. See, for example, Charles B. Keely, *U.S. Immigration: A Policy Analysis*, Public Issues Paper no. 2 (New York: The Population Council, 1979); and Edwin P. Reubens, "Immigration Problems, Limited-Visa Programs, and Other Options," Chapter 7, this volume.

2. See James W. Singer, "Controlling Illegal Aliens—Carter's Compromise Solution," *National Journal*, September 3, 1977, pp. 1379–83. For a detailed critique of Carter's plan, see Rev. Msgr. Anthony J. Bevilacqua, "Legal Critique of President Carter's Proposals on Undocumented Aliens," *Catholic Lawyer* 23 (1978): 286–300.

3. On the Reagan administration proposals, see "Statement by the President," July 30, 1981; Department of Justice press release, "U.S. Immigration and Refugee Policy," July 30, 1981; and the testimony of William French Smith before the Immigration and Refugee subcommittees, July 30, 1981. For a Mexican response, see "Mexican Labor Blasts 'Guestworker' Plan," *San Francisco Chronicle*, August 19, 1981, p. 9.

4. For the text of the Universal Declaration of Human Rights and other documents, such as the European Convention on Human Rights, the International Covenant on Civil and Political Rights, the International Covenant on Economic, Social and Cultural Rights, and the American Convention on Human Rights, see Ian Brownlie, ed., *Basic Documents on Human Rights* (Oxford: Clarendon Press, 1971).

5. Sketches of such a justification are found in my papers, "Is There a Human Right to Employment?" *Philosophical Forum* 10 (1978–79): 149–170 at p. 158, and "Cultural Diversity and Human Rights," in *International Human Rights: Contemporary Perspectives*, edited by Jack Green and Vera Nelson (New York: Earl M. Coleman Enterprises Publ., 1980), pp. 43–56 at p. 48. See also Henry Shue, *Basic Rights* (Princeton: Princeton University Press, 1980).

6. Although human rights do not tell U.S. policymakers how they should weigh those interests of foreigners which are not protected by human rights, when human rights standards are relevant they are likely to provide much less controversial guides to policy than arguments, such as those used by Lichtenberg, based on ability to aid, interdependence, or past harm. See Judith Lichtenberg, "Mexican Migration and U.S. Policy: A Guide for the Perplexed," Chapter 1, this volume.

7. See Myres McDougal et al., "The Protection of Aliens from Discrimination and World Public Order," *American Journal of International Law* 70 (1976): 433.

8. Universal Declaration, 15:1; International Covenant on Civil and Political Rights, 24:3; American Convention on Human Rights, 20:1.

9. Universal Declaration, 15:2; American Convention on Human Rights, 20:3.

10. Universal Declaration, 13:2; International Covenant on Civil and Political Rights, 12:2; American Convention on Human Rights, 22:3.

11. Universal Declaration, 13:2; International Covenant on Civil and Political Rights, 12:4; American Convention on Human Rights, 22:5.

12. Universal Declaration, 14:1; American Convention on Human Rights, 22:7.

13. American Convention on Human Rights, 22:7–8.

14. Ibid., 22:6.

15. Ibid., 22:9.

16. International Covenant on Civil and Political Rights, 25.

17. International Covenant on Economic, Social and Cultural Rights, 2:1.

18. See, for example, the criticism in S. I. Benn and R. S. Peters, *Social Principles and the Democratic State* (London: Allen & Unwin, 1958), pp. 322–23.

19. Note that I do not classify rights as positive and negative; the reason for this is that most rights generate both negative and positive obligations. The distinction is between types of obligations flowing from rights. See Henry Shue, "Rights in the Light of Duties," in *Human Rights and U.S. Foreign Policy*, edited by Peter G. Brown and Douglas MacLean (Lexington, Mass.: Lexington Books, 1979), pp. 65–82. Also see Shue, *Basic Rights*.

20. United Nations Charter, 1:3, 13:1, 55:(c), 68.

21. On self-determination and nonintervention, see Charles Beitz, *Political Theory and International Relations* (Princeton: Princeton University Press, 1979), pp. 92–123; and the essays by Thomas Buergenthal, J. Bryan Hehir, and Mark R. Wicclair in Brown and MacLean, eds., *Human Rights and U.S. Foreign Policy*, pp. 111–60.

22. John Stuart Mill, *On Liberty* (1859), chaps. 1 and 2.

23. Alexander Meiklejohn, *Free Speech and Its Relation to Self-Government* (New York: Harper & Row, 1948).

24. See Maurice Cranston, *What Are Human Rights?* (London: Bodley Head, 1973), pp. 65–72; Charles Frankel, *Human Rights and Foreign Policy* (New York: Foreign Policy Association, 1978), pp. 38–49; and Robert Nozick, *Anarchy, State, and Utopia* (New York: Basic Books, 1974), pp. 149–275.

25. For a fuller treatment of these issues see my paper, "Is There a Human Right to Employment?"

26. As evidence for this claim I would cite the fact that Mexican migrants to the United States are disproportionately young and male—and hence not in great need of welfare services. See James T. Bennett and Manuel Johnson, "Illegal Aliens: Economic and Social Issues," *Akron Business and Economic Review* 9 (1978): 11–16 at p. 12.

27. For the US, see Bennett and Johnson, "Illegal Aliens." On Venezuela, see John Enders, "Venezuela: Country of Non-Citizens," *Christian Science Monitor*, November 28, 1979, section B, p. 6, col. 1.

PART II

Historical Precedents

3

The Importation of Mexican Contract Laborers to the United States, 1942–1964: Antecedents, Operation, and Legacy

MANUEL GARCÍA Y GRIEGO

The *bracero* program, also known as the Mexican contract-labor program, was a mechanism by which Mexicans were sent to work in certain agricultural areas of the United States under a series of bilateral agreements with Mexico that spanned two decades. It began in 1942 as an emergency program to satisfy perceived labor shortages created in agriculture by World War II. By the time this growing and increasingly controversial program reached its peak in the late 1950s, it had become an institutionalized feature of U.S. and Mexican agriculture.

Although the contract-labor program has been defunct since 1965, it has left an important legacy for the economies, migration patterns, and politics of the United States and Mexico. Since 1980, the possibility of again admitting temporary workers from Mexico has become a significant element in the ongoing debate over the direction of U.S. immigration policy. Various interpretations of what occurred during the program have figured prominently in arguments raised for and against the future admission of temporary workers. This chapter will describe the operation and development of the program in historical context and assess its legacy for the current policy debate.[1]

Antecedents

The roots of twentieth-century Mexican migration to the United States, characterized chiefly as a mass movement of rural laborers from specific regions in north-central Mexico to the U.S. Southwest and Midwest, can be found in late nineteenth-century Porfirian Mexico. During the period 1880–1900 the mass of the rural population became proletarianized as a result of Porfirio Díaz's policies; also during this period most of the current south-north railroad grid was constructed and the internal migration of temporary agricultural laborers, especially young adult males, became noticeable. By 1900, Mexico's economy and society had evolved in a manner which met the preconditions for mass labor migration to the United States.[2]

The birth of the twentieth century was marked by a sudden increase in the volume of Mexican migration to the United States. Slightly more than 100,000 Mexican-born persons were censused in 1900. By 1910, this number had doubled to 222,000; it more than redoubled by 1920 (to 486,000), and possibly doubled yet a third time between 1920 and 1930.[3] Although there is some debate concerning the size of the Mexican-born population in 1930—some would revise the census count of 641,000 upward toward one million—there can be no doubt that during the first three decades of the century a substantial growth in the stock of Mexican immigrants residing in the US took place.[4]

The relative impermanence of Mexican settlement in the United States was demonstrated by events following the onset of the Great Depression. As the fourth decade began, economic activity ground to a halt. Mexicans, as well as others, were thrown out of work. Immigration to the US slowed to a trickle, and a mass return movement to Mexico began. According to Mexican government statistics, 345,000 Mexicans—almost the number of immigrants counted in the US in 1920—returned to their homeland between 1929 and 1932. By 1940, the Mexican-born population had been reduced to a fraction of what it had been in 1930.[5]

An overview of the history of Mexican migration to the United States during the years 1900–1940 suggests that four themes may be stressed: (a) the characterization of much of the flow as the movement of temporary or seasonal laborers; (b) the operation of formal labor recruitment systems; (c) the utilization of established repatriation mechanisms at selected points in time, especially during U.S. economic slowdowns; and (d) the involvement of U.S. and Mexican government agencies in influencing the nature and volume of the flow. These themes are interrelated to some extent, although it is useful to discuss them separately in order to describe how pre-bracero-program migration developed.

Without a doubt, a dominant feature of the period 1900–1930 was the presence of a strong component of seasonal labor migration between Mexico and the United States. Although the average annual *net* flow of Mexican immigrants during the first three decades of this century has been estimated to be between 18,000 and 30,000, the average annual *gross* flow was estimated to be between 60,000 and 100,000.[6] These estimates imply a return flow of 42,000 to ₁0,000 annually. Mexican government statistics regarding the return of its citizens seem to substantiate this figure. They show an average annual return flow of 57,000 over the second and third decades of the century.[7] Prior to 1930, the number of entries to—and departures from—the US seems to have been considerably larger than the number of individuals who entered and remained.

The largely menial occupations found by Mexicans in the United States directly contributed to the seasonal nature of Mexican migration. Immigrants were principally occupied in the railroad industry, as maintenance-of-way workers, and in agriculture, as field hands. They were also employed as miners, quarrymen, copper workers, waiters, waitresses, laundresses, and in other casual laborer-type occupations.[8] Labor demand in these occupations was subject to great fluctuations, which encouraged not only seasonal international migration from Mexico but also internal migration of Mexicans within the United States. Since by 1920 the majority of Mexican immigrants were working at agricultural occupations, crop time tables obviously contributed to sharp seasonal fluctuations in labor demand.[9]

To ensure that the rise in labor demand would be met by an adequate supply of Mexican workers, formal as well as informal labor recruitment systems came into being. They first appeared early in the twentieth century when the railroads monopolized substantial numbers of workers. They were later supplemented by small agencies and labor contractors who undertook the task of channeling Mexican labor to specific employers, particularly to farmers near the border willing to pay a higher wage than that offered by the railroad.[10]

By 1920, it appeared that the internal migration of Mexicans to points at the border was self-sustained; thereafter, employers directed much of their efforts toward the recruitment of labor *within* the United States among those Mexicans who had trekked north on their own. They could be found in such migrant entrepôts as El Paso, the lower Río Grande Valley, San Antonio, and even Los Angeles.[11] Such employers included the Detroit automobile industry in 1918, the Bethlehem Steel Corporation in 1923, the US Steel plant in Lorain, Ohio, in the same year, and Alaskan fish canneries at about the same time.[12]

Among the efforts of employers to recruit Mexican labor, perhaps those of the Great Western Sugar Company of Colorado were most noteworthy. This company relied upon thousands of Mexican laborers to cultivate and harvest its northern Colorado sugarbeet crop every season. In 1920 the company sent advance agents throughout the states of New Mexico, Texas, Colorado, Kansas, Nebraska, and Missouri, who worked from house to house in Mexican communities, held public meetings, ran newspaper ads, and offered free transportation to the fields. That same year the company opened an office in El Paso to recruit laborers throughout the season, whereas in Fort Worth and San Antonio it used established labor agents.[13]

Even though this aggressive recruitment effort by Great Western was not typical of the process, it helps to illustrate that recruitment was crucial in assuring an adequate labor supply. This pattern was a general one; labor contractors, or *enganchadores*, appeared frequently in the life-story of Mexican immigrants. Much of the recruitment effort in the United States took place along the Texas border. Small wonder that by 1929 the Texas legislature had adopted a law that levied a tax on the recruitment of laborers by out-of-state employers.[14]

One result of this extreme recruitment program and of the seasonal or temporary occupation of Mexican laborers was that they occasionally found themselves out of work. Economic recessions, a cyclical phenomenon, exacerbated the seasonal unemployment of foreign workers and brought them into competition with U.S. workers. Erratic drops in the economy thus contributed to sporadic expressions of local hostility against Mexican workers and aroused the concern of Mexican consular officials. The repatriation, or return of Mexican immigrants to their homeland, dates back to the nineteenth century.[15] During the period 1900–1940, formal mechanisms for the repatriation of Mexicans were set up. Two historical events—the brief depression of 1921–1922 and the Great Depression of 1929–1933—stand out as times when unusually intense efforts were made to return immigrants to Mexico.

The recession of 1921 reinforced the normal interest of the Mexican government in the repatriation of its citizens, although few organizations outside the consular network and Mexican border officials participated directly. Consular officials were authorized to offer free return transportation to the Mexican interior and subsistence to any repatriate who desired it.[16] The government created a special *Departamento de Repatriaciones* within the *Secretaría de Relaciones Exteriores (SRE)** to administer these efforts.[17] One estimate places the number of repatriated Mexicans during 1921 at 100,000, one-fifth of the Mexican-born population residing in the United States in 1920. With the decline in the number of workers seeking to repatriate, the program was suspended in 1923.[18]

At the beginning of the Great Depression the Mexican government again became formally involved in the repatriation of its citizens from the United States. A *Comité Nacional de Repatriación* was created, duties on goods obtained in the US were waived for returning migrants, and repatriates were included in the accelerating land distribution program of the revolutionary government.[19] Mexican consular officials linked their efforts to those being undertaken by U.S. local governments and charities, who were organizing repatriation programs of their own. The motivations of U.S. agencies in promoting repatriation were twofold: to reduce the number of persons subsisting on relief, and to remove a segment of the population increasingly perceived as a burden to the local community and as undesirable competition in the workplace. Between 1931 and 1934 the county of Los Angeles repatriated 13,000 Mexicans at its own expense; other communities, such as St. Paul, Minnesota; East Chicago, Indiana; Detroit, Michigan; Douglas, Arizona; and the states of Ohio and Michigan organized similar, though less ambitious efforts.[20]

Mexican officials expressed mixed reactions to this repatriation. President Ortiz Rubio (1930–1932) issued a public invitation for emigrants in the United States "to come to their homeland to assist in the economic reconstruction of Mexico."[21] The consulates provided limited repatriation assistance as part of their overall mandate to protect Mexican citizens abroad. But the Mexican government also expressed the view that the ongoing repatriation was symptomatic of how the migration process benefited the United States at Mexico's expense. As the Secretary of *Relaciones Exteriores* put it, his government should evaluate its policies with respect to the emigration of Mexican citizens

*See the end of the text for abbreviations used.

in order to avoid that this type of difficulty repeat itself, given that it would be disastrous for our national economy to . . . on the one hand, establish the precedent of facilitating the departure of our better workers when their services are demanded abroad, and on the other, have these contingents of laborers forced back upon us when they are no longer necessary abroad and when we, too, are economically unable to absorb them.[22]

From the point of view of the Mexican government, the United States and, specifically, U.S. employers had benefited from the "hard labors" of Mexican workers which had "sapped their strength," and it was the responsibility of the US to provide for their "subsistence during this period of depression."[23] Consistent with this view, Mexican consulates encouraged would-be repatriates to pressure their employers for assistance in making the return trip.[24]

North of the border, the view was quite different. United States officials were increasingly concerned about the deepening depression, which had shown no signs of improvement by December 1930, when newly appointed Secretary of Labor William Doak arrived in Washington. The new secretary proposed simply that "one way to provide work for unemployed Americans was to oust any alien holding a job and to deport him."[25] The agency responsible for the enforcement of immigration laws, the Bureau of Immigration, undertook a campaign to deport aliens found in illegal status. Statistics suggest that the actual number of Mexicans deported was small—a few thousand annually— but the effect was magnified by the expulsion of persons who waived deportation proceedings and by the tactic of rounding up large numbers of persons in community sweeps accompanied by massive doses of local publicity.[26]

The official enthusiasm with the repatriation of Mexicans, forced or otherwise, was not shared by the employers who had expended much effort in bringing them north.[27] This led some observers to note that large employers, recruiters, and labor contractors imported Mexicans for what were known to be temporary jobs, and after the work period ended, set them adrift.[28] Others— local charities, community organizations, local governments, the U.S. and Mexican governments, and the immigrants themselves—assumed the burden of providing for unemployed workers and repatriating Mexicans. Regardless of who was responsible for the transportation of Mexican workers north and south, the established pattern of recruitment and repatriation underscores the fact that movement in neither direction was left to chance.

As has been noted, each of the two governments intervened in determining the course of this migratory flow. At times the U.S. government acted to attract Mexican immigrants; at others it acted to restrict their entry and to expel those already here. The Mexican government was more consistently opposed to emigration, although it did not always act vigorously to retain or return its citizens. Emigration was perceived, particularly in the two decades before the bracero program, as a symbol of what was wrong with prerevolutionary Mexico.[29] Both repatriation and domestic socioeconomic reforms served legitimating functions for the early regimes trying to consolidate their power. These policies were intensified during the Cárdenas administration (1934–1940).

Other actions not directly connected with repatriation policies, such as the massive distribution of land that was carried out in the north-central region of the country, had the indirect effect of temporarily restraining Mexican emigration to the United States.[30]

Mexico's official position on this matter emerged from the 1917 Constitutional Convention, where legislation was passed in the form of Article 123 of the Constitution to provide safeguards for emigrant workers. Popular views in Mexico correctly held that emigrant workers in the United States suffered serious abuses. In the late teens, Mexican border officials were ordered to discourage the departure of workers who did not have labor contracts meeting the standards of the newly enacted legislation. The consulates in the United States were directed to become more active in protecting the rights of Mexican citizens, which they did, to a limited extent. Throughout the 1920s, the Mexican government exhorted emigrants to stay at home, and provided return transportation to others with the hope that the return migration would be permanent.[31]

By 1929, it had become abundantly clear that Mexican unilateral efforts to restrain emigration had failed.[32] From this failure, and from the sudden realization in the early 1930s that the U.S. economic downturn—and not Mexican government policies—was causing emigrants to return in record numbers, emerged a view that the emigration of unemployed Mexicans was a "safety valve" for Mexico's polity.[33] In a move that would foreshadow the institution of the bracero program a decade later, the Mexican government in 1929 proposed to the United States that it consider an international agreement for the purpose of jointly managing the flow of workers between the two countries. The proposal was ill timed and not acted upon.[34]

In contrast, the changing policies of the U.S. government seemed to be a function of fluctuating economic conditions. In 1909, when there was apparently a need for sugarbeet workers in Colorado and Nebraska, Presidents Taft and Porfirio Díaz arrived at an executive agreement authorizing the migration of a thousand Mexican contract laborers to those states.[35] In 1917, as the United States entered World War I, the prohibitions against contract labor that had just been legislated were suspended for about 73,000 Mexican workers.[36] Some authors have referred to the World War I temporary admissions as the "first bracero program."[37]

During the years 1917–1924, Congress passed a series of laws for the purpose of restricting immigration and tightening government control over border crossings. Literacy tests and a head tax were imposed upon entering immigrants, a numerical limit for each country was set, visa fees were levied, and the Border Patrol was created. (Mexicans and immigrants from other Western Hemisphere countries were exempted from the quota limitations until 1968.)

The enforcement of immigration laws was stepped up, and by the mid-1920s deportation raids had become common among rural communities in the Southwest. Because these raids occasionally deported workers at critical times, many employers voiced strident complaints about these enforcement activities to any authorities who might be in a position to pressure the nearby office of the Bureau of Immigration. The district director of the El Paso office testified:

From the time I came on as district director in March 1926, nearly every year at cotton-chopping or cotton-picking time, the farmers would send a complaint to [Washington] I am certain for no other purpose than to cause an investigation that would result in one of two things: Either I get the word from some higher official to go easy until cotton-chopping . . . or cotton-picking time was over; or the men who were doing the work would be so upset by the investigation that they would go easy on their own.[38]

Moreover, he expressed the view that it was not until 1937 that he received support for carrying out his enforcement duties.[39] Other research on the enforcement of immigration laws in the 1920s and 1930s suggests that the situation with the El Paso office may have been typical of enforcement activities along the Mexican–U.S. border.[40]

If the implementation of U.S. government policy at the border with respect to Mexican undocumented immigration seems to have been flexible, it is clear that the legislation providing for the admission of legal immigrants was similarly pragmatic. Two mutually antagonistic provisions were continued from prior legislation: the prohibition against contract labor and the exclusion of immigrants "likely to become a public charge." These restrictions allowed for wide latitude in administrative discretion. When Mexican immigration was restricted administratively after the mid-1920s, these two provisions made it possible to reject visa petitions from immigrants with no history of residence in the United States. Many Mexicans who were "admitted" as legal immigrants in the late 1920s and 1930s by U.S. authorities were *already* residing (after having entered illegally) in the United States.[41]

In the United States, the entry of Mexicans during the period 1900–1940 was regarded chiefly as a *labor* migration. This is symbolized by the themes highlighted by contemporaneous researchers in their work: Clark (1908) and Taylor (1927–1934) wrote not about Mexican *immigration*, but about Mexican *labor* in the United States. The public and government officials on each side of the border shared this view. Indeed, the historical record shows that Mexican migration to the US before 1940 cannot be separated from such labor-related themes as seasonal migration, labor recruitment, repatriation, and certain types of government intervention. Some of the mechanisms associated with labor migration during the first four decades of this century were to become institutionalized in the period of the Mexican contract-labor program, 1942–1964.

War-time Cooperation, 1942–1946

On August 4, 1942, the governments of the United States and Mexico embarked upon a program unprecedented in the history of both nations: the large-scale, sustained recruitment and contracting of temporary migrant workers under the aegis of an international agreement. This agreement was renewed several times during World War II, and in 1946, a year after the war ended, its termination was proposed by the State Department. Also in 1946, Congress provided the first legislative authority for a postwar contract-labor program. Since the succeeding international agreement, that of March 10, 1947, introduced some substantial changes in the operation of the program, 1946 marks an appropriate terminus for what may be considered the first and simplest phase of the bracero program. (For a chronology of the contract-labor program, see the appendix.)

What the 1942 agreement did was to create a labor recruitment and contracting system administered by a number of government agencies on both sides of the border. On the Mexican side the program first involved the *Dirección General del Servicio Consular*, the *Oficialía Mayor* and, later in the 1950s, the *Dirección de Asuntos de Trabajadores Agrícolas Migratorios (DATAM)* of the *Secretaría de Relaciones Exteriores (SRE)*; officials of the *Secretaría de Gobernación*, and the *Secretaría del Trabajo y Previsión Social*; the offices of the state governors; and the *presidentes municipales* of the counties where migrant workers resided. First an agency of *Gobernación*, then *DATAM* served as the principal administrative center, where operating decisions were made and information relative to Mexico's role in the international agreements was gathered. This agency was also responsible for assigning quotas to the Mexican states and for making sure that the requisite number of workers assembled at the recruitment centers (Mexico City during 1942–1944 and Guadalajara and Irapuato during 1944–1947). The functions of some of these agencies changed several times during the life of the program.[42]

On the U.S. side, four departments were involved in the administration of the program: State, Justice, Agriculture, and Labor. The federal agencies most actively involved were the U.S. Employment Service (USES) of the Department of Labor (DOL) and its state branches, and the Immigration and Naturalization Service (INS) of the Department of Justice. The principal administrative responsibility was assigned initially to the DOL in 1942; this was quickly transferred to the Department of Agriculture in 1943 and then returned to the DOL at the end of the war.[43]

The Mexicans who were accepted by their government as bracero candidates were turned over to the Department of Labor (USES) representatives who, acting as agents for employers, selected those they thought fit for agricultural work. Next, INS officers took fingerprints and prepared documentation for those accepted, and the candidates were transported to U.S. contracting centers at the border. There they were screened by the U.S. Public Health Service and were left to be considered by visiting employers and their agents.[44]

This process of labor recruitment and distribution, created during the war, remained in operation for 22 years. To be sure, the names and duties of the government agencies involved changed throughout this period; for several years after World War II, the labor contracts were made directly between U.S. employers and Mexican workers, and the bureaucratic machinery to enforce their provisions was scaled back drastically. But even then, the program was operated within the framework of an international agreement, and either one or both governments were involved in the recruitment and distribution of workers. Thus, the wartime program represented the beginning of a process Ernesto Galarza aptly calls "managed migration"—a process sustained virtually without interruption from 1942 to 1964. In a number of other respects, however, the period 1942–1946 is unique. First, World War II represented a period of extraordinary growth in the demand for labor in the United States. Yet, by comparison to the years after 1946, the number of workers involved in the wartime program was the smallest ever. Another feature of the period 1942–1946 is that contract laborers were employed in activities other than agriculture. Finally, it was the only sustained period during which the Mexican government seems to have had the upper hand during the bilateral negotiations.

As noted above, wartime labor demand and economic growth were impressive. This was particularly true in California, where employment in the shipbuilding and aircraft industries increased, respectively, from 31,000 and 96,000 in 1941 to 274,000 and 236,000 in 1943. Those previously unemployed due to the depression went back to work, and the traditional barriers against the industrial employment of certain groups—women, blacks, nonunion workers, and members of certain ethnic groups, such as Mexicans—disappeared momentarily. The trickle of workers from agriculture to the growing wartime industries, which was noticeable as early as 1941, became a torrent.[45]

Thus, at a time when the wartime demand for agricultural products was growing rapidly, the available agricultural labor force was shrinking. Agricultural wages began to rise, although they remained below industrial levels, and farms began to compete for labor. No longer applicable were the informal wage agreements that had been negotiated among growers in the past; these gave way to the "stealing" of workers employed by other growers, which brought cries of "labor piracy" by the affected employers. Lloyd Fisher, describing the economics of this process, noted: "Whether a 'shortage' of agricultural labor had developed by 1943 depends upon the definition given to the term 'shortage' . . . but the labor market had clearly begun to change from a buyer's to a seller's market."[46]

This "shortage" of labor and the critical importance of certain agricultural products in wartime were the essential elements which provided the justification—from the U.S. point of view—for the creation of the wartime emergency contract-labor program. Whether labor "shortages" actually existed or not, as Fisher has noted, is a matter of definition, but evidently there was a general *perception* in the United States that there was a labor shortage in agriculture, particularly in California.

Notwithstanding such perceptions, it is noteworthy that the number of workers imported during the critical years of World War II was smaller than the number contracted for any comparable postwar period. Depending upon whether one uses Mexican or U.S. statistical sources, the average number of contract workers that entered per year during 1943–1946 was 49,000 or 82,000.[47] Regardless of which of these two numbers is correct, or what precisely each data set indicates, there is no doubt that the wartime period involved the smallest volume of recorded bracero migration. During the later period of 1947–1954, the average annual number of contracts issued was at least 116,000 and could have been as high as 141,000. During the final ten years of the program, the average annual number of contracts recorded was 333,000. Of the total 4.6 million contracts issued during the life of the program, about 72

Table 3.1   Indicators of Mexican Labor Migration to the United States, 1942–1964

Year[a]	Mexican contract workers departed, according to Mexican authorities[b] (Col.) 1	Contracts issued to Mexican workers by U.S. authorities[c] 2	Mexican immigrants admitted to U.S.[d] 3	Deportable Mexicans apprehended[e] 4
1942	4,152	4,203	2,378	na
1943	75,923	52,098	4,172	8,189
1944	118,059	62,170	6,598	26,689
1945	104,641	49,454	6,702	63,602
1946	31,198	32,043	7,146	91,456
1947	72,769	19,632	7,558	182,986
1948	24,320	35,345	8,384	179,385
1949	19,866	107,000	8,083	278,538
1950	23,399	67,500	6,744	458,215
1951	308,878	192,000	6,153	500,000
1952	195,963	197,100	9,079	543,538
1953	130,794	201,380	17,183	865,318
1954	153,975	309,033	30,645	1,075,168
1955	398,703	398,650	50,772	242,608
1956	432,926	445,197	65,047	72,442
1957	436,049	436,049	49,154	44,451
1958	432,491	432,857	26,712	37,242
1959	444,408	437,643	23,061	30,196
1960	319,412	315,846	32,684	29,651
1961	296,464	291,420	41,632	29,817
1962	198,322	194,978	55,291	30,272
1963	189,528	186,865	55,253	39,124
1964	179,298	177,736[f]	32,967	43,844

[a] Calendar years for column 1, fiscal years for all other columns.

[b] *Anuario Estadístico de los Estados Unidos Mexicanos*, 1943–1954, 1964, and unpublished data collected by the Dirección General de Estadística, summarized in Moisés González Navarro, *Población y sociedad en México (1900-1970)* (México: Facultad de Ciencias Políticas y Sociales, UNAM, 1974), vol. 2, table opposite p. 146.

[c] U.S. Department of Labor, summarized in Congressional Quarterly, *Congress and the Nation, 1945-1964* (Washington, D.C.: Congressional Quarterly Service, 1965), p. 762.

[d] For the period 1942–1954, the immigrants admitted refer to persons of Mexican citizenship, and beginning in 1955, to persons born in Mexico. U.S. Bureau of the Census, *Statistical Abstracts*, summarized in González Navarro, *Población y sociedad*, pp. 133–34.

[e] Prior to 1960 these refer to actual apprehensions; afterwards, to deportable Mexicans located. INS *Annual Reports*, summarized in Julian Samora, *Los Mojados: The Wetback Story* (Notre Dame: University of Notre Dame Press, 1971), p. 46.

[f] After 1964, the following number of contract workers were admitted under P.L. 414: 20,286 in 1965, 8,647 in 1966, 7,703 in 1967, and zero thereafter. Source: U.S. Department of Labor, in George C. Kiser and Martha Woody Kiser, eds., *Mexican Workers in the United States: Historical and Political Perspectives* (Albuquerque: University of New Mexico Press, 1979), p. 219.

percent occurred between 1955 and 1964, whereas the wartime program involved only 4–7 percent of all such contracts.[48]

The only nonagricultural industry to succeed in establishing that a labor shortage existed was the railroad. The employment of contract laborers by this industry, particularly in tasks related to the maintenance of way, was unique to the wartime period and an aberration in the history of the bracero program.[49] Its administration by U.S. officials was entirely separate from the farm-labor program; and many of its logistical functions, such as defining the specifications and requirements for labor, securing food and transportation facilities, carrying out recruitment and interviewing workers, and issuing Individual Work Agreements and cards, were the responsibility of a quasi-labor agency, the Railroad Retirement Board.[50] Moreover, at the end of the war there was an immediate effort to repatriate the contract workers and terminate the program, an effort which suffered relatively minor delays.

In April 1943, when contracting for the railroad program began, the agency responsible for supervising the program, the War Manpower Commission, approved the use of construction and maintenance-of-way workers for the Southern Pacific, the Atchison, Topeka, and Santa Fé, and the Western Pacific railroads. The privilege of utilizing Mexican contract workers was extended the following year to 21 other railroads. By the time the contracting stopped in 1945, 35 railroads were involved. The majority of the railroad "braceros" worked in Montana, Washington, Oregon, California, Nevada, and southern Arizona; over half of them worked for the Southern Pacific or the Atchison, Topeka, and Santa Fé lines. At the peak of the railroad program in March 1945, 69,000 workers were employed.[51]

The position of the Mexican government on the creation and operation of the contract-labor program during the cooperative era of 1942–1946 was influenced to a great extent by its prior experiences with the repatriation of Mexican citizens, and with the unorganized recruitment that had been carried out by enganchadores (labor contractors) and private employers during the preceding decades. Controls over the international contracting of its citizens had been written into the Ley de Migración of 1932.[52] Mexico was also influenced by domestic public opinion, which opposed labor emigration to the United States,[53] and by the ideas of Manuel Gamio, a leading anthropologist who had written a seminal work on the subject in 1930.[54]

The preparation that went into the negotiation of the agreement, and the reluctance to enter into the contract-labor program in 1942, reveals the Mexican government's sensitivity to these factors and explains why it expressed serious reservations about the emigration of its citizens.[55] In addition to these concerns, opposition to the program was based on the notion that Mexican agricultural production would be harmed by labor emigration to the north.[56] Nevertheless, it is probable that emigration was perceived in some quarters of Mexican government as a potential safety valve for rural unemployment even as early as 1942. Adherents of this point of view held that the U.S.–Mexican agreement would facilitate the labor exodus in a controlled manner, one which would allow the Mexican government to influence its management. Moreover, it seems that the bracero agreement was initially conceived by Mexico as part of a package that included wartime cooperation in other areas in exchange for U.S. concessions on Mexico's foreign debt and the settlement of claims arising from the recently expropriated oil industry.[57]

In any event, when in 1942 Mexico expressed its willingness to consider an international labor agreement with the United States, it did so on the basis of a number of conditions.[58] First, recruitment would be based on a written labor contract. Second, the administration of the program would be carried out by both governments, and contract compliance would be guaranteed by the same. Third, recruitment would be based on need, i.e., Mexican laborers would not displace domestic labor nor lower its wage.[59] Fourth, employers or the U.S. government would pay transportation and subsistence costs between the recruitment center in Mexico and the work site. Fifth, contract workers would not be permitted to remain permanently in the United States. Finally, racial discrimination, of the type in which Mexicans were turned away from "white" restaurants and public facilities or sorted by color on buses, was unacceptable. Its occurrence in a U.S. community would constitute grounds for excluding braceros from that community. In the view of the Mexican government, adherence to these conditions would allow the migration to take place without the serious abuses it perceived had occurred in the past.[60]

The agreement, signed on July 23, 1942 and made effective by an exchange of diplomatic notes on August 4, incorporated all the above elements and provided contract workers with certain labor guarantees not then available under U.S. law to domestic workers. This outcome suggests a relatively strong Mexican negotiating position in 1942,[61] a further indication of which was the initial reaction by U.S. growers to the contents of the agreement. The president of the American Farm Bureau complained about the extensiveness of the program's regulations, expressed the view that they were unnecessary, and recognized that informal recruitment mechanisms already existed: "Why not just let the growers go into Mexico and get the workers they needed as they had done in the past?"[62]

Another indication of Mexico's bargaining strength was its refusal to certify braceros for employment in the state of Texas—a position it justified by reference to the discriminatory treatment historically suffered by Mexicans in that state. In response, Texas appointed its Good Neighbor Commission and lobbied strongly to be included among the areas receiving contract laborers. It was unsuccessful in effecting a change in Mexican policy throughout the war, however, and not until March 10, 1947, did Mexico lift its ban on Texas.[63] During the period when the bracero agreement was not in force in Texas, its agricultural employers relied on Mexican workers who entered without any documents at all—known then as "wetbacks."

Although the Mexican government's practice of unilaterally blacklisting Texas—and other U.S. areas where discrimination occurred—may not have reduced the discrimination its citizens suffered in the United States, it did promote a greater awareness, at some embarrassment to U.S. officials, of the problem. The Mexican government could also point to the blacklisting, in justifying the program to domestic constituencies, as a sign of its willingness to establish some limits on the abuses suffered by Mexican workers in the United States. Nonetheless, the practice became a serious bone of contention, and it ended during the negotiations for the 1949 agreement.

Despite occasional tension over the conduct of the program, the two governments managed to play down the conflicts that occurred and put the best possible light on the situation. Some of those incidents, however, were indicative of underlying tensions that were to erupt in the postwar period, during a time when the management of conflict between the two governments was to receive less attention.

One source of tension was the previously mentioned Mexican insistence that contract laborers not be sent to Texas because of ongoing discrimination against Mexicans in that region. Nevertheless, Texas growers needed labor, and they made their needs felt when Congress, in the spring of 1943, enacted Public Law 45, which gave legislative approval to the executive agreement negotiated months earlier. The act included a section authorizing the Commissioner of Immigration to lift then-existing restrictions on the entry of farm laborers so that under certain conditions an "open border" could be unilaterally declared by the United States, much as had occurred during the temporary admissions of World War I.[64] On May 11, 1943, regulations were issued authorizing Mexican laborers waiting at the border to enter for a period of one year. According to one source, Texas farmers, "harried by fears of insufficient labor to meet spring needs, rushed across the border to recruit the necessary workers."[65] This process evidently undermined the bilateral program upon which the Mexican government had staked so much, and on May 28 it threatened to abrogate the agreement. After a series of meetings between U.S. government officials and farm groups "in which some of the participants bluntly advocated disregarding Mexico's wishes," the State Department announced that the section of Public Law 45 providing for unilateral recruitment did not apply to Mexico.[66] What in 1944 might have boiled over as a crisis was averted by the adoption of a U.S. position that assigned a greater weight to assuring Mexico's cooperation in keeping the program intact than to assuaging the special interests of Texas growers in getting access to labor on their own terms.

Another source of tension was the management—or mismanagement—of the so-called "wetback" problem. When contract laborers and unilaterally recruited workers were banned from Texas, in order to assure a labor supply to the growers of that state the U.S. government acquiesced in the use of "wetback" labor by Texas farmers. An Assistant Commissioner of Immigration wrote: "At times, due to manpower shortages and critical need for agricultural production brought on by the war, the Service officers were instructed to defer the apprehension of Mexicans employed on Texas farms."[67] This practice brought Mexican protests that the United States do something about the employment of undocumented workers, and U.S. countercharges that Mexico itself was not doing enough to prevent illegal migration and to return expelled migrants to the interior.

In June 1944, the two governments agreed on a set of joint policies to address the problem, which included border enforcement by both countries.[68] According to U.S. sources, Mexico did not carry out its part of the agreement. The US did increase enforcement by the INS, but to minimize its expense, it expelled the migrants through the nearest border community; those apprehended in California were expelled through Mexicali and Tijuana, which were virtually isolated from the rest of Mexico at that time because of limited transportation facilities. These INS actions apparently created severe problems for those Mexican border communities, and in December 1944 the Mexican government unilaterally closed those two ports to the return of expelled migrants. The U.S. government responded by redirecting some of those expelled to other border ports more accessible to the Mexican interior.[69] As in the previous example, this series of events suggests a superior Mexican bargaining position.

During 1945 and 1946, Mexico and the United States continued to make limited efforts to improve the management of the legal program and to address the problem of workers who entered illegally. By this time, however, it was becoming clear that without spending additional money on enforcement—and perhaps then—these objectives would not be met. For whatever reasons, neither government increased its allocation of resources significantly. When the war came to a close, conditions were perceived to have worsened. The Mexican government refused to transport expelled migrants to the interior, U.S. officials slackened efforts to deport migrants, and unemployed Mexicans congregated in the border towns of both countries. Domestic groups in the US, which had not been vocal during the war, began to speak out against the importation of foreign labor.[70]

At the end of 1946, the posture of the U.S. government, though ambiguous, seemed to indicate that the bracero program was coming to an end. To be sure, Public Laws 521 and 707, enacted that year, extended the appropriations of the program to 1947 and provided legislative authority for what could no longer be considered an emergency, wartime program. Nevertheless, the nonagricultural component of the bilateral agreement was terminated noisily, and the State Department formally proposed an end to the agricultural program within the time frame originally established. Similarly, although two years earlier a Mexican source had indicated that the emigration of workers had been a palliative for Mexico's unemployment, the *Secretaría del Trabajo* unofficially communicated its desire that the program come to an end.[71] Thus, during the closing weeks of 1946 it appeared that the four-year program, with several hundred thousand contracts issued, was about to pass into history. It would have been difficult to imagine that 18 more years of existence and 4.3 million more contracts lay ahead.

Turbulence and Transition, 1947–1954

Almost all the significant changes that occurred in the contract program between the early war years and the late contracting system of the 1960s took place during the eight-year period 1947–1954. This interval was marked by international and domestic political conflict, the testing of alternatives, the creation of a new framework for the operation of the postwar contract-labor program, and the shifting and reaccommodation of key players in the political process. During these eight years, the bracero program evolved from a wartime to a peacetime activity where key interests and power politics were given a freer hand, the consequences of which are examined below.

A useful approach to the issues of that time is to divide them into two broad categories: (a) the general problem of illegal, or "wetback," immigration, and (b) certain specific issues of dispute between Mexico and the United States. These problem issues resulted in a number of confrontations, two (October 1948 and January 1954) of which merit discussion as events that both shaped and laid bare the reaccommodation of postwar U.S.–Mexican power relationships.

THE POSTWAR WETBACK INVASION

The entry and presence of undocumented Mexicans became an important issue that drew increased national attention and public hostility in the United States during the postwar years.[72] Since undocumented migration is a clandestine phenomenon, the public perception of the growing problem was based on data that could be only a rough index of its volume, and on its interpretation by public officials. At that time as now, this data consisted of the number of deportable aliens apprehended by INS. A rapidly growing number of such apprehensions led the President's Commission on Migratory Labor to argue in 1951: "The number of deportations and voluntary departures has continuously mounted each year . . . In its newly achieved proportions, [the wetback traffic] is virtually an *invasion*."[73] The magnitude of the arrests increased rather than declined after the commission's report, and in 1954, an INS official characterized the phenomenon as "the greatest peacetime invasion complacently suffered by a country under open, flagrant, contemptuous violation of its laws."[74]

The views expressed by the commission in 1951 reflected a position that was slow to develop in the United States. Earlier, public opinion had countenanced the illegal entry and employment of undocumented Mexicans. Thus, some of the proposals of the commission—the imposition of penalties for those who harbored, concealed, or transported illegal aliens, fines and imprisonment for employers of deportable aliens, prohibitions against interstate shipment of products made with the labor of undocumented aliens[75]—seemed novel or harsh. The recommendations of the commission were largely ignored. Only the criminal sanctions against "harboring" deportable aliens were approved, and at the insistence of the Texas congressional delegation, the so-called "Texas Proviso" was inserted in the 1952 anti-wetback legislation, which explicitly exempted the act of offering employment from its penalties.[76]

By contrast, since the early 1940s the Mexican government had expressed the view that the extralegal emigration of its workers was a threat to the bracero system, to domestic agricultural production, and to the agricultural interests who wanted assured access to an ample domestic labor supply. Early in the operation of the program Mexico pressed the United States to effectively penalize employers of undocumented labor. It also promoted cooperative efforts to control the clandestine migration to the north, but it stopped short of costly enforcement measures.[77]

Critics of Mexican anti-wetback policies have pointed out that other than consistently to pressure the United States to penalize employers, Mexico itself did little to stop the undocumented flow.[78] The reasons for this have yet to be adequately explored. Certainly, Mexican officials were juridically correct in pointing out that Mexican legislation on this issue provided the government with few legal instruments to interfere with the free transit of its citizens. Also, Mexican policymakers probably had not forgotten that there were limits to the effectiveness of Mexican government intervention in this process, as evidenced by the failure of Mexican efforts in the 1920s to stop labor emigration. Moreover, the thrust of Mexican government actions throughout the bracero program suggests an awareness by political elites that the government had little domestic "policy space" in this issue area.[79] But there is also evidence, as is mentioned below, to show that Mexico's stake in the continuation of emigration to the United States seems to have become more visible in the postwar years, raising the question whether it was consistent with its objective interests to stop the clandestine flow. Nevertheless, Mexico's perceived interests, as well as its formal position, were consistently expressed in opposition to the uncontrolled emigration of its citizens.

The United States was more equivocal. "Even in 1952 and 1954, when the wetbacks were in full tide," wrote Ernesto Galarza, "senators and representatives from the border states took the lead in cutting back appropriations for the Border Patrol. With the purse half shut the gate could remain half open."[80] Testimony of Border Patrol officers indicates that immigration law enforcement, particularly along the Texas border, was deliberately lax and selective. As early as 1949, Senator Clinton P. Anderson of New Mexico had introduced a bill (S. 272) arguing for an "open border" and virtually unrestricted recruitment from Mexico.[81] The following year, the chief inspector at the port of Tucson, Arizona, testifying before the President's Commission on Migratory Labor, noted that he "received orders from the District Director at El Paso each harvest to stop deporting illegal Mexican labor."[82] A report from south Texas at about the same time indicates that a senior officer kept his force of Border Patrolmen away from certain farms and ranches in his district.[83] The explanation for this flexible approach to the enforcement of immigration law was expressed in testimony before Congress in 1951 by the chief INS official responsible for this enforcement in a bald-faced assertion of authority to enforce the law selectively: "We do feel we have the authority to permit to remain in the United States aliens who are here as agricultural workers whether they are here legally or not."[84]

U.S. policy responses to undocumented migration can be divided into two categories: mass legalization (1947–1951) and mass expulsion accompanied by legalization (1954–1955). Both processes involved the transformation of illegal to legal (contract) labor migration. During this period, therefore, the flow of

Mexican labor was not stopped; it was regularized. The first process was called "drying out the wetbacks"; the second was a campaign run by the Border Patrol called "Operation Wetback."

Legalization was a process by which deportable Mexicans who had been in the United States for a certain number of weeks were given bracero contracts, usually to work for the same employer, without the laborer having to return to Mexico and undergo the screening process in the interior, or the employer having to pay transportation to the United States. It first occurred as a result of the 1947 bilateral agreement, when 55,000 undocumented Mexicans in Texas (which up to that time had received no contract laborers) were legalized as braceros.[85] According to the President's Commission on Migratory Labor, during the years 1947–1949, 74,600 Mexican contract laborers were imported, and 142,200 deportable Mexicans already in the US were legalized and put under contract.[86] During fiscal year 1950, only 19,813 new bracero contracts were issued; but 96,239 undocumented Mexicans already here were "dried out" as a result of the international agreement.[87] Thus, in the years following the war, more legalized "wetbacks" were contracted by employers than braceros were imported from within Mexico. By the time the commission's report was written in 1951, it had become evident that mass legalization was not curbing illegal immigration; as a result, its abolition was successfully recommended.[88] Nevertheless, the practice did convince many employers that bracero labor could be used as a substitute for undocumented labor when deportation raids threatened to interrupt access to such labor.[89]

The organization of Operation Wetback followed a tour of inspection of the U.S.–Mexico border in August 1953 by Attorney-General Herbert Brownell.[90] In April 1954, retired army general Joseph Swing, a personal friend of President Eisenhower, was named INS commissioner, and a military-style expulsion campaign was in the process of formulation.[91] After much fanfare in the US, Operation Wetback formally began on June 17 with the deployment of 800 Border Patrol officers in Mexican communities and ranches throughout southern California. The immigration authorities were able to count on the support of local and state authorities, including the police, and the local press, who created the impression that an "army" of Border Patrolmen was "invading" the area. The patrol had impressive logistical support, including the use of aircraft and boats. Most important, in California they were able to count on the farmers who employed the aliens.[92] Many were not expelled to the border as was customary, but were transported by air, sea, and land to the Mexican interior with financial support provided by the Mexican government.[93]

In the months following, the operation moved to the Midwest and Pacific Northwest, and to Texas, where it received some resistance in farm communities.[94] Operation Wetback was sanctioned by U.S. public opinion, which blamed "wetbacks" for the propagation of disease, labor strikes in agriculture, subversive and communist infiltration, border crimes, low retail sales in south Texas, and adverse effects on domestic labor.[95]

Operation Wetback was viewed by its organizers as a test upon whose outcome the future of the Border Patrol might rest.[96] Fortunately for the leadership of INS, the action was immediately successful in restoring credibility and morale to an agency which had a serious image problem with Congress.[97] The campaign had been underway for barely a month when Congress, which had cut INS's budget from the previous year, rewarded the agency with a supplemental appropriation of $3 million.[98]

Contrary to popular opinion, Operation Wetback was not merely a mass-expulsion campaign, although the deportation drives were the most visible part of this action. Had it been, history suggests that it would have accomplished little. Instead, the relative success of Operation Wetback in reducing the volume of illegal migration seems to have rested upon a unique strategy of combined rewards and punishments mostly directed at the employers of such workers. Important elements in this strategy were INS activities designed to (a) convince employers that they faced an increased risk of having the INS interrupt their use of undocumented labor,[99] (b) facilitate access to contract labor for these employers,[100] and (c) "streamline" the contract-labor program and eliminate those provisions to which employers objected most seriously.[101] Another element that seems to have been important in effecting changes in employer attitudes toward the *status* of their workers (though not toward their need for Mexican labor) was the more general pattern of anti-wetback public opinion.[102] These factors, taken together, provide plausible reasons why Operation Wetback was successful in regularizing much of the flow of Mexican labor to the United States.

As early as 1955, INS could take credit for having eradicated the "wetback problem." In his annual report of that year, Commissioner Swing wrote: "The so-called 'wetback' problem no longer exists. . . . The border has been secured."[103] The number of apprehensions of Mexicans dropped precipitously after 1954, and by 1958 the Mexican newspaper *Excélsior* was implicitly editorializing that "the era of the 'wetbacks' [had passed] into history."[104] Hindsight tells us, of course, that they editorialized too soon, but it is evident that the flow of undocumented labor was reduced substantially for a decade from what appearances suggest it had been before 1954.

The costs of this achievement were not immediately apparent.[105] One of the consequences of the "success" of Operation Wetback, as was noted, was the substitution of bracero labor for undocumented workers. In order to persuade employers to effect the substitution, the protections of the contract-labor program were dropped—formally, through negotiation with Mexico, and informally, by reduced U.S. enforcement of contract provisions.[106] In other words, after 1954 the bracero program became little more than a formally sanctioned recruitment system for the employment of "wetbacks" in U.S. agriculture.

DIPLOMACY AND DISPUTE ON SELECTED ISSUES

The period 1947–1954 witnessed a series of sharp confrontations between the governments of the United States and Mexico and a growing public debate on the formal aspects of the contract-labor program. The disputed issues, to be discussed below, were (a) the location of the recruitment centers in Mexico, (b) the practice employed by the Mexican government of unilaterally blacklisting areas and employers from receiving contract workers, (c) the wages earned by contract laborers, and (d) the relative merits of government-to-government and employer-to-worker agreements. To varying degrees, each of these issues led to breakdowns in negotiations during this eight-year period, and each contributed to the mounting tensions immediately preceding the two border incidents and diplomatic confrontations.

Out of this turbulence, three major and interconnected themes emerge: the progressive deterioration of the Mexican government's bargaining position, the assertion of control over the program by U.S. farm organizations, and the increasing importance to the Mexican government that it maintain the program for what was perceived to be a "safety valve" for domestic rural unemployment. As a result of these processes, by 1954 U.S. farm groups had managed to institutionalize a labor-recruitment program largely paid for by the Mexican and U.S. governments, which supplied them with labor on favorable terms. Also apparent by 1954 was a willingness on the part of the Mexican government to compromise, almost at any cost, its position on the operation of the program and to look the other way when the contract guarantees it had worked so hard to achieve became diluted.

The U.S. position on the location of the recruitment centers, which was largely determined by the interests of agricultural employers, was that recruitment should be done as close to the border as possible. A nearby recruitment center was attractive because it meant lower transportation and subsistence costs to the employer who participated in the program.[107] This position also recognized that, since Mexican northward migration to the border had been self-sustained since the 1920s, there was no need for a formal recruitment system to absorb the expense of transporting workers from their communities of origin.

The Mexican position held that recruitment centers should be located in the interior, hundreds of miles from the border. This position seems to have been determined by two principal considerations: first, that the labor supply of large-scale Mexican agriculturalists in the northern states of Sonora, Chihuahua, and Sinaloa might be adversely affected by border recruitment, and second, that the degree of Mexican control over the migration process was directly proportional to the distance the centers were located away from the border.[108] This position recognized that the contract-labor program was a system of managed migration; in order to reduce the effects of *stimulating* undocumented migration, the centers should be located *away* from the border, where such effects would be less pronounced.

The location of the recruitment centers gradually shifted north. During the war, Mexicans were recruited in Mexico City, Guadalajara, and Irapuato. During the 1947–1954 period, new centers were located closer to or at the border: Monterrey, Chihuahua, Zacatecas, Tampico, Aguascalientes, Hermosillo, and Mexicali. Beginning in 1955, Mexican statistics show that some braceros were officially contracted at the border, and Empalme, Sonora, also appeared as a new recruitment center location.[109]

The demise of the Mexican negotiating position on this issue had occurred as early as 1950, even though it may not have been evident to the public at the time. On August 18 of that year, the Mexican government did not seek to prevent the issuance of work certificates to Mexicans at the border. "Although Mexico expressed concern about the total withdrawal of wetback restraint," wrote Peter Kirstein, "there was no abrogation, there was no protest note—just a request that publicity of the Mexican-supported open border 'be restricted.' "[110]

Similarly, the practice of blacklisting certain areas in the United States by the Mexican government to bar the use of braceros was another source of international conflict in which Mexico's position was gradually undermined. These bans were motivated by Mexican perceptions that employers in those areas had not lived up to the terms of the agreements, and by concerns that Mexican citizens in those places were subjected to discrimination. The first concern led to a brief ban upon eight midwestern and northwestern states in 1946 because of reported violations of the agreement by sugarbeet employers.[111] The second concern led to the prohibition of Mexican contract labor in Texas until the legalization in 1947 of undocumented workers already there.[112] Mexico's perception that Texas farmers proceeded to violate the terms of the contracts conferred upon them with the acceptance of legalized labor led to its decision to close Texas to further bracero contracting on September 26 of that year.[113]

The Mexican position during the January–February 1949 negotiations held that a blacklisted area would not be allowed to receive contract workers until guarantees were offered by local authorities that discrimination would stop. In the event that these guarantees were violated, the appropriate Mexican consul was to request the participation of the USES in a joint investigation. But "if the USES and the Mexican consul differed as to the presence of discrimination, the issue was to be unilaterally resolved by the Mexican foreign minister."[114]

The United States argued for joint determination of blacklisted areas and made the execution of its part of the bargain to enforce laws against "wetbacks" contingent upon Mexico's removal of the Texas ban. By the summer of 1949, the Mexican government had given in, and the bracero program was salvaged by an agreement to determine such bans jointly.[115]

Disputes between the United States and Mexico concerning the wages to be paid to braceros by farm employers go to the heart of the conflict over the administration of the program itself. The President's Commission correctly characterized the negotiation of the agreements as a "collective bargaining situation" where Mexico represented its workers and the US its employers. And the SRE, wrote Galarza, "had never concealed its polite indignation over the low wages prevailing in the Southwest."[116] According to Galarza, Mexican pressures to raise the wages paid to braceros led to the two open-border incidents that occurred in 1948 and 1954. Mexican motives for wage increases seem to have been linked to domestic pressure by labor organizations in Mexico and the awareness that they would improve the foreign-exchange earnings of the contract workers. The U.S. response was to accuse the Mexican consuls of attempting to set the wages at rates higher than those prevailing, to blame the "wetback" influx upon Mexican intransigence, and to insist that "if farm employers were to be persuaded to give up hiring illegals 'certain modifications in the agreement and in the work contract are imperative.' " [117]

The original Mexican position during the 1942 agreements was that Mexican labor was to be paid the "prevailing wage" in the communities where braceros were sent. As the Mexican government began to realize that the prevailing wage was whatever the employers decided it would be, it developed the position that the wages paid were negotiable. [118] Its attempt to raise wages for cotton pickers in 1948, however, was unsuccessful. The death knell of the new Mexican position was sounded by the terms of the 1951 agreement, which stated that the U.S. Secretary of Labor would have the exclusive responsibility for determining the prevailing level of wages. [119] After the second major diplomatic confrontation in 1954, the Joint Determination signed that year reaffirmed the same principle. [120]

A final issue that grew out of the conflicts of the years 1947–1954 was the relative merits of government-to-government and worker-to-employer agreements. The wartime agreements were of the former type: they required close governmental supervision over recruitment, selection, transportation, the issuance of contracts, the investigation of complaints, and the assurance of contract compliance. The 1948 agreement introduced some changes that moved the program in the direction of the latter type of agreement: Individual Worker Contracts were issued on a worker-to-employer basis, and the responsibility of INS and USES for assuring compliance was removed. [121] Experimentation with less formal versions of the bracero program continued until congressional approval of Public Law 78 in 1951.

The passage of Public Law 78 had come partially as a result of Mexican insistence that a formal structure for the execution of bilateral agreements be created, and that there be a return to a government-to-government program. In pressing its demands, the Mexican government took advantage of the conjuncture afforded by the Korean War. Its position was strengthened by the President's Commission, whose report was issued as the enactment of Public Law 78 was being debated, and which also argued for an end to the worker-to-employer experiment. [122] Mexico's insistence that the experiment come to an end was motivated by the perception that U.S. employers frequently violated the terms of the agreements negotiated between 1948 and 1951. Placing the responsibility for enforcing the agreement on the shoulders of the U.S. government was perceived to be the most feasible way to assure compliance. [123] Mexican pressures for assuring accountability therefore could be expressed through the familiar channels of diplomatic protest and bilateral negotiation.

The passage of Public Law 78 and the end of the informal period of contracting could be narrowly construed to be a victory for the Mexican vis-à-vis the U.S. position. [124] However, during the postwar years the U.S. position shifted from one exclusively determined by powerful agricultural interests to one influenced by other segments of the U.S. public. These latter segments demanded that the United States assert some control over contract-labor migration and not leave it exclusively in the hands of the employers. Their views were typified by those of the President's Commission. Even so, the influence that employers had on Congress can be discerned from the fact that, despite the pressure of anti-wetback forces, the Mexican government, and others, Congress refused to legislate any penalties against employers for hiring "wetbacks."

The adoption of Public Law 78 was a hollow victory for the Mexican government. To be sure, the mechanisms to ensure contract compliance were formally in place once again, but by this time the Mexican negotiating position had so deteriorated that it mattered little. The years after the 1951 agreement, and particularly after 1954, are marked by Mexican acquiesence to a program whose specifics would have been rejected out of hand at any time prior to 1947.[125]

An important event that influenced Mexican policy responses to bracero emigration was the increasing Mexican stake in maintaining the contract-labor system. This grew out of the perception, which came to dominate the views of Mexican policymakers sometime after World War II, that bracero emigration provided much-needed dollar income[126] and "probably spared Mexico a great deal of social unrest and upheaval."[127] Juan Ramón García argues: "Even if Mexico had discontinued the program at the end of World War II, it is quite doubtful that large-scale emigration to the United States could have been prevented . . .[A]n international agreement, reasoned Mexican officials, would allow for some protection of their citizens while in the United States. If mass emigration seemed inevitable, then let it occur under government auspices."[128] While it is not clear just when the view that emigration was "inevitable" became prevalent among policymakers, it evidently gained currency in the postwar years. At the same time, emigration was becoming a source of acute embarrassment, because it was associated with the failure of the regime's land-reform program.[129]

Thus, the relationship between the Mexican government and the labor program began to be framed in the form of a dilemma for Mexican policymakers. On the one hand, the program was perceived to be increasingly important as a safety valve for domestic political and economic troubles and as an interim strategy for managing Mexico's economic underdevelopment. On the other hand, Mexico's participation in the program was itself viewed as an admission of failure in providing domestic solutions for unemployment problems and as an activity that abetted the exploitation and discrimination suffered by Mexican workers in the United States. Thus, the Mexican government found itself caught between what it perceived to be a growing stake in keeping the labor program in operation, and the political heat resulting from its participation in it—particularly the criticisms leveled at it by leftist opposition groups.[130] It acted to reduce the impact of negative publicity arising from the program and adopted public and private negotiating positions that were increasingly inconsistent.[131] As Mexico's maneuvering room with respect to the United States was shrinking as a consequence of the domestic political process, its bargaining capacity vis-à-vis its neighbor was deteriorating steadily. These complex, interrelated processes set the stage for the diplomatic confrontations of 1948 and 1954.

TWO OPEN-BORDER INCIDENTS

In the summer of 1948 the U.S. government pressured Mexico to allow recruitment along the border; Mexico yielded partially by agreeing to establish a recruitment center in Mexicali and by proposing that centers be established in interior cities of other border states. Nevertheless, according to a secret study uncovered by Peter Kirstein in the Truman Library, representatives of the DOL, INS, and the State Department met to discuss the pros and cons of opening the border to illegal entrants, thereby unilaterally disrupting the 1948 agreement. The meeting, mediated by the White House, seems to have resulted in the position that the agreement would be adhered to.[132]

Between October 13 and 18, however, the border port of El Paso was opened to several thousand undocumented Mexicans waiting to enter the United States:

> The *braceros* . . . waded the shallow river in sight of the Border Patrol, which received them with formality, herded them into temporary enclosures and immediately paroled them to the cotton growers, who trucked the men at once to the fields.[133]

The Mexican government responded by abrogating the 1948 agreement, formally announcing that it would reserve the possibility of filing claims for damage inflicted upon its agricultural production in the north from the uncontrolled exodus of border resident laborers. The US formally apologized for the incident days later.[134]

As a result of his review of the secret study, Kirstein concluded that the order to open the border did not emanate from the White House, but was a decision made within the INS and USES. He made a point to note that no disciplinary action was taken against the officials who created the "El Paso incident," as it became known, and that the United States used the incident to place new conditions on the table when negotiations were reopened during January–February 1949.[135]

In any event, the planning for the second incident clearly involved the highest levels of the U.S. government.[136] On January 15, 1954, the Departments of Justice, State, and Labor issued a joint press release announcing that braceros would be contracted unilaterally until a binational accord was reached. Mexico responded sharply by announcing that braceros could no longer be legally contracted to work in the United States and by exhorting Mexican laborers to stay at home.[137]

The situation in 1954 would seem anomalous today: the US was advocating an "open border" at its neighbor's expense. During the last week of January, hundreds of Mexican workers gathered at Mexican border cities with the expectation of entering the United States, despite the call of their government to stay at home. Mexican local police converged upon mobs, attempting to disperse them and to prevent their entry to the United States. As some of the men raced across the line they were snatched back into Mexico, while Border Patrol officers extended a helping hand from the other side. Other undocumented migrants already in the United States were brought to the border, told to step across briefly to meet the legal requirement of having been expelled, and then to re-enter so they could be admitted as contract workers by INS officials. The resulting commotion was illustrated graphically in a photograph published in February 1954, depicting a bracero pulled in a tug of war between a Mexican border official and a U.S. officer.[138]

Mexico countered with a show of force designed to prevent the emigration of its citizens. The government deployed troops to Ensenada, Nuevo Laredo, Nogales, and other points near the border. Border guards repelled the rush of illegal crossers with clubs, fists, waterhoses, and shots fired into the air. In Mexicali, 500 would-be braceros marched on the governor's palace demanding jobs or food; soldiers turned them back with fire hoses. As President Ruiz Cortines received reports that the international confrontation was turning into a domestic crisis at the border, he ordered Mexican troops withdrawn and instructed Mexican officials not to use force to oppose any citizen attempting to cross illegally. Mexico had been beaten in its brief attempt to use dissuasion and force to prevent the emigration of its workers.[139]

The Mexican defeat in January 1954 merely laid bare the end-result of a process that had been unfolding for several years. On the one hand, as close observers had known for some time, Mexico lacked either the political will or the policy instruments to withhold the labor of its workers on whose behalf it was negotiating, and its "cooperation" with the United States in this and other issue areas was no longer vital. On the other hand, domestic criticism was forcing Mexico to adopt positions which it could not sustain.[140] When it refused to compromise further its position in the fall of 1953, it apparently miscalculated in assuming that the US would not adopt a position of unilateral recruitment.[141] Once the confrontation was in process, little could be done to salvage Mexico's position or credibility.

A number of deliberately conciliatory signals sent by Mexico during the crisis were suggestive of Mexico's limited "policy space." It unilaterally extended the life of the agreement which had expired, and Ruiz Cortines made a public statement that the affront by the United States was "not a problem but only an incident that could be resolved within the norms of the good neighbor policy."[142] Simultaneously, the Mexican ambassador in Washington quietly made a request that negotiations be resumed, to which Eisenhower publicly acceded on February 11. Since the Mexican government needed a face-saving device, this was played up as a victory in the Mexican press.[143]

In the aftermath of the diplomatic crisis it was discovered that the U.S. government had no legal authority to spend federal funds on unilateral recruitment; Congress therefore passed Joint Resolution 355 on March 3, which amended Public Law 78 to provide for U.S. unilateral recruitment.[144] Although the implications of this were not lost on the Mexican negotiators (a U.S. congressman characterized it as a means of seeking an agreement "with a pistol in their backs")[145] the Mexican government publicly played down this legislative defeat.[146] Two days later, the Mexican government announced that the negotiations for a new agreement were proceeding satisfactorily. To allow Mexico some domestic maneuvering room, Eisenhower postponed signing

Resolution 355. A new bilateral accord, in which Mexico in essence ceded all its demands, was reached on March 10, and on March 16 Eisenhower signed the resolution into law.[147] Perhaps to strengthen Mexico's position before its domestic critics, or because the U.S. president had an appreciation for irony, he explained that signing Resolution 355 was "necessary for the United States government to provide Mexican braceros with the protection of its laws."[148] Not surprisingly, Mexico publicly ignored the resolution and instead played up its "success" in reaching the labor agreement, which in actuality "contained little to satisfy the Mexican demands that had prompted termination of the agreement a few months earlier."[149]

The crisis of January 1954 was a rude awakening for the Mexican public. A columnist in a Mexico City newspaper in February seemed to express this when he wrote that thanks to the "safety valve afforded by emigration, the failure of the regime's agrarian-reform policies had not provoked another revolution."[150] Another columnist wondered: "Is it possible to prevent the emigration of braceros?"[151] The answer from the Mexican public seemed to be "no." In his State of the Union address in September 1954, Ruiz Cortines "deplored the migration of laborers but concluded that it was unavoidable because the country did not have enough work to hold the braceros."[152] This view was to hold among Mexican political elites for many years after the crisis of 1954.[153]

Apogee and Demise, 1955–1964

By 1955 the bracero program was well into what Richard Craig calls the "era of stabilization"—a period with no serious disagreements between Mexico and the United States nor substantive changes in the formal operation of the program. It was also a time when the "adverse effects" of the importation of foreign workers, particularly in the agricultural labor market, emerged as a domestic issue in the US, which ultimately led to the end of the contract-labor program.

Early opposition to the importation of foreign workers, in 1947–1949, was based on claims that it undermined strikes, working conditions, and farm wages. So claimed the National Association for the Advancement of Colored People which issued public statements to that effect; and the National Farm Labor Union, affiliated with the American Federation of Labor, enlisted the support of the Federal Advisory Council of the Bureau of Employment Security with the DOL. This position apparently had limited acceptance at that time, however; although the President's Commission showed that the increased use of braceros correlated negatively with rising agricultural wages, it did *not* propose an end to the program. Instead, it argued for modifications which would assure that certifications of need would be based on actual shortages.[154] This view implicitly recognized that the realities of U.S. domestic politics did not allow for any successful opposition to the farm bloc in Congress and assumed that if the program could be held to some standard of compliance, adverse effects could be avoided.

Growers opposed such interpretations of the contract-labor program with arguments which essentially held that there were no serious adverse effects and that the labor contracts were being complied with. They argued that braceros were more efficient than native workers, and that far from constituting a source of cheap labor, they were more expensive than domestic workers since employers were responsible for transportation costs, insurance, bonds, and the like.[155] It appears that the thrust of the growers' arguments—that bracero laborers were more expensive in terms of gross outlays—would have been correct if the contracts had actually been complied with. Evidence suggests that contract compliance was most frequently observed during the wartime program, the period when the labor program was least attractive to employers.[156] Nonetheless, as contract compliance declined and the program was made more attractive to employers (after the postwar period of worker-to-employer agreements and during Operation Wetback), adverse effects from the importation of contract laborers became more visible.[157] As the number of workers involved in the program expanded, growers resorted to the fiction that bracero workers were more expensive—as indeed they had been at the beginning of the program[158]—to defend the program against those who attacked it as a means for importing "cheap labor." In assessing this expanding bracero labor force, Galarza wrote: "Contrary to the iron laws of supply and demand, which are nowhere more ironic than in agriculture, the dearer type of labor was driving out of the market the cheaper."[159]

The substitution of contracted labor for domestic labor proceeded apace throughout this final phase of the program. California farm-labor statistics tell part of the story. From December 1949 to September 1959, the peak number of braceros at work in the state shot up from 7,500 to 84,000. Peak employment of local domestic seasonal workers for the same years declined from 150,000 to 131,500. In certain crops, such as sugarbeets, and in certain areas, such as San Diego and Imperial counties, noncontract labor had virtually disappeared. Comparisons to out-of-state or nonlocal workers are more illustrative. In 1949 there were more than three noncontract workers for every contract laborer; in 1959 there were six contract laborers for every three noncontract workers. "Plainly," asserted Galarza, "the native inter-state migrant, about whose peripatetic misery a copious and sympathetic literature had accumulated, was close to extinction in California."[160]

As the number of contract workers involved in U.S. agriculture increased, so did the perception among agricultural labor organizers that the importation of farm labor had adverse effects upon the domestic labor force. Wages in the agricultural areas where they worked remained constant or dropped. Since domestic farm wages, largely determined by the employers in advance of the harvest, never got much higher than "wetback" standards in the 1950s, it was possible—and common—to find domestic, contract, and undocumented workers in the same crews.[161] Wage depression in the 1950s was facilitated by the importation of labor during a period when increased mechanization of certain crops also lowered the demand for casual labor. Given the relative immobility of many domestic farm workers between rural and urban occupations, and the absolute immobility of contract workers, it appears that increasingly both were competing for less. The National Agricultural Workers Union, a group that was persistent in its attempts to organize California agricultural workers, thus directed most of its energies not toward attacking the growers directly, but toward stopping the Mexican contract-labor program.[162]

The emphasis that the National Agricultural Workers Union gave to exposing the evils of the bracero program found expression in a research project directed by Ernesto Galarza, which was published in 1956 under the title *Strangers in Our Fields*. This report recorded the abuses of the bracero system with depth and perception, often by reproducing interviews held with the braceros in and out of work camps in California. Galarza's interviews and his review of pay stubs and receipts for camp meals and other deducted charges led him to conclude that "in almost every area covered by the International Agreement, United States law, state law, and the provision of the work contract, serious violations of the rights of Mexican nationals were found to be the norm rather than the exception."[163]

The response to *Strangers* by agricultural interests was predictably negative. The official response by the DOL, however, was silence, and its unofficial response constituted the beginning of a reassessment of its position on the contract-labor program.[164] By exposing employer non-compliance with the terms of the labor agreement, Galarza had raised the painful issue of whether the bracero program was having adverse effects on the domestic labor market.

The year that *Strangers* was published also marked the beginning of a new effort by the DOL to tighten its administration of Public Law 78 and to adopt a more skeptical attitude concerning employer compliance with the agreements. In December 1956, the department improved the standards applied to bracero housing; in the summer of 1958, a new formula for determining wages and assuring a minimum hourly rate was applied. In October 1959, the findings of what was known as the Consultants' report were released; the study recommended that the Secretary of Labor take action to reduce the adverse effects of the importation of braceros. In November, the DOL issued new regulations that set minimum standards for the wage and working conditions of domestic workers recruited through the farm placement service of the Labor Department. During this period, the actions of the department and the records of its private meetings indicate the reluctant admission that many of the allegations in *Strangers* were true.[165]

As early as 1957, farmers in the state of California began to sense that opposition to the program created by Public Law 78 was mounting and that the contract-labor system was being seriously threatened. Local grower associations began to exhort their members to "not turn down domestic labor applicants," and one demanded that its members sign a pledge of honest compliance, or be dropped. Caught between the DOL's increasingly forceful attempts to ensure compliance and minimize adverse effects, and a public opinion shifting against the bracero program, farmers became more uncomfortable with a system they had worked to create. Mechanization of the harvest, particularly for those engaged in cultivating cotton, became a sought-after alternative.[166]

Beginning in 1960, opposition to the bracero program mounted in Congress. During the session of that year, acrimonious debate postponed the vote on the extension of Public Law 78 until the last day, at which time a six-month extension was secured. This was the first effective attack on the program in Congress. In 1961, the program was extended for another two years; the anti-bracero forces had gained in strength, although they were unable to bring the program to an immediate end. In 1962 the Kennedy administration openly opposed the Public Law 78 program, and in 1963 the program was extended one final time.[167]

The final extension of the program was obtained only after pro-bracero advocates revealed that there was substantial opposition by the Mexican government to its abrupt termination. A diplomatic dispatch from the SRE dated July 21, 1963, summarized the Mexican position: to end the contracting system would not end the underlying migratory process; in other words, bracero emigration functioned as a substitute for illegal migration. In the view of Mexican political elites, the termination of the program would have serious effects on Mexico's unemployment; the dispatch argued for more time so that Mexico could reabsorb approximately 200,000 persons to "stave off the sudden crisis" that would result.[168] The dispatch was placed into the *Congressional Record* on August 15, and the program was extended for a final year.[169] On December 31, 1964, the Mexican contract-labor program formally came to an end.[170] Mexico did not experience a political upheaval; crops in the U.S. Southwest did not rot in the fields. Whatever were the effects of the termination of the program, they were not immediately apparent.

The Legacy of Debate

A phenomenon of the magnitude and duration of the Mexican contract-labor program does not end without leaving traces of its impact. The effects of the bracero program on the migration process itself have not been adequately researched, although inferences can be drawn from available data. The importation of laborers under contract largely reinforced the characteristic features of pre-bracero migration: the seasonal migration of laborers as opposed to permanent settlement, a regional concentration of migrants from about six or seven states in the north-central region of Mexico to selected areas of the United States West and border areas, and the concentration of Mexican workers in agriculture and in "stoop" labor. It is no surprise that post-1964 "illegals" come from the same regions, work for many of the same employers in the United States, and often work only a few months before returning to Mexico.[171] Clearly, the migration of braceros established continuity between the first wave of Mexican migrants during the first four decades of the century and the more recent immigration of undocumented persons during the 1960s and 1970s.

The migration of workers stimulated and regulated by the contract-labor program is not an aberration in the history of Mexican immigration to the United States. To be sure, the large-scale importation of contract labor from Mexico under the auspices of a binational agreement has not occurred before or since, but to dwell on the formal aspects of administered migration is to miss the point. The bracero migration not only continued the labor migration of the earlier period, it reaffirmed the notion that the northward movement of Mexicans is a single process. Braceros and undocumented (and, to a limited extent, legally admitted) immigrants were substituted for each other. After 1954, the "success" of Operation Wetback signified the substitution of braceros for "wetbacks"—at labor standards substantially below those afforded by contract-labor guarantees. After 1964, some braceros were replaced by "wetbacks" and others by machines; the elite within the bracero labor force immigrated legally and became either permanent residents or "green-card commuters."[172] Thus, throughout the contract-labor period and since then, the formal conditions of Mexican labor migration—i.e., the labels assigned to it—varied from time to time, but the informal patterns of migration persisted.

The termination of the contract-labor program had a pronounced effect on Mexican policymakers. One result was the creation of additional jobs in Mexico, presumably for the ex-braceros who after 1964 could not work legally in the United States. Most frequently cited in this connection is the Border Industrialization, or *Maquiladora, Program*—a system of unique binational concessions principally to U.S. corporations that located manufacturing assembly plants in northern Mexico border towns and whose production is exported entirely to the United States.[173]

A number of factors had already laid the basis for the Maquiladora Program before the end of the contract-labor recruitment, but the Mexican government gave it additional stimulation in 1965. Mexican concessions involved making a number of exceptions in its legislation to allow for wholly owned foreign subsidiaries to enter the country. This action had perceived and objective benefits to certain sectors of Mexico's society, but it also involved some risk to the government. The Maquiladora Program has been criticized within Mexico as an abandonment of revolutionary goals with respect to the control of foreign direct investment and to limitations upon landownership by foreigners; it has also been attacked as the de facto transformation of the country into a free-production zone. That Mexican political elites would knowingly embark upon such a program is in part a reflection of how seriously they viewed the elimination of the safety valve afforded by the labor program.

The border industries have not hired ex-braceros, however; instead, they have hired a young female labor force who had attained a level of education superior to the mean among local residents. This outcome apparently was unforeseen by the Mexican architects of the program. Thus, if the Maquiladora Program has acted as a substitute safety valve, it has not done so directly.

Another set of Mexican responses to the termination of the bracero program was to seek its renewal, an effort sustained over a period of ten years. These efforts were made for a twofold purpose: to reestablish the safety valve, and to adopt a control measure to manage what was perceived to be a growing problem of undocumented migration (apprehensions of deportable Mexicans grew at a geometric rate of about 25 per cent per year in the late 1960s and early 1970s). These efforts culminated in a public admission by President Echeverría in his 1974 State of the Union address that Mexican attempts to secure a labor agreement with the United States had failed. In his 1972 and 1974 addresses Echeverría stressed several familiar themes: that emigration was in part due to the lack of domestic opportunity and that development efforts were addressing that problem; that Mexican workers in the US received inhumane treatment and that Mexico expressed its concern that this be corrected.[174]

By 1975, Echeverría's position changed, to the surprise of many, when he publicly announced that Mexico did *not* want a labor agreement. According to Jorge Bustamante, a meeting between Echeverría and Galarza shortly before his announcement had persuaded the president to change his posture.[175] In his 1976 State of the Union address, Echeverría explained: "We reject the idea of a new migrant worker agreement, for such agreements have never succeeded in preventing undocumented emigration in the past."[176] This reflected a new interpretation of the potential effects of a renewed contract-labor program—one which stressed the stimulation, rather than the substitution, effects of such a program with respect to undocumented emigration.

Echeverría's sudden change in policy threw open a debate—largely conducted within government circles and the Mexico City press—which has continued to this day. The sudden de-emphasis of a search for a binational temporary-worker program may be consistent with Mexican domestic and foreign policy objectives, but it has left that government with few alternatives. Generating additional employment within Mexico continues to be an important goal of the regime, but even if drastic changes in Mexico's development model, placing more emphasis on labor-intensive activities, were to be made, the domestic employment problem would not be even close to solution during this century.[177] In falling back upon a position which stresses domestic job generation and in protesting the ill treatment of undocumented Mexicans in the United States, Mexican policymakers have continued to demonstrate that emigration touches upon sensitive domestic issues, and that it continues to be perceived as a "safety valve." This fallback position also reveals that the Mexican government has few options in this issue area that can yield short-term results.

In the United States, the termination of the bracero program has set in motion several processes which have also demanded policy responses. Three of these have been mentioned—the increased flow of "commuters" across the border, increased undocumented immigration, and the export of jobs through "runaway plants" that have relocated on the Mexican border. Thus, the termination of the program ended the legal importation of workers, but not the U.S. domestic controversy over Mexican labor migration. Of these post-bracero program issues, the perceived increase of undocumented immigration has provoked the sharpest debate and presented U.S. policymakers with a serious issue on which there seems to be no national consensus about how to proceed.[178]

It is no surprise that the policy proposals most frequently suggested to address the "illegal alien problem"—increased enforcement at the border, mass roundups of deportable aliens in the interior, penalizing employers for hiring such aliens, legalizing undocumented persons already here, and instituting a temporary-worker program—are not new. Today's proposals are but variants of those measures adopted or actively considered during the "wetback invasion" of the early 1950s. The participants in the present debate seem to be unaware of the past, however; those who advocate "sealing" the border, for example, seem to be aware neither that such options have been considered before, nor of the reasons why such responses have not been pursued in the past. Proponents of "police-type" solutions apparently do not know that no such measure has ever successfully stopped migration; at best, in the aftermath of Operation Wetback, the flow was only regularized. Even then, the mass roundup of 1954 created new problems as it temporarily solved an old one. Those who argue that the United States bears no responsibility to Mexican migrants who recently have entered illegally ignore the long-standing involvement of U.S. employers in promoting this flow, and of the U.S. government in encouraging the violation of its immigration laws in order to accomplish its foreign policy objectives. To embark upon paths that repeat errors of the past does not speak well for the capacity of this society and polity to learn from historical experience.

One area that has generated recent discussion is temporary-worker programs.[179] Early in its term, the Reagan administration itself proposed a "pilot program" by which 50,000 Mexican nationals would be admitted each year for temporary work in the United States.[180] It is noteworthy that while this proposal was included within a package of other far-reaching immigration policy proposals, it is the temporary-worker plan that has generated the most discussion thus far. That temporary-worker proposals are in themselves controversial is a legacy of a program which itself expired almost two decades ago.

It may be true, as David Gregory argues, that "the historical perspective of Mexican participation in earlier programs such as the *bracero* programs acts as an impediment to our current search for a policy to effectively deal with contemporary migration movements."[181] Certainly, current interpretations of that experience have led many to equate all temporary-worker program proposals with the bracero program, and to assume that the evils and/or benefits of the earlier program automatically carry over into the present. It is in this sense that Gregory seems to be arguing against the drawing of close parallels between the earlier experience and the present situation.

Nevertheless, it is also true that the historical experience derived from the bracero era is indispensable for an understanding of the current debate and for the formulation of an appropriate U.S. policy response to undocumented migration. The experience of the contract-labor program may not give us answers regarding what a proposed temporary-worker program will accomplish, but it does offer a framework for posing some important questions. An examination of the proposals made thus far suggests that many of these questions have received little public attention or scrutiny.

Perhaps the first question to be posed in the current debate is, to what extent is the proposed program simply a copy of the contract-labor program, and to what extent does it diverge significantly? For example, the so-called H-2 program, which currently operates through §101 (15) (H) (ii) of the Immigration and Nationality Act, is essentially a unilateral bracero program. It involves the importation of temporary workers who are admitted to work for a specific employer, largely in agriculture. The principal difference between this and the Mexican contract-labor program is that the Mexican government is not directly involved in its design or administration.

Other questions which might be considered are: If the temporary-worker program is designed to serve as a substitute for undocumented migration, what evidence is there to suggest that it will function as planned? (The earlier experience suggests that the contract-labor program functioned alternatively as a stimulator and as a substitute for undocumented migration, depending upon the circumstances.) Moreover, what additional measures will be needed to get the proposed program to function as a substitute for undocumented migration? (The earlier experience suggests that widespread employer participation in any temporary-worker scheme is necessary for it to function as such a substitute.) Will a temporary-worker program be accompanied by an expulsion campaign, a new version of Operation Wetback? Will the design of the program be such that it will constitute little more than legitimizing the current situation in which undocumented workers are employed? Will the operation of the program have the necessary safeguards for working conditions and wages, or will it result in the kinds of abuse and exploitation that occurred previously, particularly during the 1950s?

The answers to such questions will be debated for some time. The discussion about the future direction of U.S. immigration policy with respect to Mexico will unavoidably focus on undocumented migration, on temporary-worker program proposals, and on conflicting interpretations of the contract-labor program of 1942–1964.

Abbreviations Used

DATAM
: *Dirección de Asuntos de Trabajadores Agrícolas Migratorios*, of the Mexican *Secretaría de Relaciones Exteriores*, the federal agency responsible for the negotiation of the labor agreement for the Mexican government and for setting general guidelines regarding the administration of the contract-labor program within Mexico.

DOL
: U.S. Department of Labor.

INS
: Immigration and Naturalization Service of the Department of Justice, the federal agency responsible for the control of immigration, first according to the 1917 Immigration Act, and later pursuant to the 1952 Immigration and Nationality Act. Its responsibilities under Public Law 78 were minor.

SRE
: *Secretaría de Relaciones Exteriores*, the Mexican Ministry of Foreign Relations.

USES
: U.S. Employment Service of the Department of Labor, the federal agency principally responsible for the administration of the contract-labor program at the state level after World War II. Its functions ranged from the selection of candidates at the Mexican recruitment centers to the certifications of need issued to employers.

Appendix
Chronology of the Mexican Contract-Labor Program

1942 August 4	Executive agreement made effective between Mexico and the United States to contract workers. Appropriations out of (U.S.) President's Emergency Fund.
1943 April 26	Executive agreement renewed.
April 29	Public Law 45 enacted, providing appropriations for agreement of April 26. Administration of program removed from USES and placed in hands of War Food Administration and Extension Service of the Department of Agriculture; §5(g) provided for the unilateral recruitment of farm workers from Western Hemisphere countries. Non-agricultural (railroad) worker agreement entered into between Mexico and the U.S. The U.S. government paid all transportation, medical, and housing costs for the contract workers.
May 11	Commissioner of Immigration issued regulations under P.L. 45 authorizing the entry of laborers arriving at the border for a stay of up to one year. Within three days, 2,040 workers had been distributed to farmers in New Mexico and Texas.
May 28	After Mexican protests, the State Department announced that §5(g) of P.L. 45 did not apply to Mexico.
December 23	Public Law 217 extended Farm Labor Supply Program from December 31, 1943 to January 31, 1944.
1944 February 14	Public Law 229, Farm Labor Supply Appropriations Act, enacted.
1945 December 28	Public Law 269 extended the authority of the program through December 31, 1946.
1946 July 23	Public Law 521 extended appropriations of wartime program to June 1947.
August 9	Public Law 707 enacted, the first legislative authority for a farm-labor program operating in peacetime.
August 25	U.S. Embassy formally instructed to seek termination of the railroad-worker program.
November 25	Department of State notified Mexico of its desire to end wartime agreement in 90 days.
1947 March 10	Bilateral agreement renewed. New provisions on legalization of "wetbacks" already in United States and on issue of blacklisting areas from receiving bracero labor. First time Mexico allowed braceros to be used in state of Texas.
April 28	Public Law 40 extended special wartime placement program to December 31, 1947.
September 26	Contract labor banned from Texas by Mexico.
1948 January 1	End of special wartime program and beginning of the worker-to-

employer program administered by USES from 1948 to 1951. Under this arrangement, the entry of Mexican workers was made possible under government-to-government agreements, but transportation and recruitment costs were borne by the farmers.

February 21
First peacetime bilateral agreement. Ended legalization of "wetbacks" first permitted by the March 10, 1947 agreement.

July 3
Public Law 893 authorized Federal Security Agency to recruit foreign workers and administer program until June 30, 1949.

October 13–
October 23
"First open-border incident." Due to differences with Mexico in the administration of the program, INS unilaterally opened border at El Paso for a brief period to allow illegal entrants in, to legalize them as contract workers, and to distribute them among farmers in Texas and New Mexico. Mexico abrogated the agreement on October 18, and the US formally apologized for action on October 23.

1949 August 1
New bilateral agreement. Included provisions denying certification of employers who continued to use "wetbacks" and eliminated Mexican practice of unilateral blacklisting. Legalized all "wetbacks" as braceros who had entered prior to that date.

1950 June 3
Truman signed executive order creating President's Commission on Migratory Labor.

July 26
New bilateral agreement. Contract laborers were not to be imported that year; "wetbacks" already in US to be legalized instead.

1951 January–
February
Under pressure from growers' associations, U.S. government opened negotiations for a renewal of the contract-labor program. Mexico indicated its willingness to renew the program if there were a return to a government-to-government program with contracting supervised by a federal agency.

March 26
Report of President's Commission on Migratory Labor transmitted to Truman.

July 12
Public Law 78 (Mexican Farm Labor Law) enacted to administer a government-to-government labor program. The program was extended three times with little difficulty: P.L. 237—August 8, 1953; P.L. 319—August 9, 1955; P.L. 779—August 27, 1958. The last extension was scheduled to expire on June 30, 1961.

August
New bilateral agreement.

1952 March 20
Public Law 283 provided for sanctions against those who willfully imported, transported, or harbored illegal entrants. Attempts to include an employer sanctions provision failed.

June 12
New bilateral agreement. Renewed four times in a routine fashion: March 10, 1954, December 23, 1955, December 20, 1956, and August 31, 1959. The latter agreement was scheduled to expire on June 30, 1961. Extensions of the agreement were made to Decem-

ber 1961, January 31, 1962, December 31, 1963, and December 31, 1964.

June 27	The Immigration and Nationality Act, also known as the McCarren-Walter Act and Public Law 414, was passed over Truman's veto. This law superseded the 1917 and 1924 Acts, but continued many of their features, including a quota for non-Western Hemisphere country immigrants.
1953 August	Attorney-General Herbert Brownell made a tour of inspection along U.S.–Mexican border.
1954 January 15– February 5	"Second open-border incident." Negotiations suspended by US on January 15, and Departments of Labor, Justice, and State announced unilateral recruitment to begin on January 18. Mexico issued a sharp response, calling for a halt to emigration. Incidents in Tijuana and Mexicali. On February 2, U.S. Comptroller-General advised the DOL that P.L. 78 funds could not be spent legally on unilateral recruiting. Unilateral action suspended on February 5.
March 16	Public Law 309 enacted (House Joint Resolution 355.). Amended P.L. 78 providing for unilateral importation of foreign workers if bilateral negotiations broke down.
April	Retired army general Joseph Swing appointed Commissioner of Immigration and Naturalization.
June 17	"Operation Wetback" began, resulting in the arrest of 57,000 deportable Mexicans in California in June and July. The campaign moved to Texas in July, and other states thereafter.
1955 April 14	United States and Mexico concluded an agreement on illegal entrants to the US.
1956 Spring	Publication of *Strangers in Our Fields* by Ernesto Galarza. Study documented widespread violations of the international agreement by public officials and employers, and abuses of bracero systems.
December	DOL issued new regulations designed to improve housing for contract workers.
1958 July– September	DOL instituted new formula for determining prevailing wage and new method for determining piece rates so that minimum hourly rate of bracero contract upheld. Actions designed to reduce adverse effects of bracero contracting on domestic agricultural labor market.
1959 October 23	Consultants' Report issued by the Bureau of Employment Security, DOL, recommending that the use of braceros be restricted and that powers of Secretary of Labor be expanded to effect protection of domestic workers.
November	New regulations setting minimum standards for working conditions involving domestic farm workers recruited through Farm Placement Service of the DOL.

1960 September 1	The 1951 Mexican Farm Labor Law was extended for six months, to December 31, 1961 (P.L. 783).
1961 October 4	Mexican Farm Labor Law extended for two more years after bitter debate and some reluctance in Kennedy administration (P.L. 345). Some changes in the 1951 law made, barring braceros from certain types of work and requiring farmers employing contract laborers to provide certain minimum working conditions for domestic workers.
1962 March 30	DOL put into effect the 1959 recommendations of the Consultants' Report with respect to the method employed to determine prevailing wage, thus forcing farmers to bid higher for the services of U.S. domestic workers before they could be certified to employ braceros.
1963 June 21	Diplomatic dispatch from Mexico transmitted to U.S., arguing for extension of program. Dispatch made public by Senator William Fulbright August 15.
December 13	Final extension of Mexican Farm Labor Law (P.L. 203). Program terminated on December 31, 1964.

Sources:
Congressional Quarterly Service, *Congress and the Nation, 1945–1964* (Washington, D.C.: Congressional Quarterly, 1965); Richard B. Craig, *The Bracero Program: Interest Groups and Foreign Policy* (Austin: Univ. of Texas Press, 1971); Ernesto Galarza, *Merchants of Labor: The Mexican Bracero Story* (Charlotte: McNally and Loftin, 1964); Peter N. Kirstein, *Anglo Over Bracero: A History of the Mexican Worker in the United States from Roosevelt to Nixon* (San Francisco: R & E Associates, 1977); George C. Kiser and Martha Woody Kiser, eds., *Mexican Workers in the United States: Historical and Political Perspectives* (Albuquerque: Univ. of New Mexico Press, 1979); and Johnny Mac McCain, "Contract Labor as a Factor in United States–Mexican Relations, 1942–1947" (Ph.D. dissertation, Univ. of Texas, Austin, 1970).

Notes

The author gratefully acknowledges the suggestions of several colleagues, particularly the excellent comments received from Ricardo Anzaldúa Montoya in the preparation of the final version of this paper, which was written during the author's tenure as a Tinker Foundation Visiting Research Fellow at the Program in United States—Mexican Studies, University of California at San Diego. An earlier draft appeared as no. 11 in the series *Working Papers in U.S.–Mexican Studies* of that program.

1. An essay that attempts to summarize briefly the events surrounding the operation of the bracero program necessarily must be selective in its treatment. This chapter offers an interpretation of the history of the program by focusing on the public policy issues it raised at that time and which continue to be of interest today.

2. No one work describes all these processes in detail, although a composite profile can be drawn from the following: Ciro Cardoso, ed., *México en el siglo XIX (1821–1910): historia económica de la estructura social* (México: Editorial Nueva Imagen, 1980), pp. 315–36, 381–404, 437–97; Lawrence Cardoso, *Mexican Emigration to the United States, 1897–1931: Socio-economic Patterns* (Tucson: Univ. of Arizona Press, 1980), pp. 1–17; Centro de Estudios Históricos, *Historia general de México*, vol. 3 (México: El Colegio de México, 1976), pp. 231–67; John H. Coatsworth, "Railroads and Concentration of Land-

ownership in the Early Porfiriato," *Hispanic American Historical Review* 54, no. 1 (February 1974): 48–71; Arthur F. Corwin, ed., *Immigrants—and Immigrants: Perspectives on Mexican Labor Migration to the United States* (Westport, Conn.: Greenwood Press, 1978), pp. 25–37; Keith A. Davies, "Tendencias demográficas urbanas durante el siglo XIX en México," in *Historia mexicana* 31, no. 3 (January–March 1972): 481–524; Juan Gómez-Quiñones, "The Origin and Development of the Mexican Working Class in the United States: Laborers and Artisans North of the Río Bravo, 1600–1900," in *El trabajo y los trabajadores en la historia de México: ponencias y comentarios presentados en la V Reunión de Historiadores Mexicanos y Norteamericanos*, edited by Elsa Cecilia Frost et al. (México and Tucson: El Colegio de México and Univ. of Arizona Press, 1979), pp. 463–505; Moisés González Navarro, *La colonización en México, 1877–1910* (México: n.p., 1960), pp. 95–140; Friedrich Katz, "Labor Conditions on Haciendas in Porfirian Mexico: Some Trends and Tendencies," *Hispanic American Historical Review* 54, no. 1 (February 1974): 1–47; Andrés Molina Enriquez, *Los grandes problemas nacionales* (México: Ediciones Era, 1978), pp. 285–356; Fernando Rosenzweig, "El desarrollo económico de México de 1877 a 1911," *El trimestre económico* 32, no. 3 (July–September 1965): 405–54; Paul S. Taylor, *An American-Mexican Frontier: Nueces County, Texas* (New York: Russell & Russell, 1971), pp. 10–117.

3. U.S. Office of the Census, *Twelfth Census of the United States, 1900*, Part I, *Population* (Washington, D.C.: GPO, 1901), p. clxxiv; U.S. Bureau of the Census, *Thirteenth Census of the United States, 1910*, vol. 1 (Washington, D.C.: GPO, 1913), p. 781; U.S. Bureau of the Census, *Fourteenth Census of the United States, 1920*, vol. 2, *Population* (Washington, D.C.: GPO, 1922), p. 693; U.S. Bureau of the Census, *Fifteenth Census of the United States, 1930*, vol. 3, *Population* (Washington, D.C.: GPO, 1933), p. 225.

4. For a discussion of the limitations of the 1930 census count of Mexican-born persons, see L. Cardoso, *Mexican Emigration*, pp. 94–95; Corwin, *Immigrants—*, pp. 115–17.

5. Mexican repatriation statistics are reproduced in Moisés González Navarro, *Población y sociedad en México (1900–1970)* vol. 2 (México: Facultad de Ciencias Políticas y Sociales, UNAM, 1974), p. 231. Another source (Corwin, *Immigrants—*, p. 117) suggests a somewhat larger number of Mexican settlers, including U.S.–born dependents, returned during the years 1931–1940. On the same page Corwin notes that the 1940 U.S. census registered 377,400 Mexican-born persons.

6. The estimates of average annual net flow are based on the census returns of the Mexican-born population registered in 1900 and 1930, and on the hypothesis that the Mexican-born population in 1930 may have been as high as one million. The gross flow estimates are largely speculative and are mentioned in Victor Clark, "Mexican Labor in the United States," *U.S. Bureau of Labor Bulletin* 17 (September 1908): 466; and George McCutchen McBride, *The Land Systems of Mexico* (New York: American Geographic Society, 1923), p. 33.

No allowance is made for mortality in these calculations. Corrected estimates of average annual net flow would be somewhat higher than those presented.

7. According to Mexican migration authorities at the border, between January 1, 1910, and June 30, 1928, 1,050,634 arrivals from the United States were effectuated by Mexican citizens. See Paul S. Taylor, *Mexican Labor in the United States, Migration Statistics* (Berkeley: Univ. of California Press, 1929), pp. 240–41.

8. Roden Fuller, "Occupations of the Mexican-born Population of Texas, New Mexico and Arizona, 1900–1920," *American Statistical Association Journal* 23 (March 1928): 67; Mark Reisler, *By the Sweat of Their Brow: Mexican Immigrant Labor in the United States, 1900–1940* (Westport, Conn.: Greenwood Press, 1976), pp. 96–113.

9. Emory S. Bogardus, *The Mexican in the United States* (Los Angeles: Univ. of Southern California Press, 1934), p. 37; Robert N. McLean, *That Mexican! As He Really Is, North and South of the Rio Grande* (New York: Fleming H. Revell & Co., 1928), pp. 130–31. Such fluctuations also occurred in the railroad industry (Reisler, *By the Sweat*, p. 97).

10. Clark, "Mexican Labor in the United States," pp. 470–71, 476; U.S. Bureau of Immigration, *Annual Report of the Commissioner-General of Immigration* (Washington, D.C.: GPO, 1910), p. 123; Taylor, *An American-Mexican Frontier*, p. 151; John H. Burma, *Spanish-speaking Groups in the United States* (Durham, N.C.: Duke Univ. Press, 1954), pp. 39–40; Lloyd H. Fisher, *The Harvest Labor Market in California* (Cambridge, Mass.: Harvard Univ. Press, 1953), p. 31.

11. Reisler, *By the Sweat*, p. 96.

12. Carey McWilliams, *North From Mexico: The Spanish-speaking People of the United States* (New York: Greenwood Press, 1968), pp. 178–84; Paul S. Taylor, *Mexican Labor in the United States, Bethlehem, Pennsylvania* (Berkeley: Univ. of California Press, 1930), p. 2. For a discussion of agricultural labor recruitment in California, see Fisher, *The Harvest Labor Market in California*, pp. 48–55.

13. Paul S. Taylor, *Mexican Labor in the United States, Valley of the South Platte, Colorado* (Berkeley: Univ. of California Press, 1929), pp. 131–33.

14. Ruth D. Tuck, *Not with the Fist: Mexican Americans in a Southwest City* (New York: Harcourt, Brace, 1948), pp. 58–59; Manuel Gamio, *Mexican Immigration to the United States: A Study of Human Migration and Adjustment* (New York: Dover Publications, 1971), p. 10; Reisler, *By the Sweat*, pp. 3–17, 58, 88–89, 98–105.

15. Mercedes Carreras de Velasco, *Los mexicanos que devolvió la crisis, 1929–1932* (México: Secretaría de Relaciones Exteriores, 1974), pp. 43–45; González Navarro, *La colonización en México*, pp. 6, 10, 54, 63–65, 115–22.

16. Lawrence Cardoso, "La repatriación de braceros en época de Obregón, 1920–1923," *Historia mexicana* 26, no. 4 (April–June 1977): 576–95; L. Cardoso, *Mexican Emigration*, pp. 99–103; John Martínez, *Mexican Emigration to the U.S., 1910–1930* (San Francisco: R & E Associates, 1971), p. 74. For a sampling of internal correspondence (1918–1923) among heads of Mexican government agencies and consuls in the United States regarding the conditions of Mexican workers and their repatriation from the US, see *Boletín del Archivo General de la Nación* Tercera Serie 2, no. 1 (January–March 1978), pp. 6–33.

17. México, SRE, *Un siglo de relaciones internacionales de México a través de los mensajes presidenciales* (México: Publicaciones de la Secretaría de Relaciones Exteriores, 1935) [Archivo Historico Diplomático Mexicano, Primera Serie, no. 39], p. 327.

18. Martínez, *Mexican Emigration*, p. 76; Luis G. Zorilla, *Historia de las Relaciones entre México y los Estados Unidos de América, 1800–1958*, vol. 2 (México: Porrúa, 1966), pp. 373–74.

19. Carreras de Velasco, *Los mexicanos*, pp. 73–97.

20. Abraham Hoffman, *Unwanted Mexican Americans in the Great Depression: Repatriation Pressures, 1929–1939* (Tucson: Univ. of Arizona Press, 1974), pp. 122–23; Norman D. Humphrey, "Mexican Repatriation from Michigan: Public Assistance in Historical Perspective," *Social Science Review* (September 1941): 497–513; George C. Kiser and Martha Woody Kiser, eds., *Mexican Workers in the United States: Historical and Political Perspectives* (Albuquerque: Univ. of New Mexico Press, 1979), pp. 41–66. Compare Reisler, *By the Sweat*, pp. 54–55.

21. Quoted in Carreras de Velasco, *Los mexicanos*, p. 84.

22. Foreign Minister Téllez, quoted in Carreras de Velasco, *Los mexicanos*, p. 79.

23. Carreras de Velasco, *Los mexicanos*, pp. 76, 79.

24. Ibid., pp. 75–76.

25. Hoffman, *Unwanted Mexican Americans*, p. 39.

26. Hoffman (pp. 39–66) provides a detailed discussion of the Los Angeles raids of January–February 1931.

27. Reisler, *By the Sweat*, pp. 50–51, 227–33; Carreras de Velasco, *Los mexicanos*, pp. 78–79. Exceptions to this indifference were few, but some were recorded. See Martínez, *Mexican Emigration*, p. 76; Carreras de Velasco, *Los mexicanos*, p. 47.

28. For an articulation of this view, see Bogardus, *The Mexican in the United States*, p. 46.

29. L. Cardoso, "La repatriación de braceros en época de Obregón," pp. 576–95; L.

Cardoso, *Mexican Emigration*, pp. 55–65, 104; Carreras de Velasco, *Los mexicanos*, pp. 47, 49, 51–52, 76, 84; Gamio, *Mexican Immigration*, p. 176; Hoffman, *Unwanted Mexican Americans*, p. 134; Kiser and Kiser, *Mexican Workers*, p. 15.

30. Harry E. Cross and James E. Sandos, *Across the Border: Rural Development in Mexico and Recent Migration to the United States* (Berkeley: University of California Institute of Governmental Studies, 1981), p. 15. The authors stress, however, that the longer-term effects of land-distribution policies were to further impoverish would-be emigrants from the north-central parts of the country (pp. 11–13). Compare Gonzáles Navarro, *Población y sociedad*, pp. 235–39; Carreras de Velasco, *Los mexicanos*.

31. For a discussion of Mexican policies to restrain or return emigrants during the years 1910–1940, and Mexican perceptions of abuses suffered by Mexican workers in the United States, see L. Cardoso, *Mexican Emigration*, pp. 64, 107, 113–15; Corwin, *Immigrants—*, pp. 179–84, 187–88; González Navarro, *Población y sociedad*, pp. 38–41, 46, 49, 153, 207–10, 224–39; Harvey A. Levenstein, "The AFL and Mexican Immigration in the 1920s: An Experiment in Labor Diplomacy," *Hispanic American Historical Review* 47, no. 2 (May 1968): 212–14.

32. González Navarro, *Población y sociedad*, p. 208.

33. This view was expressed by José María Dávila, a member of Congress, in 1932. González Navarro, *Población y sociedad*, p. 163.

34. L. Cardoso, *Mexican Emigration*, p. 117.

35. México, SRE, *Memoria de la Secretaría de Relaciones Exteriores; septiembre de 1952–diciembre de 1953* (México: Talleres Gráficos de la Nación, 1953), p. 331.

36. Martínez, *Mexican Emigration*, p. 18; Kiser and Kiser, *Mexican Workers*, pp. 9–29; Reisler, *By the Sweat*, pp. 24–42.

37. Kiser and Kiser, *Mexican Workers*, pp. 3–4.

38. Quoted in U.S. President's Commission on Migratory Labor, *Migratory Labor in American Agriculture* (Washington, D.C.: GPO, 1951), p. 71.

39. Ibid.

40. Reisler, *By the Sweat*, pp. 60–63; L. Cardoso, *Mexican Emigration*, pp. 129–30. A similar practice was reported by Otey Scruggs, who noted that as the price dropped for farm products during the Great Depression, the Bureau of Immigration adopted the policy of apprehending only a select group of deportable migrants who "were bad citizens or had criminal records" on the theory that "low farm prices entitled farmers to cheap Mexican labor." See Otey M. Scruggs, "The United States, Mexico and the Wetbacks, 1942–1947," *Pacific Historical Review* 30, no. 2 (May 1961): 150, note 8. For a discussion of the problems of managing the El Paso and San Antonio Border Patrol offices, viewed from the perspective of a former chief of the Border Patrol, see Clifford Alan Perkins, *Border Patrol: With the U.S. Immigration Service on the Mexican Boundary, 1910–54* (El Paso: Texas Western Press, 1978), pp. 32–119, esp. pp. 104–6.

41. Hoffman, *Unwanted Mexican Americans*, p. 32; Reisler, *By the Sweat*, pp. 214–18; Kiser and Kiser, *Mexican Workers*, pp. 53–54; Robert D. Tomasek, "The Political and Economic Implications of Mexican Labor in the United States Under the Non Quota System, Contract Labor Program, and Wetback Movement" (Ph.D. dissertation, Univ. of Michigan, 1957), p. 44.

42. Ernesto Galarza, *Merchants of Labor: The Mexican Bracero Story* (Charlotte: McNally and Loftin, 1964), pp. 80–81; Henry P. Anderson, *The Bracero Program in California* (New York: Arno Press, 1976), pp. 5–9. Another source, Johnny Mac McCain, "Contract Labor as a Factor in United States-Mexican Relations, 1942–1947" (Ph.D. dissertation, Univ. of Texas at Austin, 1970), pp. 179–80, shows that the *Secretaría del Trabajo y Previsión Social* was involved in the assignment of labor quotas within Mexico for the recruitment of railroad contract workers during World War II. During the 1950s, the principal agency on the Mexican side responsible for negotiating the agreement was the *Dirección de Asuntos de Trabajadores Agrícolas Migratorios (DATAM)* of the SRE. The agency responsible for operating the recruitment centers in Mexico was the *Oficina de Trabajadores Emigrantes* of the *Secretaría de Gobernación*. See México, SRE, *Memoria de la Secretaría de Relaciones Exteriores; septiembre de 1951–agosto de 1952*

(México: Talleres Gráficos de la Nación, 1952), p. 188; José Lázaro Salinas, *La emigración de braceros: una visión objetiva de un problema mexicano* (México: [Cuauhtémoc], 1955), pp. 66–89.

43. Agencies within the Departments of Agriculture and Labor that were responsible for the administration of the program during the war were the Farm Security Administration, the Extension Service, the War Food Administration, and the War Manpower Commission (Galarza, *Merchants of Labor*, p. 80).

44. Ibid., pp. 82–83; Anderson, *The Bracero Program*, passim.

45. Fisher, *The Harvest Labor Market*, pp. 122–23; Peter N. Kirstein, *Anglo Over Bracero: A History of the Mexican Worker in the United States from Roosevelt to Nixon* (San Francisco: R & E Associates, 1977), p. 12.

46. Fisher, *The Harvest Labor Market*, p. 123; Tomasek, "Political and Economic Implications," p. 52.

47. The 1942 recruitment season began late and is excluded from the calculation of the average. According to Table 3.1, U.S. statistics indicate that 195,765 contracts were issued during 1943–1946, and in the same period, Mexican sources registered 329,821 departures (*salidas*) of contract laborers. In interpreting these figures, the reader should keep in mind that they represent an approximate measure of the *flow* of Mexican contract workers to the United States for the years indicated; they do not indicate the number of such workers in the US at any given time (stock). Contract extensions, renewals, and multiple entries by individual workers make these numbers somewhat deceptive. The reader should also note that, as yet, no one has explained the difference between the U.S. and Mexican statistics on the flow of braceros. (U.S. secondary sources cite U.S. statistics, and Mexican sources cite one of two sets of Mexican statistics; up to this point apparently no researcher has even acknowledged that the disparity existed.) There are a number of possible explanations for this disparity, but their discussion exceeds the scope of this essay. For the present case, the precise number of contracts issued in any given year is not important, and both sets of numbers will be used to indicate a range of possible values.

48. According to U.S. statistics, 1,128,990 contracts were issued between 1947 and 1954; according to Mexican statistics, this number was 929,964. Mexican statistics for 1955–1964 indicate that 3,327,601 braceros departed; U.S. statistics record 3,317,241. The total for the program, according to U.S. sources, is 4,646,199; the same total, according to Mexican data, is 4,591,538.

49. My research indicates that only railroad workers were employed through the nonagricultural labor program, although attempts to use them in the San Diego naval yards and as forge and foundry workers, food workers, sawmill operators, and in other capacities, almost succeeded. McCain, "Contract Labor as a Factor," pp. 182–92.

50. Kirstein, *Anglo Over Bracero*, p. 28; McCain, "Contract Labor as a Factor," p. 174.

51. Galarza, *Merchants of Labor*, p. 54; Kirstein, *Anglo Over Bracero*, pp. 32–33.

52. Galarza, *Merchants of Labor*, p. 46; SRE, *Memoria, 1952–53*, p. 331.

53. Mexican domestic opposition to the initiation of the wartime program and to Mexico's continued participation had several motivations and can be gleaned from a number of sources. See, e.g., a letter from a labor organization representing Mexican workers in the United States which argued against bracero emigration in April 1942, reproduced in: *Boletín del Archivo General de la Nación*, Tercera Series 4, no. 4 (October–December 1980), pp. 22–23. In the same *Boletín* (pp. 21–22) a letter written in May 1942 by the Minister of Labor and directed to the Minister of SRE is reproduced. It argued against Mexico's participation in the labor program on the grounds that a vast army of unemployed Mexicans already resided in the United States. Mexico City news articles in 1942 reflect similar apprehensions, e.g., "México necesita sus brazos," *Excélsior*, June 11, 1942. An article reporting the opposition of the U.S. League of Latin American Citizens to the program about to begin appears in "No quieren campesinos mexicanos," *Novedades*, June 16, 1942. A prominent labor leader and persistent critic of the program, Vicente Lombardo Toledano, complained to President Avila Camacho in 1943 that braceros were prohibited from joining U.S. labor organizations (noted in Jorge del Pinal, "Los trabajadores mexicanos en los Estados Unidos," *El trimestre económico*

12, no.1 [April–June 1945], p. 26). At the other end of the political spectrum was the opposition of the Sinarquista Party (Kiser and Kiser, *Mexican Workers*, p. 75). In 1944 the principal umbrella organization of Mexican labor unions, the *Confederación de Trabajadores Mexicanos*, sent an observer to the United States to inspect the working conditions of Mexican braceros. Upon return, he filed a report that criticized the manner in which the Mexican consuls were handling bracero-related problems. This report, and the reply prepared by the SRE at the request of Avila Camacho in response to these and Lombardo Toledano's allegations, appear in *Boletín* (1980), pp. 28–31. Contrasting these criticisms of Mexico's participation in the program are petitions by unemployed workers requesting permission to emigrate to the United States (*Boletín* [1980], pp. 14–16). See also Mexican public statements, accentuating the positive aspects of the labor program, in: "Cómo cumplimos lo convenido con nuestros aliados, es satisfactoria la situación de los contratados," *El nacional*, May 31, 1944, p. 8.

54. Manuel Gamio's participation in the design of the contract-labor program still has to be adequately researched. His proposal for a temporary-worker program to substitute for the northward movement of legal immigrants is expressed in his book *Mexican Immigration*, pp. 182–83. Evidence that his involvement was crucial in the formulation of a Mexican position in 1942 is provided in a reference made by Tomasek, "Political and Economic Implications," p. 29, to an interview with a Mexican official. For other evidence of Gamio's involvement in the wartime program, see his confidential report to Avila Camacho, reproduced in *Boletín* (1980), pp. 38–40.

55. McCain, "Contract Labor as a Factor," p. 77; Scruggs, "The United States," p. 151. For a discussion of the inter-agency preparation for the agreement among the Departments of State, Justice, Labor, and Agriculture in the United States and SRE, *Secretaría de Gobernación*, and *Secretaría del Trabajo y Previsión Social*, as well as Mexico's initial reluctance to participate in the program, see McCain, "Contract Labor as a Factor," pp. 6–23; Juan Ramón García, *Operation Wetback: The Mass Deportation of Mexican Undocumented Workers in 1954* (Westport, Conn.: Greenwood Press, 1980), pp. 21–23; Tomasek, "Political and Economic Implications," pp. 53–54.

56. The view that emigration harmed Mexico's rural economy seems to have emerged soon after the program began. González Navarro (*Población y sociedad*, p. 215) reports that at the outset of mass labor migration, the authorities of two states most severely affected—Jalisco and Guanajuato—sought to prevent it "because of the economic damages it caused." He also notes (p. 163) that in 1943, as bracero emigration increased, a shortage of agricultural labor developed in parts of Mexico. For samples of telegrams and correspondence opposing bracero emigration received by Avila Camacho during the years 1943–1945 from Mexican farmers' organizations, prominent businessmen in the communities from which braceros were sent, the leaders of county and state governments from the same regions, industrialists, and chambers of commerce, see *Boletín* (1980), pp. 34–36, 37. A contradictory view, which stressed the benefits of bracero emigration perceived through the remittances and foreign exchange earnings, was expressed in a 1944 letter to one of Avila Camacho's ministers by a personal friend. The letter summarized the results, both anecdotal and quantitative, of a survey conducted by its author in several sending communities. See *Boletín* (1980), pp. 36–37.

57. Centro de Estudios Históricos, *Historia general de México*, vol. 4, pp. 197–98, 264–65.

58. These are summarized from the list presented in Galarza, *Merchants of Labor*, p. 47.

59. One should keep in mind that "needs," like agricultural labor "shortages," are not absolutes, even though the initial Mexican position—accepted by the United States—assumed that they were. In a path-breaking analysis of the California harvest labor market, Lloyd Fisher noted that labor demand is best expressed not in terms of numbers of laborers, but in labor hours. Since farmers had an interest in minimizing the risks of disease, bad weather, and spoilage, and because farm labor was paid piece-rate and the farmer could not experience diminishing returns to labor, the agricultural labor market experienced sharp peaks in labor demand for short periods. Had farmers been willing to

accept those risks and some unevenness of quality in the product harvested, Fisher argues, labor demand would have been lower and the harvest season longer. Thus, a labor "shortage" in this type of agriculture is a relative, not an absolute, concept (Fisher, *The Harvest Labor Market*, pp. 6, 123, 151–60).

60. The first and fourth conditions mentioned are explicitly derived from Article 123 and pertinent Mexican labor legislation. The second, third, and fifth conditions are explicitly mentioned in Manuel Gamio's proposal, outlined in 1930 *(Mexican Immigration*, pp. 182–83). The sixth condition reflects an old concern by the Mexican public and government dating to the teens and twenties.

61. McCain, "Contract Labor as a Factor," p. 32; Richard B. Craig, *The Bracero Program: Interest Groups and Foreign Policy* (Austin: Univ. of Texas Press, 1971), pp. 43–45; González Navarro, *Población y sociedad*, pp. 240–42.

62. García, *Operation Wetback*, p. 26. The author further notes (p. 27) that this placed the growers in the anomalous position "of defending the importation of laborers while attacking the agreements that made the importation of those workers possible." It is noteworthy that after the wartime agreements expired, the program was modified significantly—although not to the complete satisfaction of the growers. Despite their complaints in the late forties, no support could be found among them for returning to a system modeled on the wartime program. See Kiser and Kiser, *Mexican Workers*, p. 115, note 5.

63. del Pinal, "Los trabajadores mexicanos," pp. 30–31; Galarza, *Merchants of Labor*, p. 56; Kirstein, *Anglo Over Bracero*, p. 71. The political salience in Mexico of discrimination against Mexicans in the United States can be discerned from fact-finding reports prepared for SRE, as well as from the fact that the ruling party (PRM) adopted a formal position critical of racial discrimination and of the failure of U.S. authorities to do something about it. See *Boletín* (1980), pp. 23–25, 31–32. That occasionally the protests of the Mexican government to the US regarding racial discrimination were measured can be seen in its reactions to the so-called zoot-suit riots in Los Angeles in 1943. See Tomasek, "Political and Economic Implications," p. 79.

64. Kiser and Kiser, *Mexican Workers*, p. 86.

65. Ibid., pp. 86–87.

66. Ibid., p. 87.

67. Quoted in Scruggs, "The United States," p. 152. The author further notes (p. 153) that in 1944, "In conversations with State Department officials, an immigration officer confessed that the Service [INS] was deporting only those workers not engaged in harvesting perishable crops."

68. Scruggs, "The United States," pp. 154, 158.

69. Ibid., pp. 154–55.

70. Ibid., pp. 156–57; Tomasek, "Political and Economic Implications," p. 51.

71. Tomasek, "Political and Economic Implications," pp. 158, 171; del Pinal, "Los trabajadores mexicanos," p. 33. Tomasek (p. 83) cites a number of Mexican sources which opposed the extension of the program and implies (p. 84) that only the president and the SRE preferred to continue with the program.

72. Many articles in the national media, in such publications as *Time, Newsweek, Life, The New York Times, The Saturday Evening Post, Business Week*, and *The Washington Post*, drew attention to the "wetback" problem in the postwar years, especially during 1951–1954. These articles stressed the threat, real or imagined, that undocumented Mexicans represented for the United States in a number of respects. A sampling of these is reproduced or referred to in American G.I. Forum and Texas State Federation of Labor (AFL), *What Price Wetbacks?* (Austin: [Allied Printing], 1953), pp. 15–16, 28–30, 46, 58; Beatriz Massa Gil, *Bibliografía sobre migración de trabajadores mexicanos a los Estados Unidos* (México: Biblioteca del Banco de México, 1959), pp. 25–31, 45–97. Since the vast majority of the U.S. population did not have contact with "wetbacks" in their daily lives, it is generally agreed that these articles—and the allegations of anti-wetback groups reported therein—were instrumental in the shaping of U.S. public opinion on issues relating to undocumented migration.

73. President's Commission, *Migratory Labor*, p. 69 (emphasis added). The report continues (pp. 69–70): "It is estimated that at least 400 thousand of our migratory farm labor force of 1 million in 1949 were wetbacks. . . . Before 1944 employment of wetbacks was largely at hand labor in agriculture; now they are *infiltrating* a wide range of nonfarm jobs and occupations" (emphasis added). Another example of a source which equated the "wetback" problem with exaggerated assumptions about their numbers can be found in a March 1954 *New York Times* article which asserted that one of every ten Mexican inhabitants had gone to the United States. (Cited in González Navarro, *Población y sociedad*, p. 200.)

74. Willard F. Kelley, "The Wetback Issue," *I & N Reporter*, January 1954, pp. 38–39.

75. President's Commission, *Migratory Labor*, p. 88.

76. Tomasek, "Political and Economic Implications," pp. 253–54; Galarza, *Merchants of Labor*, p. 62; Corwin, *Immigrants—*, pp. 152–53.

77. Craig, *The Bracero Program*, pp. 94–99; McCain, "Contract Labor as a Factor," p. 300; Tomasek, "Political and Economic Implications," pp. 204–5, 224, 239, 241–42, 248–54; Kiser and Kiser, *Mexican Workers*, pp. 129, 155–58; SRE, *Memoria, 1951–52*, pp. 17, 184.

78. Tomasek, "Political and Economic Implications," p. 224.

79. Indications of this are that, when Mexico used force to prevent emigration to the United States, as in August 1953, there was a virtual news blackout on the action. The only reference I was able to find was a four-paragraph article in the Mexico City official newspaper: "Impídese que sin contrato salgan muchos braceros; centenares, detenidos en la frontera norte," *El nacional*, August 18, 1953. (Compare Tomasek, "Political and Economic Implications, p. 257.) By the same token, when Operation Wetback was launched a year later, Mexico's active participation in it received practically no notice in Mexico City newspapers during June, July, or August 1954. (Again compare Tomasek, "Political and Economic Implications," p. 271.) It is also noteworthy that the annual report of *DATAM* played down the campaign, with only a single sentence in reference to the event. It notes that the "considerable increase in the number of formal contracts issued in [1954] is due exclusively to the well-organized and persistent campaign deployed by U.S. authorities to return to Mexico all workers that lacked a contract and immigration documentation, particularly from the state of Texas." México, SRE, *Memoria de la Secretaría de Relaciones Exteriores; enero a diciembre de 1954* (México: Talleres Gráficos de la Nación, 1955), p. 696.

80. Galarza, *Merchants of Labor*, p. 61.

81. McCain, "Contract Labor as a Factor," pp. 268–89; Kirstein, *Anglo Over Bracero*, pp. 73–74; García, *Operation Wetback*, pp. 111, 122.

82. Kirstein, *Anglo Over Bracero*, p. 90. See also President's Commission, *Migratory Labor*, pp. 75–76. Tomasek ("Political and Economic Implications," p. 141) notes that a representative announced in Congress in 1949 that the Commissioner of Immigration had assured him "that the Border Patrol would not go on the farms in search of 'wetbacks' but would confine their activities to the highways and places of social gatherings."

83. American G.I. Forum, *What Price Wetbacks?*, p. 42.

84. Quoted in Galarza, *Merchants of Labor*, p. 63. See also García, *Operation Wetback*, p. 111.

85. President's Commission, *Migratory Labor*, p. 52.

86. Ibid., p. 53.

87. Galarza, *Merchants of Labor*, p. 63.

88. President's Commission, *Migratory Labor*, pp. 88, 180.

89. Hundreds of agricultural employers joined farm-labor associations during the years 1951–1954 on the condition that deportable Mexicans in their employ would be approved for bracero contracts. (Galarza, *Merchants of Labor*, p. 64.)

90. Craig, *The Bracero Program*, p. 127; Galarza, *Merchants of Labor*, p. 70; García, *Operation Wetback*, p. 158; Tomasek, "Political and Economic Implications," p. 267.

91. Craig, *The Bracero Program*, p. 128.

92. Ibid., p. 129; Galarza, *Merchants of Labor*, pp. 70, 255; Julian Samora, *Los Mojados: The Wetback Story* (Notre Dame, Ind.: Univ. of Notre Dame Press, 1971), p. 52; Tomasek,

"Political and Economic Implications," p. 270. For a discussion of employer cooperation with Operation Wetback and the substitution of legally imported labor for "wetbacks," see Kiser and Kiser, *Mexican Workers*, p. 101; Tomasek, "Political and Economic Implications," pp. 269–70.

93. García, *Operation Wetback*, pp. 175–76, 186, 220–21; Tomasek, "Political and Economic Implications," p. 271.

94. García, *Operation Wetback*, pp. 214–15; Tomasek, "Political and Economic Implications," p. 270.

95. American G.I. Forum, *What Price Wetbacks?*, pp. 17–25, 28–32, 34–36; Craig, *The Bracero Program*, p. 126, note 80; Galarza, *Merchants of Labor*, p. 70; González Navarro, *Población y sociedad*, p. 199. García (*Operation Wetback*, p. 159) quotes a weekly magazine in the fall of 1953 which noted that the media, labor leaders, and the Justice Department had asserted that "the 'illegals' had created 'a grave social problem involving murder, prostitution, robbery and a gigantic narcotics infiltration [as well as] a malignant threat to the growth of our society.' " The Acting Commissioner of INS, while testifying on behalf of his agency's budget requests, asserted that 100 "Communists and ex–Reds [were] sneaking across the Mexican border" each day. Quoted in *Hispanic American Report* 7, no. 2 (February 1954): 10.

96. Commissioner Swing reportedly told the chief of the Border Patrol that whether or not there would be a patrol in the future depended upon the success of the campaign (García, *Operation Wetback*, p. 178).

97. The negative–image problem and low morale of the Border Patrol in the early 1950s are discussed in a number of sources. See García, *Operation Wetback*, pp. 113, 116–17, 218–19; Tomasek, "Political and Economic Implications," p. 140. García (p. 177) shows that from the outset, the planning for Operation Wetback took into account the need "to drum up public and legislative support" for INS. "Meticulous attention was given not only to publicizing the drive but also to make sure that sympathetic [news] correspondents accompanied some of the [Border Patrol] forces," and " 'Operation Wetback' was an important project for the Border Patrol, providing it with the opportunity to prove its public, private and congressional detractors wrong and to begin to change its image as an inept, slovenly, and ineffective branch of the government" (ibid.). García further notes: "By 1955 its prestige and reputation had noticeably improved, particularly in Texas" (p. 225). Its reputation had also improved in Congress. "Flushed with the 'success' of 'Operation Wetback,' " INS representatives were able to argue effectively for increased budget allocations, and "traditional opponents to increased Border Patrol appropriations were not able to utilize the Patrol's ineffectiveness as a rationale for denying them the appropriation" (p. 227).

98. Tomasek, "Political and Economic Implications," pp. 267–68, 270, 150. He notes (p. 256) that appropriations for the Border Patrol had been reduced such that in 1952 it had 1,200 men compared to 1,450 ten years earlier, when the number of apprehensions was much smaller. In early 1953 the force was further reduced to 1,000 men.

99. Indicative of this were the howls of pain raised by many growers, particularly in Texas, and the creation (accompanied by some initial grumbling) of new organizations in the lower Rio Grande Valley, Arizona, and Imperial Valley to contract braceros. See García, *Operation Wetback*, p. 219; Tomasek, "Political and Economic Implications," p. 99. One should further note that the INS media blitz, accompanied by farmer protests, exaggerated the potential enforcement impact of the Border Patrol force, and as a consequence, perceptions of increased risk of INS interference with the use of undocumented labor were strengthened. See García, pp. 177–78, 185.

100. García (*Operation Wetback*, p. 219) writes: "The anger and hostility of many employers was assuaged when they realized that many of the braceros who were being contracted were in truth 'dried–out' 'illegals.' " He further notes (p. 184) that INS put up signs in the buses used to transport expelled migrants, which stated (in Spanish): "NOTICE: The United States Needs Legal Farm Workers! The Mayor of Your Town Can Arrange for Your Contracting. WARNING: The Era of the Wetback and the Wire Cutter has Ended! From This Day Forward Any Person Found in the United States Illegally Will Be

Punished By Imprisonment." García further notes (pp. 55, 226) that many of the braceros contracted after the campaign had previously been employed as "wetbacks." The substitution of contract for "wetback" labor seems to have been particularly notable in south Texas. See Tomasek, "Political and Economic Implications," p. 270. The reader should also note from Table 3.1 in this chapter that the total number of issued bracero contracts rose dramatically after 1954, just as the number of apprehensions dropped sharply. Similarly, after 1960, as the number of bracero contracts declined sharply, the number of apprehensions began to increase, although more slowly.

101. "Streamlining" the program involved changing provisions that the Mexican government had insisted on from the outset of the program. Mexico dropped its requirement of a minimum contract work period of six weeks for "special cases," and lowered it to four weeks two days after Operation Wetback began in Texas. See SRE, *Memoria, 1954*, p. 694; García, *Operation Wetback*, p. 212. In 1955, INS unilaterally instituted a simple border-crossing card that "allowed braceros to proceed immediately to contracting centers and to bypass procedures set up by the Mexican government" (García, p. 219). "Streamlining" also involved relaxing DOL provisions designed to reduce the "adverse effects" of braceros on domestic labor, such as the contracting of specialized contract workers (García, p. 219). It was not immediately apparent how much of an impact this had on U.S. farm workers, but Tomasek ("Political and Economic Implications," p. 274) notes that the substitution of contract labor for "wetback" labor was more noticeable than the substitution of domestic migrant labor for the same. In the lower Río Grande Valley contract laborers increased from 3,000 to 70,000; domestic workers only increased from 19,000 to 32,000. Compare García, pp. 208, 209.

102. Galarza (*Merchants of Labor*, p. 70) writes: "The most influential leaders of the farming community were now regarding the Wetback with moral disapproval, giving [Commissioner Swing] occasion to remark that the drive 'would have been impossible without the generous cooperation extended . . . by farmers, ranchers and growers' who 'were never too busy to help in the enforcement of the laws of their nation.' The growers cooperated mainly by identifying Wetbacks they had not been able to recognize before." Compare Kiser and Kiser, *Mexican Workers*, p. 101; Tomasek, "Political and Economic Implications," p. 275.

103. Quoted in García, *Operation Wetback*, p. 225.

104. "La época de los espaldas mojadas' pasa a la historia," *Excélsior*, August 24, 1958. Craig (*The Bracero Program*, p. 129) also notes that when the United States and Mexico concluded an agreement relating to illegal migration in April 1955, "the wetback had, for all practical purposes, ceased to exist."

105. One of the "costs" rarely discussed in the writings on Operation Wetback, which cannot be elaborated on here but is nevertheless important, is the violation of civil rights—particularly of persons of Mexican origin—that the campaign entailed. References to the tremendous social costs borne by the Mexican community in the United States as a result of this action can be found in García, *Operation Wetback*, pp. 194–99, 216, 218, 230–31.

106. Tomasek writes ("Political and Economic Implications," p. 274): "Unfortunately, many of the growers in the lower Río Grande Valley of Texas and the Imperial Valley of California were so used to paying 'wetback' wages that the increased contract labor brought in received only 30 to 45 cents an hour. This was contrary to the agreement which stipulated that they were to receive 50 cents an hour minimum wage or the prevailing wage, whichever was [higher]. The Labor Department had only twenty men on its compliance staff [in 1955]."

107. Craig, *The Bracero Program*, p. 104; García, *Operation Wetback*, p. 39; Kirstein, *Anglo Over Bracero*, p. 67.

108. Galarza, *Merchants of Labor*, p. 77; García, *Operation Wetback*, p. 39; González Navarro, *Población y sociedad*, p. 248.

109. Galarza, *Merchants of Labor*, pp. 52, 81; González Navarro, *Población y sociedad*, table opposite p. 146.

110. An internal document prepared during the Truman and Eisenhower administra-

tions summarized the communication between the U.S. and Mexican governments on this issue during 1948–1953. This document was entitled *The Secret Study* by Kirstein, who discovered it (Kirstein, *Anglo Over Bracero,* p. 76).

111. McCain, "Contract Labor as a Factor," pp. 330–34.

112. Ibid., pp. 274, 278–79, 284, 288–89.

113. Ibid., p. 290.

114. Kirstein, *Anglo Over Bracero,* p. 70.

115. Ibid.

116. President's Commission, *Migratory Labor,* p. 50; Galarza, *Merchants of Labor,* p. 77. The position of the Mexican government may have been influenced by perceptions such as those revealed in a letter from an organization of Mexicans in the United States to President Avila Camacho in 1946. The authors of this letter argue that contract-labor wages were so low that they depressed the wage levels of other agricultural laborers. The letter appears in *Boletín* (1980), pp. 12–13.

117. Galarza, *Merchants of Labor,* p. 65.

118. Prevailing wages were determined at preharvest-season meetings, where farmers agreed in advance on what wages would prevail. See American G.I. Forum, *What Price Wetbacks?,* p. 50; Fisher, *The Harvest Labor Market,* pp. 91–116; Galarza, *Merchants of Labor,* p. 111; President's Commission, *Migratory Labor,* pp. 59–60.

119. This provision was agreed to as a compromise solution, since the growers actually wanted the Agricultural Extension Service to determine farm wage levels. In actuality, since the DOL readily accepted the interpretation that growers gave to prevailing wages, the "compromise" represented a defeat for the Mexican position. Not until the late 1950s did the DOL begin to question then-existing procedures for determining "prevailing wages."

120. Galarza, *Merchants of Labor,* pp. 77–78.

121. Kirstein, *Anglo Over Bracero,* p. 65; Scruggs, "The United States," p. 159; Tomasek, "Political and Economic Implications," pp. 224–26.

122. Tomasek, "Political and Economic Implications," pp. 239–42.

123. Galarza, *Merchants of Labor,* p. 75; Salinas, *La emigración de braceros: una visión objetiva de un problema mexicano,* pp. 11–29.

124. García, *Operation Wetback,* p. 121.

125. Tomasek, "Political and Economic Implications," pp. 226, 228–29, 241–42, 248–55, 262.

126. Tomasek (ibid., p. 84), notes that the economic importance of bracero remittances and income brought by returning migrants was an argument offered by a Mexican government official as an explanation for the desire of the Alemán administration to renew the program in 1947, notwithstanding domestic opposition to its continuation. It is doubtful, however, that bracero earnings ever had a substantial impact on Mexico's exchange of goods and services with the United States. Bracero remittances (which do not include amounts brought back by returning contract workers) reached a peak relative value of 20 percent of the U.S.–Mexican trade balance in 1955. In other years it fluctuated between 10 and 16 percent, and occasionally dropped to lower levels. Foreign exchange earnings from braceros probably were never more than a fraction of Mexico's net earnings from border transactions or tourism. (Calculations based on González Navarro, *Población y sociedad,* table opposite p. 168.) After 1955, the relative importance of bracero earnings declined, yet, paradoxically, references to their significance continued. See "Los braceros harán ingresos más de diecisiete millones de dólares," *El universal,* December 10, 1956; "800 millones de pesos envían al año los braceros," *Excélsior,* November 10, 1958. It is conceivable that the income earned by braceros was seized upon by Mexican officials as a means of *justifying* a program the government wanted to continue for other reasons, e.g., its presumed "safety-valve" function.

127. García, *Operation Wetback,* pp. 58–59. Referring to the years 1948–1951, Richard Craig writes: "One needs little imagination to visualize the extent of rural discontent that Mexico was spared as a result of the legal and clandestine northern flow during these years" (Craig, *The Bracero Program,* p. 60). True or not, this statement appears to reflect

accurately the view that was becoming increasingly prevalent among Mexican political elites during those years. See González Navarro, *Población y sociedad*, pp. 177–78. González Navarro also notes (p. 250) that as early as 1951 the Mexican government recognized the underdevelopment of Mexico's economy as an important, if not crucial, factor in causing the emigration of its workers, although it seemingly viewed that its development policies might obviate the need for emigration in the medium run. Thus, after 1951, the Mexican government renewed the labor agreement several times, but never for more than two and a half years at a time, because it considered the contract-labor program an emergency measure that was not acceptable in the long term. Compare SRE, *Memoria, 1952–53*, pp. 67–68; México, SRE, *Memoria de la Secretaría de Relaciones Exteriores: 1° de enero a 31 de diciembre de 1956* (México: Talleres Gráficos de la Nación, 1957), p. 382; México, SRE, *Memoria de la Secretaría de Relaciones Exteriores; 1° de enero a 31 de diciembre de 1957* (México: Talleres Gráficos de la Nación, 1958), p. 391; México, SRE, *Memoria de la Secretaría de Relaciones Exteriores; 1° de enero a 31 de diciembre de 1959* (México: Talleres Gráficos de la Nación, 1960), p. 388.

128. García, *Operation Wetback*, p. 59.

129. González Navarro, *Población y sociedad*, pp. 154–56. Tomasek ("Political and Economic Implications," p. 229) notes that in 1951, 20,000 would-be braceros scrambled to interior contracting centers *ten weeks before the contracting was to begin* with the hope that they would be assured a labor contract.

130. Craig, *The Bracero Program*, pp. 22–23; García, *Operation Wetback*, pp. 70–73; 79–80; Scruggs, "The United States," pp. 152, 155, 163; Tomasek, "Political and Economic Implications," pp. 165–71. Illustrative of the criticism to which the government was most sensitive were the attacks by Vicente Lombardo Toledano, a candidate in the 1952 presidential campaign. For example, see one of his speeches, "Ni un sólo mexicano más debe ir a trabajar a los Estados Unidos," delivered February 15, 1952, in Nogales, Sonora (transcript available at the Servicio de la Hemeroteca, Universidad Obrera de México, Mexico City). Compare Tomasek, "Political and Economic Implications," p. 243; Kiser and Kiser, *Mexican Workers*, p. 76. Mexico City newspaper articles during 1951 and 1952 reported the constant barrage of criticism against the government for its role in the bracero program, as well as the responses of Mexican government officials, which stressed the gains Mexico was making in its negotiations with the United States, and which underscored the demands made by the Mexican delegation regarding certain guarantees for the bracero laborers. See the collection of articles titled, "Campesinos Mexicanos en Estados Unidos," in the Biblioteca Lerdo de Tejada, Mexico City, several hundred of which were filed during 1951–1952.

131. García (*Operation Wetback*, p. 32) notes: "In confidential letters, memos, and telegrams, Mexican officials often expressed concern about problems plaguing the program, including discriminatory acts against Mexican nationals, physical abuse, inadequate grievance procedures, and violations of civil rights and contract guarantees. When news of such incidents did become public, Mexican officials wrote with concern about how such news proved damaging to their efforts to keep the contract labor program in a positive light. They informed officials of the United States that, when news of abuses or of secret agreements leaked out, it placed Mexico in a difficult situation, forcing [it] to take harsher stands than [it] ordinarily might."

132. Kirstein, *Anglo Over Bracero*, p. 67.

133. Galarza, *Merchants of Labor*, p. 49.

134. Craig, *The Bracero Program*, p. 69; Galarza, *Merchants of Labor*, p. 50; *Hispanic American Report* 1, no. 1 (November 1948): 3; Kirstein, *Anglo Over Bracero*, p. 68; Tomasek, "Political and Economic Implications," pp. 232–35. García (*Operation Wetback*, p. 77) notes that the incident aggravated Mexican public opinion, "which had always disapproved of the program," and that "Mexican officials believed they had little choice but to terminate the agreement." The text of the note of apology and the Mexican reply is reproduced in Kiser and Kiser, *Mexican Workers*, pp. 153–55.

135. Kirstein, *Anglo Over Bracero*, pp. 70, 76.

136. Craig, *The Bracero Program*, pp. 105–6.

137. Ibid., pp. 109–10; Galarza, *Merchants of Labor*, p. 66; *Hispanic American Report* 7, no. 1 (January 1954): 8; Salinas, *La emigración de braceros: una visión objetiva de un problema mexicano*, pp. 11–14; Tomasek, "Political and Economic Implications," p. 259. Examples of Mexican press statements, revealing an extraordinary degree of unanimity in condemning the U.S. action, can be found in the clippings file "Campesinos Mexicanos en Estados Unidos."

138. Craig, *The Bracero Program*, pp. 112–13; Galarza, *Merchants of Labor*, p. 66; Tomasek, "Political and Economic Implications," p. 206.

139. Craig, *The Bracero Program*, pp. 112–13; Galarza, *Merchants of Labor*, p. 68; Tomasek, "Political and Economic Implications," p. 260; "A pesar de la excitativa oficial, empezó la fuga de braceros," *Excélsior*, January 23, 1954.

140. Tomasek, "Political and Economic Implications." For a discussion of that criticism, see pp. 166–79, 257–58.

141. Craig, *The Bracero Program*, p. 119; García, *Operation Wetback*, pp. 81–82.

142. Quoted in Tomasek, "Political and Economic Implications," p. 260. Compare Craig, *The Bracero Program*, p. 112.

143. Craig, *The Bracero Program*, p. 117; Tomasek, "Political and Economic Implications," p. 261.

144. Craig, *The Bracero Program*, pp. 114, 117–18; Tomasek, "Political and Economic Implications," pp. 260–61, p. 261, note 5.

145. Quoted in Craig, *The Bracero Program*, p. 115, note 52.

146. Ibid., pp. 115–19; García, *Operation Wetback*, pp. 95–96; Tomasek, "Political and Economic Implications," p. 261.

147. García, *Operation Wetback*, p. 95; Tomasek, "Political and Economic Implications," p. 262.

148. Quoted in García, *Operation Wetback*, p. 95.

149. Ibid., p. 96.

150. Cited in González Navarro, *Población y sociedad*, p. 177.

151. Fernando Robles, "¿Será posible detener la emigración de los braceros?" [opinion column] *El universal*, February 9, 1954. For a discussion of the internal debate in Mexico about the causes of emigration, see Craig, *The Bracero Program*, pp. 118–21. Compare SRE, *Memoria, 1957*, p. 391; SRE, *Memoria, 1958*, p. 308.

152. Galarza, *Merchants of Labor*, p. 244.

153. Official references explained the inevitability of emigration in terms of "supply" and "demand." Instead of expending futile efforts to prevent it, both governments should regulate and control it. See González Navarro, *Población y sociedad*, pp. 222–23.

154. Ernesto Galarza, *Farm Workers and Agri-business in California, 1947–1960* (Notre Dame, Ind.: Univ. of Notre Dame Press, 1977), p. 114; Kirstein, *Anglo Over Bracero*, pp. 74, 83; President's Commission, *Migratory Labor*, pp. 56–59, 63, 66. Tomasek ("Political and Economic Implications," pp. 120–25) also discusses the early opposition of a number of ethnic-group, social-welfare, and religious organizations. Compare McCain, "Contract Labor as a Factor," p. 338; Congressional Quarterly, *Congress and the Nation, 1945–1964* (Washington, D.C.: Congressional Quarterly Service, 1965), p. 764.

155. Galarza, *Merchants of Labor*, pp. 103–4.

156. García (*Operation Wetback*, p. 45) notes that U.S. critics of the program seemed to perceive that things became worse after 1947. Tomasek ("Political and Economic Implications," p. 226) notes that although the grievance procedure for handling complaints "had never been very good" during World War II, its deficiencies were made up for by the fact that the number of contract laborers involved was small.

157. Tomasek ("Political and Economic Implications," pp. 226–27) notes that after the war, the number of contract laborers grew and the number of U.S. and Mexican compliance inspectors declined. After 1951 some fifty DOL compliance officers were responsible for overseeing contract guarantees for some 30,000 farmers who used Mexican contract labor. Compare García, *Operation Wetback*, pp. 45–48.

158. The issue of the relative costs of contract and "wetback" labor was fraught with

controversy throughout the duration of the program. It cannot be resolved here. It seems clear, however, that (a) braceros were generally more productive than domestic workers and (b) bracero labor became cheaper as the program wore on, such that after 1954 the wages and benefits of contract workers were equivalent to—perhaps worse than—those of "wetbacks," a fact which facilitated their employment as substitutes.

159. Galarza, *Merchants of Labor*, p. 106.

160. Ibid., pp. 94–95. It appears that undocumented farm labor was included in the category "non-local domestic seasonal workers." Thus, although this point is often ignored, part of the "domestic" labor being substituted for by contract workers was actually undocumented.

161. Ibid., pp. 101, 105.

162. Galarza, *Farm Workers and Agri-business*, pp. 356–57.

163. Ibid., pp. 252–53.

164. Ibid., pp. 253–56.

165. Craig, *The Bracero Program*, pp. 151–54; Galarza, *Farm Workers and Agri-business*, pp. 272-73.

166. Craig, *The Bracero Program*, pp. 151, 176, 180–81; Galarza, *Farm Workers and Agri-business*, pp. 271-72; Kiser and Kiser, *Mexican Workers*, pp. 100, 110–11. Tomasek ("Political and Economic Implications," pp. 266–67) gave this evaluation of the new political trend in 1957: "In general, the [U.S. labor] unions have gained in influence in the Department of Labor since 1952 on the question of Mexican labor, but still do not have as much influence as that of the growers."

167. Craig, *The Bracero Program*, pp. 155–85; Kirstein, *Anglo Over Bracero*, p. 104. In Kiser and Kiser, *Mexican Workers*, pp. 111–14, especially p. 111, a split among agricultural interests is noted between those who found mechanization a viable alternative and those who did not.

168. The text of the diplomatic note is reproduced in Kiser and Kiser, *Mexican Workers*, pp. 120–23. In the note the Mexican government also emphasized the contract guarantees offered by the program, thus implicitly arguing that bracero employment did not have adverse effects on the U.S. labor market. It also took credit for the "virtual extinction of discrimination against and segregation of persons of Mexican nationality in areas of the United States where such practices once existed" through the application of the instruments afforded by the contract-labor agreement. Compare González Navarro, *Población y sociedad*, p. 253, for a description of the increasing nervousness of Mexican members of Congress who perceived the end of the labor program at that time as a return to the earlier period of mass migration of undocumented workers.

169. Craig, *The Bracero Program*, pp. 186–87.

170. Contract labor continued to be admitted for three more years under Public Law 414 (the Immigration and Nationality Act of 1952). The number of such workers was small.

171. Not all Mexicans who currently enter illegally into the United States fit the pattern of contract-labor migrants. But one of the subpopulations in this flow—temporary, illegal, long-distance migrants—is essentially a continuation of the bracero migration. For a typology of contemporary Mexican migration, among which this group is discussed, see Wayne A. Cornelius, Leo R. Chávez, and Jorge G. Castro, *Mexican Immigrants and Southern California: A Summary of Current Knowledge*, A Report to the Human Resources Committee of the Los Angeles Chamber of Commerce (La Jolla, Calif.: Program in United States-Mexican Studies, UCSD, 1981), pp. 5–7.

172. The responses of California agricultural producers to the termination of the bracero program varied widely, as discussed in David Runsten and Phillip LeVeen, *Mechanization and Mexican Labor in California Agriculture*, Monographs in U.S.–Mexican Studies, no. 6 (La Jolla, Calif.: Program in U.S.–Mexican Studies, UCSD, 1981). These responses ranged from ceasing production (white asparagus, pp. 92–93), utilizing share-croppers (strawberries, pp. 75–76), mechanization (canning tomatoes, pp. 103–111), and "labor rationalization" schemes (organizing the harvest to make labor more productive and reduce its demand, for lemons and lettuce, pp. 79–82, 85). Some agricultural

producers in strawberries and tomatoes simply left California for northern Mexico, where they once again began to produce these crops for the U.S. winter-vegetable market (pp. 72, 106). Runsten and LeVeen also note that some of the braceros who had found repeated employment in small farms were brought in as legal immigrants through the labor certification preference category (pp. 73–74, 78–79, 87–88). For a discussion of the "green card commuters" who reside in Mexican border cities and work in the United States, a group that seems to have expanded significantly since 1964, see Kiser and Kiser, *Mexican Workers*, pp. 215–56.

173. This discussion on the Border Industrialization Program is based on María Patricia Fernández Kelly, *Women and Multinational Corporations: The Ciudad Juárez Maquiladoras* (Albany: SUNY Press, forthcoming); Kiser and Kiser, *Mexican Workers*, pp. 257–84; Antonio Ugalde, "Regional Political Processes and Mexican Politics on the Border," in *Views Across the Border*, edited by Stanley R. Ross (Albuquerque: Univ. of New Mexico Press, 1978), pp. 109–11; Mitchell A. Seligson and Edward J. Williams, *Maquiladoras and Migration: A Study of Workers in the Mexican–United States Border Industrialization Program* (Tucson: Univ. of Arizona, Department of Political Science, 1980), a study prepared for the Employment and Training Administration of the DOL.

174. For a discussion of Mexican efforts to renew the contract-labor agreement until 1974, see Jorge A. Bustamante, "La migración mexicana en la dinámica de las percepciones." Paper presented at the Seminar on Economic and Social Aspects of Relations Between the United States and Mexico, Stanford Univ., Stanford, Calif., November 15, 1980, pp. 19–29; and Corwin, *Immigrants—*, pp. 157, 197–99. Excerpts from Echeverría's State of the Union addresses in 1972 and 1974, dealing with the issue of undocumented emigration, are reproduced in Kiser and Kiser, *Mexican Workers*, pp. 124, 196.

175. Bustamante, "La migración mexicana," p. 28; Corwin, *Immigrants—*, pp. 198–99; Kiser and Kiser, *Mexican Workers*, pp. 125–26.

176. Kiser and Kiser, *Mexican Workers*, p. 126.

177. Wayne A. Cornelius, "Immigration, Mexican Development Policy, and the Future of U.S.–Mexican Relations," in *Mexico and the United States*, edited by Robert H. McBride (Englewood Cliffs, N.J.: Prentice-Hall, 1981), pp. 113–14. Also see the chapters in this volume by Lourdes Arizpe and August Schumacher.

178. Symptomatic of that lack of consensus is the content of the final report of the Select Commission on Immigration and Refugee Policy, and particularly the "supplemental statements" of the Commissioners. See U.S. Select Commission on Immigration and Refugee Policy, *Immigration Policy and the National Interest* (Washington, D.C.: GPO, 1981), pp. 331–419.

179. See, e.g., Chapter 7, this volume, by Edwin Reubens; David Gregory, "A U.S.–Mexican Temporary Workers Program: the Search for Co-determination," in *Mexico and the United States*, edited by Robert H. McBride (Englewood Cliffs, N.J.: Prentice-Hall, 1981), pp. 158–77; Warren C. Sanderson, "The Problems of Planning for the Expected: Demographic Shocks and Policy Paralysis." Paper presented at the Seminar on Economic and Social Aspects of Relations Between the United States and Mexico, Stanford Univ., Stanford, Calif., November 15, 1980; Wayne Cornelius, "Legalizing the Flow of Temporary Migrant Workers From Mexico: A Policy Proposal," *Working Papers in U.S.–Mexican Studies, No. 7* (La Jolla, Calif.: Program in United States–Mexican Studies, UCSD, 1981). Cornelius also issued a statement ("Statement of Cornelius Position on Guest-Worker Programs," May 5, 1980, Program in U.S.–Mexican Studies, UCSD) where he clarifies some of the distinguishing features of his proposal.

180. See "White House Asks a Law to Bar Jobs for Illegal Aliens," *The New York Times* July 31, 1981, pp. 1, 9, and "Plan on Immigration," p. 9, in the same issue. See also "Testimony of William French Smith before the Senate Subcommittee on Immigration and Refugee Policy and the House Subcommittee on Immigration, Refugees, and International Law," July 30, 1981. A critique of the Reagan proposals, including the temporary worker plan, is discussed in Wayne A. Cornelius, "The Reagan Administration's Proposals for a New U.S. Immigration Policy: An Assessment of Potential Effects," *International Migration Review* (December 1981).

181. Gregory, "A U.S.–Mexican Temporary Workers Program," p. 160.

4

Guestworker Employment in Selected European Countries—Lessons for the United States?

W. R. BÖHNING

Introduction and Summary

In the search for the right elements for U.S. immigration reform, some observers preoccupied with the illegal influx of Mexicans have looked for guidance to the experience of Western European countries with foreign or migrant workers, there commonly called "guestworkers." Western Europe appears to have controlled well a phenomenon that has so far proven uncontrollable in the United States. Not all observers, however, understand the law and practice prevailing in Europe today, partly because newspapers have highlighted certain extreme features and partly because the discussion in the United States wrongly equates temporary worker with guestworker policies. Section I will therefore elaborate the relevant characteristics of postwar policies in Western Europe.

Temporary foreign workers enter for a limited time and leave voluntarily or involuntarily when the time is up. H-2s in the United States or seasonal workers in France and Switzerland are of this type, although moves to a more permanent status have been allowed on both sides of the Atlantic. Guests, as a rule, are invited to stay as long as they wish; they are generally expected to leave eventually but, barring misconduct, are not forced out. Guestworker employment rather than temporary worker programs is the hallmark of Western Europe. Although the term is not official—"foreign employees" or "migrant workers" is most frequently used—it is very popular, and I will apply it here in the sense in which it should be used.

The practice of admitting aliens *subject to restrictions* (regarding, for instance, access to jobs) raises yet another issue. Programs of restricted admission differ from temporary worker programs, because restricted admission does not entail forced exit. Restrictions are, unfortunately, ubiquitous in the case of both temporary and guestworkers, but most restrictions, fortunately, come to an end sometime. One central but frequently unacknowledged element of the Western European make-up has been what one might call a progressive adjustment system, where restrictions on economic and social rights are gradually lifted.

Western European policymakers have been plagued by the problem of the permanence of the influx of foreigners—or how temporary it could be made to be. This is also the key issue in the current U.S. debate, especially as regards Mexicans. The main aim of this chapter, therefore, is to examine what happened in Western Europe and why, with a view to assessing whether future labor inflows into the United States could be so managed to assure the workers' temporary visits, should the country opt for a guestworker policy.[1]

Such trans-Atlantic comparisons can be useful only if the determining factors are identical, or at least similar. I assume the noncommunist countries north of the Alps and the United States are sufficiently similar as regards their forms of government and economies. But is the migration phenomenon the same? Is it perhaps a comparison of apples with oranges if, as has been said, Western Europe's migration movements are determined by the demand for labor in the country of employment,[2] while the U.S. movements are determined by the supply of labor in the country of origin?[3] Section II attempts to shed some light on this question analytically and by means of simple regressions. It proceeds to make the all-important distinction between necessary and sufficient factors. Supply pressure falls in the former category and labor demand in the latter; both factors are operative on both sides of the Atlantic; our exercise in cross-national policy comparison is therefore valid.

Section III begins by measuring how many of the guestworkers admitted during the prime migration periods have stayed or returned home. In the Federal Republic of Germany the rate of return is about two-thirds, and in Switzerland it is more than four-fifths. There are intriguing differences among the major nationalities. In Germany, about nine out of ten Italian, eight out of ten Spanish, seven out of ten Greek, five out of ten Yugoslav, and three out of ten Turkish workers returned.

These national differences will be examined. First, migrants' intentions are reviewed. In Western Europe, fewer workers were either short-term return-oriented or target workers, and more were either permanent emigrants or undecided than was generally believed. Many changed their mind. Intentions, which in any case require sophisticated methods to classify, do not predict reliably whether a nationality tends to return. Neither is the second examined predictor, family migration and family reunification, very helpful, nor a host of personal, social, economic, and behavioral determinants that are analyzed through ranked data. None of the factors at which policies might aim, such as skills or rural origin, fulfills the expectations that have generally been placed in them. The level of GNP per capita is perhaps an exception: it corresponds to the nationality differentials, and it is plausible in that low incomes reattract less than high incomes; yet it has limited utility for policymaking when there is not much choice about whose migrants to admit. Nevertheless, the analysis clearly reveals that propensity to return is nationality-related. Regardless of which group the Mexicans fall into, the theoretically conceivable manipulation of intentions, family reunification, or selection criteria would probably change the secular tendency little and is unlikely to be worth the political and administrative effort.

In the concluding section I briefly discuss whether the United States should institute a proper temporary worker program or whether it should restrict the rights of workers admitted for the purpose of nontemporary work.

I. Selected Aspects of Guestworker Policies in Western Europe

A short essay obviously cannot go into the details of the social, economic, political, and other dimensions of guestworker policies. Only characteristics that have a bearing on the question of temporariness will be dealt with.

A selection of countries must be made.[4] Some are too small (Liechtenstein, Luxembourg) or too little documented (Austria, Denmark, Norway); others are too heterogenous (the Netherlands, the UK) or have too short and checkered a history of labor immigration (Belgium, Sweden and, once more, the UK) to be suited to the analysis here. This leaves the Federal Republic of Germany, France, and Switzerland, the three countries which have regularly absorbed the great majority of foreign workers in Western Europe. They are also fairly similar in their orientation toward migrants and are as nearly representative of Western Europe's experience in this field as a selection of countries can be. For example, the progressive adjustment system mentioned earlier that enables—in some cases even entitles—guestworkers to enjoy unrestricted economic rights and/or permanent resident alien status fixes the qualifying periods for free choice of employment at five to ten years in Switzerland (depending on nationality), five years in Germany, and four in France. This compares with eight years in Austria, four in the UK, three in Belgium and the Netherlands, and one year in Sweden.

It should also be mentioned that the bulk of the Western European population is authorized to move and work freely in member states of the European Economic Community (EEC)[5] and the Common Nordic Labour Market.[6]

In the following analysis of the three countries selected, I will examine only the salient points in each country.

FEDERAL REPUBLIC OF GERMANY

Successive Federal governments have only themselves to blame for the reputation they have earned for the treatment of *Gastarbeiter*. Although they never officially implemented a temporary or rotation policy vis-à-vis the major migrant-sending countries,[7] they received the workers who were actively recruited by proclaiming publicly, stridently, and repeatedly, *Deutschland ist kein Einwanderungsland* (Germany is not a country of immigration); and they tolerated, even fostered, a climate of legal and material insecurity that has made many a guestworker feel unwelcome.[8] One or two *Länder* governments flew "trial balloons" in the early seventies, but the Federal government did not accept administratively enforced departure or even financial inducement to return. It proclaimed in one of its basic policy statements, "The limitation of the duration of stay of foreign employees will not be effected through [police] measures under the law relating to foreigners."[9]

One telling statistic may elucidate the situation. During the high unemployment years 1974–1978, foreign workers (other than EEC citizens) submitted 6,370,000 requests for new or renewed work permits, of which 152,000, or 2.4 percent, were refused.[10] Some of these workers may have been successful in a subsequent request. Many will have signed on to the unemployment register. Others who felt discouraged may have left for home or for a third country. At any rate, being without gainful employment did not force departure.

On the other hand, the proclamation of a public policy does not ipso facto mean that it is implemented by every subaltern official in the country, without regard to personal prejudices or preferences (which can act either in favor of or against an individual foreigner). Several court cases have publicly revealed that a few lower, labor-exchange officials or sections of the police were more than keen to expedite the return of foreigners. Illegal entrants were in any case usually deported when caught; foreigners considered a threat to the political order were also given short shrift.

Policymakers assumed that the volume of guestworker employment could be regulated by the interplay of market forces and the migrants' short-run return orientation. Operatively, this policy was given effect through strict control of entry of non-EEC citizens (with active recruitment being discontinued after November 1973). The market forces were expected to act indirectly upon the number of foreign workers present: it was taken for granted that rational workers would decide to go home when the economy ran out of steam.

The official attitude can be summed up as follows: "Given past experience, the Federal Government continues to proceed from the assumption that the overwhelming number of foreign employees will not stay permanently in the Federal Republic."[11] Politicians and officials have always refused to state precisely what rate of settlement they expected in the 1950s or early 1960s, when the large-scale recruitment of foreigners began, or what rate they might find comfortable today. I have reason to believe that in the beginning it was no more than 10 percent of the numbers admitted. At any rate, to state a definite rate or number would entail repatriating the excess and would be extremely unwise politically if prior public declarations ruled out the forced exit of foreigners.

FRANCE

France, in contrast to her neighbors to the east, has been able to project a welcoming and nonrestrictive image of her migrant worker situation. Yet, beneath the thin veneer of a population-oriented policy, which throughout the postwar period was always something of a myth, was the harsh reality of work and residence permits, police checks, strikes, and some very ugly racial confrontations (the latter did not occur in France's eastern neighbors!). Entry control has been tightened in stages since 1968; previously the majority of the people receiving annual permits had entered as illegals in that they circumvented the cumbersome official recruitment machinery and were subsequently regularized. The share of regularizations in total admission dropped to 39 percent in 1971 and 27 percent in 1972, while 11 percent and 23 percent, respectively, of the requests for regularization were denied.[12] Large-scale recruitment was discontinued in summer 1974, and admissions are now down to exceptional cases, dependents who have joined breadwinners or who have grown up in France, EEC citizens, and seasonal workers. The inflow of seasonals has, in fact, remained fairly stable during the last twenty years.[13] With very few exceptions, France's seasonal migrants work in agriculture.

If one excludes seasonals, it would be true to say that France pursued a guestworker policy as opposed to either a temporary worker program or a traditional immigration policy. In the face of growing unemployment, the French government recently attempted to change policies. In mid-1979 it proposed that work and residence permits be withdrawn from foreigners who were unemployed for more than six months; that the qualification period for permanent resident aliens be raised to twenty years; and that the number of foreigners in the country be reduced by 200,000 each year.[14] There was an immediate outcry in national and international fora, and it appears that the government plans have quietly been shelved.

The circumvention of the official recruitment procedures by the employers' direct hiring of entrants and their later regularization has been a peculiar feature of France's postwar history. Leading politicians have not been averse to rationalizing it. As Minister of Labor, M. Jeanneney said: "L'immigration clandestine n'est pas inutile car si l'on s'en tenait à l'application stricte des règlements et accords internationaux, nous manquerions peut-être de main-d'oeuvre."[15]

Illegal immigration in the full sense of the word happens in Western Europe, too. Outside the UK (where numbers are probably very small but public opinion jumps on each individual case as though it were the tip of an iceberg), the most widely accepted figure puts illegals at one-tenth of all foreigners legally present in Western Europe. The public is not exercised by the scale of the problem. Civil penalties for employers of illegals are now much harsher than they used to be, and imprisonment is included in the range of sanctions.[16] Amnesties in Belgium, the Netherlands, and the UK have drawn fewer illegals out of hiding than had been expected.[17]

SWITZERLAND

To be given leave to enter Switzerland as a worker presupposes, as elsewhere, that nationals are not available to fill the vacancies. This has not been difficult to demonstrate, given the virtual absence even of frictional unemployment in Switzerland.[18] In the early fifties the economic boom was judged to be a passing phenomenon, to be followed by a depression on the lines of the inter-war period. Foreigners were, therefore, not encouraged to settle. When boom followed boom with only the slightest interruption, popular misgivings emerged about the burgeoning foreign population, along with economic fears about dependence on foreign workers and the labor intensity that appeared to be associated with them. Beginning in 1963, the Federal Council decreed limits on the numbers of workers and their dependents. Successive policies tried, somewhat unsuccessfully, to set ceilings on the number of foreigners in enterprises or sectors. Reduction was the order of the day during the early seventies, when several referenda were pending. (They were eventually defeated with the support of government and employers' and workers' organizations.) Today, stabilization of the reduced numbers is the leitmotif, along with assimilation of long-term stayers. It is achieved in the main by fixing quotas for the inflow of annual permit holders. In other words, the *stock* (the numbers present) is held constant by manipulation of the *inflow* (the numbers admitted from abroad).

The postwar period witnessed a gradual easing of the restrictions on new entrants; this process was general throughout Western Europe. Switzerland's restrictions were perhaps more draconian than those in other countries. For instance, the Italians—who represented some 90 percent of the new entrants in the early fifties and still comprise 50 percent of today's stock—were restricted to one canton and bound to an employer or occupation, or both, for at least five years. They needed ten years of continuous employment to qualify as resident foreigners on a par with Swiss nationals in matters of economic and social rights. Family migration was not foreseen. Annual permit holders could apply for family reunification only after a ten-year residence, and seasonal permit holders had no such rights. Today, annual permit holders can change cantons, employers, and occupations, after one year's employment, and family reunification is possible after one year. Seasonal workers who have accumulated 36 months of employment during four consecutive seasons can have their status changed to that of an annual permit holder without restrictions regarding canton, employer, or occupation; they can also request family reunification when they obtain an annual work permit. Adjustment to resident alien status still presupposes ten years of employment (five in the case of Austrians, French, and Germans), and naturalization, twelve years.

There are five basic categories of foreigners in Switzerland: residence permit holders, annual permit holders, seasonal work permit holders, frontier workers, and international officials and dependents. Annual permit holders are a dying breed, as more and more of them are entitled to resident status while fewer and fewer are admitted. For instance, the numbers admitted amounted to 137,700 in 1960, 70,400 in 1970, and 26,800 in 1979. The inflow, properly speaking, was 9 percent smaller in 1970 and 14 percent in 1979, because the overall figures include the seasonal permit holders, whose status has been adjusted to that of an annual permit holder.[19]

Seasonal workers have always been a point of contention, particularly between Swiss and Italian authorities. For instance, a number of employers hired foreigners registered as seasonals, who in fact were engaged in permanent positions and were sent home once a year for an extended holiday (*faux saisonniers*), a practice now clamped down upon by the Swiss government. Seasonal workers are employed chiefly in construction or hotel and catering. They have long been allowed to adjust their status to annual permit holders, even before the recent legislation eased the conditions of change-over. The statistics gain added weight when it is noted that the average annual proportion of seasonals who have never before worked in Switzerland amounts to about one-third.[20] Some make the journey only once, others come back each year, and still others see their seasonal permits as springboards to better employment in the host country. In France it has not actually been possible *de jure* to change from seasonal to a better status, but exceptions were made *de facto*. (The Federal Republic of Germany and other Western European countries do not grant seasonal permits.)

Seasonal employment is, by definition, of limited duration. Seasonal workers seem to have accepted their unenviable lot. Similarly, annual work permit holders who found themselves without a job and a permit to stay also returned home regularly and apparently quite naturally, unless they decided to claim local unemployment benefits, which in Switzerland was rarely the case. It was relatively easy for an Italian, for instance, whose home country was within a short driving distance, to pack up his belongings and wait for next year's call from the employer.

To most people living in the triangle bounded by the Scandinavian countries in the north, Portugal in the southwest, and Greece in the southeast, the expiration of one's permit signifies that one should go home. To challenge government authority in the form of a foreign bureaucracy, let alone a policy apparatus, hardly comes naturally to inhabitants of this triangle. Furthermore, it requires information, communication, and financial and human resources. But these are all now increasingly available, and habits are changing. I mention this because, contrary to many publications, the considerable return flow of Mediterranean workers from countries north of the Alps is seldom the result of administrative enforcement in the true sense of the word.[21] To shore up this contention, one can point to Swiss statistics which show that residence permit holders, i.e., foreigners whose exit cannot be forced, form an important part of the return flow. During the six years 1974–1979 there were 189,500 (including 95,100 active) cases of return from this category, compared with 326,800 (173,500 active) from among the annual permit holders.[22]

Western European countries may not deserve much praise in immigration matters, but they are certainly not the black sheep they are often depicted to be.

II. Determinants of Contemporary Labor Migration

The degree of settlement that might be associated with a future U.S. guestworker-type policy can, in principle, be predicted on the basis of Western Europe's experience, provided, first, that sufficient structural similarities exist between the polities and economies on both sides of the Atlantic, and, second, that their labor inflows are determined by the same factors. The first assumption is generally accepted with reference to democratic, pluralistic forms of government and high-income market economies buttressed by advanced technology, a broadly based industry, and a wide network of trade relations. The second assumption is debatable. I maintain that the demand for labor in the immigration countries is the key to explaining contemporary international migration movements;[23] prominent American authors have claimed that it is the supply of labor in the emigration countries.[24]

This controversy cannot be resolved here. One can merely explore the ground to see whether there is a reasonably firm basis for cross-national policy comparison. First, different schools of thought will be critically reviewed; next, I will briefly present my own views and exemplify them empirically (with data from the Federal Republic of Germany, because other statistics are unavailable or insufficiently valid to underpin the analysis); and finally, I will examine comparable research undertaken in the United States.

DIFFERENT SCHOOLS OF THOUGHT

Marxist authors have attributed a peculiar hunger for "cheap" foreign labor to "early" as well as "late" capitalism.[25] Although Marxists have been diligent unravelers of the intricacies of employers' attempts to keep down labor costs—as well as furthering migrant workers' struggles for equality of opportunity and treatment—their causal explanations are unconvincing for several reasons.

First, they cannot explain the characteristic differences between countries (say, between Canada, France, and Japan). Second, they cannot explain the differences within countries as regards (a) differential recourse to migrants by different types of employers or industries, (b) different statuses for one nationality in the same country of employment, or (c) different treatment of various nationalities. Third, they cannot explain a host of other international labor movements, such as those between South American countries, or the movements between the socialist countries of Eastern Europe, or the truly temporary migration system instituted between a developing North African country, Algeria, and the technologically advanced German Democratic Republic.[26] Regardless of the political merits of the Marxist analyses, their broad causal interpretations lack validity.

Two sectoral explanations have been offered by *Lutz* and by *Portes. Lutz's* influential model sees selective opening of the borders as a way of postponing wage adjustments in an inflation-prone environment.[27] His sector I contains industries with high productivity growth and wages; sector II, low productivity and wages. Today's labor force, being increasingly educated, aspires to sector I jobs. Scarcities occur in sector II which, in Lutz's view, are

> ultimately a wage (or price) question. The scarcity implies one or both of two things. Either the *general* wage level is lower than the country can afford while providing full employment for its domestic labor force. Or the structure of *relative* wage rates as between different industries and occupations is

"wrong." I shall argue that the primary reason for the recent large-scale importation of foreign labor by the European countries concerned is that relative wages have been out of line with conditions on the supply side of the domestic labor market.[28]

Valid and invalid points are mixed in Lutz's two-sector model. Among the invalid ones are

a. the supply-determined engagement of nationals in sector I—as though it was not the general demand for labor that enabled them to find jobs there;

b. the fact that wage differentials within each sector (industry or occupation) tend to be larger than between them—as though intrasectoral differentials would not have the effects ascribed to intersectoral differentials;

c. the mechanical view of "just" or "wrong" wage levels—as though the real world corresponded to the atomizing, homogenizing, and conflict-free world of neoclassical assumptions, where rational economic man disregards all but pecuniary rewards or accepts disutilities after a suitable top up of his pay;[29] and

d. the related supposition that national labor was not really numerically short but merely failed to come forward—as though people have an obligation to work and, given a little incentive, should work whether they want to or need to or not.

Portes has offered a somewhat different two-sector model.[30] His key line of reasoning is also worth reporting at length because it contains a number of basic and valid observations:

Other things being equal, the rate of return to capital is inversely related to the costs of labor. . . . Advanced capitalist societies tend to be characterized by scarcity of labor either in the absolute sense of exhaustion of the domestic labor supply or in the relative one of exhaustion of labor willing to work for low wages. . . . Smaller industrial and service firms cannot readily pass on their labor costs. In addition, many continue to be labor intensive since there is no available technology to increase labor productivity or it is beyond their means. In this situation, the only available alternative is to seek a reduction of the share of the product going to labor as wages. The search for new sources of low-cost labor takes two major forms: 1) exporting the production process to where such labor sources are found; and 2) importing low-cost labor to replace or supplement the domestic work force. . . . There are a number of firms which, by their very nature, cannot easily export themselves abroad. Agricultural enterprises are the most obvious and best publicized examples, although certainly not the only ones. A wide variety of urban services cannot be "produced" except in place and, hence, require a readily available supply of low-cost labor.[31]

Portes's explanation has two basic shortcomings: first, in the United States, where illegals seem to cluster in the secondary labor market among small-scale employers,[32] it is clear that only a relatively small portion of the said employers actually hires illegals. Second, in Western Europe, foreign workers are more often than not employed by the larger firms (see Tables 4.1 and 4.2). Portes's reasoning might appear to stand up to verification in the agricultural sector, yet the nature of family enterprises predetermines average firm size. And agriculture is—with the exception of France and Switzerland—the least important European employer of foreigners. For instance, in the Federal Republic of Germany it accounts for only 1 percent of all guestworkers. As regards the commercial and private service sector, Portes's contentions would be supported by the German, but not by the French, data. At any rate, in the Federal Republic manufacturing employs the most foreigners (61 percent in 1968 and 59 percent, according to the most recent data of June 1979). In the case of France it is manufacturing and construction (47 percent and 33 percent, respectively, in 1976). On balance, therefore, Portes's arguments fail the empirical test.

One *macro-sociological* attempt to explain contemporary international migration should be noted in passing. *Richmond and Verma* have constructed a global systems model where economic determinants are combined with political and administrative controls.[33] Migration is one of the ways in which people

Table 4.1 Proportion of Employed Foreign Workers by Size of Firm in Different Sectors of the Economy of the Federal Republic of Germany, Autumn 1968

| | Size of firm (number of employees) | | | | | | | |
| | 1–49 | | 50–199 | | 200–499 | | 500 and larger | |
	Men	Women	Men	Women	Men	Women	Men	Women
Agriculture	72	—	—	—	—	—	—	—
Mines and quarries[a]	24	—	23	—	12	—	41	—
Manufacturing	10	—	13	14	12	13	65	68
Construction	33	—	35	—	17	—	15	—
Commerce	53	49	24	—	—	—	—	—
Private services	66	71	—	13	—	—	—	—
Transport	—	—	—	—	—	—	74	—
Public services	—	25	—	30	—	19	42	26
Total	21	20	21	20	15	17	43	43

[a] Including energy sector.

Note: Blank indicates that sample survey results are too small to yield reliable results.

Source: Bundesanstalt für Arbeit, *Ausländische Arbeitnehmer: Beschäftigung, Anwerbung, Vermittlung—Erfahrungsbericht 1969*, Beilage zu Nr. 8 der *Amtlichen Nachrichten* vom 28 August 1970, p. 79.

Table 4.2   Share of Foreign Workers in Total Employment by Size of Firm in Different Sectors of the Economy of France, October 1976

	Size of firm (number of employees)				
	10–49	50–199	200–499	500 and larger	Average
Mines and quarries	12	11	7	7	9
Manufacturing	9	10	9	12	10
Construction	19	27	33	41	27
Commerce	5	6	5	7	6
Transport	4	6	10	5	5
Private services	4	8	7	4	5
Total	8	11	11	12	11

Note: Firms with less than ten employees are excluded, as are agriculture, public administration, public services, and domestic services.

Source: Ministère du Travail et de la Participation, *Résultats de l'enquête sur la main-d'oeuvre étrangère effectuée en October 1976* (Paris, July 1979), Table 2.

and societies adapt to changing conditions, among them the continuing high requirement for geographic and labor mobility in industrial and postindustrial societies. In essence, migration is supply-determined. The model is seductive but, at least in its present form, unverifiable on account of its generality and broadness.

The latest line of advance is associated with the *secondary labor market* model and *Piore*.[34] I shall trace Piore's rejection of other schools of thought before explaining his own secondary labor market concept. I have tested some of his contentions with ordinary least-square regressions, using absolute numbers of foreign workers, vacancies, unemployed, etc., from the Federal Republic of Germany over the period 1961–1976. Logarithmic transformations were not used, to prevent complicating the basically straightforward lines of reasoning. Relevant coefficients of determination have been assembled in Table 4.3. When tests are subsequently designated as "correct" or "incorrect," it means that the regression results shown in Table 4.3 support or contradict his arguments.

Piore states that migration cannot be explained as a response to general labor shortages that eventually feed through to bottom-rung jobs, because—to the contrary—the labor demand model (a) cannot explain why there are X rather than Y numbers of foreign workers, and (b) it cannot explain why market or administrative forces do not achieve a lasting reduction in foreign worker employment. As the determination of the inflow is not specified in Piore's demand concept, one can only test his *a contrario* arguments relating to stocks and return. On the first of these, the coefficients of determination prove Piore

Table 4.3 Coefficients of Determination of Least Square Regressions Relating Flows and Stocks of Economically Active Foreigners to Demand Variables in the Federal Republic of Germany, 1961–1976

Active foreigners[b]	Demand variables							
	Vacancies			Unemployed			Workseekers[a]	
	Stock[c]	Change in stock[d]	Registrations[e]	Stock[c]	Change in stock[d]	Registrations[e]	Stock[c]	Registrations[e]
Inflow[f]	0.96*	n.a.	0.44*	0.66*	n.a.	0.90*	0.64*	0.65*
Change in inflow[d]	(0.11)	0.96*	0.09	(0.04)	0.52*	(0.06)	(0.02)	(0.00)
Stock[g]	(0.02)	n.a.	(0.47)*	(0.14)	n.a.	(0.03)	(0.18)	(0.32)**
Change in stock[d]	0.16	0.52*	0.49*	0.12	0.65*	0.18	0.15	0.35**
Outflow[h]	(0.10)	n.a.	(0.01)	(0.29)**	n.a.	(0.20)	(0.29)**	(0.07)

Bracketed figures indicate that the regression coefficient has the wrong sign; n.a. = not available or analytically spurious link, * = coefficient of determination significant at 1-percent level, and ** = coefficient of determination significant at 5-percent level.

[a] Workseekers comprise registered unemployed plus employed wage and salary earners who register to seek new jobs.

[b] Including frontier workers.

[c] Annual average of monthly data (16 observations). Stock in the case of vacancies means vacancies remaining unfilled at end of month. In the case of unemployed and workseekers they similarly represent those "remaining on the books." Unregistered unemployed etc. are disregarded.

[d] Year to year changes (15 observations which include a half-year lag where related to stock data).

[e] Annual sum of vacancies, etc., notified to labor exchanges (16 observations).

[f] Annual sum of foreigners granted leave to enter for the purpose of employment (16 observations).

[g] End of year data, including unemployed since 1969.

[h] Adjusted for deaths, naturalizations and unregistered unemployed. For method of calculation see Table 4.4 below (where frontier workers are excluded).

Source: Amtliche Nachrichten der Bundesanstalt für Arbeit (various); author's own calculations.

correct (see row relating to "stock" in Table 4.3). On the second, the results are somewhat mixed, but Piore is by and large correct (rows relating to "change in stock" and "outflow"). Demand variables predict badly or not at all the size of the foreign workforce, changes in it, or return movements.[35]

Next, Piore elucidates the bottom-rung or dead-end jobs concept.[36] Verification of this model runs the risk of becoming circular: because certain jobs are bottom-rung/dead-end, migrants are employed in them, therefore they are bottom-rung/dead-end jobs, ad infinitum. Regressions do not help here. It is obvious visually and statistically that foreign workers in Western Europe are overrepresented in unskilled, low-status jobs with poor working conditions.[37]

Finally, in his dual labor market hypothesis Piore posits the uncertainty and variability of demand for labor as the "underlying explanation of the adverse job characteristics,"[38] and job security arrangements for nationals, especially skilled workers, as the impetus of the employers' search for foreigners to satisfy additional, variable demand for labor.[39] Although Piore's reasoning is full of stimulating insights, I am certain that few, let alone many, labor markets in Western Europe can be characterized in this way. Inherent in Piore's theory is a bimodal distribution of jobs which is almost nonexistent in reality. One reason is that, where industry-wide rather than craftsman-type trade unions are prevalent (as in many parts of Europe), job security is an industrial rather than a hierarchical matter in collective bargaining. Moreover, beginning in the late sixties and gathering momentum in the seventies, there were moves on the side of workers' organizations to assure disproportionate gains in wages and working conditions for low-skilled workers. In other words, the wage and salary earners at the bottom were deliberately favored by Piore's primary labor force! Furthermore, Western Europe's foreign workers have become passive as well as active members of trade unions, in large numbers.[40] That they nevertheless suffer disproportionately from unemployment results primarily from the differential incidence of layoffs by sector, marital status, age or seniority, and lack of knowledge of the local language. Skill differentials also play a role, but this does not, as such, signify the existence of secondary labor markets.

DEMAND DETERMINATION REVISITED

International labor migration is determined, in my view, as follows:[41] in a world of nation states there are borders over which nonbelongers may step only with explicit or tacit consent. Whether or not, and if so by how much, the borders open to economically active foreigners depends on how the nation's influential members and groups satisfy the wants and promote the welfare of nationals and, in so doing, command nonutilized or underutilized capital. If such capital articulates a demand for labor that cannot be satisfied sufficiently quickly (because there is a physical shortage of nationals in the sense that there are not enough people, or a relative shortage in the sense that not enough unemployed or inactive can be attracted to the jobs), and if the political power structure sanctions it, borders will be opened to foreign workers.

Demand, then, is caused economically, screened politically, and given effect administratively. Of course, it is *necessary* that there be candidates for migration. As a rule, their supply is infinitely elastic. This is not a logical, but an empirical, proposition, characteristic of the world today and, as far as can be foreseen, of the world tomorrow. The relative attractions of the area in which the demand arises and the area in which the supply originates are *conditioning* factors, but not the *cause* of labor movements. Whatever the cause may be in particular circumstances, for international migration to occur it is *sufficient* that a country signals its willingness to employ foreigners. A tap provides a good analogy. As there is always pressure in the pipe, it suffices to turn the tap to ensure the flow of water.

One way of clarifying the argument is to compare refugees with economic migrants. Refugees are persons who leave their country because of a well-founded fear of persecution for reasons of race, religion, nationality, political association, or social grouping. Their flows are supply-determined. No country in this world articulates a demand for refugees, although many accept them. In contrast, many countries wish to admit certain categories or numbers of active foreigners, both of which can be highly variable; in others, politics and administration produce illegals. Recruitment and border or residence control match candidates with aims. The *volume* and *socio-economic characteristics* of the resulting migration are demand-determined in the sense outlined here. The *nationality composition* may well be influenced by the interplay of distance (cost) and differential "push" factors (of an economic or political kind), or by the comparative attractions of home and immigration country; but that is another question.

The presence or absence of economic demand can be checked with the help of the regressions already presented in Table 4.3. Given a guestworker-type policy, i.e., a policy that operates on the inflow rather than the stock of migrant workers, one must hypothesize that the demand for labor determines (a) the numbers admitted during any period and (b) the change in numbers admitted between periods. Both contentions are proved correct, at least when demand is expressed in the form of vacancies.[42] Ninety-six percent of annual admissions in the Federal Republic of Germany resulted from variations in unfilled vacancies, and 96 percent of the differences in numbers admitted from one year to the next were accounted for by the changes in the annual number of unfilled vacancies. This leaves no room for supply factors![43]

The lack of specification of the political framework in Piore's work is responsible for his mis-specification of the demand model. If policies link demand for labor with numbers coming in rather than with numbers present or numbers returning, one should not in the first instance expect any correlation between the stock or outflow of foreign workers, on the one side, and demand variables, on the other. Properly specified, demand determination relates to the inflow, which it explains satisfactorily, both analytically and empirically.[44]

When the inflow of foreign labor is demand-determined,[45] resources that were waiting to be used will be brought into productive use and value added will be created, internal and external demand will be generated, and the whole will turn into a self-feeding process where a portion of the additional labor will come to form an increment to the national labor force with structural, rather than conjunctural, characteristics.[46] Recessions will not necessarily cut down jobs in the same numbers, sectors, or occupations as were previously offered to foreigners; and voluntary return movements in excess of needs will call for new immigration.[47] The flaw in the Western European guestworker concept was the apparent belief that a migrant worker arrived and performed a job, and goods or services were supplied as though this were a discrete and finite event, at the end of which the guest would have worked himself out of a job. It is small wonder, therefore, that the stock and outflow figures correlate badly with the ups and downs of demand for labor.

THE UNITED STATES: DEMAND OR SUPPLY? NECESSARY VERSUS SUFFICIENT FACTORS

In theory, the United States should fit the framework I have developed about demand determination, in both illegal and other labor inflows. Two pieces of comparable empirical research appear to contradict this assumption.

Frisbie and Jenkins ran a variety of regressions chiefly on the basis of INS apprehension data as a proxy for inflows. Frisbie concluded that Mexican supply factors have greater explanatory power than U.S. demand factors.[48] Jenkins's regression coefficients relating to U.S. employment and unemployment had, *inter alia*, the "wrong" sign, which he took as a refutation of the demand model.[49]

In actual fact, INS apprehension figures are not by any means a true approximation of the labor inflow. It is widely accepted that enforcement efforts are inversely related to the state of the labor market and that INS officers turn a blind eye to certain situations of illegal employment.[50] INS Commissioner Castillo confirmed—officially, as it were—that his staff responds even to the sectoral or regional incidence of unemployment.[51] Generally speaking, in good times when U.S. employment goes up, INS apprehensions take on a routine or lenient character; in bad times when unemployment goes up, apprehension efforts are intensified and the numbers detained increase. The "wrong" signs of Jenkins's coefficients confirm this reasoning! The size of his coefficients indicate that the good times/bad times relationship is weak, which is not surprising because apprehension efforts are undertaken all the time.

Both Frisbie and Jenkins fail to make an essential conceptual distinction. They should have distinguished between necessary and sufficient determinants of international migration. Of course, it is *necessary* that there are Mexican candidates for migration. It is, indeed, highly plausible that "push" factors influence their number and composition.[52] If this determinant of international moves were inoperative in the case of Mexico, the INS would apprehend only a random number of Mexicans. But the Mexicans found in the United States are not there because of "push" factors in their village or country. Other Mexicans and, more importantly, many other nationalities are "pushed" a great deal more, and yet they never come near the US. The Mexicans who are caught by the INS, as well as those who slip through, are there in essence because US employers hire them, often seeking them out, and because the employers are exempted by law (section 274[a] of the 1952 Immigration and Nationality Act, the so-called Texas Proviso) from penalties for so doing. The U.S. demand takes effect through this hole in the law, and this demand factor is the *sufficient* condition for the illegal inflow of Mexicans and others. If U.S. employers stopped hiring them voluntarily or in the face of dissuasive penal-

Table 4.4 Number of Economically Active Foreigners Admitted to Employment in the Federal Republic of Germany, and Percentage Leaving the Country, by Selected Nationalities, 1961–1976 (in thousands)

			1961–1976	1961–1968	1969–1976	1969–1973	1974–1976
Greeks	Stock at begin.	number	28.0	28.0	155.0	155.0	245.0
	Inflow	number	561.7	353.0	208.6	205.4	3.3
	Outflow	%	68	63	76	53	1,482
	Stock at end	number	178.0	155.0	178.0	245.0	178.0
Italians	Stock at begin.	number	157.2	157.2	282.0	282.0	428.0
	Inflow	number	1,987.9	1,160.5	827.4	717.4	110.0
	Outflow	%	91	89	94	78	200
	Stock at end	number	286.0	282.0	286.0	428.0	286.0
Spaniards	Stock at begin.	number	27.4	27.4	119.0	119.0	184.0
	Inflow	number	564.6	366.6	198.0	195.6	2.4
	Outflow	%	82	74	96	65	2,681
	Stock at end	number	108.0	119.0	108.0	184.0	108.0
Turks	Stock at begin.	number	3.0	3.0	170.0	170.0	610.0
	Inflow	number	875.7	293.5	582.2	571.5	10.7
	Outflow	%	30	42	24	21	159
	Stock at end	number	542.0	170.0	542.0	610.0	542.0
Yugoslavs	Stock at begin.	number	5.0	5.0	148.0	148.0	520.0
	Inflow	number	923.6	245.9	677.7	664.9	12.8
	Outflow	%	52	41	56	43	757
	Stock at end	number	390.0	148.0	390.0	520.0	390.0
Subtotal	Stock at begin.	number	200.6	200.6	874.0	874.0	1,987.0
	Inflow	number	4,913.4	2,419.6	2,493.9	2,354.8	139.1
	Outflow	%	69	72	66	51	321
	Stock at end	number	1,504.0	874.0	1,504.0	1,987.0	1,504.0
Other	Stock at begin.	number	125.4	125.4	226.0	226.0	513.0
	Inflow	number	1,058.4	433.8	624.6	505.3	119.2
	Outflow	%	66	75	59	41	136
	Stock at end	number	416.0	226.0	416.0	513.0	416.0
Grand total	Stock at begin.	number	346.0	346.0	1,100.0	1,100.0	2,500.0
	Inflow	number	5,971.8	2,853.3	3,118.4	2,860.1	258.4
	Naturalizations	number	62.5	16.0	46.5	24.9	21.6
	Deaths	number	59.4	11.7	47.7	26.3	21.4
	Withdrawal	%	74	74	74	51	324
	Outflow	%	68	73	65	49	236
	Stock at end	number	1,920.0	1,100.0	1,920.0	2,500.0	1,920.0

(See next page for footnote and sources.)

Note: Economically active (excluding frontier workers) = employed + registered unemployed. Calculation of "withdrawal" from German labor market = stock of active at beginning of period + inflow during period – stock of active at end of period. Result is percentage of inflow. Calculation of "outflow" (approximate return of active foreigners) from German labor market = stock at beginning + inflow – naturalizations – deaths – unregistered unemployed (change from active to inactive status) – stock at end. Result as percentage of inflow. The presumably negligible number of retirements taking place in Germany is disregarded because of lack of hard data. Also disregarded is the small number of changes to self-employed status because (1) it is not known, and (2) the table is conceived in terms of economically active status, even though all raw data actually relate to wage and salary earners. Estimation of naturalizations and deaths of active foreigners = rising share of overall number of naturalizations and deaths published by Statistisches Bundesamt; a few data gaps were closed by interpolation and extrapolation. The share was assumed to be 10 percent in year 1961 and increased by 5 percent each year, thus rising to 85 percent in year 1976. The naturalizations and deaths for each nationality were estimated as follows: the proportion of each nationality in each year's average number of employed foreigners was obtained and this proportion was applied to the previously calculated total number of active foreigners who had been naturalized or who had died during that year.

Unregistered unemployed foreigners = nil until 1973; 36,000 in 1974; 156,000 in 1975; and 181,000 in 1976. Source: *Mitteilungen aus de Arbeitsmarkt- und Berufsforschung* 12, no. 1 (1979), p. 28. These semiofficial figures, which at heart reflect the ups and downs of the economy, appear to include many young people who had joined their parents in Germany but were prohibited from taking up employment. Not forming part of the inflow (or work permit) statistics used here, this group had to be taken out of the calculation of outflows of people admitted for the purpose of employment. It was assumed that this group amounted to 50 percent of the overall number of unregistered unemployed foreigners. Each nationality's share was then estimated as corresponding to its proportion in the average number of employed foreigners during each year, i.e., on the same lines as naturalizations and deaths.

Sources: Published and unpublished information of the Bundesanstalt für Arbeit; Statistisches Bundesamt, *Wirtschaft und Statistik* (various); author's own estimates.

ties, there might still be numerous surreptitious movements across the border, as well as visa abusers, but this would not entail significant employment in the United States.

In view of these observations, we can accept as a working assumption that the structural features of the migration are sufficiently similar to permit policy learning across the Atlantic.

III. Measurement and Explanation of Temporariness

What happened in Western Europe? How many economically active migrants later returned home? What are the determinants of temporariness? Can any policy-relevant factors be singled out and, in future, applied to modify the extent of spontaneous settlement? These questions will be investigated in this section. Fortunately, the data base is broader than it was for the preceding section, and the statistics used have been made comparable to the greatest extent possible. Seasonal workers have been eliminated in the measurement of temporariness because they are limited-time rather than guestworkers.

THE EXTENT OF TEMPORARINESS

Figures on several nationalities are presented in Table 4.4 for the Federal Republic of Germany, and overall rates in Table 4.5 for Switzerland. Two measures are developed: first "withdrawal," and second "outflow." "Withdrawal" is a rough estimate of the number of foreigners who have dropped out of the labor market of the country of employment. "Outflow" is a refined estimate that takes account of the foreigners who died, were naturalized, or pulled out without appearing in the unemployment statistics. "Outflow" equals return from the point of view of the country of employment; but since a portion of the migrants involved tends to move to a third country rather than to the country of origin, "outflow" does not necessarily mean return from the point of view of the country whose nationality the migrants bear. The economic status and nationalities of foreign deaths and naturalizations in the Federal Republic and Switzerland are not known in sufficient detail for most of the years under consideration. Therefore, a plausible and logical estimation procedure was used that affects all nationalities and the total figures in the same way. The discrepancies with reality probably make themselves felt only after the decimal point and can for all practical purposes be neglected.[53] Migration streams gain in maturity in the course of time, i.e., they change their characteristics, especially with regard to the question "Stay or return?" Therefore, several periods have been distinguished to permit comparisons between the countries over the same periods, or during different periods within both Germany and Switzerland. Since the Federal Republic clamped down on the inflow of foreign workers at the end of 1973, and Switzerland effectively after 1970, the last columns in Tables 4.4 and 4.5, showing percentage figures about 100 under "withdrawal" and "outflow," indicate that more people withdrew or

Table 4.5   Number of Economically Active Foreigners Admitted to Employment in
Switzerland and Percentage Leaving the Country, 1949–1978 (in thousands)

			1949–1978	1949–1960	1961–1976	1961–1968	1969–1976
Grand total	Stock at begin.	number	175.0[a]	175.0[a]	337.0[a]	337.0[a]	586.1
	Inflow	number	2,529.4	968.6	1,509.7	1,082.4	427.3
	Naturalizations	number	58.3	3.1	40.9	8.9	32.0
	Deaths	number	43.4	6.1	31.6	12.8	18.8
	Withdrawal	%	86	83	88	77	116
	Outflow	%	84	82	83	75	105
	Stock at end	number	489.4	337.0[a]	516.0	586.1	516.0

[a] Estimate. Table excludes seasonal workers, frontier workers, and international officials. Withdrawal and outflow are calculated as in Table 4.4. Result as percentage of inflow. Estimation of naturalizations and deaths of active foreigners = rising share of overall number of "naturalisations ordinaires" and deaths published by the Office Federal de la Statistique. The share was assumed to be 2.5 percent in 1949 and increased by 2.5 percent per year, thus rising to 75 percent in 1978. Naturalizations prior to 1954 were not taken into account, however.

As there are no hard data on unregistered unemployed foreigners and because their numbers are generally held to be very low, the calculation of the outflow disregards this group.

Source: *Annuaire statistique de la Suisse* (various); author's own calculations.

returned than were admitted to employment. As the statistics and the calculations derive from administrative acts, an individual migrant might be counted several times; this does not affect the basic question or the interpretation of the empirical results.

The highlights from the two tables may be summarized as follows: more than two-thirds of the foreign workers admitted to the Federal Republic, and more than four-fifths to Switzerland, have returned. The future will probably witness a continuing small trickle of return migrants who still figure in the 1976 or 1978 stock data, thus tending to raise the proportion of temporariness. Whether or not this corresponds to the assumption of German policymakers quoted earlier (that the "overwhelming number of foreign employees will not stay permanently in the Federal Republic,") is not really possible to say. Yet it is defensible to say that neither German nor Swiss policymakers, among others, expected to admit so many foreign workers over such a long period of time. Therefore, one could conclude that twenty or thirty years ago none of the Western European countries opting for a guestworker policy foresaw as many foreign workers on its soil as there are today. I believe Western European policymakers have been proved wrong regarding the *volume* of guestworker employment rather than its *temporariness*.

Table 4.4 reveals impressive differences between nationalities, for example

Italians (9 in 10 of whom returned) compared with Turks (of whom only 3 in 10 returned). If one applies the results of the calculations for (a) Italians, (b) Spaniards, and (c) others to the Swiss data, i.e., if one weights the German rates of return by the proportion of Italian, Spanish, and other nationalities in Switzerland's foreign workforce for the period 1961–1976, one obtains almost exactly the overall Swiss rates shown in Table 4.5. This would seem to suggest two conclusions. First, a nationality's propensity to stay or return is not greatly influenced by where it is employed abroad nor by the degree of welcome or hostility in the country of employment. Second, host countries must choose the nationality of their foreign workers carefully, depending on whether it is desired that they settle or return. In the case of return there is the further task of efficiently handling the recruitment, selection, admission, etc., of what will undoubtedly be large numbers of people.[54]

MIGRANTS' INTENTIONS

Given the key role assigned to them by Western European policymakers, motivations and intentions can be used to predict whether an individual, a distinct group, or a nationality stays or returns. European policymakers actually based their views on assumptions; they did not commission enquiries until well after the movements had settled into a pattern. Had they done so earlier they would probably have been surprised by the gap between their assumptions and reality, or by the lack of certainty on the part of the migrants.

Five basic categories can be distinguished: (1) the seasonals who have their time horizon fixed by the legislation of the country of employment, (2) the emigrants who intend to stay abroad for good, (3) the target workers whose expatriation is linked to the accumulation of a certain sum of money for some purpose back home, (4) the nonseasonals who have a clearly limited expatriation of X numbers of years in mind, and (5) all others who do not have a well-defined time horizon.

Several intimate observers of Western European migration have pointed out the huge proportion of migrants who had no clear idea of the duration of their migration. For example, a quarter of the Greeks interviewed in 1960–1962 in Belgium, France, and Germany were undecided at the moment of emigration;[55] nearly half of those to whom a questionnaire was administered during a journey home over Christmas 1964 planned to stay abroad for an indefinite period.[56] Half the Italians surveyed by Braun in 1964 in German-speaking Switzerland had no idea when they left home how long they would stay in Switzerland; after many years of expatriation, more than a quarter still fell into this category.[57] It was estimated by Baučić that 55 percent of the Yugoslavs left without a concrete idea of the length of their out-migration, although it was believed that most people in this category hoped to return home when their country's development offered attractive wage-earning opportunities.[58] Such a high proportion of waverers seems remarkable for the one migrant-sending country in the Western European–Mediterranean context which has conceived all external labor movements as *temporary* employment abroad.[59]

Table 4.6 documents a range of intentions, changes therein, and actual length of stay.[60] It speaks for itself. The notion popularly bandied about in the 1950s and 1960s—that migrants from Mediterranean countries cross the Alps in order to work for one, two, or at most three years and then return—is visibly a myth, or an ideology. The German figures in Table 4.6 can be corroborated by a few survey data from Switzerland. Braun found that 29 percent had originally intended to stay up to five years and 7 percent longer or permanently, and 11 percent had materially determined targets; at the time of his 1964 interviews, 58 percent had been resident for up to five years and 17 percent for ten years or more; 20 percent envisaged a further five years in Switzerland and 27 percent intended to stay longer/permanently or to fulfill their material ambitions before returning.[61] Hoffmann-Nowotny interviewed economically active male Italians in 1969, 44 percent of whom had been resident for up to five years and 15 percent for more than eleven years; half tended toward leaving Switzerland, 41 percent toward staying, and about 10 percent were undecided.[62]

The target workers form the most intriguing but least understood group. There is no doubt that some migrants have specific and limited material or monetary goals, but I do not believe that they have played an important role in Western Europe. (Occupational or educational objectives or the evasion of national service obligations may be neglected here in order not to complicate the picture unnecessarily.) Target workers are certainly a minority. What is more, target workers are not easily identifiable. As Braun's 1964 data show (see Table 4.7), their personal, social, and economic characteristics do not differ greatly from those of other migrants. One may suspect that target workers are overrepresented among married men, possibly older ones, and perhaps among migrants from rural areas with an above-average education. In the Federal Republic a 1976 survey discovered a group that was economically highly motivated and paid little attention to improvements regarding quality of life in Germany. This definition comes close to the notion of target workers, and the group was indeed characterized by intentions to remain a comparatively short time. Thirty-six percent of the Yugoslavs, 34 percent of the Turks, 24 percent of the Greeks, 21 percent of the Italians, and 17 percent of the Spaniards formed part of it.[63] Still, neither the notion nor the quantity would seem to justify the policy assumptions which have been placed in them.

Data ranked visually can tell us whether the nationalities' propensity to return as recorded in Table 4.4 accords with the intentions reported by survey researchers. Table 4.8 contains the ranked data. Even when allowance is made for the fact that the 1976 predictors measure the intentions and proportions of those who have stayed rather than those who returned, there is little correlation between intentions and realities. I believe that the intentions of migrants were both more complex and more fickle than policymakers allowed for, which further complicates the difficulty of finding out exactly what people's intentions are. To build policy on *intentions* of migrants, whether revealed or unrevealed, is to build a house on sand. It is much easier simply to rely on how intentions crystallize into *secular patterns of behavior*.

Table 4.6 Originally Intended, Actual Duration, and Envisaged Future Duration of Stay of Economically Active Foreigners of Selected Nationalities in the Federal Republic of Germany (percentages recorded in surveys held between 1968 and 1976)

	Original intentions				Actual duration							
	Don't know or no response	Up to 5 years		10 years or more	Up to 5 years				8–10 years or more			
	Men 1968	Men 1968	1976	Men 1968	Men 1968	Men 1971	Women 1971	1976	Men 1968	Men 1971	Women 1971	1976
(Col.)	1	2	3	4	5	6	7	8	9a	10b	11b	12c
Italians	6	62	62	24	54	43	65	23	11	20	7	47
Spaniards	19	67	78	7	45	37	41	28	6	16	10	42
Greeks	5	79	74	3	45	42	54	9	6	14	5	57
Yugoslavs	n.a.	n.a.	66	n.a.	n.a.	82	83	28	n.a.	4	2	20
Turks	7	83	69	4	84	69	85	31	1	3	0	27

Envisaged future length of stay

(Col.)	Short Men 1968 (13[d])	Short 1976 (14[e])	Medium 1976 (15[f])	Long Men 1968 (16[g])	Long 1976 (17[h])	No idea or no response Men 1968 (18)	Shorter than originally foreseen Men 1971 (19)	Shorter than originally foreseen Women 1971 (20)	As long as originally foreseen Men 1971 (21)	As long as originally foreseen Women 1971 (22)	Longer than originally foreseen Men 1971 (23)	Longer than originally foreseen Women 1971 (24)	No idea Men 1971 (25)	No idea Women 1971 (26)
Italians	45	52	25	17	23	38	13	14	7	9	41	30	39	47
Spaniards	51	58	18	10	24	39	5	4	13	19	62	54	20	23
Greeks	70	62	29	8	9	22	6	11	12	11	38	37	44	41
Yugoslavs	n.a.	46	33	n.a.	21	n.a.	6	6	6	7	25	31	63	56
Turks	77	44	36	9	9	14	6	0	26	28	32	30	36	42

n.a. = not available; a = 8 years and longer; b = 10 years and longer; c = 9 years and longer; d = up to 5 years; e = up to 4 years; f = 5–16 years; g = 5 years and longer or permanently; and h = 17 years and longer.

Source: Columns 1, 2, 4, 5, 9, 13, 16, and 18, see R. Hentschel et al., *Die Integration der ausländischen Arbeitnehmer in Köln*, Tabellenband, mimeographed (Cologne, 1968), Tables 1, 7a, and 52. Columns 3, 8, 12, 14, 15, and 17, see Forschungsverbund, *Integrierter Endbericht*, pp. 231 ff. Columns 6, 7, 10, 11, and 19–26, see U. Mehrländer, *Soziale Aspekte der Ausländerbeschäftigung* (Bonn–Bad Godesberg: Neue Gesellschaft, 1974), pp. 24f and 122.

Table 4.7 Envisaged Future Duration of Stay of Italians in Switzerland, by Category (percentage recorded in 1964 survey)

Intentions regarding future	Sex		Age			Marital status		Origin		Education		
	Men	Women	Under 25	26–35	Over 35	Single	Married	Rural[a]	Urban[b]	Below average	Average	Above average
Stay 5 years or longer	9	6	12	6	6	9	7	9	7	6	9	6
Stay permanently	18	20	5	20	31	18	19	13	24	30	16	20
Target workers	34	19	29	24	32	23	30	31	24	15	27	33

	Reason for emigrating				Occupational status			Years of residence in Switzerland				
	Poverty and need	Higher earnings	Reunifi-cation	Other	Unskilled	Skilled	Foreman	Less than 2	2–4	4–6	6–10	10 and longer
Stay 5 years or longer	6	9	7	10	8	7	0	19	5	8	7	6
Stay permanently	20	21	18	15	15	31	27	9	10	10	30	42
Target workers	25	30	21	33	27	29	27	26	25	42	24	26

[a]Proxy. Source records geographical origin southern Italy.
[b]Proxy. Source records geographical origin northern Italy.

Source: Braun, *Sozialkulturelle Probleme*, p. 489.

Table 4.8 Predicting the Propensity to Return with Migrants' Intentions, Federal Republic of Germany (ranked data)

Ranking	Propensity to return 1961–76 1 = highest (Col.) 1	Proportion with originally short-term intentions 1976 1 = highest 2	Proportions with future intentions		Proportion of target workers 1976 1 = highest 5
			short 1976 1 = highest 3	long 1976 1 = lowest 4	
Italians	1	5	3	5	4
Spaniards	2	1	2	4	5
Greeks	3	2	1	1	3
Yugoslavs	4	4	4	3	1
Turks	5	3	5	2	2

Source: Column 1, see Table 4.4. Column 2, see Table 4.6, column 3. Column 3, see Table 4.6, column 14. Column 4, see Table 4.6, column 17. Column 5, see text; Forschungsverbund, *Integrierter Endbericht*, pp. 237–38.

FAMILY MIGRATION OR REUNIFICATION

If breadwinners emigrate with their dependents or if the dependents join them later, such migration could herald immigration or settlement in the traditional sense of the word. Family migration or reunification was viewed in the 1950s and 1960s with equanimity in France, but with considerable unease in the Federal Republic of Germany and Switzerland. Demographic, economic, social, and ethnic reasons played a role, sometimes reinforcing each other in one country at one point of time, and sometimes contradicting each other. Today, Western Europe's nonseasonal guestworkers who have a job and accommodations can, as a rule, count on having members of the nuclear (as opposed to extended) family join them once they have worked for twelve months in the country of employment, provided their dependents are free of certain diseases that constitute a danger to public health.[64] Austria, Belgium, Sweden, and the UK are more liberal; they do not subject family members to any period of qualification. France introduced a one-year waiting period in 1976, but Greeks, Spaniards, and Portuguese in nonseasonal employment in France are treated leniently in accordance with the provisions of earlier bilateral agreements.

Popular beliefs notwithstanding, the proportions of economically inactive individuals in the migrant population tend to be similar in the Federal Republic (see Table 4.9), France (see Table 4.10), and Switzerland (see Table 4.11); and the same holds true for particular migrant nationalities in each of the three countries. Marked differences disappear in the course of time. Remaining differences can be explained by the relative lack of fresh labor immigration in

Table 4.9   Number of Foreigners in the Federal Republic of Germany and Percentage of
Economically Inactive, by Selected Nationalities, 1961–1976 (in thousands)

		June 6 1961	Sept. 30 1968	Sept. 30 1973	Sept. 30 1976
Greeks	% inactive	10	32	39	51
	total number	42.1	211.8	407.6	353.7
Italians	% inactive	17	33	29	51
	total number	196.7	454.2	630.7	568.0
Spaniards	% inactive	22	34	34	51
	total number	44.2	175.0	287.0	219.4
Turks	% inactive	34	26	34	59
	total number	6.7	205.4	910.5	1,079.3
Yugoslavs	% inactive	26	30	24	39
	total number	16.4	169.1	701.6	640.4
Subtotal	% inactive	12	31	31	49
	total number	306.1	1,215.5	2,937.4	2,860.8
Other	% inactive	49	64	45	58
	total number	380.1	708.7	1,028.9	1,087.5
Total	% inactive	33	43	35	51
	total number	686.2	1,942.2	3,966.2	3,948.3

Source: 1961 = Census. Other "total" figures from Statistisches Bundesamt. Figures of
economically active (not represented here) from Bundesanstalt für Arbeit. The statistics of
active published by the Statistisches Bundesamt, based on residence permits, and those of
the Bundesanstalt für Arbeit, based on work permits, often differ slightly; this impediment
to strict comparability does not affect the order of magnitude.

France and the greater maturity of some migration streams, i.e., the longer
periods of family reunification. For instance, the Yugoslavs in Switzerland are
newcomers compared with the Italians in that country, or compared with the
Yugoslavs in France. The migrants' decisions about family members' accompanying or joining them may be influenced by the perceived degree of public or
private hostility toward them, but this influence bends rather than breaks
human bonds.

A different set of data underlines the historical evolution. Shortly after the
immigration had gathered momentum in the Federal Republic of Germany,
Hollenberg estimated that 7½–9 percent of the foreign workers resided with
their families there.[65] Twelve years later the situation had changed dramati-

Table 4.10 Number of Resident Foreigners in France and Percentage of Economically Inactive, by Selected Nationalities, 1962-1976 (in thousands)

		March 1962	March 1968	Feb. 1975	Oct. 1976
Algerians	% inactive	42	44	53	54
	total number	350.5	471.0	710.7	792.0
Italians	% inactive	52	57	57	62
	total number	629.0	585.9	462.9	465.9
Moroccans	% inactive	42	33	41	40
	total number	33.3	88.3	260.0	299.9
Portuguese	% inactive	40	43	52	53
	total number	50.0	303.2	758.9	823.0
Spaniards	% inactive	52	55	59	64
	total number	441.7	618.2	497.5	507.3
Tunisians	% inactive	57	50	48	50
	total number	26.6	60.2	139.7	147.1
Turks	% inactive	n.a.	51	39	37
	total number	15.7	7.6	50.9	57.9
Yugoslavs	% inactive	n.a.	33	40	42
	total number	21.3	48.2	70.3	74.0
Subtotal	% inactive	48	50	53	55
	total number	1,568.0	2,182.6	2,950.9	3,167.1
Other	% inactive	60	58	61	62
	total number	601.7	481.5	491.5	532.9
Total	% inactive	51	51	54	56
	total number	2,169.7	2,664.1	3,442.4	3,700.0

n.a. = not available.

Source: 1962, 1968, and 1975 = Census (the 1962 Census counted all Algerians, including members of the French army). 1976 = Groupe de travail interministériel sur les statistiques de population étrangère, *Mesure de la présence étrangère en France* (Paris, May 1979).

Table 4.11 Number of Resident Foreigners in Switzerland and Percentage of Economically Inactive, by Selected Nationalities, 1968–1978 (in thousands)

		1968	1973	1978
Italians	% inactive	n.a.	n.a.	(46)
	total number	522.6	551.8	442.7
Spaniards	% inactive	n.a.	n.a.	(36)
	total number	87.7	119.1	96.1
Yugoslavs	% inactive	n.a.	n.a.	(29)
	total number	16.1	31.6	37.7
Total	% inactive	38	43	46
	total number	933.1	1,052.5	898.1

n.a. = not available. Figures exclude seasonal workers, frontier workers, and international officials and their families.

The figures of the total population and all grand total figures relate to the end of 1968, 1973, and 1978. The figures for inactive Italians, Spaniards, and Yugoslavs were approximated by deducting the stock of active in April 1979 from the end-of-1978 population figures (statistics by nationality are not published for earlier years).

Source: Annuaire statistique de la Suisse (various); *La Vie Economique* 52, no. 6 (June 1979).

Table 4.12 Indicators of Family Migration and Reunification in the Federal Republic of Germany, by Selected Nationalities in 1976 (percentages)

	Single, divorced, and widowed	Married		Families in Germany with			Families that have children: proportion with one or all children in home country
		without spouse in Germany	with spouse in Germany	no children	one or two children	three or more children	
Italians	25	6	69	12	37	18	25
Spaniards	22	10	68	19	n.a.	11	31
Greeks	17	3	80	16	52	12	26
Yugoslavs	18	23	60	24	29	6	51
Turks	9	19	72	15	35	21	53

n.a. = not available.

Source: Forschungsverbund, *Integrierter Endbericht*, pp. 56 ff.

Table 4.13 Predicting the Propensity to Return by Degree of Completed Family Reunification, Federal Republic of Germany (ranked data)

	Propensity to return	Proportion of inactive in migrant population		Complete families	
				proportion among married	proportion among all migrants
	1961–1976	1968	1976	1976	
	1 = highest	1 = lowest		1 = lowest	
Ranking	1	2	3	4	5
Italians	1	4	2	4	4
Spaniards	2	5	4	3	3
Greeks	3	3	3	5	5
Yugoslavs	4	2	1	2	1
Turks	5	1	5	1	2

Source: Column 1, see Table 4.4. Columns 2 and 3, see Table 4.9. Columns 4 and 5, see Forschungsverbund, *Integrierter Endbericht*, pp. 56 ff.

cally, as Table 4.12 demonstrates. Of the married migrants, about three-quarters of the Italian and Greek nuclear families were united, about seven-tenths of the Spaniards, and just under half of the Yugoslavs and Turks.

Rank orders should indicate whether different degrees of completed family reunification predict a nationality's tendency to stay. The answer is clearly no (see Table 4.13), and the explanation must be sought largely in the complex web of economic, social, and human factors that make people move. It is quite possible, for example, that a target worker may ask his spouse to join him to help earn the desired nest egg, rather than to settle abroad. If a group has a strong attachment to family life, hostile attitudes and policies on the part of the country of employment (other than an inhuman policy that totally prohibits families coming together) will only delay, rather than stop, family reunification.

OTHER EXPLANATIONS?

Can other factors be identified that would help to explain why a nationality returns? Continuing with visual rank correlations, Table 4.14 examines personal and socio-economic determinants; Table 4.15 screens economic determinants relating to the countries of origin; and Table 4.16 takes earnings or incomes obtained in the country of employment and refracts them under different behavioral assumptions, i.e., it assumes first that all migrants behave as people are ordinarily said to behave, and it then assumes that all migrants behave as though they were target workers.

Table 4.14 Predicting the Propensity to Return by Personal or Socio-economic Factors, Federal Republic of Germany (ranked data)

Ranking	Propensity to return 1961–1976	Personal factors					Socio-economic factors				
		Relative proportion of longer-term stayers[a]		Proportion of single, divorced and widowed		Youthfulness = percent under 25 years	Proportion of rural origin	Proportion of skilled prior to emigration		Proportion of skilled in German employment	
	1 = highest	1 = lowest		1 = highest		1 = highest	1 = highest	1 = lowest		1 = lowest	
	1961–1976	1968	1976	1968	1976	1971	1971	1971	1976	1968	1976
(Col.)	1	2	3	4	5	6	7	8	9	10	11
Italians	1	5	4	2	1	1	3	1	2	2	1
Spaniards	2	4	2	3	2	5	1	4	4	3	3
Greeks	3	3	5	4	4	4	2	2	1	1	4
Yugoslavs	4	1	3	1	3	2	4	5	5	5	5
Turks	5	2	1	5	5	3	5	3	3	4	2

[a] 1968 = proportion in excess of four years of stay; 1976 = proportion in excess of five years of stay. Data refer to economically active persons. 1968 data refer to the autumn of that year; 1971 and 1976, to the summer.

Source: Column 1, see Table 4.4. Columns 2, 4, and 10, see Bundesanstalt für Arbeit, *Ausländische Arbeitnehmer*, pp. 45, 49, 53–54, and 86; and author's own computations. Columns 3, 5, 11, and 13, see Forschungsverbund, *Integrierter Endbericht*, pp. 56–58, 94, 117, and 231. Columns 6, 7, and 8, see Mehrländer, *Soziale Aspekte*, pp. 24, 28, and 36.

Table 4.15 Predicting the Propensity to Return by Economic Factors, Federal Republic of Germany (ranked data)

			Per capita income in countries of origin		Economic factors			
	Propensity to return 1961-1976	Distance between capitals (cost)			Average annual growth of per capita income in countries of origin		Average annual growth of the labor force in countries of origin	
			1960	1976	1960-1976	1970-1976	1960-1970	1970-1977
Ranking	1 = highest	1 = shortest	1 = highest		1 = highest		1 = highest	
(Col.)	1	2	3	4	5	6	7	8
Italians	1	1	1	1	5	5	5	4
Spaniards	2	3	3	2	3	3	3	3
Greeks	3	4	2	3	1	4	4	5
Yugoslavs	4	2	4	4	2	1	2	2
Turks	5	5	5	5	4	2	1	1

Source: Column 1, see Table 4.4. Columns 3–6, see World Bank Atlas (various). Columns 7–8, see World Bank, *World Development Report*, 1979 (Washington: August 1979), Table 19.

Table 4.16 Predicting the Propensity to Return with Different Behavioral Assumptions Relating to Earnings/Income Factors, Federal Republic of Germany (ranked data)

	Propensity to return 1961–76	Earnings/income factors									
		ordinarily: high earnings = low return					target workers: high earnings = high return				
		Proportion with earnings higher than expected		Proportion with earnings lower than expected		Average net income	Proportion with earnings higher than expected		Proportion with earnings lower than expected		Average net income
		Men 1971	Women 1971	Men 1971	Women 1971	1976	Men 1971	Women 1971	Men 1971	Women 1971	1976
Ranking	1 = highest	1 = lowest		1 = highest		1 = lowest	1 = highest		1 = lowest		1 = highest
(Col.)	1	2	3	4	5	6	7	8	9	10	11
Italians	1	4	(4)	3	(3)	1	2	(2)	3	(3)	5
Spaniards	2	5	(5)	5	5	5	1	(1)	1	1	1
Greeks	3	3	3	4	1	3	3	3	2	5	3
Yugoslavs	4	1	2	1	(4)	2	5	4	5	(2)	4
Turks	5	2	1	2	2	4	4	5	4	4	2

Data refer to economically active persons. The bracketed ranks in columns 3, 5, 8, and 10 are identical scores that have been arranged to make the ranks of men and women as equal as possible.

Source: Column 1, see Table 4.4. Columns 2–5 and 7–10, see Mehrländer, *Soziale Aspekte*, pp. 113–4. Columns 6 and 11, see Forschungsverbund, *Integrierter Endbericht*, p. 130.

Other than the recent level of GNP per capita (Table 4.15, column 4), no single variable predicts the various nationalities' differential propensity to return. Moreover, what one determinant indicates at one point of time, or for one sex, may be quite different from what it indicates at another time, or for the other sex. Furthermore, there is not as much coherence between factors as is assumed when one of them is taken as a proxy for another. For instance, youthfulness and proportions of single workers do not go well together; proportions of rural origin do not predict skill levels, either before departure from home or at the place of work abroad; per capita income levels do not correlate with either the growth rates of income or the growth rates of employment, nor do the growth rates of income and employment correlate among themselves.[66] The policy variables that are generally mentioned in this context, namely marital status, rural origin, or skills, are too unsatisfactory to inspire confidence as criteria to maximize the numbers returning.

GNP per capita at recent levels does appear to explain the various nationalities' rate of return. It is indeed plausible that the lower income of, say, Turkey should be less attractive than the higher income of Italy. Yet I have certain misgivings about the explanatory power of this factor, quite apart from the fact that, in the case of the United States, it does not really represent a policy variable, since the candidates for migration mainly come from middle-income Mexico, rather than from low-income Malawi, India, or other countries. The GNP explanation could well be spurious. First, in principle the underlying income concept should also show up well—but does not—in its other forms, such as the socio-economic variables that are at least in some way associated with incomes (rural origin, skills prior to migration, skilled employment abroad, in Table 4.14, columns 7–11) or the income differentials in the country of employment (Table 4.16). Second, the influence of income should be confirmed—but is not—in the correlations with the rates of growth of income in the countries of origin (Table 4.15, columns 5 and 6), for one must expect any single nationality to be decisively influenced by the progress achieved in its own country, rather than by a learned comparison of different countries' well-being. Why should almost every Italian return to his home country's stagnating economy, whereas Turks show a remarkable tendency not to go back to a relatively flourishing economy?[67] The level of GNP per capita may be one facet of the explanation, but there must be other factors at work.

Single ranks do not, of course, capture composite factors that might explain return. For instance, young, unskilled target workers of rural origin may be expected to exhibit a lower propensity to settle than older, skilled, ordinary workers of urban origin. This brings us back to the realm of speculation that ruled Western Europe for many years. And the policy relevance of cumulative variables is limited because multiple selection criteria are difficult to administer. As far as the crucial target worker dimension is concerned, it is probably impossible to have bureaucrats—or even sociologists or economists—determine reliably who is or is not a target worker. In any case, target workers can change their minds, and often do.

I have the firm impression that nationality, as such, is a better indicator than any other factor whether migrant workers tend to stay or return.[68] This finding tallies with other attempts to explain migrants' behavior. Large-scale survey research in the Federal Republic of Germany came to the following conclusion:

> It is almost completely immaterial to the future duration of stay envisaged by foreign workers whether their occupational status is high (skilled worker and above) or low (unskilled worker), whether the conditions at the place of work are good or bad, whether the general social climate at the place of work is perceived as positive or negative, whether social mobility is desired or not, or whether the people concerned have resided in the Federal Republic for a short or long while. Even if all these factors are jointly accounted for, they explain barely 6 percent of the variation in the planned duration of stay. Moreover, the larger part of this marginal power of explanation derives from the more subjective valuation and judgment of the social climate at the place of work and the desire to climb up the social ladder, rather than the objective factors such as occupational status or work-place conditions.[69]

It is clear that some nationalities have on average a low, others a high, propensity to return. A historical pattern or secular tendency has evolved. Neither incentives nor constraints seem to have a marked influence. Raw political force might, but Western democracies are neither domestically nor internationally free to proceed with brute force.

If guestworkers' propensity to return voluntarily cannot be predicted with accuracy on the basis of selection criteria other than nationality, what can this fact teach the United States? The key lesson is that one should accept high or low temporariness rather than try to manipulate it. A further lesson is that one should not create expectations regarding the return of guests that are not substantiated by hard facts. If one were to announce to the public that Mexicans, for instance, tend to return rather than to stay, one should be sure about the facts first—and in my view the facts are highly debatable in the case of Mexicans. If expectations turn out to have been unrealistic, the policy will be in ruins.

IV. In Lieu of Conclusions

Should the United States institute a massive temporary worker program instead of a guestworker or an enlarged traditional immigration program? I believe that temporary worker programs for nontemporary jobs are incompatible with the fundamental tenets of Western democracy, the charter of the United Nations, the constitution of the International Labour Organization and, most of all, the Universal Declaration of Human Rights.[70] It is perfectly legitimate to argue that foreigners do not have a right to enter a country. Yet those who are voluntarily admitted—except perhaps foreigners destined to work in truly temporary activities[71]—should be entitled to what the Universal Declaration of Human Rights calls free choice of employment (article 23[1]) and to security in the event of unemployment, sickness, disability, widowhood, old age, or other lack of livelihood (article 25[1]) as well as to the protection of their family (article 16[3]). Western Europe's guestworker policies, by and large, respect the social rights of article 25 (1) of the Universal Declaration of Human Rights; they freely admit and thereby protect families in some, albeit not yet all, cases; but they still subject the free choice of employment to a qualifying period (outside the EEC and the Common Nordic Labour Market). The trend of policies has been toward closer conformity with the principles of Western democracy, and the recent French attempt to reverse it has met with powerful domestic and international resistance.

Temporary worker programs and restrictions are not only morally offensive but politically less and less tenable in Western plural societies. Much domestic political and administrative commotion and loss of international political capital can be avoided by adopting an initial position in conformity with democratic values, rather than having to yield in inauspicious circumstances to domestic and international pressures.

Notes

1. As opposed to an expanded H-2 program on the lines proposed by E. P. Reubens, *Temporary Admission of Foreign Workers: Dimensions and Policies*, National Commission for Manpower Policy Special Report No. 34 (Washington, D.C.: U.S. Government Printing Office, March 1979).

2. W. R. Böhning, "The Differential Strength of Demand and Wage Factors in Intra-European Labour Mobility: With Special Reference to West Germany, 1957–1968," *International Migration* 8, no. 4 (1970): 193–202.

3. See R. Marshall, "Employment Implications of the International Migration of Workers," in *Illegal Aliens: An Assessment of the Issues*, edited by the National Council on Employment Policy (Washington, D.C.: National Council on Employment Policy, October 1976), pp. 23 and 63; and P. L. Martin, *Guestworker Programs: Lessons from Europe*, prepared for the Joint Economic Committee, U.S. Congress (Washington, D.C.: The Brookings Institution, June 1979), p. 61ff.

4. The law and practice of (im)migration in the world at large has recently been documented in ILO, *Migrant Workers: Summary of Reports on Conventions nos. 97 and 143 and Recommendations nos. 86 and 151*, International Labour Conference, 66th Session, Report 3 (Part 2) (Geneva: International Labour Organization, 1980); and ILO, *Migrant Workers: General Survey by the Committee of Experts on the Application of Conventions and Recommendations*, International Labour Conference 66th Session (Geneva: International Labour Organization, 1980).

5. Whose original six members were Belgium, the Federal Republic of Germany, France, Italy, Luxembourg, and the Netherlands. Denmark, Ireland, and the UK joined in the early 1970s. Greece entered in January 1981. Spain and Portugal hope to do so before the mid-1980s, and Turkey occasionally presses hard for membership. See also W. R. Böhning, *The Migration of Workers in the United Kingdom and the European Community* (London: Oxford University Press, 1972).

6. Established 1954 by agreement among Denmark, Finland, Norway, and Sweden. See also J. Lönnroth, "The Common Nordic Labour Market: Background and Developments," in *Finnish Contributions to the IUSSP Conference on Economic and Demographic Change: Issues for the 1980s*, edited by the Demographic Society of Finland (Helsinki, 1978), pp. 63–77.

7. One exception for minor migrant-sending countries was the 1970 agreement concerning the admission of miners from the Republic of Korea for temporary employment in colleries. At present, it involves some 600 workers.

One historical oddity is also worth mentioning. The original recruitment agreement with Turkey of October 1961 had features of a temporary worker program. Initial work permits could be extended, but the text stated categorically that "the residence permit will not be extended beyond a total duration of validity of two years" (*Amtliche Nachrichten* der Bundesanstalt für Arbeit, vol. 9, no. 12 [December 1961], p. 589). An exchange of notes in 1964 deleted this clause, however (text ibid., vol. 13, no. 1 [January 1965], pp. 1–2). Germany's only major limited-time program was therefore abandoned before it had really started.

8. Cf. R. C. Rist, *Guestworkers in Germany: The Prospects for Pluralism* (New York: Praeger, 1978).

9. Bundesminister für Arbeit und Sozialordnung, *Politik der Bundesregierung gegenü-ber den ausländischen Arbeitnehmern in der Bundesrepublik Deutschland*, Deutscher Bundestag, 6. Wahlperiode, Drucksache VI/3085, 31. January 1972 (Bonn), p. 4.

10. Bundesminister für Arbeit und Sozialordnung, "Bundesregierung beschliesst Integrationsprogramm für junge Ausländer," *Sozialpolitische Informationen* 16, no. 6 (March 1980).

11. See note 9.

12. G. Tapinos, *L'immigration étrangère en France 1946–1973* (Presses universitaires de France, 1975).

13. The annual average number of foreign workers admitted to seasonal employment in France has been: 1955–1959—53,800; 1960–1964—104,800; 1965–1969—124,600; 1970–1974—138,000; 1975–1979—120,000. *Revue des Affaires Sociales*, vol. 32 (April–June 1978); Ministère du Travail, *Elements statistiques sur l'immigration en France en 1979* (Paris, May 1980).

14. See *Le Monde*, June 15, 1979.

15. *Les Echos*, March 29, 1966, which roughly translates as: "Clandestine immigration itself is not without its uses, because if we were to insist on the strict application of international regulations and agreements we might perhaps be short of labor."

16. D. S. North, "Foreign Workers: Unwanted Guests?" *Transatlantic Perspectives* 1 (June 1979): 19–23.

17. D. S. North, "The Canadian Experience with Amnesty for Aliens: What the United States Can Learn," mimeographed, restricted World Employment Programme Research Working Paper (Geneva: ILO, October 1979).

18. The Swiss rate of registered unemployment briefly touched the 1-percent level during the depth of the mid-seventies recession. It had fallen back to 0.5 percent by the end of the decade.

19. The number of seasonal work permit holders given annual permits has been: 1968—3,500; 1969—7,700; 1970—6,000; 1971—8,300; 1972—11,900; 1973—11,600; 1974—9,600; 1975—7,900; 1976—9,200; 1977—5,800; 1978—4,100; 1979—3,700. Letter of Eidgenössische Konsultativkommission für das Ausländerproblem, dated November 20, 1979; and *La Vie Economique* 53, no. 3 (March 1980).

20. A similarly high rate is found among frontier workers.

21. Only Austria has clear legal reserve powers to enforce departure on economic grounds. Residence permits may not be renewed or canceled when a foreigner is not engaged in regular employment or is not entitled to unemployment insurance benefits, and when he consequently appears to be without means of support. If in this event the foreigner does not leave Austria voluntarily, or does not comply with an order for his departure, he may be forbidden to stay in the country and be expelled to his country of origin.

In Switzerland, the 1931 Federal Act respecting the residence and settlement of aliens provides that an alien may be deported if he or a person for whose maintenance he is liable becomes permanently and, to a substantial degree, dependent on public relief. The act makes deportation subject to the condition that the return of the alien to his country of origin is practicable and may reasonably be demanded of him. The Aliens Bill now before Parliament further limits the scope for deportation.

The Swiss government has tried on three occasions to rid the country of whole groups of foreign workers who did not possess resident status. In 1952 work permits were revoked in the textile industry and in 1958 in the watch-making industry; and in 1975 firms were instructed not to make redundant nationals or resident foreigners as long as they employed foreign annual permit holders in comparable jobs. No follow-up research has come to my knowledge.

22. *La Vie Economique* 53, no. 3 (March 1980), Table 3.

23. W. R. Böhning, "Regularising Indocumentados," mimeographed, restricted World Employment Programme Research Working Paper (Geneva: ILO, April 1979); and "Elements of a Theory of International Migration to Industrial Nation States," in *Global Trends in Migration: Theory and Research on International Population Movements*, edited by M. M. Kritz, C. B. Keely and S. Tomasi (New York: Center for Migration Studies, 1980), pp. 28–43; also Böhning, "The Differential Strength of Demand and Wage Factors."

24. See note 3.

25. See, for instance, S. Castles and G. Kosack, *Immigrant Workers and Class Structure in Western Europe* (London: Oxford University Press, 1973); C. Mercier, *Les Déracinés du capital: Immigration et accumulation* (Presses universitaires de Lyon; [1977]); and M. Nikolinakos, *Politische Okonomie der Gastarbeiterfrage* (Reinbeck: Rowohlt, 1973).

26. See S. Adler, "Co-operation or Coercion? Algerian Migrant Workers in the German Democratic Republic," *Studi Emigrazione/Etudes Migrations* 15, no. 50 (1978): 246–61.

27. V. Lutz, "Foreign Workers and Domestic Wage Levels: With an Illustration from the Swiss Case," *Banca Nazionale del Lavoro Quarterly Review* 16, no. 4 (March 1963): 3–68.

28. Ibid., p. 7.

29. My own view of the origin and development of wage differentials (W. R. Böhning, "Determinants of Labour Immigration in Industrialised Countries of Western Europe," in "Basic Aspects of Immigration and Return Migration in Western Europe," mimeographed, restricted World Employment Programme Research Working Paper [Geneva: ILO, July 1975], pp. 5–23) resembles Piore's (M. J. Piore, *Birds of Passage: Migrant Labour in Industrial Society* [Cambridge University Press, 1979]) in that it places emphasis on the social determination, function, and perception of income differences. There is much casual evidence that, e.g., Frenchmen or Germans who are not marginal labor market participants are little influenced by attempts to make low-status jobs more attractive in terms of pay and/or working conditions. If a town cannot get, say, local garbage collectors, it is usually not on account of low pay. Evidence on the failure of the ambitious French policy of giving manual workers a better image and pay is beginning to appear. See Y. Moulier, "Le Secteur de l'industrie automobile," in "Possibilités de transfert d'emploi vers les pays d'émigration en tant qu'alternative aux migrations internationales des travailleurs: Le cas français," II, edited by G. Tapinos et al.: Etudes Sectorielles, (Geneva: ILO, April 1978; and R. E. Verhaeren, *Revalorisation du travail manuel dans le B.T.P. et la substitution immigrés-nationaux* (Grenoble: Université II, Institut de Recherche Economique et de Planification, 1978).

30. A. Portes, "Towards a Structural Analysis of Illegal (undocumented) Migration," *International Migration Review* 12, no. 4 (Winter 1978): 469–84.

31. Ibid., pp. 472–3.

32. D. S. North and M. F. Houstoun, *The Characteristics and Role of Illegal Aliens in the U.S. Labor Market: An Exploratory Study* (Washington: Linton & Co. Inc., March 1976); and M. J. Piore, *The Role of Immigration in Industrial Growth: A Case Study of the Origins and Character of Puerto Rican Migration to Boston*, mimeographed MIT Department of Economics Working Paper (Cambridge, Mass., May 1973).

33. A. H. Richmond and R. P. Verma, "The Economic Adaptation of Immigrants: A New Theoretical Perspective," *International Migration Review* 12, no. 1 (Spring 1978): 3–38.

34. Piore, *Birds of Passage* and *The Role of Immigration*.

35. As far as return migration is concerned, the lack of correlation with economic factors points, *a contrario*, to the importance of personal and family factors, which has been revealed time and again by survey research.

36. Whereby he attributes to me a supposed key characteristic of jobs, namely the personalized as opposed to institutionalized relationship between supervisor and mi-

grant subordinates (Piore, *Birds of Passage*, p. 17, fn. 6), by referring to a publication (Böhning, "Determinants of Labour Immigration") which makes no mention of it and apparently without knowing that I have explicitly rejected this feature for Western Europe on analytical and empirical grounds. (W. R. Böhning, "Elements of a Theory of International Migration and Compensation," mimeographed, restricted World Employment Programme Research Working Paper; [Geneva: ILO, November 1978], p. 7, fn. 1).

37. See, for instance, W. R. Böhning, "Migration from Developing to High-Income Countries," in ILO, *Tripartite World Conference on Employment, Income Distribution and Social Progress and the International Division of Labour, Background Papers, Vol. II: International Strategies for Employment* (Geneva: 1976), Table 3; and Forschungsverbund "Probleme der Ausländerbeschäftigung," *Integrierter Endbericht* (n.p. [Bonn], Bundesminister für Forschung und Technologie, July 1979).

38. Piore, *Birds of Passage*, p. 45.

39. Ibid., pp. 35–43.

40. G. Minet, "Spectators or Participants? Immigrants and Industrial Relations in Western Europe," *International Labour Review* 117, no. 1 (January–February 1978): 21–35.

41. See Böhning, "Elements of a Theory of International Migration."

42. The stock of vacancies remaining on the books and the change therein (columns 1 and 2 of Table 4.3) are, for Germany, the most appropriate indicators. They reflect better than the flow nature of registrations (column 3) the labor market test required by law, i.e., the search for national workers before foreigners are admitted. The lower power of explanation of the unemployment/work-seeker variables is probably a result of nonregistration of women, youngsters, etc. Tests indicated a steady (inverse) relationship between vacancies and unemployment in the course of the period of 1961–1976.

43. It is interesting to note that the coefficients of determination for 1961–1976 are practically identical with the ones I had earlier calculated for 1957–1968 with minutely different data and after double log transformation; see Böhning, "The Differential Strength."

44. Unfortunately, the statistics of demand for labor cannot be decomposed to investigate which proportion of the overall demand results from physical as opposed to relative shortages of nationals. The given regressions cannot, therefore, tell us anything about the origin of the demand for foreign labor. Nor is my analytical framework designed to do that. In the real world, one must expect physical and relative shortages to appear together.

45. Wage differentials, which do influence movements between developed countries, are totally eclipsed by the demand factors in migration from developing to developed countries; see Böhning, "The Differential Strength of Demand and Wage Factors." H.-M. Geck, *Die griechische Arbeitsmigration: Eine Analyse ihrer Ursachen und Wirkungen* (Königstein/Ts.: Hanstein, 1979), regressed the importance of Greek wages and employment as "push" factors compared with German wages and employment as "pull" factors. He was forced to the conclusion that, whereas wage differentials may have been a necessary condition, Germany's demand for labor was the sole determinant of Greek movement to the Federal Republic. W. Künne, *Die Aussenwanderung jugoslawischer Arbeitskräfte: Ein Beitrag zur Analyse internationaler Arbeitskräftewanderungen* (Königstein/Ts.: Hanstein, 1979) undertook a comparable analysis for Yugoslav migration to Germany and came to similar results. F. Butschek, "Die Verwendung formalisierter Modelle in der Osterreichischen Arbeitsmarktforschung," in *Die ökonomischen Aspekte der Arbeitsmarktpolitik,* edited by F. Butscheck (Vienna: Bohrmann, 1975), demonstrated that demand was crucial in the Austrian context.

46. For details of the economic and social aspects of the self-feeding process, see W. R. Böhning, "The Economic Effects of the Employment of Foreign Workers: With Special Reference to the Labour Markets of Western Europe's Post-Industrial Countries," in OECD, *The Effects of the Employment of Foreign Workers* (Paris: OECD, 1974), pp. 43–123.

47. As happened, for example, in the Federal Republic of Germany both in the 1967

recession and after the 1973 rise in oil prices. U.S. employers voiced demands for Mexican labor even during the Great Depression; see G. C. Kiser and M. W. Kiser, *Mexican Workers in the United States: Historical and Political Perspectives* (Albuquerque: University of New Mexico Press, 1979), pp. 50–51.

48. P. Frisbie, "Illegal Migration from Mexico to the United States: A Longitudinal Analysis," *International Migration Review* 9, no. 1 (Spring 1975): 3–13.

49. J. C. Jenkins, "Push/Pull in Recent Mexican Migration to the U.S.," *International Migration Review* 2, no. 2 (Summer 1977): 178–89; Jenkins, "The Demand for Immigrant Workers: Labor Scarcity or Social Control?" *International Migration Review* 12, no. 4 (Winter 1978): 514–35.

50. See, e.g., Kiser and Kiser, *Mexican Workers;* and E. R. Stoddard, "A Conceptual Analysis of the 'Alien Invasion': Institutional Support of Illegal Mexican Aliens in the U.S.," *International Migration Review* 12, no. 4 (Winter 1978): 469–84.

51. Television interview conducted by William F. Buckley, Jr.; script in *Population and Development Review* 5, no. 2 (June 1979): 358–71.

52. Lourdes Arizpe argues in Chapter 6, this volume, that conditions in Mexico largely determine which sorts of people come (sex, age, etc.), while conditions in the United States largely determine how many come.

53. It appears, for instance, that more Italians but fewer Turks are naturalized in Germany than estimated by the procedure used in Table 4.4.

54. Assuming the Federal Republic had opted for Italians only, and given the 90 percent rate of return indicated by Table 4.4, Germany would have had to admit 19 million Italian workers, *ceteris paribus*, in order to reach a 1976 stock of 1.9 million.

55. E. Dimitras, *Enquêtes sociologiques sur les émigrants grecs: Deuxième enquête lors du séjour en Europe occidentale* (Athens: National Center for Social Research, 1971), p. 28.

56. E. Dimitras and E. Vlachos, *Sociological Surveys on Greek Emigrants: Third Survey upon the Return to Greece* (Athens: National Center for Social Research, 1971), p. 53.

57. R. Braun, *Sozio-kulturelle Probleme der Eingliederung italienischer Arbeitskräfte in der Schweiz* (Erlenbach-Zürich: Rentsch, 1970), pp. 473 and 488.

58. I. Baučić, "Migration temporaire ou définitive: Le dilemme des migrants et les politiques de migration," *Studi Emigrazione* 11, no. 33 (March 1974): 126.

59. This to the extent that Yugoslav trade unionists told their counterparts in the Federal Republic that they would look with disfavor on German moves to give municipal voting rights to Yugoslav migrants or to ease naturalization requirements for the second generation. See O. N. Haberl, *Die Abwanderung von Arbeitskräften aus Jugoslawien* (Munich: Oldenbourg, 1978), pp. 20 and 128.

60. Many of the interview schedules used in surveys appear to press migrant responses into predefined categories or to repress the "don't know/no response" category for fear of showing untidy results. Migrants can be assumed to bias their answers to the short-term end of the range, so their attitudes and behavior can be seen to correspond to what is expected of them.

61. Braun, *Sozio-kulturelle Probleme*, pp. 60, 80, and 473. By comparison, the Greeks interviewed by Dimitras, *Enquêtes sociologiques*, pp. 28–29, comprised 34 percent who initially intended to stay up to five years, 20 percent, longer or permanently, and 11–18 percent who had materially determined targets.

62. Hoffmann-Nowotny, *Soziologie des Fremdarbeitersystems*, pp. 184 and 256.

63. Forschungsverbund, *Integrierter Endbericht*, pp. 237-8.

64. Citizens of the EEC and the Nordic countries are in any case entitled to have their families move within the two groups of countries.

65. W. A. Hollenberg, "Der Familienwohnungsbedarf ausländischer Arbeitnehmer," *Bundesarbeitsblatt* 14, no. 5 (May 1965): 222.

66. Unemployment rates could not be standardized sufficiently to order the data by ranks. It appears as though they would not correlate well with the propensity to return.

67. Compare particularly the 1969–1976 rates of return in Table 4.4 with the

1970–1976 rates of growth and employment in Table 4.15, columns 5–8. There are indications that Italians (as well as Spaniards and Greeks) are repeat migrants to a greater extent than Turks; i.e., they return home and after one or several years they leave again to work abroad. See W. R. Böhning, "The Social and Occupational Apprenticeship of Mediterranean Migrant Workers in West Germany," in *The Demographic and Social Pattern of Emigration from the Southern European Countries,* edited by M. Livi Bacci (Florence, 1972), Table 32. Nevertheless, this differential does not by any means explain why Italians return at a much higher *rate* than Turks.

68. It could be argued that the full implementation of the EEC's free movement provisions since 1968 is responsible for the high rate of return among Italians in the Federal Republic of Germany. I think it has been an enabling or contributing factor, but not the cause. How else is one to explain the apparently identical return rate of nonseasonal Italians from Germany and Switzerland when the latter country does not form part of the EEC? Distance may be assumed to be the enabling or contributing factor that takes the place of the institutional factor in the case of Switzerland. But the distance does not really favor Switzerland all that much, and Table 4.15 (column 2) does not actually lend much credence to the predictive power of the distance or cost factor.

69. Forschungsverbund, *Integrierter Endbericht,* p. 235.

70. See also W. R. Böhning, *Regularising indocumentados;* and "International Migration in Western Europe: Reflections on the Past Five Years," *International Labour Review* 118, no. 4 (July–August 1979): 401–14.

71. Such as (a) artists and members of the liberal professions entering on a short-term basis; (b) persons coming specifically for purposes of training or education; and (c) employees of organizations or undertakings operating within the territory of a country who have been admitted temporarily to that country at the request of their employer to undertake specific duties or assignments, for a limited and defined period of time, and who are required to leave that country on the completion of their duties or assignments. In these cases one is likely to find positive discrimination to compensate the migrants for the geographical displacement and temporary nature of the job.

PART III

Current Situation

5

Agricultural Development
and Rural Employment:
A Mexican Dilemma

AUGUST SCHUMACHER

Introduction

Following the Cárdenas presidency (1934–1940), Mexico achieved a high rate of agricultural output, accompanied by extensive levels of rural underemployment. But the Mexican bi-modal route to this growth in agricultural output[1]—investment in irrigation to benefit commercial agriculture, with minimum support to the majority of Mexico's farmers—severely bifurcated rural society. By the mid-1960s underemployment in rural Mexico reached 35–45 percent of the 5.5 million persons in the total workforce, e.g., some 2.5 million villagers averaged less than 100 days worked. Only in the past decade has Mexico begun to consider a more "uni-modal" approach to developing its rural society, with the evolution of such programs as PIDER, CUC, COPLAMAR, and Distrito de Temporal.

This chapter traces the development of postwar rural development policies in Mexico; the cumulative impact of the dual agricultural development policy on rural society, employment, and income by the early 1970s; and the beginnings of a more uni-modal policy approach in the later years of the past decade. The essay hypothesizes that while public attention has focused on efforts to raise small farm productivity to achieve national food self-sufficiency goals,[2] analysis of the public investment budget since 1973 indicates that substantial funding has been directed toward creating a large and geographically dispersed labor-intensive rural works program. With the expanded CUC and COPLAMAR programs, temporary job creation in rural areas has been significant. Yet little analysis has been done on these rural works programs, with the exception of the rural roads program.

The chapter also postulates that this rural works policy (temporary job creation) is a sensible macro-strategy, both politically and economically. Efforts to reach food self-sufficiency and to create substantial numbers of permanent jobs in rural Mexico based on smallholder farming systems will take more than a decade to achieve. These conclusions are based on empirical evidence from two decades of applied agronomic trials under Plan Puebla, a decade of work in the Yucatan, and more recent experience with Plan Zacapoaxtla. Achieving the major policy goal of self-sufficiency in maize production, even by the middle of this decade, would have little impact on rural employment, as maize cultivation is relatively labor-extensive. An alternative job creation strategy via a widespread rural enterprise program would also take considerable time to plan and implement, as most *ejidos* to date have had little management or entrepreneurial experience with starting or operating labor-intensive businesses.[3]

With these smallholder production and employment constraints, the current government rural works strategy (CUC, COPLAMAR, elements of PIDER) is a reasonable public policy to gain time until the organizational and technical research bottlenecks to a more vibrant smallholder-based food system are dealt with, a process which empirical evidence indicates is clearly possible, but which needs a longer time frame to be implemented.

Postwar Rural Development in Mexico

For four decades following World War II, the Mexican government equated rural development with investment in commercial irrigated agriculture. This policy led to high rates of output. Paul Lamartine Yates labeled the 1940–1965 output of Mexican agriculture "a magnificent performance,"[4] where output rose at a rate of 5.7 percent annually, not only feeding a rising population, but leaving substantial surpluses for export. This approach was also given the patina of academic approbation in the early 1970s. "This pattern of agricultural development in Mexico can be characterized as bi-modal because large-scale, highly commercial farm units in northern Mexico have accounted for the bulk of the increase in farm output and an even larger fraction of the growth of commercialized production."[5]

This bi-modal strategy received additional support from Clark Reynolds. "The 'dual strategy' for agriculture was advantageous because the policy of redistributing land in small parcels to millions of *ejidatarios* satisfied income security and distribution criteria essential to maintain political stability, while the policy of public investment satisfied productivity criteria designed to spur the rate of growth of agricultural production."[6]

But the "golden age" of the dual Mexican agricultural strategy came to an abrupt halt in the mid-sixties. In the ensuing decade, production of such basic crops as maize, beans, and sugar fell off substantially, well below the population growth rate. Overall, the rate of agricultural growth fell to 1.5 percent.

The result of this bi-modal policy was the impoverishment of the majority of the rural population, through lack of employment, lack of farm income, and lack of basic rural infrastructure and services. By the advent of the Echeverría administration in 1970, the accumulated impact of this postwar strategy could no longer be ignored. Migration to the cities was expanding faster than metropolitan governments could provide even minimum services or productive employment opportunities.

During these decades, rural development in Mexico went through several contradictions: on the one hand, achieving the best output of food production in Latin America, and on the other hand, "setting in motion a process of pauperization . . . in the way of life of most rural people."[7] Population growth, declining soils, and little technological development suitable for rainfed production resulted in "much of the rural poor [becoming] not only objectively poorer than in immediately preceding decades . . . but also subjectively so."[8]

Despite this post-Cárdenas deterioration in rural Mexico and the start of the major rural exodus to its cities, rural Mexico still may have sustained almost double the number of people for whom it could provide full-time employment.[9] This tendency was reinforced by the rapidly growing landless segment of the rural population. Rural output was especially skewed with "as many as 81% of all small holdings contributing a scant 3.6% of national production, while 3.3% of the largest commercial farms produced 81% of the total output."[10] For the rural—and urban—poor, nutrition standards fell, despite the success of the bi-modal policy in gross food output.[11] This decline in nutrition may have been accelerated in the past decade. "The high rate of inflation during the early 1970s, combined with a declining *per capita* availability of basic grains, may have reduced nutritional levels among low-income families as much as 20% more since that time."[12]

The Transitional Strategy of the 1970s

Faced with the bi-modal pattern's failure to provide benefits for the bulk of the rural population and with a drastic decline in the rate of food production, in its early days the Echeverría administration (1970–1976) decided to review these past rural development strategies. Until the early 1970s, the principal public investment effort for rural development had been primarily functional, e.g., irrigation, roads, and some directed credit. These programs were not well coordinated or focused. There were also some larger-scale river basin programs such as Plan Lerma, the Commission de Rio Balsas, and the Papaloapan River Basin Commission. But once the principal dams and infrastructure were completed, the interest of these commissions lagged in ensuring that distribution canals functioned and that water actually reached and was effectively applied to farmers' fields.[13]

PIDER (INTEGRATED RURAL DEVELOPMENT PROGRAM)

In response, a new approach was unveiled on a modest scale in 1973. This was later to be called PIDER (*Programa Integral Para el Desarrollo Rural*). Its unveiling marked the beginning of a major departure from earlier programs. PIDER was explicitly designed to channel federal funds to small projects in villages in the poorest regions of the country. Ceilings on project and village size (300 to 3,000 persons) were established.[14] Also, the program was explicitly multi-sectoral, involving by 1979 some 38 federal line agencies. It was a strategy similar to what Sterling Wortman later called "defined area development": "Defined area development builds understanding of a rural community—its resources, and its potentials—and permits subsequent changes in the community to be measured."[15] Among its other goals, PIDER was devised to correct spatial and economic polarization by channeling larger amounts of investment using an integrated development approach. PIDER staff defined the specific goals of its program in 1980 as follows:

PIDER is a productive, multi-sectoral, decentralized and participatory program.

It is considered *productive* because it places emphasis on productive projects, considering them to be the driving force of PIDER's development strategy, since they generate the economic surplus necessary to finance other projects desired by the community.

The program is considered *multi-sectoral* because it finances programs of many sectors, including the agricultural, fisheries, agroindustrial, tourist, transport, communications, educational, and health sectors.

PIDER is a *decentralized* program: all of its phases, from programming through evaluation, are carried out at the state level.

It is *participatory* because the executing agencies, the state and municipal governments, and the program's beneficiaries are intimately involved in the distinct phases of the program. In this regard, it is important to emphasize that the active and organized participation of the community's members has long been an important part of PIDER's strategy.[16]

PIDER's geographical coverage expanded greatly from 41 regions in 1973, when it first started operations, to 131 in 1980, distributed throughout all thirty-one Mexican states. PIDER is currently engaged in works and services in about 50 percent of the countryside, serving 22 percent of the total rural population in 8,473 rural communities with 6.5 million inhabitants.

Investments authorized during the 1973–1980 period totaled M$32,928 million (U.S. $1,860 million), at current prices, equivalent to M$14,208 million (U.S. $800 million) at 1973 prices. Investment distribution by state was targeted to benefit those least-developed states with the largest number of poor persons. Oaxaca, Guerrero, Zacatecas, and Chiapas, which are among the country's poorest states, thus received 23 percent of PIDER's funds.

The average investment received per region between 1973 and 1980 was M$117.3 million in 1973 prices (U.S. $6.5 million). A study of investment per community shows that the average amount received between 1973 and 1979 was M$1.3 million (U.S. $72,000) or M$1,858 per person (U.S. $103).

During the 1973–1979 period, 44 percent of investments were devoted to production projects, 41 percent to support projects, and 15 percent to social projects. The trend between 1973 and 1979 showed an average annual increase of 24 percent in directly productive investments, while investments in support projects increased 11 percent and those in social projects, 3 percent. Of the thirty investment programs funded by PIDER, ten received 75.5 percent of total funding. The main ones were rural roads (16.2%), irrigation (15.6%), and livestock development programs (11.1%).

As PIDER expanded in the mid-1970s, the organizational lessons of a regionally focused rural development program became apparent to a number of line agencies, of which the most important was the Ministry of Agriculture and Water Resources. Using many of the lessons of PIDER, it developed a regionally focused national rainfed extension program, called Distrito de Temporal (Rainfed District), that now covers 123 districts, compared to PIDER's coverage of 131 macro-regions.[17] There is considerable overlap in district and micro-region boundaries that both agencies responsible, SARH (Secretariat of Agriculture and Water Resources) and SPP (Secretariat of Programming and Budget), are now trying to resolve. Resolution may be difficult.

Overlying this major shift to a regional focus on rural development was a concurrent change in the government's rural development objectives. Mexico's main policy objectives were altered to increase basic food grain production and to create temporary and permanent employment. Secondary objectives were focused on income distribution to and within poor regions, income and employment diversification, and the creation of more viable rural growth poles.

While PIDER was the first of several new "defined area strategies," it now competed for funding with three decentralized, regional, rural development programs (CUC, COPLAMAR, and Rainfed District). From 1971–1979 the PIDER program represented 1 percent of total public investment and 26 percent of public investment in poverty-oriented rural development programs. From 1973 to 1977, PIDER was the main public investment instrument focusing on the problems of rural poverty; it accounted for 8.8 percent of public investment in rural development and agriculture during this period. More importantly, PIDER investment represented more than 50 percent of *all federal investment* in such poor states as Oaxaca, Zacatecas, Chiapas, and the Yucatan. But as other programs were developed (such as CUC, COPLAMAR, and Distrito de Temporal), PIDER's overall share of federal investment in these states declined after 1977. Nevertheless, PIDER remains one of the very few multi-sectoral programs that emphasizes, in particular, decentralization and beneficiary participation. The other new poverty-oriented projects have had a single-sector orientation, with more emphasis on the importance of basic needs.

With the advent of the Lopez-Portillo administration in 1976, expectations were that programs like PIDER would be severely curtailed or even eliminated. On the contrary, in real terms, PIDER was expanded. At the same time, a number of programs deriving from the PIDER experience were started. These used PIDER's successful lesson of directly targeting a small spatial area of rural Mexico with a mix of small-scale investments. The first program started, CUC, was designed as a form of revenue sharing for small public works. It rapidly reached PIDER funding levels. Then the government decided to focus more directly on the small farmer in rainfed areas, developing a Rainfed District program based in large part on PIDER and Plan Puebla experience. Finally, as the magnitude of the rural poverty problem began to be fully recognized by the president—and as oil revenues began to expand—a fourth program, COPLAMAR, was created and substantially expanded to address the basic needs of the most "marginal" groups of rural Mexico.

CUC (COORDINATED DEVELOPMENT AGREEMENT)

The CUC (*Convenios Unicos de Coordinacion*) system began in 1977, with the objectives of decentralizing programming, executing small-scale infrastructure works, and encouraging the states to share in the programming and the financing of these projects. (Earlier, the federal government had both financed and programmed such projects.) Directly productive projects have not been part of this program. The principal programs financed (60% federal, 30% state revenue, and 10% village cash, materials, or labor) were divided as follows:

	Percentages
Village roads	45
Schools	27
Water supply system	8
Public buildings, sports facilities, and health clinics	12
Other small works	8
Total	100

In budget terms, the CUC program was financed as shown in Table 5.1. This program is administered by the General Coordination of Regional Delegations (SPP), the same area office responsible for PIDER.

Table 5.1   Financing of the CUC Program, 1977–1980 (in M$ billions)

	Federal	State	Local	Total
1977	4.2	1.7	0.4	6.3
1978	5.1	2.2	0.6	8.0
1979	7.5	3.9	0.9	12.4
1980 (est.)	9.1	4.6	1.2	14.8

In assessing the CUC "revenue-sharing" program, an outside observer commented that despite a few well-publicized problems, the CUC record since 1977 has not been, in fact, disastrous. The Ministry of Public Works, for example, has proposed to SPP that additional programs be added to the CUC decentralized administrative system. As a result of this generally favorable prognosis on the viability of a decentralized system, the government is pressing for the continuation of further program devolution to the states. The government is aware that during the transition period, there will be risks and mistakes. An experienced commentator views these risks as part of the administrative learning process of the previously moribund state bureaucracies. It involves breaking a vicious circle, since without administrative capabilities states cannot take on responsibilities, and without responsibilities they cannot acquire capabilities.

COPLAMAR (COORDINATING PROGRAM FOR MARGINAL ZONES)

COPLAMAR was started·on a limited scale in late 1977 by the former minister of the presidency and one of the former directors of the PIDER program. Its purpose was to coordinate the many agencies involved in improving living conditions in the marginal areas of Mexico, often areas where rainfall or productive potential was so poor that such programs as PIDER and Distrito de Temporal had little possibility of success. In 1979, Mexico's president approved the broad lines of the program and increased its allocation to nearly U.S. $3 billion to be spent over the 1980–1982 period. In addition, he gave authority for the COPLAMAR staff to enter three-year "commitment" agreements with executing agencies. This permitted these agencies to program more rationally over the medium term rather than strictly on a year-to-year budget basis, as is common for all other investment programs in Mexico. The major sectors to be supported by COPLAMAR during this period are shown in Table 5.2.

Table 5.2   1980–1982 Budget Allocation by COPLAMAR (in M$ billions)

Rural roads	16.8
Drinking water	20.8
Forestry	9.5
Food distribution facilities	8.7
Health clinics	5.8
Housing improvements	.9
Total (which is equivalent to U.S. $2.7 billion)	M$62.5 billion

THE RAINFED DISTRICT PROGRAM (DISTRITO DE TEMPORAL)

Initiated in 1977, the purpose of SARH's Rainfed District program is to coordinate all the government agricultural activities in the nation's 123 rainfed districts. In recent years, there has been a gradual policy shift in Mexico away from undertaking large-scale irrigation projects and toward the promotion of rainfed agriculture. Since 1945, these rainfed areas had received only 10 percent of all public investment funds for the agricultural sector. About 70 percent of Mexico's farm families live in rainfed areas; of this group some 50–60 percent are subsistence farmers with reasonable potential for improvement because of good weather conditions. The reasons for increased attention to rainfed areas are threefold. First, in areas of adequate rainfall (above 700 mm annually) the potential exists to increase productivity of rainfed crops and livestock through application of available technology and to increase cropped areas through improved drainage. The average costs of bringing about these changes are considered to be lower than investing in large-scale irrigation programs. Second, investments in rainfed agriculture are also considered an important means to redress the social imbalance now evident in Mexican agriculture; while rainfed areas produce only 50 percent of the value of agriculture output, they contain 87 percent of all farmers. Third, the government has been particularly concerned about the increasing imports of basic staples, especially maize, beans, and wheat, as a result of stagnating domestic production of these commodities; of the total cropped area under rainfed conditions of 11 million hectares, 8.6 million hectares are under maize and beans, with average yields that have changed little in the last decade.

The Rainfed District program's objective is to make these rainfed districts as autonomous in a budgetary sense as Mexico's successful irrigation districts. More than twenty agencies are directly or indirectly involved in promoting agricultural production in rainfed areas, and their performance varies: execution on infrastructure (i.e., roads, small irrigation systems, water supply) has generally been better than on other development activities, at least in rainfed areas. Unfortunately, lack of coordination among these agencies at the field level has reduced the productive impact of investments both in infrastructure and in new technology generation. In view of this, the government's decision to create the Rainfed District program with the main objectives of (a) reinforcing extension, credit, and research services in rainfed areas and (b) obtaining maximum coordination and participation of all groups involved at the local level (farmers, government agencies, banks) is an important step. SARH's 123 rainfed districts now cover 70 percent of the country. Each district is composed of a number of municipalities in a given state which share similar ecological conditions.[18] Activities in these districts are coordinated through a directing committee supported by a technical committee.

The Rainfed District program and PIDER do not on the surface appear to compete. Staff members of both realize that at the field level there is substantial interdependence. For example, most administrators of the rainfed districts perceived their initial task as primarily agricultural, rather than broader rural, development. A number of these administrators now realize that without a wider rural development perspective (i.e., rural roads, water supply, farmer organization schools) narrower food production goals are difficult to attain.

The development programs of these 123 rainfed districts vary according to climate, population density, accessibility, and agricultural specialization. The main planned activities, however, can be grouped as follows:

a. the promotion of various extension packages to combine available improved cultivation and animal-husbandry methods with the provision of short- and long-term credit;

b. production system research and on-farm testing of new technology;

c. a soil and water conservation program, including various types of terraces, contour furrows, and small water storage reservoirs;

d. a rural works program, including the construction or improvement of farm to market roads, small irrigation schemes, and drainage works; and

e. a forestry program, covering pine plantations, on-farm woodlots, and windbreak trees.

SAM (MEXICAN FOOD SYSTEM)

In March 1980, the president announced a new national food policy calling for self-sufficiency in maize and beans by 1982 and in overall food imports by 1985, as well as a major effort to reverse declining nutrition standards for some 35 million rural and urban Mexicans. It is probable that PIDER will play an important part in implementing some aspects of SAM, especially in areas where PIDER micro-regions overlap with SAM's "critical nutrition zones." Developed by the Office of the President, the analysis underpinning this policy announcement is called Sistema Alimentario Mexicano (SAM), the Mexican Food System. The basic document is an analysis of food-related problems in Mexico. By the end of 1982, the policy has called for the production of maize to increase from 10 to 13 million tons, and the production of beans from 1.1 to 1.5 million tons.

To the surprise of its critics, SAM has nearly achieved its target. Mexico is unlikely to import significant quantities of maize or beans in 1982. A combination of good weather and a very favorable price support policy were the main contributors to this success. The SAM strategy emphasized an expansion of applied research, credit, use of inputs—especially fertilizer and insecticides—and technical assistance. A new feature outlined in SAM is a government-sponsored crop insurance program that would guarantee not only the repayment of the cost of inputs, but also the value of the crop if it were lost during the season. This crop insurance program would encourage farmers to use more inputs and to plant maize in areas whose inadequate rainfall has made the sowing of maize a high-risk proposition. Other policies for stimulating production include annual increases in the guaranteed prices of maize and beans, and readjustment of the guaranteed price ratios between maize and beans and competing crops, so that cultivation of maize and beans would be more attractive. The target group of farmers will be peasant farmers in rainfed areas, who at present are producing for their own subsistence, but who have additional productive potential.

Critical Nutrition Zones. Concurrent with the studies on production, the Advisory Group to the President undertook research on the scope of the malnutrition problem and some of its causes. SAM identified 699 municipalities which were grouped into "critical zones"; these are areas "in which the federal government should take the responsibility for supplying food—either gratis or at subsidized prices—in order to eliminate malnutrition in those groups whose alternatives for improvements are severely limited."[19] In the urban areas, the critical zones include the "belts of poverty" surrounding the major cities, areas in which inadequate distribution of food and low income make malnutrition a serious problem. In the rural areas, the zones primarily include areas where agricultural productivity is limited by soil and terrain or is highly vulnerable to drought. In both situations the production of food is insufficient to feed the family, either directly or through inadequate ability to purchase foodstuffs. The sisal-producing areas of the Yucatan and semiarid areas such as Zacatecas, Durango, and much of Oaxaca are typical of the rural areas classified as "critical zones" by SAM. The SAM strategy for eliminating malnutrition consists of production components, increased distribution of food, and nutrition education. At the household level, small family gardens and the raising of chickens or pigs would be encouraged by the provision of seeds, technical assistance, and improved stock. The distribution of food would be improved by an expansion of the network of rural stores run by CONASUPO, the buying and marketing agency for agricultural produce within the Secretariat of Industry and Commerce. Both rural and urban families would have greater access to more food products at subsidized prices, and if the savings from the subsidized prices are used for purchasing more food, food consumption would again increase. In those areas where there is little chance of increasing production or generating income, food distribution programs for the most vulnerable groups (i.e., preschoolers and lactating mothers) are contemplated. A nutrition education program would complement all these programs to assure that the utilization of food and the distribution of food within the family result in real improvements in the diet of the vulnerable family members.

Federal Investment in Agriculture and Rural Development

In the past ten years, Mexican public investment in agriculture and rural development programs has changed in three significant ways (see Table 5.3).

1. Overall investment in agriculture and rural development may be approaching 25 percent of total federal investment in the early 1980s, up from less than 15 percent in a comparable period in the mid-1970s.

2. Federal investment in the commercial agriculture sector seems to have been constant at approximately 14 percent of total public investment.

Table 5.3 **Mexican Federal Public Investment in Agriculture and Rural Development, 1971–1982 (in M$ billion)**

	1971–1973 (average)	1975–1977 (average)	Estimated 1980–1982 (average)
Total federal government investment	35.1	119.0	550.0
Federal investment in agriculture and rural development	5.2	22.4	130.7
Percentage of total	14.8	18.8	23.7
Federal investment in agriculture	4.8	18.3	77.2
Percentage of total	13.8	15.8	13.71
Federal investment in rural development	0.4	4.1	53.5
Percentage of total	1	3	10

Source: SPP, IBRD, and author's estimates.

3. The major change seems to be occurring in federal investment in rural development, rising from 1 percent to 10 percent of total public investment.

These changes are significant both as a reflection of relative changes in budgetary priorities and, equally important, as a reflection of the recent administration's efforts to increase food production and broaden income distribution to affect a larger portion of the rural populace. If current budget trends continue into the next administration (1982–1988), Mexico will have shifted back again to the uni-modal policies first articulated in the Cardenas presidency.

In analyzing government budget data over the past decade, several additional developments occurred.

1. Within government funding of agriculture, there appears to be a recent shift from funding irrigation (75% of investment) to a more balanced investment in both rainfed and irrigation development. Rainfed agriculture has historically been virtually ignored by Mexican agricultural planners in favor of attention to irrigated farming. This imbalance seems to be changing (see Table 5.4).

2. Within the rural development sector, PIDER was the primary investment vehicle during the Echeverría administration (1970–1976). The Lopez-Portillo

Table 5.4   Mexican Federal Public Investment in Agriculture by Program, 1971–1977 (in M$ billion)

Program	1971	1972	1973	1974	1975	1976	1977
Irrigation	2.5	3.6	4.1	7.1	10.0	9.9	8.3
Percentage of total	76	74	65	71	66	70	32
Rainfed production	0.4	0.7	1.5	2.2	3.0	2.2	15.3
Percentage of total	13	14	24	22	21	16	60
Livestock production	0.09	0.2	0.2	0.3	0.8	0.8	1.2
Percentage of total	2	4	3	2	5	5	5
Forestry	—	—	0.2	0.2	0.5	0.4	0.6
Percentage of total			3	2	3	3	2
Fishery	0.3	0.4	0.3	0.3	0.8	0.9	0.3
Percentage of total	9	8	5	3	5	6	1
Total	3.3	4.9	6.3	10.1	15.1	14.2	25.7

Source: SPP.

administration has added two additional rural development programs, CUC and COPLAMAR, while continuing to expand PIDER investment in real terms.

In dollar terms, public investment in rural development is likely to rise from an annual average of U.S. $120 *million* from the 1973/75 period to a possible annual average of U.S. $2.3 *billion* for the 1980/82 period. For the two million families classified as the rural poor, this is an average public investment of U.S. $1,150 for each peasant family, a significant sum in any international comparison.

Impact of a "Targeted Uni-Modal" Strategy on Food Output and Employment Creation

Given this analysis of the recent changes in budgetary priorities and the various agricultural and rural development programs being supported by these changing priorities, what is the time frame of the likely effect of these efforts, both on food production and on temporary and permanent employment creation?

FOOD PRODUCTION

The national food system plan (SAM) called for self-sufficiency in maize and beans by 1982 and in all basic foods by 1985. The 1979–1980 drought increased the difficulty of meeting these near-term targets. Even without the drought, the negligible national experience with the time frame of productivity increases in rainfed agriculture (chiefly the well-known Puebla program) indicates that achieving progress will be excruciatingly slow. For the majority of farmers in the Puebla area to achieve significant yield increase (from 1.3 tons to 3 tons of maize per hectare), a thirteen-year time frame is required, even for literate farmers who already have available most of the basic physical infrastructure. It is likely that it will take at least a decade for the majority of Mexico's smaller rainfed farmers to achieve significant national productivity gains from rainfed agriculture.

Yet, within the basic grain sector, a major reduction in maize and bean imports may be achieved through a combination of improved weather, much higher price supports, and credit for maize and bean producers relative to other grain, especially sorghum, production. Mexican policymakers have apparently decided to greatly encourage foodgrain production, particularly maize, and to rely more on the international grain markets for feedgrain supplies for the burgeoning livestock industry. This is causing a major shift by larger grain producers in rainfed areas from feedgrain production of sorghum to maize production. The result should be a continuation of current levels of total grain imports, but a shift in their composition from foodgrains (maize and beans) to more feedgrains (sorghum, soybeans).

The productivity gains from installation of tube-well irrigation by small farmers is much more favorable, with average yields jumping from 600 kilograms to 3.5 tons per hectare in Zacatecas. A constraint on tube-well irrigation is the lack of adequate aquifer studies to determine well spacing and pumping rates.

EMPLOYMENT IMPACT

The rural employment impact of this more uni-modal approach to rural society is likely to be reflected initially in temporary job creation caused by construction activities. Permanent job creation is likely to depend primarily on the extent of new small-scale irrigation works.

In 1980, some 24 million persons were living in Mexico's rural areas, of which about 23 percent, some 5 million, were in the economically active labor force. At least 2 million and perhaps as many as half the agricultural labor force were underemployed, however, working on marginal farms earning or producing less than a minimum subsistence wage. If 500,000 to 750,000 of the underemployed in the smaller rural towns (2,500 to 50,000) are added, a total of 2.5 million to 3 million rural workers probably worked less than 100 days in 1980.

Some 177,000 annual new jobs in the agricultural (see Table 5.5) and rural work force of a *permanent nature* are estimated with present levels of public investment annually from 1980 to 1982. This is a modest provision in permanent employment against the above backlog of rural underemployment.

The estimate of temporary job creation in rural Mexico is more significant

Table 5.5   Permanent Job Creation Content of Federal Public Investment in Agriculture and Rural Development, 1971–1982

	Annual average 1971/73	Annual average 1975/77	Annual average (estimated) 1980/82
Total federal investment in agriculture and rural development (cost per job)	M$325,000 (US$14,100)	M$655,000 (US$28,480)	M$736,000 (US$32,000)
Total man-years of permanent employment	16,000	34,200	178,343
Public investment in agriculture (cost per job)	M$312,500	M$621,000	M$690,000
Total man-years of permanent employment	15,400	29,500	111,884
Public investment in rural development (cost per job)	M$350,000	M$736,000	M$805,000
Total man-years of permanent employment	1,142	5,570	66,459

Source: Author's estimates derived from SPP & SARH data.

(Table 5.6). If the projected federal investment in rural Mexico were attained over this 1980–1982 period, as many as 1.6 million temporary jobs, mostly in construction, would be created each year. This is a little more than half the backlog of underemployed. This (and the figure is optimistic) would still leave almost 1.4 million rural persons who would have access to no more than 75 to 100 days of work a year. It is from the better-educated segment of this latter underemployed group that much of the seasonal and some of the permanent exodus from rural areas is taking place.

EMPLOYMENT CONTENT

More analytical research on the employment structure of this current "spatial uni-modal" investment strategy is currently being done. Early data indicate that the permanent and temporary employment content of all agricultural and rural development investment shifted and expanded over the past decade. Tables 5.5 and 5.6 provide some interesting, but speculative, trends. First, the great expansion in rural development expenditures projected for the remaining period of the Lopez-Portillo administration will have its main impact on temporary employment creation. Permanent jobs are likely to develop from

Table 5.6   Temporary Job Creation Content of Federal Public Investment in Agriculture and Rural Development, 1971–1982 (estimates)

	Annual average 1971/73	Annual average 1975/77	Annual average 1980/82
Total federal investment in agriculture and rural development, per man-year of temporary jobs created	M$50,000	M$88,550	M$80,000
(US$ equivalent)	($4,000)	($3,850)	($3,500)
Total man-years of temporary employment	104,000	253,000	1,625,000
Federal investment in agriculture, per man-year of temporary work created	M$53,000	M$95,000	M$95,000
Total man-years of temporary employment	90,566	192,000	812,000
Federal investment in rural development, per man-year of temporary work created	M$40,000	M$70,000	M$60,000
Total man-years of temporary employment	10,000	58,571	813,000

Source: Author's estimates derived from SPP & SARH data.

this only in a ratio of one to ten, e.g., the annual labor of ten workers in constructing federally funded investment projects in rural areas is necessary to provide one new, permanent, rural job.

Second, the projection of temporary rural employment creation annually for the 1980–1982 period in Table 5.6 seems beyond a realistic expectation of what the government can administer. Yet, if even half the program is achieved, the creation of 800,000 temporary jobs in the rural sector would be a major accomplishment.

And third, the projection of permanent employment creation seems low, but probably realistic given the expansion of two major programs with low permanent employment possibilities, rainfed agricultural development and the COPLAMAR program of basic social infrastructure.

Conclusions

In summary, Mexican rural policy shows signs of altering its postwar bi-modal "trickle down" strategy to a more spatially targeted uni-modal effort, incorporating more of the poorer rural population in the economy. The key test of this shift will be the early investment budgets of the next administration. If the present trend continues of allocating a quarter of total public investment to the rural sector, with half of this targeted directly to poverty areas, by 1985 a shift to a more uni-modal pattern will have begun. Even so, there may be strong voices in the next administration which would, as Bruce F. Johnston wrote in 1975, "argue that the success already achieved in expanding farm output under a bi-modal strategy will compromise the prospects for a successful (and long term) shift to a more uni-modal approach." The constraints, Professor Johnston felt in that year, "imposed by the rate of growth of effective demand make it doubtful whether the Mexican government will be prepared to commit substantial resources to an expanded effort to promote increased output by smallholders."[20] On the other hand, unexpected oil revenues are generating an economic growth rate (8.5% real increase in GNP) which if added to population growth of more than 3 percent is creating a great demand for feedgrains and livestock products. This income-led demand seems to have overtaken Johnston's "lack of effective demand" thesis, with imports of basic grains soaring in recent years. The more fundamental question, it seems now, is not "lack of effective demand," but how the current demand is to be structurally supplied, a return to the Cárdenas uni-modal pattern or a continuation of the divisive bi-modal strategy. The implications for employment creation and well-being for 75 percent of Mexico's rural society hang in the balance on this choice—and the methods by which it is implemented.

As Johnston concluded, "It could be argued with considerable cogency that Mexico's bi-modal strategy was well suited to the particular set of circumstances that the country faced."[21] Yet the circumstances facing Mexico in the 1980s are vastly different from those prevailing in the administrations immediately following the Cárdenas administration. Even if very recent (since 1979) uni-modal trends are continued, does the political will exist in Mexico for the great long-term effort necessary to reverse four decades of neglect of three-quarters of Mexico's rural society?

As the SAM documents reveal, their authors felt that basic self-sufficiency could be reached in a very short time frame. In calling for this self-sufficiency, the SAM proponents appear to have overlooked not only the long gestation of the 1940–1965 "golden age," but also fundamental agricultural investment cycles.[22] Lamartine Yates writes: "Land and animals have rhythms of their own which by inherent nature of the agricultural production process have a much longer time-span than the processes of manufacturing industry, so that problems which superficially appear to be short-term in character require in reality long-term measures for dealing with them . . . efforts to attain (agricultural) goals may have to be more far-reaching and certainly more sustained than has hitherto been generally recognized."[23]

Yet an analysis of the past decade of public federal investment in the rural sector indicates that possibly such a recognition is taking place despite the day-to-day call for "immediate remedies." The real question remains, however, whether a new administration will continue these necessary investment levels which require up to a decade before significant results occur. Can short-term political support be welded into the longer-term constituency necessary to achieve the food output and rural employment generation required by 100 million Mexicans living in 1990? Given a lead time of a decade or more, is a federal investment allocation of 25 percent of the total investment budget sufficient for this task, or are even higher levels necessary, say 40–45 percent over the decade of the eighties,[24] if even a moderate impact on food output and rural permanent employment creation is to be achieved by 1990?

Appendix Table 5.1 Federal Public Investment in Agriculture and Rural Development in Mexico, 1971–1982

Year	Investment in agriculture ($M billion)	%	Investment in rural development ($M billion)	%	Total investment in agriculture and rural development	%	Total investment
1971	3.3	100	—	—	3.3	14.7	22.4
1972	4.9	100	—	—	4.9	14.7	33.3
1973	6.3	85	1.1	15	7.4	14.9	49.8
1974	10.1	89	1.3	11	11.4	17.6	64.8
1975	15.1	86	2.5	14	17.6	18.3	95.7
1976	14.2	87	2.1	13	16.3	15.0	108.6
1977	25.7	77	7.6	23	33.3	21.6	154.0
1978	30.9	66	15.7	37	46.6	21.0	221.7
1979	45.0	67	22.7	33	67.6	19.8	340.7
1980[a]	65.7	62	40.9	38	106.6	24.6	433.0
1981[b]	75.6	57	57.0	43	132.7	24.5	541.0
1982[b]	90.3	59	62.5	41	152.8	22.6	676.0

[a] Authorized.
[b] Estimates.

Source: Secretariat of Programming and Budgeting, IBRD, and author's estimates.

Appendix Table 5.2   Agricultural and Rural Development Investment Co-efficients of Labor Intensity in Mexico

	Labor-intensity of construction		Permanent job creation
	%	US$/Man-year	US$/Man-year
Irrigation			
Large scale	15	6,500	20,000
Small scale	35	3,000	6,500
Rainfed development			
Extension and demonstration	10	—	—
Soil and water conservation	70	1,500	30,000
Forestation	70	1,500	20,000
Livestock	20	5,500	35,000
Fisheries development	15	6,500	10,000
Feeder roads	40	2,800	50,000
Rural industries	20	5,500	5,000
Village water supply	40	2,800	75,000
Rural housing improvement	75	1,200	—
Village electrification	10	7,500	165,000
Village school and health clinics	40	2,800	25,000

Source: Author's analysis, based on SPP and SARH data.

Appendix Table 5.3   Integrated Rural Development Program

Regions in Operation and Investment
Authorized, 1973–1980

Year	Regions		Millions of pesos		Annual increase
	New	Accumulated	Current	Constant[a]	%[a]
1973	41	41	1,104	1,104	—
1974	13	54	1,274	1,026	−7.1
1975	26	80	2,513	1,736	69.2
1976	6	86	2,101	1,193	−31.3
1977	14	100	3,451	1,484	24.4
1978	4	104	5,138	1,882	26.8
1979	14	118	7,401	2,542	35.1
1980	13	131	9,948	3,241	27.5
Total			32,930	14,208	

[a] Constant prices of 1973.

Source: Ministry of Programming and Budget, General Directorate of Integrated Rural Development.

Notes

The discussion and analysis in this chapter derive from fieldwork on Mexican agriculture and rural development programs undertaken from 1972–1980 as part of the World Bank's lending operations to this sector. Colleagues in Mexico who contributed greatly to this dialogue were Arturo Diaz Camacho, Kim Conroy, Miguel Cuadra, Jorge Echinique, Fernando Hriart, Cassio Luiselli, Jaime Mariscal, Eduardo Pesquiera, Carlos Vidali, and Arturo Warman. Colleagues in this dialogue outside Mexico included Richard Anson, James Austin, Curt Carnemark, D. B. Dutt, Carmen Hamann, and Dan Lindheim. An early draft of this essay was prepared while the author was a Visiting Scholar at the Bellagio Center of the Rockefeller Foundation. The analysis is the author's personal view and should not be considered as representing any official position of the World Bank.

1. Bruce F. Johnston developed this bi-modal and uni-modal theme in comparing Mexico to a more balanced policy of output, employment, and rural development in Korea, Malaysia, Greece, Taiwan, and Japan during the same postwar period (Bruce F. Johnston and Peter Kilby, *Agricultural and Structural Transformation: Economic Strategies for Late-Developing Countries* [New York: Oxford University Press, 1975]). He recently updated and revised his thinking with special reference to Mexico in a paper titled "The Design and Redesign of Strategies for Agricultural Development: Mexico's Experience Revisited," Food Research Institute, Stanford University (1981), mimeographed.

2. See Office of the President (Oficina de Asesores), *Sistema Alimentario Mexicano* (Mexico City, March 1, 1980); and Johnston, "The Design and Redesign of Strategies."

3. The term *ejido* is derived from the Spanish equivalent of the village "common." The ejido is basically a group of families with joint—and thus inalienable—rights to till land. The head of such a family is called a *ejidatario*. He may not sell or subdivide his land, but he can pass the usufruct rights to his offspring, thereby subdividing those rights.

4. Paul Lamartine Yates's two-volume book *El Campo Mexicano* (Mexico DF.: Ediciones el Caballito, 1978) is one of the best analyses of the limited literature on the rural sector of Mexico.

5. Johnston and Kilby, *Agriculture and Structural Transformation*, p. 137.

6. Clark Reynolds, *The Mexican Economy* (New Haven: Yale University Press, 1970), p. 137.

7. Cynthia Hewitt de Alcantara, "Mexico: A Commentary on the Satisfaction of Basic Needs," in *Another Development: Approaches and Strategies*, edited by Marc Nerfin (Uppsala, Sweden: Dag Hammarskjöld Foundation, 1977), p. 162.

8. Ibid., p. 163.

9. Ibid., p. 169.

10. Ibid., p. 167.

11. "Agricultural production grew rapidly enough during the postwar period to increase the per capita availability of calories from roughly 2,000 to 2,600 and that of protein from 54 to 80 grams. If more people were undernourished in 1970 than in 1940, it was because the gap in consumption of foodstuffs between higher and lower income groups grew wider, not because the total supply of foodstuffs was inadequate to satisfy the public requirements of all the population" (ibid., p. 201).

12. Ibid., p. 179.

13. David Barkin and Timothy King, *Regional Economic Development* (Cambridge: Cambridge University Press, 1970).

14. The PIDER regions are composed of entire municipalities, which are the basic unit of the Mexican government's political and administrative organization. Within the municipalities, the program has been reaching communities with populations between 300 and 3,000 inhabitants. This parameter was recently modified with the objective of covering basic social services; the range was changed to include communities of 500 to 5,000 inhabitants. Nonetheless, productive projects will continue to be financed in localities with populations less than 500. With the aim of contributing to a more

equitable distribution of the nation's wealth, PIDER's productive projects are directed to those ejidatarios, *communeros,* small farmers, and landless agricultural workers who annually earn less than 250 times the minimum salary of the region. Secretariat de Programacion y Presuepuesto (SPP), "Program Integral Para el Desarrollo Rural" (Mexico City, SPP, 1980), mimeographed.

15. Sterling Wortman and Ralph Cummings, Jr., *To Feed This World* (Baltimore: Johns Hopkins University Press, 1978), p. 10.

16. SPP, PIDER.

17. Micro-regions comprise from two to seven contiguous municipalities. Rainfed districts are also municipal-based and cover seven to fifteen municipalities, defined primarily to a similar ecological base for the purposes of rainfed research and applied extension program.

18. Like PIDER, the Rainfed District program uses the municipality as the primary instrument of local budgeting. As more and more programs adopt this convention (CUC and COPLAMAR in some cases), this decentralized municipal-level budgeting tool will be given a strong impetus as further development planning and programming efforts are devised in the rural sector.

19. Office of the President, *Sistema Alimentario Mexicano.*

20. Johnston and Kilby, *Agricultural and Structural Transformation,* pp. 274–75.

21. Ibid., p. 275.

22. Improved seed, large-scale irrigation, and area expansion all have a three-to-seven-year lead time.

23. Lamaratine Yates, *El Campo Mexicano,* p. 15.

24. During the decade 1935–1945, Mexico invested 44 percent of its public investment in irrigation and rural highway networks. It was this long gestation period of the thirties and forties that fueled the high output growth in the fifties and sixties. (Johnston and Kilby, *Agricultural and Structural Transformation,* pp. 262–63).

Additional References

Cernea, M. "Measuring Project Impact: Monitoring and Evaluation in the PIDER Rural Development Project—Mexico." Staff Working Paper No. 332. Washington, D.C.: World Bank, 1979.

Eckstein, S., et al. "Land Reform in Latin America: Bolivia, Chile, Mexico, Peru and Venezuela." World Bank Staff Working Paper No. 275. Washington, D.C.: World Bank, 1978.

Hansen, Roger D. *Mexican Economic Development: The Roots of Rapid Growth.* Washington, D.C.: National Planning Association, 1971.

———. *The Politics of Mexican Development.* Baltimore and London: Johns Hopkins University Press, 1971.

Hewitt de Alcantara, Cynthia. *Modernizing Mexican Agriculture: Socioeconomic Implications of Technological Change 1940–1970.* Geneva: United Nations Research Institute for Social Development, 1976.

Korten, D.C. "Community Organization and Rural Development: A Learning Process Approach." *The Public Administration Review,* 1980.

Venezian, E. L., and Gamble, W. K. *The Agricultural Development of Mexico: Its Structure and Growth Since 1950.* New York: Praeger, 1969.

Vernon, Raymond, ed. *Public Policy and Private Enterprise in Mexico.* Cambridge: Harvard University Press, 1964.

———. *The Dilemma of Mexico's Development.* Cambridge: Harvard University Press, 1963.

Whetten, N. L. *Rural Mexico.* Chicago: University of Chicago Press, 1948.

6

The Rural Exodus in Mexico and Mexican Migration to the United States

LOURDES ARIZPE

Introduction

Migration out of rural areas, a pervasive movement in most developing countries since the fifties, began in Mexico after the turn of the century and greatly intensified in the last three decades. During this same period, as Bustamante's and García y Griego's historical research has shown, labor conditions in the United States attracted Mexican migrants, mostly from rural areas, in sharply fluctuating patterns of active recruitment, laissez-faire, or repatriation. Because these two movements have varied simultaneously and because they are interrelated, it has been assumed that the rural exodus in Mexico generally explains the flow of migrants across the border to the United States. This chapter will argue that they must be analyzed instead as two distinct movements. Data will be presented to show that most of the migrants created by the prevailing conditions in Mexican rural villages settle within Mexico, and that only specific types of migrants are attracted over the border.

This distinction between the general rural outflow in Mexico and Mexican migration to the United States is crucial for an understanding of who the U.S.–bound migrants are in Mexican rural society. This is particularly necessary because, in spite of greatly improved data and research on communities sending migrants to the United States, the patterns, reasons, and rhythms of the movement still tend to become buried under broad generalizations that seek simple villains, such as population growth, unemployment, or poverty, for what is a highly complex social and economic process.

A finer knowledge of the texture of these two flows can be important in formulating policy for all sides concerned. Most policy proposals, with a few exceptions, seem to envisage uniform solutions to what is in fact, in the case of Mexican migration to the United States, a heterogenous flow. Different types of migrants, displaying diverse strategies and targets, which for them involve difficult personal ordeals, require, if not special policies, at least an acknowledgment of their differences in any assessment of the impact of their migration on sending and receiving communities.

I begin by discussing some of the basic issues in the analysis of rural outmigration in developing countries. Then I examine the diversity of conditions that create potential outmigration in Mexican rural villages, as a context in which to understand which migrants are being attracted to the United States.

Rural Outmigration and Development: A Few Historical Hints

It is important to begin by stating that the experience of countries with early industrialization should incline us not to be surprised by rural outflows that lead to internal and international migrations. All industrial nations recruited the bulk of their industrial workforce from surplus agricultural labor that flowed to industrial regions where capital investments allowed greater productivity.

The rate at which labor flows out of agriculture, stimulated by multiple factors, usually outstrips the rate at which it is absorbed into the new industries. During the period when Europe was industrializing, for example, it was unable to absorb all the surplus labor being released from agriculture: between 1846 and 1932, it sent 51 million emigrants overseas.[1] Each of the four great outflows of migrants from Europe between 1844 and 1913 was for the most part a rural exodus. As examples, part of the outflow in 1849–1854 came from the break-up of the rural economy in the southwest of Germany; that of 1881–1888 was brought about by the agricultural crisis that resulted from cheaper wheat imports from the United States.[2]

More than half these migrants were welcomed into the United States, which took in more than 32 million European immigrants between 1821 and 1932. Most came from rural hinterlands, as the U.S. Immigration Commission stated for the 1903–1913 inflow of 10 million migrants: "Before coming to the U.S. the greater proportion were engaged in farming or unskilled labor and had no experience or training in manufacturing industry or mining."[3]

The export of redundant labor in the European case had been made possible by the vast spaces opened overseas for European domination and colonization during the previous two centuries. This option, of course, is not available for developing countries today.

Several features of rural outmigration are worth noting here. First, the outflow of rural migrants during Western Europe's industrializing period occurred in spite of slow population growth in its rural areas. This suggests that the high population increase in developing countries today cannot always be singled out as the unique cause of rural outmigration. Instead, this difference points to how much more critical a situation developing countries are facing today, where policies similar to those applied for Western European industrial growth are bringing about similar patterns of rural-urban migration, but with greatly increased population burdens and fewer employment or overseas migration options.

Second, blaming poverty as the main cause of rural outmigration explains very little. Poverty existed long before massive rural-urban migration began. Moreover, it is as much a symptom of underlying economic processes as rural outmigration is.

Third, ethnic differences, except in cases of political strife, invasion, or war, are usually reflected only indirectly in migration. Granted, the ethnic factor is crucial in channeling the distribution of land, wealth, and political influence, thus creating a pattern of class stratification that is reflected in the selectivity of migrants. Its influence is more direct, then, in the *patterns* of migration, since economic and social bonding strengthened by a common ethnic identity shape a distinctive behavior in migrants of that particular group. This is especially true in the case of Mexico.[4]

Understanding Migration

The close association between the growth of industrial capitalism, especially in countries with a highly centralized pattern of industrialization, and large-scale rural-urban migration suggests that this type of labor migration can be considered the geographical expression of an economic process. It would be inappropriate, however, to turn the truism that the rural exodus is generally the result of the development of capitalism into an abstract principle to explain migration. Such a view fails to make the theoretical distinction between the creation of a relative surplus population and the process of migration. Beyond doubt, the release of labor through higher levels of capital investment in agriculture is the necessary condition for massive outmigration. But it is another thing to say that the workers thus released automatically become migrants. Many alternative moves are possible. Workers may turn to other local salaried or income-generating activities; cultural and ethnic prescriptions may deter or change the selectivity of migrants; the labor redundancy may be transferred from one sex to another—for example, young women of the household may be sent away to work to offset the deficit in the predominantly male agricultural activity, or young men may migrate if rural factories seeking low labor costs prefer to employ young women.

Thus, migration must be examined at two levels of analysis. At a general level, it must be understood within the context of industrialization, urbanization patterns, the transformation of a peasant economy into a market economy, and state policies influencing economic and social change. These channeling forces shape migration, but this level of analysis can yield only broad, hypothetical explanations of migration. It is still necessary to explain why some rural inhabitants stay while others migrate, when they all face similar pressures to leave. This means that, since rural migrants are not a random sample of rural inhabitants, their *selectivity* must be explained.

Migrant selectivity can be explained only at another level of analysis, *by shifting the focus of analysis from the migrants themselves to what is happening in the social structure of rural towns and villages.* This implies bypassing their personal idiosyncracies (whether they are psychologically the most adventurous or the most passive, etc.) and the way they explain their reasons for migrating, and instead examining their position within the household, (i.e., if they are the eldest or youngest offspring, male or female) and within the community (i.e., whether landowners, wage laborers, craftsmen, traders).

The essential point here is that the characteristics of migrants become significant only within a given social structure. *It follows, then, that who migrates will almost certainly vary with each generation and, in even more cases, according to the pace of social change.* Rural outmigration thus can be fully accounted for only by looking closely at historical processes and specifically at the variations occurring in regions and communities undergoing rapid social change.

To summarize, there are two basic questions to be asked about rural outmigration in any developing country. The question of *why* migration occurs will be related to policies of agricultural and industrial development. But the particular features of migration can be explained only by asking *how* rural communities and individuals are coping with the pressures to migrate inherent in centralized industrial capitalism.

With these analytical instruments at hand, I will try to explain the major forces behind the rural exodus in Mexico. It would be beyond the scope of this essay to analyze fully Mexico's economic development of the last few decades, and Schumacher's chapter in this volume deals with Mexican agricultural development. Therefore, the macroeconomic changes most relevant to explaining migration will be mentioned only briefly, and analysis will focus on the changing social structure of rural villages.

Development Policies and the Rural Exodus in Mexico (1940–1980)

The drift from the land began long ago in the Mexican countryside—and even in the last century part of it involved migration to the United States—but it took on a definite pattern only in the early forties.[5] During the previous decade, President Cárdenas had carried out an agrarian reform that favored rural peasants by redistributing land extensively. This set off an era of rural prosperity, which many consider the backbone of the successful 5.7 percent annual growth of Mexican agriculture from 1940 to 1965. By the end of the sixties, however, agricultural growth had dropped below the level of the rural population increase, staple grains had to be imported, and a flood of migrants was coming to the cities and crossing the border. What had happened? What turned the production of food into the production of migrants?

In the beginning, the success of the agrarian reform and the favorable balance for agriculture in the national economy—the price of food increased more rapidly than the general price index between 1929 and 1945[6]—were reflected in improved nutrition and greater access to medical services that lowered mortality rates and created an unprecedented population growth of more than 3 percent per year.

Beginning with Aleman's regime in 1948, a new strategy of development was adopted, which directed government efforts and investments toward import-substitution and large-scale irrigation agriculture.[7] Although federal expenditure in agriculture grew progressively after that time, it was unevenly distributed within the agricultural sector.[8] By 1960 the proportion of federal investment in irrigated agriculture was double that directed toward rain-fed agriculture, and by 1966 it was seven times as great.[9]

Government policies encouraging rapid industrialization were at the same time fostering the growth of urban centers, which increasingly attracted people from rural regions. Employment was created at a very rapid rate in the major cities, particularly in Mexico City. There, for example, 503,000 jobs opened up in the forties, 686,000 in the fifties, and 679,000 in the sixties.[10] Migrants could find formal employment easily since jobs had low entrance requirements, and they could be trained on the job. For those seeking temporary income, the construction boom of expanding housing and urban infrastructure offered ample opportunities of taking up and leaving jobs as needed. Not only Mexico City, but other cities like Guadalajara and Monterrey, although on a much more moderate scale, were also building up an industrial workforce from the influx of rural migrants.

The forties and early fifties, then, were the golden age for rural migrants in Mexico, the era that created the myth of plentiful work and money that continues to exercise a strong influence in fostering migration from rural villages in the hinterland. Because of conditions in both irrigated and small landholding agriculture, government policies were successful in providing cheap food for the cities, in shifting labor from agriculture to manufacturing industry, and in creating urban employment.

Nevertheless, in spite of its spectacular growth, agricultural development was very uneven, both in its exchange with the industrial sector and internally. Agriculture provided the exports and the cheap food needed to set Mexico on the path toward industrialization, but in the process it lost too many resources. Through fiscal mechanisms, more money was taken from agriculture through taxes than was put back from 1940 to 1963.[11]

The unevenness becomes most evident in the structure of prices. From 1940 to 1966, the net balance of the fluctuation of agricultural prices in relation to the general price index showed that 2,905 million pesos (at 1960 prices) were transferred to the rest of the economy.[12] In recent years, massive government investment in the agricultural sector has offset the long-term loss of resources so that, overall, the balance is now equal.

But it was the prolonged, fluctuating imbalance in the exchange between agriculture and industry, which transferred a total of 2.3 percent of agricultural production between 1942–1962, that first began to erode the economic base of small farms.[13] It particularly undermined small landowners because of the uneven development inside the agricultural sector.

The increased irrigation of arable lands benefited only a limited group of capitalist entrepreneurs and displaced smaller producers, and the Green Revolution further polarized this development, as it did in other developing countries.[14] As Hewitt de Alcantara has explained for Mexico, the hybrid seeds could produce higher yields only when used with other high-technology inputs of insecticides, chemical fertilizers, and irrigation. Only a minority of farmers were able to benefit from the new strains and irrigated land. As a result, technology and capital began to concentrate in larger estates.[15]

By 1960 this uneven development of Mexican agriculture was evident in the following figures: 50.3 percent of land plots had less than five hectares of land, which amounted to 13.6 percent of the total arable land. These *minifundios* produced 4.2 percent of agricultural production and owned 1.3 percent of agricultural machinery. By contrast, the top 0.5 percent of land plots took in 28.3 percent of the arable land (including 37.6 percent of irrigated lands), produced 32.2 percent of agricultural production, and owned 43.7 percent of agricultural machinery.[16]

But the hardest blow to the minifundios, which subsisted on rain-fed maize cultivation, came in 1957 when the price of maize was artificially regulated. Since 1925, the price of maize had risen steadily in cycles, but in 1957, on the basis of a policy of "stabilizing development" *(Desarrollo Estabilizador)*, the rising price cycle was stopped with massive imports, a procedure that was repeated in 1963 when the price of maize again began to rise.[17] This regulating mechanism worked until 1969 because the increased yields of the Green Revolution allowed large farms to offset the loss in price. The government-guaranteed price of maize was maintained from 1957 until 1973, during which time the Mexican economist Gomez Oliver estimates that maize lost 33 percent of its value.

This loss affected small rain-fed farms much more severely than large irrigated farms, and thus the former have felt the unevenness of development within agriculture and the transfer of resources to industry much more directly. Warman states that the balance between monetary costs of production, prices, and mean salaries in rural areas was broken in 1966.[18] Minifundio farmers then lowered their "investment" in agricultural production and increased their dependence on finding seasonal wage labor. By 1974, two million hectares of rain-fed land, which had been cultivated in 1965, had been abandoned;[19] hence the crucial shortage in staple grain production in Mexican agriculture in the seventies. When one also recalls the decline of wage employment in rural areas in this period, it becomes clear how dependent the minifundio farmers became on migratory wage labor. The farmers relied increasingly on seasonal and temporary labor in the cities and in the expanding agricultural regions in the Northwest.

Male and female wage laborers represented 36.7 percent of the agricultural workforce in Mexico in 1950, 48.0 percent in 1960, and 54.0 percent in 1970.[20] Of landless agricultural workers, 58 percent live in the central-northern states of Puebla, Queretaro, San Luis Potosi, Tlaxcala, Morelos, Michoacan, Mexico, Jalisco, Hidalgo, Zacatecas, Guerrero, Guanajuato, and Oaxaca. These are the main regions of rain-fed agriculture. Many of these laborers work in the prosperous regions of irrigated agriculture in the Northwest. Several annual circuits have been established between these central areas and the Northwest, along which agricultural laborers migrate most of the year, returning to their home base only a few weeks or months a year. Others have resettled in regions where work is available all year long. In Zamora, Michoacan, for example, the strawberry export agribusiness has brought in 50,000 agricultural laborers, women and men, who settled there in the seventies.

At the same time that labor was being released from agriculture—as small farmers needed more wage labor to perform and large farms began to mechanize—the rate at which employment was being created in industrial centers began to fall. In Mexico City it decreased from 4.9 percent for men and 5.0 percent for women in the fifties, to 3.2 percent and 3.3 percent in the sixties.[21] Many reasons account for the decline in the number of jobs being created in manufacturing industry in Mexico, including restricted markets, insufficient reinvestments, high costs of imported technology, repatriation of profits by multinationals, and capital-intensive forms of production.

Migrants thus increasingly entered the service sector, which was responsible for 30.1 percent of new jobs in the forties, 33.2 percent in the fifties, and 55.5 percent in the sixties.[22] But it has been the informal sector, that is, non-contractual, low-paid jobs usually in self-employment, that has overwhelmingly taken in the rural migrants since the sixties.[23]

In this section, some of the major indicators of the crisis of small landholdings in Mexico have been mentioned, but these give only a partial picture of rural outmigration. In the end, it is the way in which these major economic pressures are absorbed at the local level that contributes decisively to migration patterns. One must look at their *local effects* as well as at the community organization, the local political structure, and the division of labor within the peasant household. These are the conditions that most clearly explain the different types of migrants who have left and are leaving the Mexican countryside. Now we can ask, given these necessary conditions for migration, what have been the sufficient conditions that have selected certain groups and individuals for migration?

Social Structure in Rural Communities and Outmigration

The integration of peasant communities in Mexico into the national market economy in the last three decades has entailed a total reordering of economic and social relations; single factors alone cannot account for these changes, or for their consequences. This explains, as I hope will become clear in the analysis that follows, why correlation analysis of variables of village and municipal conditions and outmigration fails fully to explain migration.[24]

An example can help illustrate this problem. A cash-crop has been found in some cases to *deter* migration, as it both enables peasant families to obtain much-needed cash locally and stabilizes seasonal fluctuations of employ-ment.[25] The more dynamic commercial flow that is produced may bring to the villages some of the goods and amenities that make cities so attractive. On the other hand, a cash-crop may *encourage* migration, when its introduction has the consequence of centralizing land and capital. This displaces small land-holders and, by fostering capital intensification of cultivation, also makes agricultural laborers redundant. It can also force peasant households to send out migrants in order to get cash needed to plant and harvest the commercial crop.

This example emphasizes the extent to which the social and political structure of a town or community will soften or sharpen the negative aspects of integration into the market economy. Thus, a uniformly structured abstract "rural community" cannot be assumed.

Another example of this kind is road building. One of the more notable achievements of the Mexican government has been the building of hundreds of kilometers of paved and gravel roads that have opened the way for a dynamic exchange of migrants and commodities to even the most remote villages. Clearly, a new road will create new migrants or ease the discomforts of traveling for old migrants, but this in itself need not be negative. That is, it is necessary to assess the optimal point at which a "healthy" outmigration, which may ease pressures on community resources and move laborers to more productive jobs, turns into a damaging drain on the community, as the most able migrants as well as vital resources start leaving by the road. Such variation in the impact of road building has been reported by Cornelius for Mexico and by Connell and Dasgupta for India and other developing countries.[26]

Against this background, I will summarize the way in which greater integra-tion of peasant communities into the Mexican economy has influenced the rural exodus in the past three decades.

First, the peasant economy in Mexico is not as "traditional" as some may think. The agrarian reform in the thirties brought about a considerable reset-tling of the rural population, making it possible for communities to reconstitute a peasant economy based on self-subsistence production in households closely linked by reciprocity within the community. Two characteristics of the agrarian reform land distribution were to have important repercussions in later outmi-gration. The first was that in many *ejidos*, that is, the newly formed cluster of allocative lands, the claim to the usufruct of land was granted on a collective basis, with no individual allotment of land plots. The *ejidatarios* could cultivate as large a plot as they were able to care for, provided enough land was available. Since at that time most of them had little agricultural machinery, it happened that those with larger households, especially with a larger number of sons, had an advantage over others in being able to cultivate more land. Thus, "human capital," even in this initial period, was far more reliable in the eyes of the farmers than "economic capital," which was extremely scarce in any case.

In highly populated areas, the average allotment of land granted in the ejido was sometimes less than the 6.5 hectares considered a minifundio, that is, a plot of land that does not allow an average farming household to make its livelihood from it. In Santiago Toxi, a community in the state of Mexico, the ejidatarios started out with 2.5 hectares of land in 1929; by the seventies, most of the ejido plots, and even the private plots of land, were hardly one hectare on average.[27] Many young men wanted to stay in the village and continue to farm, but as the twenty-year-old son of Pascual de la Luz put it: "I do want to work on the land, yes, but tell me, what am I going to do with a few furrows?"

Second, in the land distribution programs no provision was made for the natural population increase of ejidatario households, as Cornelius has also pointed out. In fact, sons of ejidatarios frequently do not have legal title to their ejido lands, making it extremely difficult for them to set up guarantees for agricultural credit and allowing all sorts of irregularities in the reassignment of land.

Population growth in Mexico has been translated directly into fragmentation of lands (as happened in France, in contrast to England and parts of Germany), due to partible inheritance, the principle drawn up in the Mexican Constitution directly from the Napoleonic Code. In theory, all offspring, including women, have a right to inherit patrimonial land. In fact, women rarely inherit land since they are expected to marry a husband who will provide land and, indeed, they were legally barred from holding ejido rights to land until 1975. Daughters usually receive a few belongings, animals, or some money as inheritance. But all male offspring do have a right to land. The fragmentation of ejido lands has already gone through at least two and, in most places, even three or four generations. In Huecorio, Michoacan, the average size of land-holdings had shrunk from 5.2 hectares in 1960 to 2.8 hectares by 1976.[28]

Yet population growth by itself explains neither the crisis of agriculture nor the high rate of rural outmigration. Proof of this is that the amount of arable land per capita in Mexico has not changed since the 1930s.[29] As Connell and his coauthors note for several developing countries, the crude man: land ratio "tells us nothing about the productivity of the soil, the cultivation and, importantly, its distribution among the resident population."[30]

As noted in the previous section, the concentration of land has continued in Mexico, and the rain-fed farming sector has suffered acutely from demographic pressure on land. Even so, some communities with high population pressure, such as Santiago Toxi, were able to maintain a viable economy based on rain-fed agriculture *because they had other options that allowed them to diversify the household economy.*

In communities with land scarcity, such as Toxi, the search for alternative sources of income began as early as the forties. Many households could still rely on old-time sources of income: petty trade, crafts, and cottage industries. Some communities in fact depended primarily on such activities. In many regions, villages had specialized in certain crafts which they traded with other villages through weekly markets. Such intricate traditional systems of exchange were highly developed, for example, in the Patzcuaro region of the state of Michoacan. Similar systems have been amply described in the states of Puebla, Oaxaca, Tlaxcala, Hidalgo, Queretaro, and most other central and southern states.

In other regions "traditional" cash-crops for the internal as well as international market still provided a steady inflow of cash. *Ixtle* fibers made from agave and used for rope-making were a mainstay in the states of Hidalgo, San Luis Potosi, Guanajuato, and others. The hard, fibrous root of the *zacaton* plant had been exported abroad since last century in regions of the states of Mexico, Michoacan, Oaxaca, and Jalisco.

Crafts had ample demand since they provided the bulk of clothing, housewares, agricultural tools, furniture, horse and oxen apparel, cargo equipment, containers, and toys. So did the cottage industries of brewing, cooking, tanning, weaving, and others. The great advantage of such activities, as well as of petty trade, was their adaptability to the seasonal needs of labor by distributing the various activities among the household members by sex and age.

Local sources of wage labor were also available in agriculture during planting and harvesting seasons and in government projects, such as road and dam building programs that were developed in the forties and fifties.

Labor migration was one option among many. Up until the end of the fifties it was mainly seasonal (father and/or sons working in construction work in the cities, or in cash-cropping areas) and temporary (sons and daughters working in the city, males mainly as market porters, handymen, and servants and females as resident servants). Another possibility in regions where recruitment centers had been set up was, of course, migration to the United States through the bracero program.

All these labor options meant that the larger the household, the higher its income, as household members combined agricultural and other activities. Again, it shows that their "human capital" was clearly an asset. The lowering of the mortality rate, especially infant mortality, enhanced the possibility of survival and accumulation of resources for these households.

If peasant communities were contributing mostly seasonal and temporary migrants, who were the migrants taking up permanent jobs in the cities? It is interesting that during the forties and fifties they were mostly young people with schooling from regional cities and rural towns. They were the first to feel the full force of attraction of the industrial cities.[31] Part of the reason for their leaving was that the highly centralized pattern of industrial development in Mexico had a stagnating effect on provincial cities and towns. Employment in rural areas was expanding very slowly in nonagricultural jobs, although standards for schooling and social mobility were rising. Thus, young people with secondary or preparatory school education were keen to go to Mexico City where they could live the modern life. There were, of course, a few permanent migrants who did come from peasant communities during this "pioneer" stage of migration, mostly on an individual basis, out of ambition or adventurous impulse or because of conflicts back home.[32]

During the fifties, as the move to incorporate the peasant sector into the internal market gathered strength, irreversible economic changes began to occur in small rural communities. Previously, the exchange of goods and services within the communities had ensured that any surplus produced would remain within the region. Other socially prescribed mechanisms helped ensure that the surplus of individual households was roughly redistributed among the households of the community. The most important redistributive mechanism was the *cargo* system, whereby the wealthier members of the community were expected to serve the collective social and religious life of the community by spending on fiestas and ceremonies.

Kinship and residential arrangements also allowed this redistribution. Any household or family group in economic distress could be bailed out for some time or could simply be reattached or its members redistributed among the more prosperous households. Uxorilocal marriage (where the groom lives with the bride's parents), compound families, and ritual kinship could also achieve this end.

The crucial point here for understanding outmigration is that maintenance of a high degree of interdependence and leveling off of wealth inequalities within the community lessen the economic risks for any given household, thus inhibiting the bankruptcy and landlessness of farming families. This is not to say that inequalities did not exist in such communities. Of course they did, and political power was unevenly distributed due to the *cacicazgos*, but in a self-subsistence economy such social pressures did inhibit the creation of extremes of wealth and poverty.

When these social mechanisms of redistribution are altered and ultimately destroyed, a process begins within the community, leading toward increased social and economic inequality, including landlessness, all of which sets the stage for outmigration. This happens, in my view, not so much as a result of the modernization of agriculture—or, I would add, the modernization of social values—but from the monetization of the economy, as Young has argued for a community in Oaxaca.

The ripple effect of monetization can be most clearly understood in villages where a cash-crop at some point suddenly offers vast amounts of cash. A case in point is the cultivation of coffee, which increased its price 22-fold from 1938 to 1954.[33] In one community in the Sierra of Puebla, Zacatipan, the sudden boom in coffee brought about the fragmentation of patrimonial estates owned by several kin-related households, as young sons could now become economically independent of the parental household. They could obtain cash immediately, whereas before, with maize cultivation, agricultural inputs and reciprocal labor could be obtained only by belonging to the kin-based labor groups. As a result, the young neo-local households became entirely dependent on the income of coffee sales, and with the fall of the price of coffee were at greater risk of having to sell or lose their land and to migrate.[34]

The same process was analyzed by Young in Copa Bitoo, in the state of Oaxaca. Young reports that wage labor became prevalent during the peak of the coffee boom. When coffee prices in the international market fell in the mid-fifties, households were unable to revive the traditional *manovuelta* system of labor exchange; they had to revert to unpaid family labor, since they could no longer pay for laborers. But by then many households had had to send sons and daughters outside the community to sell their labor. This seasonal and permanent outmigration further eroded the system of exchange of labor within the community. A large majority of households then had to decrease the amount of maize cultivated to conform with the labor they could rely on within the household.[35]

Changes flowing from the monetization of the rural economy were often slower than in these examples but were pervasive in all rural areas in Mexico. The increase in cash needed to pay the production costs of maize was the most crucial development. By 1973 in Santiago Toxi 80 percent of the production costs of maize had to be paid for in cash, compared to 30 percent a decade earlier. Kin-based labor and plough-sharing groups disappeared, as did the exchange of seed among kin-related groups. Now, because of soil erosion from constant cultivation, fertilizer was indispensable and expensive. Now a plough and oxen had to be rented, as well as mules for other cultivation tasks.

Meanwhile, income from the sale of maize and other agricultural products bought less and less on the market. The farmers perceived that their growing deficit hinged on the price of maize. "Everything goes up (in price), but not maize. Why do you think that is?" asked Raul Martinez. Another farmer quickly summarized the whole situation: "It is not viable to plant maize anymore because the prices of everything have gone up. Take fertilizer, one year it costs 600 pesos, the next 700 pesos. Meantime, the price of maize had not gone up for fifteen or twenty years. That's why people don't want to plant anymore and they'd rather go to Mexico City to work."[36]

During this same period local cottage and crafts industries greatly declined. Manufactured products poured into rural areas; some were more durable than their local counterparts, for example, tin pots instead of pottery; or cheaper, such as factory-woven blankets; or had greater prestige, such as plastic flowers compared to handwoven decorations. Bottled beer swept away locally brewed beverages such as *pulque*, a formerly very popular alcoholic drink which lost 80 percent of its price value, while junk foods and soft drinks replaced women's sales of tortilla savories, *quelites* (edible plants), and quick-fried foods. Tule raincapes were replaced by plastic sheets, leather sandals by plastic shoes, reed mats by mattresses, ixtle and sisal ropes by synthetic fiber ropes, zacaton brushes by those made also with synthetic fibers—the list can go on and on, region by region. Importantly, the old cash-crops mentioned—zacaton, sisal, ixtle, candelilla and others—were no longer in demand in the internal or the international market. Also important, the major income-generating activities of women—weaving, sewing, pottery-making, the sale of food and gathered products, petty trade, etc.—all declined, thus lowering poorer households' income and making it almost impossible for women in female-headed households, or on their own, to make a living in these communities.

The critical economic imbalance created in these communities is made even more evident by the fact that at the same time they were losing traditional sources of cash, their cash needs were soaring. New services had to be purchased: electricity, potable water, transport. And the "modernizing" attitude spread by the urban-educated teachers and the mass media, aggressively and with contempt for the rural way of life, has fostered the consumption of urban prestige goods: fashionable clothes, sumptuous consoles, record players, and so on.

As the national culture became more geared toward the urban, industrial setting, which acquired prestige as the more "modern" way of life, many young men and women came to see agriculture and life in rural towns and villages as an "uncivilized" and certainly unsophisticated existence. As one wealthy farmer put it: "(Young people) don't want to work here anymore. The boys come along with wristwatches and bracelets. Agriculture is dead, there aren't any laborers. . . . You can't find a puny little maid anymore. The girls who go to school get full of ideas." It is not only a question of "ideas," however, but also of a direct contrast of the rewards—social and economic—offered by rural and urban work. An example is a young migrant's view of working on the zacaton root: "Pulling the root out of the zacaton is very hard work. You have to get up at 6 a.m. and keep loosening the plants with the stake. Then you have to take off all the lumps of soil. You get covered with dust, you suffer a lot to get it out."

In the city, one rural migrant explained, "life is much better. There you can go to the movies and you don't have to kill yourself to make a living. Here, in the countryside, you don't have the security of a salary, because in cultivating maize, many times you end up losing, since you don't get back what you put in, in costs of fertilizer, oxen, and the laborers you have to pay. That's why many from the village go there (Mexico City) with their women and sometimes even take their children. Over there, the woman and the man can work, and the money is certain." This is how rural men and women have perceived the changes around them inherent in the policies described in the previous section and the way they have reacted to them. It shows that for all their "traditionalism," rural people will not endure a hopeless, exploitative situation for long. But other factors made it extremely difficult for people in the communities to improve the situation locally.

Once the amassing of goods became the main source of prestige—and of political power—the wealthy in communities began a pattern of conspicuous consumption. But access to credit and to business concessions runs through political channels. The political and the economic elite thus reinforced each other by drawing a closer circle of overlapping power and wealth, while the subordination of the judicial system to the political class gave no standpoint from which to check abuse. Thus was consolidated a rural ruling class which centralized agricultural, financial, commercial, and political capital. Against this formidable clique, neither the small landholders, the ejidatarios, nor the agricultural laborers have any political leverage.

Significantly, this rural ruling class also has a high incidence of sons and daughters migrating for a better education or to live in more fashionable surroundings. The same phenomenon has been reported in other developing countries.

In the conditions described, households become increasingly reluctant to fulfill community ritual and social obligations. The maxim of *"que cada quien se rasque con sus propias uñas"* ("let everyone scratch with his/her own fingernails") is quickly becoming the pervasive value for social behavior. As a consequence, the services and goods provided by people in the community for social rituals are no longer in demand. Gone are the dancers, the musicians, the costume-makers, the prayer women, the chapel decorators, the makers of ritual ornaments. Gone is the free eating and drinking for the poorer members of the village.

In sum, work opportunities in the villages were stripped to the barest bones. Local wage labor provided neither expanded opportunities nor adequate amounts of cash. In Huecorio, Michoacan, the day wage in agriculture was 6 or 7 pesos (U.S. 48¢ or 56¢) in 1962; by 1976, that is, fourteen years later, when agricultural revenues in rain-fed farms had plunged and cash needs had gone to the stratosphere, the daily wage in agriculture had soared to 8 pesos (U.S. 64¢) a day![37]

But the discrepancy with urban wages and salaries had the greatest effect on migration, particularly in regions within a 500-kilometer radius of the cities. In regions outlying Mexico City (states of Hidalgo, Tlaxcala, Puebla, Morelos, Mexico, and Queretaro) the official minimum salary was 18 to 21 pesos (U.S. $1.44 to $1.68) per day in 1972; the wage actually paid in these areas was 8 to 10 pesos (U.S. 64¢ to 80¢) for women and 10 to 15 pesos (U.S. 80¢ to $1.20) for men. Meanwhile, the minimum wage in Mexico City—only two hours away by bus—was 41 pesos (U.S. $3.28); a construction worker could easily make 25 pesos (U.S. $2) a day and a street vendor at least 20 pesos (U.S. $1.60) a day.[38]

Needless to say, the discrepancy with wages across the border has been even more blatant. In 1976 Cornelius reported that local agricultural wages in Jalisco were 25 to 30 pesos (U.S. $2.00 to $2.80) per day and their equivalent in the United States, $2.50 to $3.00 an hour. In U.S. factories wages were as high as U.S. $4.00 and $5.00 an hour.[39]

The differential between agricultural income levels and wage levels in urban areas and in the United States, in my view, was the crucial pull factor that accelerated outmigration and determined the farming households' strategy. As their deficit in maize cultivation grew, minifundio households turned to a multiplication and diversification of wage earnings. Since circumstances did not allow economic investments in a dwindling agricultural enterprise, households directed their meager surplus to investment in "human capital."

This does not mean that parents consciously try to have more children. It means only that they have encountered no reasons to limit their fertility now that more children survive. Indeed, to the contrary, they have found that more children enhance the household's chances of surviving as an agricultural enterprise.

Table 6.1 shows the internal labor composition of households in a sample of 150 households in the villages of Toxi and Dotejiare.[40] In Toxi, local sources of income have disappeared, and land plots are so small that they provide work for only one full-time agricultural worker. As can be seen in the table, at least a third of the household workers are in migratory wage labor all along the developmental cycle of the household. Many unpaid domestic laborers in Toxi, all of them women, also work locally in nonresident, paid, domestic service.

The contrast with Dotejiare is very marked: there, land plots are slightly larger, and two local sources of cash still bring money periodically into the households. These are the brewing and selling of pulque and the sale of the

Table 6.1   Percentage of Workers in Households, According to Type of Work Performed and to the Stages of the Domestic Cycle, in Two Mexican Rural Villages

Domestic cycle[a] (mother's age)		Agri-culture	Unpaid domestic work	Local wage labor	Migratory wage labor
18–25	Toxi	0	42	25	33
	Dotejiare	50	45	5	0
26–30	Toxi	7	47	3	43
	Dotejiare	51	38	4	7
31–38	Toxi	18	39	8	35
	Dotejiare	61	34	0	5
39–44	Toxi	27	30	9	34
	Dotejiare	61	26	0	13
45–50	Toxi	22	30	7	41
	Dotejiare	43	32	6	18
50 and older	Toxi	35	19	10	35
	Dotejiare	54	32	4	10

[a] Insufficient information on four cases (2.8 percent) in each village. Data was estimated by dividing the total number of household workers by the number of household workers in specific types of work, for each household, which was then averaged among the households in each stage of the domestic cycle.

root of the zacaton bush, a communal cash-crop. Consequently, migratory wage labor does not occupy more than one-fifth of the workers in the household at any time during the domestic cycle.

The vital role of migration for the survival of Toxi households and the pattern of what I have called *relay migration* become even clearer in Table 6.2.

There is no clear pattern of outmigration in Dotejiare. In Toxi, on the contrary, it follows a stepwise progression of the first son/daughter at each particular developmental stage taking up migratory wage labor, substituting for the father or the elder siblings as they separate from the household. Remittances from migrants are used primarily to buy fertilizer and to pay for tractor or plough rental, and also for food.

This pattern of relay migration may apply only for some regions, but it helps explain why the bulk of seasonal and temporary migrants are either small landholders or sons and daughters of such households. It also warns against the danger of pointing at the "population explosion" as the culprit of rural outmigration, when, in fact, this may very well be a major life-line for impoverished farmers.

Table 6.2   Percentage of Household Members Who Migrate, According to the Stages of the Domestic Cycle

Domestic cycle[a] (mother's age)		Father	First son/ daughter[b]	Second son/ daughter	Third son/ daughter	Others[c]
18–25	Toxi	84	—	—	—	16
	Dotejiare	—	—	—	—	—
26–30	Toxi	100	—	—	—	—
	Dotejiare	—	80	—	—	20
31–38	Toxi	66	29	5	—	—
	Dotejiare	33	33	33	—	—
39–44	Toxi	9	43	43	5	—
	Dotejiare	—	84	16	—	—
45–50	Toxi	8	55	21	11	5
	Dotejiare	—	70	—	10	20
50 and older	Toxi	4	61	23	12	—
	Dotejiare	17	50	17	16	—

[a] Insufficient information on four cases (2.8 percent) in each village.
[b] This refers to *resident* offspring age order.
[c] Includes father's brothers, adopted offspring, sons- and daughters-in-law, and nephews and nieces.

The Rural Exodus and the Selectivity of U.S.–bound Migrants

Data from the surveys conducted on Mexican migration to the United States, set against the background of the rural exodus analyzed in the previous pages, clearly show that those migrating across the border are specific types of migrants.[41] In other words, just as migrants are not a random sample of rural inhabitants in Mexico, so U.S.–bound Mexican migrants are not a random sample of people leaving the Mexican countryside.

Several community studies in Mexico have shown that many of the poorest, landless people generally tend to stay on in rural areas or to migrate to other rural destinations within Mexico. In Oaxaca, Young did find that the poorest migrated, first expelling children, then as whole households, but practically all went only as far as Mexico City or Oaxaca City. Dinerman, from fieldwork in Michoacan, explains it in this way: "The landless, those without the resources to build and maintain wide social networks linking them to other households, those who are not prominent in community affairs and thus lack economic allies, do not sponsor migrants."[42] My own research in the states of Puebla, Mexico, and Michoacan supports this conclusion. The same deterrents seem to apply even more strongly for migrants going to the United States. As Cornelius points out, those at the bottom cannot afford to pay the travel fare or the cost of the "coyote" to get across to the United States.[43]

It does seem to be the case that the landless migrate more from villages that have established routes and communities in the United States, as Cornelius reports in his study in Jalisco. This could mean that the village already provides the social networks whose absence, in Dinerman's view, otherwise deters migration of the landless.

Few migrants from middle- and upper-income groups leave Mexico, because they seek social and economic mobility and most already have favorable kinship or social contacts in the cities. For different reasons, widowed, divorced, or unmarried women also tend to settle in Mexican cities, unless the village migratory network makes it possible for them to travel across the border. Elderly people leaving the villages go to live with the offspring who have attained the highest standard of living, usually in Mexican cities; few venture to the United States because of the barriers to their crossing and their preference for their more familiar surroundings.

Who are the U.S.–bound migrants, then, and why do they leave? The motive most frequently expressed for migrating to the United States is higher wages. The importance of the effect of wage differentials has been established. On the basis of a longitudinal analysis of Mexican migration to the United States, Jenkins concludes that "it is fluctuations in wage differentials, created largely by changes in Mexican wages, that shape migration (to the United States)."[44] This is in line with Todaro's model of migration where "migrants are induced to move even though there is a high probability of unemployment, as long as the product of the wage and the probability of employment exceeds the rural wage by a sufficient margin to offset the cost of moving."[45] This seems indeed to be borne out in the case of rural outmigration in Mexico. It may even happen, as data from recent fieldwork in Zamora, a booming industrial town in Michoacan, have shown, that young men to whom factory employment is available still prefer to migrate to temporary jobs in the United States.

This does not mean that the flow of Mexican migrants to the United States is made up primarily of workers who choose between two wage packages. Jenkins adds that "overall changes in agricultural productivity and capital investment, not labor conditions, have the major impact on both illegal and bracero migration."[46] Significantly, he found that the official bracero program enlisted more wage laborers while undocumented migration takes in more landholders. The *CENIET* study also showed a majority of landholders among migrants to the United States, bearing out Bustamante's observation that farmworkers have been progressively decreasing among such migrants.[47]

Thus, the evidence strongly indicates that *the bulk of Mexican migrants to the United States comes from the crisis of small-landholding, rain-fed agriculture—the minifundios, both private and belonging to ejidos—*that has been described in this chapter.

Why should farmers be more interested than landless laborers in seeking temporary employment in the United States? Some reasons are, probably, that the security of a land base makes these small-holder migrants more willing to risk—and lose—several years of uncertain and seasonal work in the United States, while laborers (male and female) need to find more stable conditions for making a living and, therefore, might prefer Mexican cities and other rural areas. Also, laborers living on a day-to-day basis find it more difficult to scrape together the money needed to travel and to cross the border. Finally, it is very probable that the social networks and information channels necessary for successful migration to the United States can be maintained in a stable way only by land-based migrants.

But although Mexico's agricultural crisis makes available migrants for the U.S. job market, not all of those needing jobs or better prospects end up in the United States. To understand why we must look at the selectivity of these migrants. Among migrants of small-landholding families we find, then, (a) the father who has no one else to substitute for him in migrating; his is a seasonal or temporary migration and rarely does he remain in the United States permanently; (b) eldest sons who are sending back remittances and who are expected to fend for themselves in the world since they will not be inheriting land; they go temporarily, but tend to stay if conditions allow them to and if they like it; (c) younger sons who will be sending remittances, but who will be certain to inherit some land; they most probably return unless they find very good fortune in the United States; (d) daughters who are also to send remittances, but who go only if they can travel with the father, a brother, or other close related kin; and (e) collateral members that the farming household can no longer afford to employ or to keep; these relatives (e.g., nephews, nieces, cousins) are especially prone to migrate.

Conclusions

The intensity with which rural outmigration has occurred in Mexico in the last three decades has resulted from the simultaneous effects of, on the one hand, the demand for labor in the expanding industrial and commercial centers in Mexico and in U.S. agriculture and low-grade urban employment, and on the other, the gradual undermining of the Mexican rural economy based on small-holding rain-fed agriculture. Population growth in rural areas in Mexico, far from being at the root of the problem, is itself the result of the desperate need in poor households for wage earners. Because opportunities for wage labor are not available in rural areas in the numbers needed, many household members have to become migrants.

The economic mechanisms behind the exodus—the monetization of the rural economy, the fluctuations and decline of agricultural prices, the destruction of rural industries and occupations—are not unlike those that expelled millions of European migrants overseas, during the mid-nineteenth and early twentieth centuries. Massive rural outmigration, then, is not a new phenomenon in Western industrial capitalism and is by no means an unfamiliar one for the United States.

But the speed at which rural migration has occurred since the fifties in Mexico, as well as in many developing countries, has been undoubtedly influenced by development policies that encouraged industrialization and urbanization at the expense of agriculture. Many believe that the present rural crisis in these countries can be traced back to the uncritical acceptance of such policies on the part of national governments and international finance institutions.

In the Mexican case, it is clear that the break-up of small-landholding agriculture created the conditions for massive rural outmigration. Specific actions, such as the holding down of the price of maize between 1957 and 1973, only accelerated a process of economic change that was implacably under way. This is not to imply that this process is irreversible or that it cannot be modified. Already, some changes are in view, notably massive government programs in support of rain-fed agriculture, as Schumacher shows in Chapter 5. The rate of population growth has also begun to decline; this will not solve the crisis but will help alleviate some of its symptoms. Other specific changes are also taking place. For example, Warman reports that some farming households in the state of Morelos are reverting back to the extended family arrangement because they have been able to intensify their agricultural production in vegetables. Another example is the new demand for handicrafts among the urban middle-class, which is enabling rural artisans to make a living once again.

Even given the release of agricultural labor, though, migration will occur only if strong factors of attraction arise elsewhere, and these determine the rate of outmigration and the destination of migrants. From the forties to the mid-sixties, growing employment in irrigated agriculture and in the urban industrial and service sectors in Mexico incorporated several million rural migrants. Since the beginning of the sixties, though, the modern sector has been unable to offer employment at the rate required, in the same way as Western European early industries were unable to retain all rural migrants, who were thus forced to migrate overseas. It is important to stress, then, that in the Mexican case the fact that new industries and new agricultural enterprises tend not to be labor-intensive has directly affected migratory flows. In other words, given the availability of migrants in rural communities, the conditions in the place of destination, such as a potential job or family and village networks, determine who will go where.

It is not surprising, therefore, that migration to the United States, both official and undocumented, attracts only certain kinds of migrants. Compared to the general outflow of rural migrants, the group going to the United States contains a lower proportion of the poor and landless, fewer women, fewer elderly people, and fewer young men and women from middle- and higher-income rural households. The bulk of migrants to the United States are adult men attached in some way to small-landholding units. And, which is important, not all of them are unemployed, which means that the pull factors override the push factors in encouraging part of the Mexican migration to the United States.

Thus, since the United States is not receiving all the potential migrants let loose by the rural decline in small-holding farming areas, there is reason to conclude that it is not bearing the brunt of the rural crisis in Mexico. Rather, U.S. employers are benefiting from the crisis by reaping the best gains for their labor market. The case for this is strengthened by noting that these able-bodied, enterprising migrants have been fed, clothed, and educated by the already weakened Mexican rural communities. While it is clear that, for the time being, the Mexican economy, both rural and urban, is unable to accommodate all rural migrants productively, it goes without saying that it is unacceptable that Mexican rural households should become the providers of nursery, social security, and unemployment services for workers in U.S. jobs—workers who can be sent back in periods of economic recession, overburdening an already burdened Mexican rural economy.

Therefore, if it can be ensured that Mexican migrants do not damage the position of U.S. workers, the movement of migrants between Mexico and the United States can constitute a partnership that benefits both sides. But this means that a policy scheme must be sought that gives proper acknowledgment to both partners' needs and benefits.

As to future trends, looking into the crystal ball—with the evidence and figures close by—it would seem that the pattern and rate of this migratory flow will not vary greatly in the years to come. It will not decrease as long as there is demand for such migrant labor in the United States, a fact quite independent of conditions in rural areas in Mexico. It will not intensify if the Mexican government is successful in helping small-holding agriculture, as it has pledged to do through multiple rural development programs. Nevertheless, the massive pouring of financial resources into such communities will take many years to rebuild community social and economic organization in a way that will begin to have an effect on outmigration. It is clear that what is needed is not only an economic policy, but a comprehensive social policy toward rural agricultural areas.

Under a broader, long-term perspective, it becomes clear that Mexican migration to the United States, involving the lives of thousands of men and women seeking better opportunities, is only part of a more complex relationship between the two countries. The way this relationship evolves overall will set the conditions for solving mutual problems in the future on the basis of reciprocal cooperation.

Notes

1. This is the estimate reported by Brinley Thomas, *International Migration and Economic Development* (Paris: UNESCO, 1966).

2. Ibid., p. 10.

3. Quoted in Thomas, *International Migration*, p. 11.

4. See Douglas Butterworth, "Migración Rural-Urbana en América Latina: El Estado de Nuestro Conocimento," in *América Indígena* 21, no. 1 (June 1971): 52–85; and Lourdes Arizpe, *Migración, Etnicismo y Cambio Economico* (Mexico: El Colegio de Mexico, 1978), pp. 188–214.

5. See Chapter 3, this volume, by Manuel García y Griego and the chapter by Jorge Bustamante in *The Border That Joins*, vol. 2, forthcoming.

6. Leopold Solis, "Hacia un Analisis General a Largo Plazo del Desarrollo Economico de México," in *Economía y Demografía* 1, no. 1 (April–June 1967): 57. For more recent trends, see his "Cambios Recientes en la Economía Mexicana," in *Investigación Económica* 30, no. 17 (1970): 23–70.

7. The import-substitution policy advocated that developing countries begin their industrialization by producing commodities which they previously imported from abroad.

8. Banco Nacional de Comercio Exterior, *Facts, Figures, Trends. Mexico 1976* (Mexico: BNCA, 1976), pp. 146–48.

9. Ibid. In Chapter 5, this volume, August Schumacher gives other related figures on government programs toward agriculture, so they need not be discussed here.

10. Enrique Suarez Contreras, "Migración Interna y Oportunidades de Empleo en la Ciudad de Mexico," in *Perfil de Mexico en 1980* (Mexico: Instituto de Investigaciones Sociales, Universidad Nacional Autonoma de Mexico, 1972), p. 393.

11. Luis Gomez Oliver, "Crisis Agricola, Crisis de los Campesinos," *Comercio Exterior* 28, no. 6 (June 1978): 718.

12. Ibid.

13. See also Sergio Reyes Osorio et al., *Estructura Agraria' y Desarrollo Agricola en Mexico* (Mexico: Fondo de Cultura Economica, 1974).

14. Susan George, *How the Other Half Dies* (Montclair, N.J.: Allanheld, Osmun & Co., 1977).

15. Cynthia Hewitt de Alcántara, *La Modernización de la Agricultura Mexicana*, Siglo 21 (Mexico, 1979).

16. Reyes Osorio, *Estructura Agraria'*, p. 220.

17. Gomez Oliver, *Crisis Agricola*, p. 727.

18. Arturo Warman, "Politica Agraria o Politica Agricola," in *Comercio Exterior* 28, no. 6 (June 1978): 681–87.

19. Ibid.

20. Luisa Pare, *El Proletariado Agricola de Mexico*, Siglo 21 (Mexico, 1977).

21. Suarez Contreras, "Migración Interna," p. 393.

22. Ibid., p. 408.

23. Lourdes Arizpe, *Indígenas en la Ciudad: El Caso de las 'Mariaso' Sep-Setentas* (Mexico, 1975) and Larissa Lomnitz, *Como Sobreviven los Marginados*, Siglo 21 (Mexico, 1978).

24. Joseph P. Stoltman and John Ball, "Migration and the Local Economic Factor in Rural Mexico," in *Human Organisation* 30, no. 1: 47–56.

25. This, for example, was the case of San Francisco Dotejiare, a community that still derives income from the traditional crop of the zacaton root, reported in Arizpe, *Migración*.

26. Wayne Cornelius, "Outmigration from Rural Mexican Communities," in *The Dynamics of International Migration*, vol. 2, no. 5, Occasional Monograph Series, Smithsonian Institution, p. 23. This variation was reported by John Connell and others after an extensive review of village studies on migration. John Connell, Biplab Dasgupta, et al., *Migration from Rural Areas: The Evidence from Village Studies* (Delhi: Oxford University Press, 1976). The same has been reported for many regions in Africa. See for example, Audrey I. Richards, ed., *Economic Development and Tribal Change* (Cambridge: W. Hefter & Sons, 1954) and the more recent Helen I. Safa and Brian M. Du Toit, *Migration and Development* (The Hague: Mouton Publishers, 1976).

27. Arizpe, *Migración*, p. 98.

28. Ina Dinerman, "Patterns of Adaptation Among Households of U.S.-Bound Migrants from Michoacan, Mexico," in *International Migration Review* 12, no. 4: 491.

29. Craig Jenkins, "Push-Pull in Recent Mexican Migration to the U.S.," in *International Migration Review* 11, no. 2: 186. He quotes Rodolfo Stavenhagen and others' extensive work on Mexican agriculture at the Centro de Investigaciones Agrarias during the sixties.

30. Connell, Dasgupta, et al., *Migration from Rural Areas*, p. 8.

31. Humberto Muñoz, Orlandina Oliveira, and Claudio Stern, *Migracion y Desigualdad Social* (Mexico: El Colegio de Mexico, 1978).

32. Jorge Balan, Harvey Browning, and Elizabeth Jelin, *Men in a Developing Society* (Austin: University of Texas at Austin, 1973); Robert Kemper, *Migration and Adaptation* (Beverly Hills: Sage Publications, 1977).

33. Reported in K. Young, "The Creation of a Relative Surplus Population: A Case Study from Mexico," in *From Dawn to Dusk*, edited by L. Beneria, International Labour Office, forthcoming.

34. Lourdes Arizpe, *Parentesco y Economia en una Sociedad Nahua* (Mexico: Instituto Nacional Indigenista, 1972).

35. Young, *The Creation of a Relative Surplus Population*, pp. 24–25.

36. Arizpe, *Migración*, p. 110.

37. Dinerman, "Patterns of Adaptation," p. 491.

38. Arizpe, *Indigenas en la Ciudad*.

39. Cornelius, "Outmigration from Rural Mexican Communities," p. 23.

40. Lourdes Arizpe, "Relay Migration and the Survival of the Peasant Household" in *Why People Move: Internal Migration and Development*, edited by Jorge Balan (Paris: UNESCO, forthcoming).

41. I base this analysis on data from Wayne Cornelius and Ina Dinerman's fieldwork, as well as on the following surveys: the CENIET survey; and those reported in Jorge Bustamante, "Undocumented Migration from Mexico: A Research Report," in *International Migration Review* II, no. 2: 149–78, and in Francisco Alba, "Mexico's International Migration as a Manifestation of Its Development Pattern," in *International Migration Review* 12, no. 4: 502–13.

42. Dinerman, "Patterns of Adaption," p. 498.

43. Cornelius, "Outmigration from Rural Mexican Communities."

44. Jenkins, "Push-Pull," p. 184.

45. Todaro's model is useful in explaining why migrants leave, but he is open to criticism for not incorporating into his model the informal or traditional urban sector that takes in a majority of migrants in many cities in developing countries. Michael P. Todaro, *Internal Migration in Developing Countries* (Geneva: ILO, 1976).

46. Jenkins, "Push-Pull," p. 184.

47. See chapters by Jorge Bustamante and Carlos H. Zazueta in *The Border That Joins*, vol. 2, forthcoming.

PART IV

Conflicting Solutions

7

Immigration Problems, Limited-Visa Programs, and Other Options

EDWIN P. REUBENS

Introduction

International migration flows ramify through the entire economic and social structure of the countries involved. This is evident whether we look at a causal model of migration in terms of push/pull forces, or at a consequences model of the impacts and feedbacks of migration with all their benefits and costs. Equally, migration challenges some of our deepest values, since it concerns personal welfare and satisfaction, human rights, individual and collective responsibilities, and the privileges of citizenship, the sovereignty of the state, equality and cooperation among states, and other standards by which we organize our lives and approve or disapprove of particular activities.

This chapter focuses on limited-term movements, i.e., temporary foreign workers (TFW). These are treated as one stream in the whole flow of migration that includes temporary and permanent, legal and illegal, economically active and nonworking persons, etc. TFWs, as both a stream and a stock, are of widely differing importance in various countries at present, but are of growing importance in relation to the needs for foreign workers and the problems of absorbing them in the host economy and society. In some views, TFWs offer the most promising postive-sum solution to those needs and problems.

In this essay, a first section summarizes the dimensions of immigration, both legal and illegal, into the United States in recent years, from all countries and particularly from Mexico. The second section reviews the forces underlying and sustaining the emigration of Mexicans and their inflows into the US. A third section indicates the major impacts—benefits and costs—of migration, primarily as regards the U.S. labor force and social system, but also taking account of the source countries as well as the migrating individuals and their families. The fourth section outlines the range of alternative approaches for dealing with the migration: among them the direct restriction of aliens, the development of native substitutes for aliens, enlargement of immigrant quotas, and a new TFW program. Section five sketches U.S. experience with TFW programs, specifically the "H-2 visa" operation. Section six proposes a revised and enlarged treatment of H-2 visas as a new LVFW (limited visa foreign workers) program; this is intended to maximize the benefits and minimize the costs of alien inflows, taking account of the lessons of the bracero program of 1942–1964, as well as the lessons of guestworkers in Western Europe during the past two decades. Finally, section seven assesses the advantages and disadvantages of this LVFW program in comparison with alternative lines of action—whether by administrative rules or by new legislation—and in the context of alleged rights and duties on the individual, national, and international levels.

Background

MAGNITUDES OF ALIEN WORKERS IN THE UNITED STATES

Basic to all discussions of the significance of immigration is the always vexing question of the numbers, or more exactly the relative magnitude, of the stocks and flows of alien workers. Enumerations are needed for all three of the main categories of aliens: the ordinary legal immigrants, approximately 400,000 entries annually during the 1970s, but averaging 460,000 annually during 1978–1981, plus refugees averaging approximately 230,000 annually over 1979–1981; the temporary workers, who enter legally for limited periods, approximately 100,000 entries annually; and the illegal aliens, the undocumented workers who enter surreptitiously or overstay their authorized entry, in the hundreds of thousands every year. The data are firm only for the gross inflows of the first two categories, however; little is known about the return flows of legal entrants, and much less is known about the gross entries and the return flows of illegals. The available data must therefore be supplemented by estimates applying plausible ratios on evasions and duplications, return flows, labor-force participation, representativeness of small samples, and other features.

The existing estimates vary widely and frequently fail to reconcile the net inflow figures (i.e., the annual gross inflow of any group less their current return flow) with the stock accumulation figures (i.e., the sum of the net inflows of the group over any selected span of years, plus their natural increase/decrease), inasmuch as the net accumulation must equal the change in their census-reported stock between the initial year and the final year of the selected span. During recent years some spokesmen for affected American social groups have tended to magnify the numbers and alleged dangers of immigration; but defenders of immigrants have tended to minimize both the accumulated stock and the current net inflows of migrants. At the extremes, the present population of illegal aliens (workers and nonworkers together) in this country has been estimated at anywhere from less than 2 million to 8 or even 12 million persons.

My own estimates—using reasonable middle-of-the-road ratios and focused on the number of workers within the whole alien population—make use of an explicit interrelation of the flow and stock data for recent years, centering on 1979. The net inflow figure combines 180,000 workers from reported legal immigration, plus 100,000 workers from the reported current special refugee admissions, plus 100,000 reported temporary workers (for a one-year stay, on average), plus an estimated 600,000 illegal workers (full-year-equivalent workers staying on here); the total comes to nearly 1 million for 1979.[1]

My stock figure on foreign workers in 1979 is calculated mostly by net accumulations (gross inflows less returns and nonlabor-participation) over the preceding eight years (1972–1979, inclusive). This yields 1.44 million reported legal immigrants, .12 million reported refugees, .10 million temporary workers (averaging a one-year stay, or an annually revolving stock), and 3.84 million stay-on illegal-alien workers (eight years of an annual average of .48 million). The total comes to 5.5 million as of the end of 1979.[2]

Relating these aggregate numbers to the corresponding American magnitudes, we find that the recently accumulated stock of alien workers amounts to not quite 6 percent of our whole labor force (or about 7 percent of all employees in the United States). Nevertheless, this small proportion is often ignored in favor of a more dramatic, but more misleading, comparison focused on our numbers of unemployed. When our measured average unemployment is estimated at 6 million persons, it is almost equaled by the stock of alien workers here. Furthermore, if our unemployment figure is written down by about 3 million for voluntary idleness and unavoidable "labor float" in our mobile society, so that the estimated real shortfall of jobs is about 3 million, then the alien stock appears to be about double our shortfall. In addition, the involuntary unemployment indicated here is concentrated among particularly vulnerable groups in our society, notably teenagers, the aged, housewives newly entering or reentering the labor force, and ethnic and social minorities. Regionally, such unemployment is concentrated in the older cities in the Northeast, as shown in U.S. Labor Department reports.[3] In contrast, the bulk of the illegal alien population is believed to be concentrated in the Southwest, plus the New York area, the Miami area, and a few other northern and eastern cities. In fact, all such comparisons must be strongly qualified as to real availabilities of the various types and locations of workers—as will be discussed in more detail below.

In another aggregate comparison using the flow data, the net inflow of alien workers, estimated at 1 million per year, adds only 1 percent to our labor force annually. But if the comparison is made at the margin, against the annual growth of 2 million in our reported labor force, the net alien inflow shows up as half of that measured increment. Here again, the real issue is the types and locations of the allegedly competing groups.

The Mexican share of the current net inflow of alien workers is about one-half of the total, or some 500,000 workers annually.[4] If the Mexican share is also one-half of the recently accumulated total of alien workers, namely 5.5 million, then their number comes to some 2.75 million workers here (legals and illegals together).

The credibility of these estimates for the Mexican portion of the alien stock and flows in the United States might be questioned on the basis of labor-force data, with the specific argument that any estimate of several million Mexican workers resident in the US must be out of line with the estimate of 5 million economically active persons in the eight Mexican states which provide 80 percent of the migrants. Unfortunately, this argument confuses a stock with a flow. The 2.75 million Mexican workers, as given in my estimate, is a stock which was accumulated by annual migrations and natural increase over some eight years, net of returns during those years. The only relevant comparison is to set my annual net flow figure against the Mexican regional labor-force stock from which it is drawn each year. My net flow estimate is currently 500,000 Mexican workers per year; this becomes 400,000 to represent just those coming from the eight states of 80-percent-concentrated origin; and this 400,000 per year shows up as merely 8 percent of 5 million economically active persons in those states. Few observers would consider this 8 percent annual net emigration to be in any way incredible.

The 1979 CENIET study of Mexico's population and migration, by means of a household survey in Mexico during December 1977–January 1978, claimed that the total stock of Mexican workers in the United States but who are "habitually domiciled in Mexico" is 405,467. A very different statement is given by Alfred Stepan in an article citing CENIET figures for the Mexican worker stock in the United States at less than 1.8 million.[5] Even this figure seems low, and may be attributable to the methodology used by CENIET: their surveys were all done inside Mexico; they made very low assumptions regarding the ratio of voluntary returns to actual expulsions by the INS; their household survey simply asked persons whose families are "committed to residence in Mexico" to give information on other persons who might be in the US; the household survey was conducted in the December–January period when many expatriated Mexicans were visiting their relatives for the holidays. In an analysis of existing studies of illegal migrations, done for the Select Commission on Immigration and Refugee Policy by specialists of the U.S. Census Bureau,[6] the CENIET procedures were severely criticized, ending in a contrast between the CENIET household survey's estimate of 400,000 and the somewhat larger numbers of Mexican workers who registered in 1977 as legitimate permanent residents of the U.S., and concluding that perhaps "the Mexican survey succeeded in counting only those Mexican nationals who were legal residents of the United States." If that comment is correct, the CENIET figures missed all the illegals! CENIET also states that the Mexicans' stay in the US is seldom longer than a year; if so, CENIET figures represent only one year's migration and implicitly deny an accumulated stock of Mexicans illegally resident in the US.

The above-mentioned Census Bureau specialists, after reviewing CENIET and other direct surveys of the illegals, as well as several studies that used analytic or indirect methods, declare that all of them "depend on broad untested assumptions and are subject to other major limitations." Nevertheless, they "offer the following cautious speculations":

> The total number of illegal residents in the United States for some recent year, such as 1978, is almost certainly below 6.0 million, and may be substantially less, possibly only 3.5 to 5.0 million. . . . The Mexican component of the illegally resident population is almost certainly less than 3.0 million, and may be substantially less, possibly only 1.5 to 2.5 million.[7]

It may be noted that the estimates of illegal workers in the United States from Mexico and from all countries, as developed in the present essay, fall well within the upper limits suggested by the Census Bureau specialists (after applying reasonable rates of labor-force participation by these groups).

CAUSES OF MEXICAN INFLOWS INTO THE UNITED STATES

Mexican entries into the United States nowadays are, according to our estimates, preponderantly unauthorized persons. Legitimate immigrant entries total about 58,000 a year (taking the quota and nonquota immigrants together), resulting in a net inflow of about 33,000 Mexican workers per year. Mexican entries on temporary work visas (mostly H-1, H-2, and exchange visitors) are in negligible numbers. The large magnitudes are the illegals. All proposals to deal with the problem of Mexican inflows into the US must confront these breakdowns of the migration, the sources thereof, and the underlying pressures of push and pull on the two sides of the border.

The Mexican inflows first attained massive numbers under the authorized *bracero* program, which operated in varying forms from 1942 to 1964 under joint governmental sponsorship by Mexico and the United States. This program brought Mexican farm workers into this country, initially to cope with the labor shortages of the World War II era, in numbers that eventually exceeded 400,000 a year during the bracero peak period of the late 1950s. The number of illegal entrants at that time was evidently quite low, as they were presumably supplanted by the legal temporary-worker braceros. When the bracero program declined and was terminated in the mid-1960s, the illegal inflow soared, which suggests that illegals were replacing the former braceros. The crude but trend-significant measure of INS apprehensions (not adjusted for duplications, evasions, return flows, labor-force participation, etc., but notably about 90 percent surreptitious border-crossers) rose from less than 90,000 a year during 1963 and 1964 to approximately 300,000 a year in 1969 and 1970, and then to nearly one million a year in the late 1970s. In the course of these years, the employment of these entrants diversified from primarily agricultural work to a predominance of nonfarm occupations.

The principal source of emigration from Mexico, as from most other sending countries, is the condition of surplus labor—i.e., the large portion of the labor force which remains idle, or if employed earns less than the "subsistence wage," after all actual absorption into jobs or emigration.[8] It is widely recognized in Mexico that as much as half of the labor force is either overtly unemployed (having no means of earning) or severely underemployed (in part-time or full-time work with earnings near or below local "subsistence" levels). To reduce that surplus, let alone eliminate it, is an enormous task, since it amounts to some 9 million workers and is deeply rooted in Mexico's economic and social structure.

On the labor supply side, the natural increase of population has been running at 3.5 percent a year. At this high rate, the population doubles every twenty years. It already totals more than 65 million, and thus will reach 130 million before the end of the century. The labor participation rate of the whole population has actually been quite low—about 30 to 32 percent. It is likely to rise as women expand their economic roles, which have been very limited to date.

It seems obvious that a program of birth control is needed to limit this flood of people. In 1973, the Mexican government finally introduced a moderate form of family planning, over much religious and social opposition; this program was subsequently strengthened and extended to rural areas, and recently the government claimed a notable drop in the population growth rate to below 3 percent. But of course, no reduction in births now can diminish the numbers who will be entering the labor force over the next fifteen years or so. (On the contrary, a decline in births may quickly increase the number of women seeking jobs.)

On the labor demand side, what is the capacity of the Mexican economy to absorb the actual labor force? Like other less-developed countries, Mexico suffers from a low basic economic level and capital shortages. But the situation is much worsened by underlying structural and operational features: economic dualism, in which expanding modern sectors exist side by side with lagging traditional sectors; high capital intensity in the modern sectors; the industrial policy of promoting domestic products as substitutes for imports behind protective tariffs and quotas; and the resulting severely skewed distribution of the national income in favor of the upper brackets of the industrial sectors.

The secular problem has been exacerbated by special adverse developments abroad during the 1980s: soaring oil import prices; fluctuating grain import prices; shrinking export markets due to the worldwide recession-cum-infla-tion; and finally, the foreign exchange crisis of 1976, which led to the sharp devaluation of the peso and loans from the International Monetary Fund under stipulated conditions of austerity, which further depressed the Mexican econ-omy by restricting credit, reducing deficit spending, curtailing luxury imports, and like constraints.

The deficiency of labor absorption in Mexico is not to be blamed on aggregate growth, since the gross domestic product (GDP) increased at a rate of 7 percent a year during the 1960s (although more slowly under the special external adversities of the 1970s). A 7-percent rate is among the world's highest growth rates for developing countries and can hardly be accelerated more. Likewise, domestic saving has been high, and capital formation has taken place at about 20 percent of the GDP. Transformation of the economy has proceeded vigor-ously along lines of industrialization and urbanization.

But Mexico has the same problem as other comparable developing countries: a concentration on fields and technologies in the modernizing sectors that use relatively little labor. Investment outlays per new job created in modern industry are found to range (in 1970 dollar prices) up to $25,000 or more in a number of fields, and to average about $15,000 per new job for all modern industries (equivalent to $30,000 in 1980 prices). Meanwhile, small and traditional labor-intensive firms are starved for funds. Even in the agricultural sector (where nearly half the population still lives and works) there is a vast disparity between the irrigated, fertilized, capital-enriched, high-productivity domains, and the traditional agriculture of the smallholders and the *ejidos* (communal holdings) to which the celebrated Green Revolution has not extended. The annual labor-force increments of 700,000 or more are not fully absorbed into satisfactory jobs. Consequently, surplus workers are accumulating in the hinterlands of agriculture, industry, and services, where they can find only part-time work or bare-subsistence earnings.

It is therefore no wonder that millions of Mexicans are migrating from the countryside to the already overcrowded cities; many then move on from the cities, or directly from the rural areas, to try to cross into the United States over a thinly guarded 2,000-mile-long border. Here they see opportunities for jobs at least no worse and usually better than those they vainly seek at home; at pay rates up to seven or eight times Mexican rates; and with amenities hitherto unattainable. Nor are they deterred by reports that these great improvements for them will often be below prevailing American standards.

Absorption of labor within Mexico has been aided in recent years by the *maquiladora* program, which serves as a kind of halfway house linking industrialization and trade in locations mostly just south of the Mexico–U.S. border. This program permits the duty-free shipment of industrial component parts, mostly from the United States, into Mexico for processing and assembly there at relatively low costs of wages, fuel, and other inputs. If the resulting products are reexported to the US, duty is paid only on the (relatively low) value added in Mexico; while if the products are sold into the Mexican economy, duty is paid to Mexico only on the value of the U.S.–made components. This program has proved attractive to a number of U.S. companies seeking to reduce manufacturing costs, and the percentage rate of growth of maquiladora plants has been rapid since 1977. Yet as of early 1980, only about 500 such plants were in operation, most were small (averaging some 220 workers per plant), and their total employment was 110,000 workers. Even if this employment figure were to double in the next few years, it would provide little help to Mexico's underemployed millions.[9]

The big new factor affecting possible labor absorption is the recent Mexican oil discoveries and the prospect of large export revenues, which are now planned by Mexican officials at about $15 billion a year (in present prices) for the next few years. Nonetheless, the costs of exploration, extraction, and development by Pemex (the national oil corporation) will take up at least one-third of that gross revenue, and some 40 percent will be allocated by the government to the social sector, local governments, and other current expenditures. This leaves only about one-fourth, or $3.75 billion, for job-creating investment, according to the parameters in the government's Global Plan for 1980–1981. Moreover, the funds would not be easily converted into millions of actual new jobs because of obstacles in the mobilization of resources, in deficient infrastructure, in weak management, in the availability of markets, in inflationary pressures, in the hostility of vested interests, and in prevalent national priorities. Indeed, the New National Industrial Development Plan, issued in March 1979, mostly resists various labor-intensive suggestions, and instead continues and even intensifies the emphasis on "heavy" and "basic" industries, especially petrochemicals and capital goods. In such fields, with a capital cost of about $37,000 per new job, only 100,000 posts will be created each year: this is a small absorption of labor.

As for the agricultural sector, estimates by August Schumacher (see Tables 5.5 and 5.6) show that even a large agricultural and rural investment (as much as 25 percent of the Mexican government's total investment budget) would probably generate annually only 177,000 permanent jobs, although providing 800,000–1,625,000 temporary jobs in constructing the permanent facilities. Thus there would be very meager permanent absorption of the underemployed labor that has accumulated in the countryside and now numbers over 4 million males of working age.

In fact, we find that illegal entries (measured simply by a time-series of the "apprehensions" of all kinds by the INS, unadjusted) are in a strongly rising trend ever since the early 1960s. Furthermore, this rising trend has persisted through the most rapid period of Mexico's growth (see Figure 7.1 for two different measures of Mexican emigration to the United States, compared to Mexico's industrial activity). To be sure, emigration accelerated somewhat when Mexico's industrial growth slowed in the early 1970s; and emigration dipped in 1975 with the U.S. recession, but rose to a new peak in 1976 and 1977 when Mexico's GDP growth slowed down to a mere 2 percent a year and industrial output actually dropped. Evidently even *rapid growth*, if it is of the *capital-intensive* kind, is not sufficient in Mexico to reduce the workers' drive to seek better opportunities across the border, although *slower* growth may indeed step up the emigration.

ALIEN WORKERS IN THE UNITED STATES: CONTRIBUTIONS AND BURDENS

The impact of alien workers in this country is found in two distinct though interrelated aspects: their labor market functions and their sociocultural role. The former aspect, which is mostly a matter of the real "needs" for foreign workers, will be discussed first.

Aliens in the U.S. labor market. The U.S. labor market is not homogeneous or perfectly competitive, but instead shows considerable segmentation. Even in the face of considerable unemployment, vacancies exist for workers with special skills in upper-bracket occupations, and for manual workers in low-level occupations. At the same time, an influx of foreign workers presents problems of absorption and adjustment.

The relative magnitudes of alien workers seem to support a widespread

Figure 7.1

Gross Migration and Economic Growth, Mexico 1960-1976

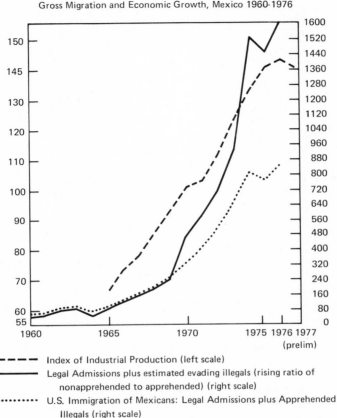

- - - - Index of Industrial Production (left scale)

——— Legal Admissions plus estimated evading illegals (rising ratio of
nonapprehended to apprehended) (right scale)

•••••••• U.S. Immigration of Mexicans: Legal Admissions plus Apprehended
Illegals (right scale)

Sources: United Nations, *Yearbook of Industrial Statistics*; and U.S.
Immigration and Naturalization Service, *Reports*, annual.

belief that there must be severe competition, particularly over entry-level jobs, between Americans and aliens trying to enter and stay in the workforce. Yet it does not automatically follow that the jobs filled by aliens would be appropriate and attractive to our unemployed, let alone our employed, workers. In fact, a breakdown of the alien workforce by industry, occupation, region, type of firm, and regularity of employment, indicates a limited area of competition with Americans. To a marked degree, the aliens are found in "noncompeting groups."

The occupational list ranges from high-level PTK ("Professional, technical, and kindred" workers, in the usage of the Census Bureau), through medium-level and semiskilled work in agriculture, manufacturing, and services, down to the unskilled, hard, unpleasant jobs with low productivity, low pay, and no future. Low-level jobs are found to persist even in advanced economies—either in distinct industries (e.g., fruit growing, food preparation, rubber manufacturing, sanitation, domestic service) or in low-level occupations supporting higher-level functions (e.g., sewing in garment manufacturing, cleaning in restaurants and hospitals). The demand for this kind of labor arises and persists in part from stages in the technology of production, in part from the patterns of consumer demand (especially the continuing shift to services of all kinds), and in part from competitive relations among the firms (most of the low-level work is done in small, intensely competitive firms with narrow profit-margins, little capacity to absorb cost-increases or to pass them along to consumers, limited access to investment capital, and heavy pressure from foreign producers).

Aliens are found working at virtually all levels of skill, but the great majority are in the lowest levels. The high-level aliens are mostly professional and technical personnel; they present few problems because their entry is mostly legal and is largely governed by the INS occupational preference systems for immigrants and distinguished visitors, supplemented by persons who are admitted on family, refugee, and other grounds.

Most of the legal and illegal aliens have no skills other than peasant farming and simple crafts. They are accustomed to heavy labor, eager for jobs, hardworking, reliable, and docile. In the now-celebrated phrase of Labor Secretary Marshall, "They work scared and hard." Farming was once the main U.S. field for these immigrants, but they are now predominantly in urban jobs.

In relation to the jobs held by most *employed* American workers, there is certainly no attraction in the aliens' jobs in most cases. To be sure, most of the low-level jobs are still filled by Americans—who are switching out of them as fast as they can. Less obvious is the question of the interest and availability of our *unemployed* workers and of persons not now in the labor force. Their availability depends on their skills, attitudes, and "reservation prices" (wage stipulations); and the latter in turn depend upon their alternatives to work—which may include unemployment compensation, family welfare support and food stamps, support by relatives and friends and charitable agencies, earnings by hustling, and by criminal activities not counted as "work." It is noteworthy that these factors, which tend toward unwillingness to accept low-level jobs, have been operative since long before the 1970s, when the large inflow of aliens first raised a really troublesome issue of job competition. These factors are conveniently ignored by some writers on immigration, who play up measured unemployment without attention to types, locations, and preferences of the workers.

In interviews reported in the press, and supplemented with first-hand investigations by the present writer, many employers claim that American workers simply are not available for the low-level jobs, or that they are not as efficient, reliable, or teachable as aliens, especially for intermittent and laborious work. In New York City, businessmen in garment manufacturing, laundries, restaurants, and other fields have flatly stated that if it were not for the illegals, they would have to close up, thereby disemploying their American personnel as well as the foreigners. Businessmen and their attorneys in Miami, Houston, and Los Angeles have made similar statements. The native labor supply for sewing operations, cleaning work, unskilled heavy labor, and similar jobs is shrinking, particularly as young Americans decline to enter these occupations. Shortages of American workers in agriculture, for hand-harvesting and other laborious work, are more prominent than ever, as native migrant workers and part-time farm help are shrinking in numbers and some crops are left to rot. When orchards recruit workers from the West Indies under the H-2 program, an official of the New York State Department of Agriculture recently declared, "It's a fact of life that New Yorkers don't want to pick apples!" Similarly, we see a shortage of household help, even when wages have increased to $5 an hour in metropolitan areas. Higher up on the occupational scale, many big-city hospitals declare they cannot function without their (mostly legal) alien doctors and nurses, and their legal and illegal alien orderlies and cleaners.

These are the labor market realities that Professor Briggs wants to deny by his assertion that "it is precisely because of the presence of sizable numbers of illegal immigrants that citizen workers are more difficult to recruit."[10] In actual fact, the recent trends in garment manufacturing, housework, restaurants, nursing homes, even fruit and vegetable harvesting show that American workers have been withdrawing from these occupations for their own reasons, independent of the illegals and long before the latter came to take their places. To be sure, some increase of wages in the low-level occupations, up to say $25,000 a year, might well put them all into the status of sanitation workers in New York City, where occasional job vacancies for collecting garbage do evoke lively response from local citizens. One wonders about the orientation of Professor Briggs and others who are implicitly calling for unlimited wage increases, entirely detached from productivity. Are they ready to give the U.S. inflationary spiral another big twist? And to force our cities finally over the edge of bankruptcy? Or to accept corresponding reductions in their own real incomes? No doubt some redistribution of income among our income classes is highly desirable, but there are severe limits in terms of economic, fiscal, and incentive relationships.

Looking at the labor market in a larger perspective, a projection by Harold Wool and Bruce Phillips concerning trends in domestic labor supply and demand in 1985, by occupation and assuming full employment, indicates "potential surpluses of workers for higher-level occupations and potential shortages for lower-level occupations." Subsequent studies confirm that projection.[11] Thus, aside from possible severe recessions, there seems to be a definite prospective need for aliens willing to fill the vacancies.

Taking a regional view, we see that currently in the South and Southwest, the so-called Sunbelt, lower-level employment is expanding vigorously. These are the very regions where the huge inflows of illegal aliens are concentrated. Many immigrants stop first in the border towns, then spread throughout the Southwest and into other areas; separate concentrations are found in Miami and in the New York metropolitan area. The big, stagnant pools of American unemployment are in the inner cities of the Northeast, where the number of low-level manual jobs has receded and is hard to restore. If the unemployed of the Snowbelt were more mobile—whether on their own or with governmental assistance—they might then compete effectively with the aliens in the Sunbelt, and some parts of the labor market there might indeed become flooded. As it is, the unemployed in the Snowbelt cities remain alongside the aliens, but they do not compete vigorously for the same jobs.

Do aliens take jobs away by accepting lower wages and worse working conditions than Americans would, and thereby undercut American labor standards? This is seldom the case for high-level professional and technical personnel, although it may be a factor for younger professionals. It is probably also rare for middle-level alien workers employed in large plants, shops, and other enterprises alongside American workers, and subject to prevailing conditions and uniform pay schedules (although some cases of wage discrimination have been reported). A mistaken impression that aliens are underpaid may have arisen simply because they work in the lower ranks of various skilled occupations and accept correspondingly lower salaries.

Likewise, there is little undercutting by the foreign temporary workers who are recruited under the H-2 visa program jointly administered by the Immigration and Naturalization Service and the Labor Department. As described more fully below, these workers are brought in for limited terms (usually one year or less), mostly from the West Indies, and mostly for seasonal agricultural work (apple harvesting in the North, sugarcane cutting in Florida), although some others are recruited to do short-term work or to fill temporary vacancies in industrial and urban locations. Their admission is conditional on specific findings by the Labor Department that American workers are not available for those vacancies, and that the aliens will not have an "adverse effect" upon wages and working conditions here, and that their wages will be at or above the prevailing hourly wages for U.S. labor. At the end of their specified stay, virtually all are reported to return to their homelands.

The really controversial category is the illegals. There are many reports of economic exploitation and inhumane conditions imposed on illegal aliens, chiefly in firms where they are the majority of the workforce—certain farms, construction work, small factories, household service. Adequate evidence is lacking, but some sample studies indicate that illegals are paid on average only about 60 percent of prevailing wages, and about one-fourth of them are paid less than the minimum wage. Vernon Briggs, in Chapter 8, which is generally opposed to any foreign worker programs, concedes that "most illegal immigrants do receive at least the federal minimum wage and many receive much more."[12] The newly reported revival of "sweatshops"—especially in the garment industry—represents in part the industry's effort to cope with cheap imports made abroad with a combination of very low-wage labor and modern techniques and equipment. But in many cases, low wages in U.S. jobs probably reflect differentiation of tasks, with low pay regularly going to work of low value-product.

Many of these relationships may be clarified by applying the concept of "non-competing groups." Insofar as alien workers fill the low-level jobs that native workers despise and avoid, the former neither compete with nor displace the latter, nor undercut their wages and working conditions. Indeed, if natives withdraw from those occupations, aliens simply take their vacant places. This action will *not depress* labor conditions, although it may well *prevent improvements*. The effect does not benefit the natives remaining in those jobs, but it does help to fight against inflation in general. Furthermore, insofar as the alien workers are more hard-working than native workers, and more responsible, regular, and reliable, they tend to raise productivity, and therefore actually tend to reduce inflation and to promote exports.

To be sure, alien workers do compete to some extent with American workers in certain higher-level jobs and in some strong, expanding industries (e.g., electronics assembly work, or house-painting in growth areas). Such jobs and industries, however, can afford to pay at least minimum wages and meet standard working conditions; they frequently offer attractive pay and are susceptible to unionization; in short, good labor conditions can be obtained there. They are in contrast with the weak, unpleasant, low-productivity, internationally impacted firms and industries that cannot easily meet high labor standards, and accordingly do not attract American workers, and will cut down their U.S. operations unless they have access to low-wage alien workers.

There is probably more substance to the charge that the presence of alien workers tends to stave off unionization. Foreigners in a strange environment are often docile and grateful to be hired at all. The illegals in particular tend to be servile toward employers because they fear being denounced to the INS. This is not the stuff of militant unionism. Some labor unions, to be sure, now willingly enroll illegals in order to fill the ranks of dues-paying members, while also meeting the employers' needs. Dr. Wayne Cornelius has reported that in Texas only 3 percent of the undocumented aliens are unionized at present, but in California about 25 percent, and in Chicago some 50 percent. Unionization is particularly active in garment manufacturing and in vegetable crop harvesting. But other unions, especially in construction, are vehemently opposed to illegals and are in line with the top-level policy declarations of the AFL/CIO.

In Professor Briggs's view,

> The real cause for exploitation is that foreign workers can be expected to be docile workers. . . . The probability that foreign workers will be less likely to make demands for job rights or to join unions will make them highly prized. Thus, these will be the critical considerations that will provide, as they now do, the crucial advantages for employers in hiring illegal immigrants. [13]

Here Professor Briggs ignores all those features, of definite economic importance, which are valued by employers of foreign workers: regularity of work, diligence, teachability, cooperation, and job satisfaction. Likewise, Professor Briggs ignores the considerable recent success in unionizing foreign workers in several fields.

The severest opponents of immigration, however, claim that our own citizens can be trained for jobs now held by supposedly "noncompeting" aliens. They say that hostile American attitudes toward certain jobs can be overcome by giving those jobs higher status and providing better wages and working conditions: in part by technologic advance and in part by setting higher legal minima. Moreover, they say that upgrading of jobs is precluded now by the very presence of the aliens willing to work at a low level of wages and other conditions. According to this view, persistent vacancies can be filled by increasing the supply of qualified American personnel (e.g., if more doctors are trained, presumably some of them will be obliged to take the lower-rank posts and specialties and the less desirable locations; and similarly for training more sewing-machine operators and giving them higher pay). As for the tendency to exploit the fears of aliens in order to pay low wages, this can be eliminated, it is said, by an amnesty that would grant full civil rights to illegal workers already here.

Many such steps to transform existing conditions are conceivable, so the issue is what would be involved in practical terms. Most of the firms where jobs might be "Americanized" and taken from aliens are small in scale, intermittent or seasonal, labor-intensive, low in profitability, severely competitive, and subject to price-sensitive demand for their product or service. Such firms are among the least progressive in technologic research and development, but are driven by competition to adopt all the known, feasible, technical advances. If some of the suggested or mandatory steps listed above were taken, we could expect rising costs, higher consumer prices, reduced sales and production, increased mechanization and power-usage to replace workers, and more do-it-yourself household work (aided by new electrical appliances). We could also expect increased migration of firms from old central-city locations in the North and East to more remote areas in the South and West or to foreign locations, and the closing of some firms along with the rise of cheap imports. Most of these tendencies are undesirable in themselves and also reduce jobs, in this country generally or in some of its regions, for Americans as well as for aliens.

Over the long run, of course, the economy would adjust. But in the short run, there would be reduced employment, aggravated inflation, enlarged use of power, and intensified trade deficits, with the heaviest burden borne by the troubled cities and the most disadvantaged groups of citizens. Meanwhile, the jobs at the bottom of the scale in pay, quality, and prospects would be little more acceptable to Americans than before. They would largely remain for aliens.

Aliens in U.S. society. The social impact and adjustment of foreigners is comparable to the economic relationship in complexity and timing. Foreigners are almost always very different from the native groups they enter, and their reception ranges from curiosity and interest in the exotic, to suspicion, hostility, antagonism, and discrimination. The huge inflows of illegal aliens today, mainly from Mexico, Colombia, and the Dominican Republic, are Spanish in name and language, Hispanic in culture and values, largely Mexican in politics, and for the most part rural, even peasant, in their habits and lifestyles. Even the inflows of H-2s and illegals from the black populations of the Caribbean, although English-speaking and educated in the British tradition, often bring a tropical and village quality in their habits and life-styles. To be sure, some of the legal immigrants are in close accord with the WASP culture which they enter. But on the whole, the currently entering foreigners tend to be alien in appearance and behavior. Even when Hispanic foreigners settle among Hispanic-Americans, whether in the North or in the South, antagonisms and conflicts emerge.

The grounds for these antagonisms—aside from the competition for jobs already discussed—often consist in competition for social facilities and services. First is an alleged or fancied scramble for limited supplies of low-rent housing, community schools, hospital services, etc., in the localities where the foreigners tend to concentrate. A second ground for antagonism is the supposition that foreigners do not pay fully, or at all, for those social facilities and services. Now, it can be shown that some of these native beliefs are unwarranted extrapolations from some special cases to the whole category, while some other aspects are myths reflecting xenophobia rather than facts.

The class of immigrants admitted for permanent settlement, comprised largely of family members (about 60 percent are dependents), certainly does present some demand for apartments, schools, and hospitals. But these immigrants amount to only some 400,000 annually, spread widely across the country. In contrast, the temporaries and the illegals, who together greatly outnumber the immigrants, consist mostly of young, single adults without dependents (in considerable contrast to the European guestworkers). Accordingly they have little need for schools or hospitals, and their housing needs run usually to single- or multiple-occupancy rooms of minimal quality. Furthermore, since they usually find jobs, they are not candidates for welfare or other public assistance. In any case, the illegals are usually too fearful to seek such services.

At the same time, foreigners do pay considerable taxes. The legal immigrants are of course subject to the same tax system as U.S. citizens, particularly those in the same occupations, income brackets, and localities; and while immigrant families may use social facilities somewhat more than average American families, they probably do not exceed the per capita usage among the comparable segments of the U.S. population. As for the illegal aliens, they do pay expenditure taxes in the form of excise taxes, sales taxes, and property taxes (included in rents), although their expenditures are comparatively small because they live cheaply and save much of their income for remittance to their home country. Many of them, who are using bogus Social Security cards, also have income taxes withheld (although some tend to exaggerate their exemptions). They also pay Social Security taxes, which will be useless to many illegals who will be unable to apply for their benefits.

To be sure, unauthorized aliens do use some costly public services: for example, a Los Angeles county hospital has sued the INS in an effort to recover the cost of services rendered to persons alleged to be illegals. But a more representative picture of public services used and taxes paid by illegals is suggested by the sample responses in the Labor Department study by North and Houstoun, shown in Table 7.1.

Table 7.1   Percentages of Illegals Using Services and Paying Taxes

	Percentages of Respondents
Services obtained	
Hospitals or clinics	27.4
Unemployment insurance	3.9
Public schools	3.7
Job training programs	1.4
Food stamps	1.3
Welfare payments	0.5
Taxes and fees paid	
Social security taxes withheld	77.3
Federal income taxes withheld	73.2
Federal income tax returns filed	31.5
Hospitalization insurance withheld	44.0

Source: David S. North and Marion F. Houstoun, *The Characteristics and Role of Illegal Aliens in the U.S. Labor Market,* March 1976.

In short, removal of the illegals would not greatly reduce the total volume of public services rendered. Admittedly, still-larger tax revenues might be collected and smaller expenditures might be made for unemployment and welfare payments to citizens, if idle Americans could be induced to take over the jobs now held by aliens.

Another ground of antagonism to foreigners concerns population growth, ecology, and the environment. America has long been considered a sparsely populated land capable of absorbing huge amounts of immigrants, urbanization, deforestation, waste disposal, and other spatial factors; but nowadays we are worried about pollution, conservation, exhaustion of our resources, and other similar rising pressures as the population increases. While it can be argued that these concerns really relate to our technology and life-style, which can be changed, rather than to landspace and population, any rapid rate of population growth still seems a menace to many.

At first glance, the demographic impact of immigration seems strong. The gross inflow of legal permanent settlers, at the current rate of nearly 400,000 a year, amounts to one-fourth of our recent reported yearly population increase of about 1.6 million. Adding in the temporary workers and the much larger numbers of illegals gives a total gross inflow of 1.5 million a year, which is greater than our natural growth, the excess of births over deaths. Our special refugee programs currently are adding a little more than 200,000 a year. Furthermore, the legal aliens have a higher rate of natural increase than the American population generally and thus tend to raise our growth rate.

In reality, however, several adjustments are required. If about 20–25 percent of the annual gross inflows of legal immigrants are migratory return flows, and if that rate is applied to the gross inflow of 1.5 million, the new inflow comes down to 1.1 million. But if the illegals have a return rate of 40 percent, the whole foreign net inflow falls below 1 million. Either figure is a relatively small increment to our population of 220 million persons—an annual increase of about one-half of 1 percent. Moreover, the measured rate of population growth already includes many immigrants (although it is not known how many illegals were counted) and has already declined to less than 1 percent a year. As the measured domestic increase shrinks, the estimated foreign inflow will automatically seem large in comparison. But the sum of the domestic and foreign increments, after duplications are discounted, evidently amounts to about 1 percent annual population growth. Whether this overall measure is "large" or "small" depends on one's anticipations and values concerning labor supply, job competition, ecology, etc. It also depends on the degree that foreigners are concentrated in small areas and little communities, which may indeed need and deserve outside aid.

If immigration were allowed to rise without limit, however, the impact would undoubtedly be very serious. Most illegal immigrants come from Mexico, other parts of Latin America, and the Caribbean (which area has a total population of more than 200,000,000 and is rapidly growing and plagued with poverty and underemployment). Given an "open border," their inflow could become overwhelming, even without considering migration from the still vaster poor populations of Asia. The dilemma is whether our borders should be controlled against the potential of future inflows, in the face of assertions that "economic refugees" have a "natural right of migration."

At the same time, some consideration should be given to the plight of the immigrants in this country. Even the legal settlers will inevitably feel some regrets over their deracination, as well as difficulties in acculturation and other adjustments in their new land. Even worse is the situation of the illegals: despite high earnings, by their standards, and the ability to send relatively large remittances to their families back home, the illegals feel themselves isolated, threatened, preyed upon by the "coyotes" (Mexican organizers of border-running schemes), by American extortionists and robbers, by exploitative employers, and by the agents of the INS. With no recourse to the police and the courts, they are well-nigh universal victims. It is a measure of their urgent economic need for jobs and earnings that they willingly endure all kinds of social hardships and psychological stresses, accept disagreeable tasks, and still work in a regular, diligent, teachable, efficient way.

Conversely, the plight of the illegals underscores the importance of reforming their situation, particularly by converting them into legitimate foreign temporary workers, on TFW status.

Programs

POLICY ALTERNATIVES ON IMMIGRATION

From an economic perspective, the immigration problem involves the danger of a shortage or surplus of personnel (domestic plus foreign) relative to the demand or capacity of the domestic economy to absorb them. Our analysis has suggested that at present, while there is a measured aggregate surplus, it is not severe; and that vacancies persist in the low-level occupations and are likely to grow. Yet unlimited immigration—drawn from a vast pool of poverty beyond our borders—might be disastrous. To cope with such prospects, three main approaches are available: (a) direct restriction of aliens; (b) development of native workers to displace aliens; and (c) legitimation of unauthorized aliens at suitable rates of inflow, under either temporary or permanent visas.

a. The first of these approaches would tighten our traditional "restrictive" treatment. Special preferences for foreign professionals—for temporary or permanent stay—under the present immigration laws would be reduced or eliminated, and the general quotas under which most of them enter for settlement would be reduced. This approach would also return alien professionals to their homelands; prevent the adjustment of students and temporary workers to permanent-resident status; and encourage and assist foreign governments to keep their professional, technical, and kindred personnel at home (whether by cutting training programs, raising salaries and other benefits, or expanding job opportunities in these countries). But such a drastic exclusion of alien professionals would be harmful or expensive, or both, to the United States in the various fields where trained personnel are scarce, as well as painful to source countries with persistent surpluses of personnel.

Under this restrictive approach, all illegal aliens already here would be rounded up and deported; our borders would be tightly sealed against unauthorized entries; business firms would be forbidden to employ undocumented persons, and would be held responsible for screening them out. These procedures would be very difficult and expensive, and also a threat to human rights. Moreover, such a policy would ignore the contributions that many aliens make to our economy and to their homelands, and would assume that replacements for them could easily be obtained from our domestic labor force without adverse economic repercussions.

b. The second available policy would be the "import-substitution" approach, which relies more on the market than on simple exclusionary quotas. In order to phase out the dependence on foreign workers, professional training facilities in the United States would be expanded, as would the number of domestic graduates, whose distribution among specialties, regions, and clientele would be improved through careful controls.

The dangers of this approach are evident from the example of the medical profession. From 1955 to 1965, medical schools in the United States showed almost no growth. But during the next decade, they nearly doubled their annual graduations, and they are continuing to expand. In response, Congress concluded that there was no longer a "doctor shortage" and passed a new law in 1976 declaring that "there is no further need for affording preference to alien physicians and surgeons." Nonetheless, the latest reports[14] and my calculations indicate little if any surplus of physicians by 1990.[15] This in turn implies a continuing shortage at least until 1985.

In past years, foreign medical graduates (FMGs) alleviated the shortfalls in the total numbers of practicing doctors and in specific regions and specialties (especially in inner-city public hospitals and clinics, in old-age nursing homes, and even in pediatrics). Nowadays, few alien doctors are admitted, whether as Preference 3 immigrants, as H-1 temporary workers, or as exchange visitors. Meanwhile, medical fees have soared, far beyond most other elements in the cost of living index (at least until 1979, when new housing and transportation costs suddenly zoomed), although allowance must be made here for factors other than a shortage of doctors, particularly the cost-push force of large malpractice settlements and of insurance against them. Possibly the doctor shortage will be alleviated in the future by the new supplies of "physician's assistants" and "para-medicals." Another contribution will be made by the new practice of service assignments—by function and by location, for a few years—imposed on new medical graduates whose education received federal assistance. Nevertheless, the nation will probably need FMGs to fill in the remaining vacancies and to minimize cost increases, as became evident in the spring of 1980 when New York City officials were obliged to press for federal legislation to extend the "waivers" on new FMG admissions that were allowed until 1980 under the 1976 law to "avoid substantial disruption of health services."

As far as illegal aliens are concerned, an import-substitution approach would at least avoid the arbitrary and harsh features of sheer exclusion. The aim would be to improve the wages and working conditions of the jobs (mostly in the lower brackets of employment) now held by illegal aliens, in order to attract American workers and thereby discourage the aliens. But such an approach could easily backfire. Illegal aliens, eager to work, would probably be more strongly attracted than ever if job conditions were to improve. Moreover, since a substitution policy would tend to raise labor costs, it would probably have unacceptable economic repercussions on particular industries and firms, as well as on the aggregate economy.

Related to an import-substitution effort in the United States would be a developmental effort in Mexico and other source countries, in the hope of their absorbing redundant labor in their own economies. Actions might include technical as well as capital assistance and relaxation of our trade regulations for their products. Yet such development, while highly desirable for the long run, is likely to prove slow, expensive, and difficult to accommodate, for the reasons I outlined above. Certainly it would be too slow to alleviate our current immigration problems.

c. The third approach would involve "legitimizing" immigration and closely adjusting admissions to the changing needs of the domestic economy, over the business cycle and over eight- to ten-year trends. It would also take account of conditions in the source countries, where surplus labor is not likely to disappear for decades to come. Such a flexible adjustment system would provide more equitable and more realistic treatment than the other two approaches, but would also involve more complex regulation and administration.

One aspect of this approach would be to provide compensation to the source countries for all professional, technical, and kindred personnel authorized to emigrate here. The questions of how much compensation to pay (including a calculation of education costs and remittances sent home, as well as the alleged losses suffered by the countries of origin), and how to collect and transfer the payment, raise complicated issues. Some of these issues are examined in the symposium edited by Bhagwati and Partington, although most of the papers take a neo-classical approach and assume scarcity, overlooking the surpluses of unemployed or underemployed professionals who emigrate from most of the source countries.[16]

Under the legitimizing approach, unauthorized aliens already living here would be granted amnesty. Thus they would acquire parity with the authorized aliens and American citizens generally, in matters of wages and working conditions, job security, access to social services, and equal protection of the laws.

Looking to future flows, the legitimizing approach would be expressed in a new and expanded version of the temporary foreign worker (TFW) admissions on the H-2 visa, but might also take the form of enlarged immigration quotas (EIQ).

THE RECORD OF H-2 VISA ADMISSIONS

The admission of H-2s—temporary foreign workers, mostly other than high-level professionals—has recently become an urgent policy issue far beyond their small annual numbers, which are approximately 30,000 a year. For many years, this program has provided modest numbers of authorized foreign workers to fill job vacancies for temporary work here: mostly seasonal work in farming, in entertainment, and in various services, and mostly at a low level of skill and pay, but also including some short contracts at high levels.

There is a growing demand for such foreign workers, who are chiefly sought by farm operators in increasing numbers and in new fields and locations. This trend has evoked numerous protests against the program, from labor unions, farmworker associations, and community organizations, who allege that H-2s cause job competition, debasement of labor standards, and pressure on social facilities and services. At the same time, the growing public concern over the far larger inflows of "undocumented aliens" (UAs) has led to a proposed remedy in the form of a revised and greatly enlarged H-2 program that might preclude unauthorized entries (i.e., "dry up the wetbacks").

Thus the H-2 operation, which originated in a very small section of the economy, has become a "mouse that roars": it involves our entire policy on immigration and population; on labor markets, wages, unemployment, inflation, and our foreign relations with Mexico, Jamaica, other Caribbean nations, and other sources of entries into this country.

The Immigration and Nationality Act of 1952 authorized the U.S. Attorney General, acting through the Commissioner of the Immigration and Naturalization Service (INS), to admit nonimmigrant aliens to "perform temporary services or labor, if unemployed persons capable of performing such service or labor cannot be found in this country. (Sec. 101 (a) (H) (ii)). Admissions are subject to the requirement that "the employment of such aliens will not adversely affect the wages and working conditions of workers in the United States similarly employed" (8 CFR 214.2 (h) (3) (i)).

To implement this requirement, the Certification Division of the DOL sets "adverse effect" wage rates and working conditions, which must be offered to all the workers of the employer seeking H-2s, and which are designed to avoid depressing the labor market and to support progressive improvements for the workers. These stipulated wages and conditions include recruitment procedures, round-trip transportation for the recruits, free housing, fixed-price meals, free use of tools, and eligibility for workmen's compensation.

The recruitment procedures allow for group contracts of aliens and employers, and the participation of the aliens' government in screening the recruits and other arrangements (e.g., the withholding of part of their earnings for direct transmission to their families back home).

In determining the "adverse effect" wage rates, the DOL each year sets specific dollar-and-cents rates per hour for agricultural and logging jobs; all other H-2 jobs are required to conform to "prevailing wages" for each type and location of job, as determined by the regional administrator in each case. The specific rates for agriculture and logging in each state are computed by applying an average actual wage change to the rates stipulated by DOL for the previous year.

The current inflow of H-2s, as regulated by the INS with the collaboration of the DOL, comprises about 30,000 admissions a year. These are authorized for specified stays ranging from a few weeks to eleven months, and are renewable up to a maximum of three years. Virtually all the H-2s are reported to return home at the end of the specified stay. These are small numbers in comparison with some 400,000 annual admissions of permanent immigrants; they are even smaller compared to the undocumented alien group, whose gross inflow is roughly estimated at close to 1 million a year (although the net number remaining in this country each year is probably much smaller.)

Earnings of the H-2s are generally at or close to prevailing wage rates and are well above the national standards for minimum wages and poverty levels. H-2s are usually sought for seasonal work; occasionally for emergencies, special locations, or rare skills, but mostly for "secondary" or low-level jobs.

The chief focus of H-2 controversy in recent years has been the farmworkers. Such controversy occurs despite, and in part because of, intensive efforts by DOL to apply the regulations concerning the "adverse effect" on U.S. wages and working conditions. The apple growers and sugarcane growers contend that even with earnings at or above the adverse-effect levels, and with efforts to recruit American workers (including crews from Puerto Rico) as required by DOL, there are severe shortages of competent American workers to meet the harvesting needs. The labor supply appears to be restricted by unattractive features of the jobs in question, combined with the attitudes of American employed and unemployed workers and the real alternatives open to them. Conversely, the labor union argument claims that the level of wages and working conditions has been so depressed by the use of H-2s (or UAs, in some regions) as to repel most American workers of good quality, and to preclude upgrading the work.

The actual statistical record shows that wages have been rising for hired farmworkers as a whole during the period in question, with these wages rising somewhat faster than nonfarm wages and considerably faster than the cost-of-living index; but that they are today still about 30 percent below nonfarm earnings.[17] Meanwhile, farm employment has been progressively curtailed by labor-saving technological changes that raised the productivity and earnings of the reduced number of workers retained on the farms. Such long-term developments may eventually resolve the operating problems of farming and provide full employment to the U.S. labor force by absorption in nonfarming occupations. Nevertheless, the shorter-term outlook for the fruit and vegetable growers—if H-2s and other aliens were not available—is a painful dilemma: they would face either a physical shortage of workers needed for the harvest, or a huge rise in costs to attract more American workers or to reduce the need for them.

A NEW TFW PROGRAM

Can a TFW-type program be devised for urban as well as rural work that will both maximize the benefits (meet the "needs"), which we have noted in the case of present inflows of foreign workers, and minimize the damages ("absorption" process) likewise noted? We suggest that a program suitably modified and enlarged from the present H-2 visa practice, and accordingly called the LVFW program (limited visa foreign workers) might meet our requirements. The following paragraphs are largely a point-by-point response to the issues we raised in the earlier section on burdens and contributions of alien workers.

The suggested program would admit several hundred thousand foreign workers annually, on H-2–type visas, for limited periods (mostly for three years). These visas would be issued by State Department consular staff, or by INS agents, to individuals most of whom had previously been screened by their own governments. The visa would specify the authorized occupations and locations, by broad categories of occupation and by region of the United States. Holders of such a visa would be entitled to full civil status before the law, but not necessarily entitled to all public services. Dependents of the worker would not be authorized for admission; instead the visa would permit unlimited home visits by the worker, and arrangments might be made to facilitate those visits. The total number of visas to be issued each year might be put on a sliding scale; it could decline over the years, or otherwise be variable according to changing U.S. conditions (whether cyclical changes or structural alterations), and according to the possible future disappearance of surplus labor in the source countries. Under ordinary circumstances, the total number would be set below the present volume of illegal entries, but it must be large enough to replace most of the undocumented workers.

The LVFW program is intended to discourage and curtail illegal entries by diverting most of their jobs to authorized, legitimate foreign workers. It follows that a program limited to some 50,000 guestworkers a year—as proposed by the Reagan administration in fall 1981, to provide an "experiment"—would be neither necessary nor sufficient: the experimentation has already been done successfully in the form of the H-2 program, and a limited expansion of that program would fail to take over most of the jobs that now attract and reward illegal entrants and overstayers.

The U.S. interest. These features of an LVFW program are intended to serve specific U.S. goals.

1. The program assures a supply of efficient labor for low-level, low-paying jobs. Accordingly, it promises most of the desired economic consequences of such labor (preserves threatened U.S. firms and the jobs of American workers in such firms and industries, provides goods and services in desired types and locations, holds down costs, and thereby restrains inflation and imports, etc.). Furthermore, the possibly declining scale of admissions—whether overall or in particular occupations—provides for gradual expansion of American employment or gradual upgrading of the work, as well as gradually increased pressure on Mexico and other source countries to improve their absorption of their own labor. This variability also provides a bargaining point in the negotiations with Mexico and the other countries.

2. Having the candidates screened by the source-country government—as is done at present by the government of Jamaica for H-2 workers—enlists the interest and responsibility of the home government and elevates the caliber and preparation of the workers, thereby holding down costs to the U.S. employers and official agencies. Conversely, to minimize corruption of officials, along labor boss lines, some openings for temporary admissions should be provided outside of official screening.

3. The three-year revolving term extends the opportunities to a wider range of Mexicans than at present, when only the more agile, risk-taking person slips across the border, or the more prosperous pays a "coyote" to help him across, or the better-dressed and more cultivated can enter on a visitor's permit which he then overstays. The three-year term makes it worthwhile for a labor union to undertake organizing such workers. It also makes it more feasible for civil rights organizations to come to the aid of mistreated individuals.

4. The specification of certain occupations and regions open to the LVFW is intended as a middle way between restriction to a particular employer (which proved to be the basis for harsh exploitation of these workers in the old bracero days) and unrestricted internal movement and choice of occupation (which is the practice with guestworkers in Europe but has led to local job conflicts, charges of debasing labor standards, and actual predominance of aliens in certain occupations that become tagged as "fit only for aliens"). In our scheme, the LVFW could change employer at will and could move from one to another of the *specified* occupations, and could travel freely *within a broad region* of the country.

5. The collection of income taxes would surely be more widespread and

more uniform among LVFWs than among illegal aliens at present. Social Security taxes, however, need not be imposed upon the LVFW worker, since his stay is specifically limited and he will therefore never draw the benefits; but the employer might be required to pay at the usual rate into the Social Security and Unemployment Insurance funds, chiefly to equalize labor costs with other firms employing only American workers.

6. The exclusion of the dependents of LVFWs may seem harsh and inhumane but is likely to prove beneficial all around. Experience in both the United States and Europe indicates that the dependents are the chief cause of social conflicts involving housing, schools, hospitals, and other facilities: sometimes a competition for limited capacity, sometimes a bidding-up of the rents and fees, and sometimes claims that the foreigners do not pay fees and taxes—at all, or adequately—for the services they use. On a deeper level, these conflicts represent the impact of a population inflow upon a resident stock that either is nearly stationary and has correspondingly limited its social facilities (as in our northeastern cities) or is already growing rapidly and has outstripped the available social facilities (as in our Southwest). This issue has been much debated in Western Europe, where the passage of time has produced a second-generation problem—the guestworkers' teenage children who are now seeking employment and careers and encountering discrimination and other resistance. The Europeans find that foreign workers who bring in their family dependents become rather immobile in times of recession and redundancy; efforts to repatriate them have not been very successful. The implication for U.S. policy would seem to be to forestall the entry of the dependents in the first place, unless we are prepared to accept these additions to our population as legal immigrants for settlement.

Lest the exclusion of dependents seem heartless and contrary to human rights the practice of frequent home visits during the three-year residence should be encouraged. Travel-cost loans, charged against earnings, might be arranged.

Of course there is always the incentive for an LVFW to marry a U.S. citizen, to settle down here, and abandon his family back home. Possibly such marriages should be excluded from conferring residence rights on LVFWs. Such marriages are already the aim of some of the present illegals—who are mostly young adults and presumably would be replaced by LVFWs in somewhat older age-brackets—but the phenomenon does not seem to have reached large proportions.

7. Several administrative problems need attention. In the present author's recent study of the H-2 program on behalf of the National Commission for Manpower Policy, a number of procedural improvements are recommended on recruitment of Americans for low-level jobs, and certification procedures on H-2 visas, and possible replacement of admissions quotas with a head-tax on foreign workers.[18] That study deals with the existing procedures, criteria, and administrative limitations of the Immigration Service, along lines which Professor Briggs simply ignores when he asserts of the foreign-labor proposals that "none has scratched the surface of such critical issues."[19]

6. A statutory basis must be established for the program, insofar as some of the work to be done might be of a "permanent" character, while other jobs are strictly "temporary" or "seasonal." This matter, in relation to the language of the existing legislation on temporary workers, is treated as a big issue in an ILO paper by Mark Miller and David Yeres.[20] In actuality, the desired statutory authority might readily be found in the existing legislation (Sec. 101(a) of the Immigration and Nationality Act of 1952, with subsequent amendments), by simply reformulating the INS administrative interpretation which was made many years ago; indeed, several categories of H-2s are currently admitted by INS for work which is not of a "temporary" character. Otherwise, if a large new LVFW program is deemed desirable, and would be strengthened by a clear statutory base, appropriate new legislative authorization should be obtainable from Congress.

9. Another remaining problem is the incentive to counterfeit the LVFW visa and other documents. The remedy may be to put these documents on "safety paper," and to include in them the individual's photograph, physical measurements, and fingerprints.

10. A more recalcitrant problem is the tendency of aliens to overstay the visa at the end of the authorized term instead of returning home. One offset here is the expected effect of the LVFW program to dry up the job market for illegals, as mentioned earlier. A second offset should be the cooperation of the Mexican authorities in tracing the individuals involved, since a large proportion of overstays would lead to reduction in the numbers of new visas granted by the United States in subsequent years. Finally, a suitable deposit of "security money" might conceivably be required of each visa-user—either in advance of entry, or as a withholding on his earnings in this country—to ensure his return home at the designated time, when the security money would be returned to him at his home.

Mexico's interest. Why should the Mexican government cooperate in a new LVFW program, and correspondingly curtail the flow of their illegal entrants? Some observers have suggested that the Mexican government is tolerably satisfied with the present inflow of illegals into the United States and would not make serious moves to curtail it. It is our suggestion that an LVFW program would offer substantial and effective inducements to the Mexican government to cooperate in the new program and to curtail the present migration on their side of the border, for the following reasons:

1. The present migration is an embarrassment to the Mexican government. The nightly patrols, arrests, and returns of Mexicans on the border; the intermittent sweeps rounding up illegal Mexicans inside the United States; the occasional fights and sporadic killings of Mexicans (involving criminals of both Mexican and American nationality along with the migrants); the spread of crime and corruption on both sides of the border; the general offense to notions of law and order—all these phenomena of the present situation are troublesome to the Mexican authorities.

2. The present migration is largely responsible for the heavy build-up of population in the border towns on the Mexican side, as people wait for their chance to try to slip across. Disease, squalor, crime, and social unrest are particularly troublesome features here.

3. The Mexican government wants to retain the present benefits from the migration: the outlet for economically redundant population, and the return flow of remittances amounting to billions of dollars a year. If no substitute program is developed, and the US goes to forcible closure of the border and roundups of illegals inside the country, Mexico will lose the present benefits. A substitute program of a legal kind, even if at somewhat lower volume than the present flows, would assure some continuation of the migratory benefits.

4. A new LVFW program would strengthen the role of the Mexican government vis-à-vis its own people. The operation of screening the candidates, and defending them against adverse treatment inside the US, would bolster the government's status as protector and advocate of its citizens.

5. An incidental benefit from Mexico's participation in an LVFW program is the opportunity for restricting the flow-through of Colombians and other Latins who are now apparently moving through Mexico on their way up to the U.S. border. This flow of unauthorized aliens through Mexico is disturbing the authorities there.

6. Agreements between the United States and Mexico on the common problem of illegal migrations, coupled perhaps with agreements on shipments of Mexican oil, might also be linked with general trade agreements widening U.S. markets for Mexican agricultural and industrial products, possibly including special concessions on tariffs and quotas (under the Generalized System of Preferences or other auspices). Capital investments might also be facilitated, notably via U.S. government guarantees for private investors against certain risks. Perhaps most attractive to Mexicans among all these arrangements, the transfer of advanced technology might be positively facilitated.

Given this list of features of interest to the Mexican authorities, it seems likely that LVFW programs would elicit their cooperation. President Lopez Portillo is reported to have expressed his interest to President Carter in Mexico City in February 1979.[21]

POLICY ISSUES CONCERNING LVFW PROGRAMS AND OTHER OPTIONS

Whether the balance of strengthened benefits and alleviated drawbacks in LVFW programs, such as we have outlined, is sufficient to justify this program, or exceeds the balance of benefits over costs in alternative programs, depends upon our system of values, as well as upon the empirical connections delineated so far. The material and behavioral connections show the consequences of alternative choices, but the choice itself depends upon our valuations, our affirmations and rejections. In the present context of changing values and disordered preferences, it is not easy for either the individual or our society to set up priorities. Many people shrink from making strong or sustained affirmations and rejections, or simply cling to many of their traditional valuations—despite inconsistencies.

Likewise, in our closeknit society any given action may have widespreading repercussions that are hard to anticipate, and hard to evaluate even when anticipated. Conversely, the presence of such "externalities" provides an opportunity to cope with features of the given action by deliberately improving or offsetting their repercussions in the externally related areas. For example, the impact of foreign workers may be offset by resulting reductions in the cost of living, or by programs to retrain and relocate the affected native workers, or by payments to compensate foreign countries if they are damaged by our migration policies. Indeed, the field of migration illustrates all these dilemmas and responses in complex array.

National versus international rights. To affirm a "right to migrate,"—as stated by advocates of the Vietnamese and Haitian boat people— would seem to reject all national barriers and to deny the converse "right" of nations to protect the welfare of their own citizens at the cost of the welfare of other peoples. A more limited affirmation holds that refugee status extends to "economic refugees." At first glance, this assertion seems to call for nothing different in kind from the refugee status that most governments have provided for foreigners suffering from political persecution, or from physical disasters, etc. But a second look at the vast numbers of persons suffering from severe poverty around the world— more than 2.5 billion people, in contrast to the total of about one billion in the distinctly prosperous countries, and omitting some intermediate cases—suggests the staggering potential of a "right to migrate as economic refugees." That is, the prosperous nations would have to accept unlimited responsibility for all the world's poor and fully share their welfare with them. A responsibility of this magnitude seems unlikely to be accepted very soon.

It is common to state as a premise that we are a nation of immigrants, which suggests that we are especially sympathetic and receptive to foreigners seeking asylum from political oppression, poverty, and adversity of all kinds. This is perhaps no less accurate, and no more accurate, than the assertion that we are a nation conceived in revolution. Isn't it true that we have become, in our evolution, a middle-class society? Are we not as defensive against immigrants who might want shares in our employment and prosperity as we are hostile to radicals of the Left or the Right, or to culturally different groups, who might subvert our established way of life?

Indeed, once we start to formulate notions of international responsibility along these lines, we are brought to face fundamental issues of human rights as such, in which each person must consider his responsibilities not only for himself, his immediate family, his neighbors, and the fellow-citizens of his nation, but for all human persons everywhere, irrespective of national boundaries. More specifically in the context of this volume, we must consider alleged rights to subsistence and welfare, rights to employment with a free choice of jobs, and rights to live in a chosen family, community, and culture. In effect, we are led into a single worldwide society. As long as the world's peoples are not ready for such a global society, and as long as nationalism—and the governments which express and implement it—continues to command allegiance, we must adapt our policies to these existing values.

Chapter 2 by James Nickel, "Human Rights and the Rights of Aliens," deals with many of the foregoing ethical questions from a realistic viewpoint on social institutions. Professor Nickel affirms the proposition that "rights to the minimal requirements of a decent life . . . are possessed independently of whether one is a native or alien. States have the same prima facie obligation to grant these rights to aliens in their territory that they have to grant them to citizens." This strong support of "human rights for aliens," even illegal aliens, nevertheless runs afoul of Professor Nickel's own earlier concession that he is "prepared to allow that governments have wide discretion in deciding whom to admit to their territories." For this concession, in effect, denies the widely alleged "right to migrate," accepts national limits on the total numbers admitted per year, and permits criteria of "discrimination" among applicants for admission. Once a national government is conceded to have these stringent exclusionary powers toward would-be immigrants, then it becomes only secondary—although still important—that "once a person is present in a territory the main obligation of upholding that person's rights must fall on the government and people of that territory." Exclusion of millions of aliens from a country is far more crucial than making sure that the few thousands who are duly admitted get full parity with the natives in that country.

Preferential versus uniform treatment of foreigners. Even the nationalist political values comprise a range of priorities affecting migration policies. It is frequently stated that "the United States and Mexico have a special relationship"; that the US has a "special responsibility" toward Mexicans (i.e., toward "citizens of an immediately contiguous, economically interlocked, and less developed nation"); and even that the US "bears guilt" toward Mexico for past behavior and "owes compensation" to that nation.[22] The material connections and social values postulated here have seldom been examined overtly and need clarification.

In particular, should any nation accept more responsibility for the citizens of a nearby country than for human beings anywhere in the world? Is the economy of Mexico any more "interlocked" with that of the United States than are the economies of Canada, U.K., Japan, Taiwan, Jamaica, etc.? Is Mexico's status as a less-developed nation in any way prior to the status of Taiwan, South Korea, or Brazil, not to mention the many other nations elsewhere that are far less developed and far more stagnant? Furthermore, what is the preferable form of accepting "responsibility" for foreigners and paying "compensation" to them or to their country? Why should the emphasis fall on migrational access, rather than on payment per foreign worker, or provision of trade, finance, grant aid, technological transfers or assistance, educational and training opportunities, and the other avenues of international intercourse? Indeed, in Western Europe today there is a growing concern with devices to "export jobs" to the less-developed countries as a superior alternative to bringing their workers into the European countries. In summary, the notion of opening special or exclusive migrational opportunities to Mexicans because of a supposed "special relationship" with the United States seems to have a weak base and some dangerous repercussions in both material and moral terms.

Actually, the main content of the notion of "special responsibility" toward Mexico may be the pragmatic recognition of the great difficulties of policing the common border with that country, as well as the urgent need for Mexican oil and gas, and the possibility of joint solutions that would include migration. These are important practical questions, but they do not seem to depend upon a lofty moral argument. They can perhaps be best handled through preferential magnitudes of admissions for Mexicans while still extending some volume of LVFW access to other countries as a matter of principle.

The moral dilemma of migration control. While the decision on proper numbers and types of foreigners to admit into our country is difficult, the implementation of our decision is even more troublesome. Indeed, we have found that implementation devices usually cause a moral dilemma: a choice between liberal values on the micro-level and social interests on the macro-level.

Essentially, the problem is how to keep out the apparently large numbers of foreigners who would attempt to enter or overstay without authorization. But most of the available control devices, and most other conceivable devices, violate deeply held and hard-won values as to privacy, mobility, nonviolence, and civil rights generally. In this situation, we may ask whether the social benefits of controls are worth the moral cost.

The usual methods—actual or proposed—for restricting illegal immigration consist of (a) sealing the borders, (b) scrutinizing those admitted on visitors' and other temporary visas, (c) rounding up illegals—either in their jobs or in their homes—and imprisoning or repatriating them, and (d) prohibiting employment of illegals with penalties for employers who fail to obtain from job applicants proof of either U.S. citizenship or legitimate alien presence. Method (a) calls for all degrees of violence, including killing the trespassers. Methods (b) and (c) involve deep invasion of personal privacy, and (c) also entails considerable violence. Method (d) invades the privacy of both U.S. citizens and aliens, as well as imposing on employers certain law-enforcement duties and bureaucratic supervision. Taken all together, these four methods approach perilously close to the anathema of a "police state." They also tend to put the employment of illegal aliens into the "prohibition" category, along with alcohol under the Volstead Act and narcotic drugs today, with consequent tendencies toward evasion, adulteration, conspiracy, and corruption.

It is worth noting that in Western European countries many of the same control devices are utilized with less outcry and with apparently greater effectiveness than in the United States. One reason for the difference is the common European tradition of a close recording and control of all persons and their movements, reinforced by housing scarcity and pervasive local police functions. That way of life, generally taken for granted in Europe, is not generally acceptable in the United States. Another, and related, reason for the inter-continental contrast is—paradoxically enough—the greater degree of existing diversity in the U.S. population. This diversity, which helps the illegal alien to hide in this country, also exposes legitimately resident aliens to harsh treatment on suspicion of being illegals. Hispanics, in particular, protest that every wave of action against illegals subjects many of them to abuse simply on the basis of Spanish surname, accent, or appearance, even when they are U.S. citizens. Other factors, which may play a role in these contrasts, are the higher rates of unemployment usually prevalent in the US, particularly among the youth and minorities who are the chief competitors for the low-level jobs taken by illegal aliens, and the quite recent emergence of housing shortages in the particular areas where illegals seek jobs and shelter.

The LVFW solution. The existence of the foregoing administrative problems tends to limit us to simple programs, ignoring diverse needs and capabilities for the sake of minimally viable administration. Consequently, one of the main appeals of the LVFW program is that it helps to avoid many of the drawbacks of controls over illegals and the moral dilemma into which they lead.

The LVFW program offers to Mexicans and other foreigners a legitimate access to this country, its available jobs, and comparatively high earnings, albeit for a limited term and possibly for a limited range of jobs and areas. If dependents are excluded, there will be minimal pressure on housing, hospitals, and schools, and strong pulls to return home, with reinforcement by way of security deposits. If American employers can obtain desirable foreign workers in this legitimate fashion, they will presumably reject sheer illegals, who are not as easily underpaid or maltreated in urban jobs nowadays as in rural jobs formerly. At the same time, American workers will be protected against adverse effects from aliens. In effect, the job market for the illegals will be dried up in considerable degree.[23]

Furthermore, a foreigner considering whether to try an illegal entry may be deterred by the prospect that he may soon be granted a legal entry, for which he would not want to disqualify himself. The supposed danger, adduced by Professor Briggs and some others, that the LVFW program itself would stimulate more Mexicans to enter the United States, is beside the point, since that desire is already strong and spreading as hundreds of thousands try their luck each year.[24]

The EIQ approach: Enlarged immigration quotas. For all the desirable features of the LVFW program, it remains more complex, expensive to administer, authoritarian, and subject to loopholes than the simple enlargement of immigration quotas for settlement.

If we accept the economic argument used for TFWs—viz., that the U.S. economy has a need and capacity to absorb a certain number of additional workers of low-skill types to fill low-level job vacancies—then a corresponding admission of additional workers on regular immigrant basis might serve to meet the economic need without imposing new types of regulations or invidious distinctions among classes of workers and their rights. These additional workers would then find their way to jobs, housing, social services, etc., like any other immigrants and indeed like any other persons, native or foreign.

Direct and simple as this proposal may seem, the EIQ approach raises serious problems of its own. First, it is necessary to estimate the optimal number of persons to admit as additional workers to fill all genuine vacancies without generating unemployment of either the aliens or Americans. The data for this purpose are deficient, making it difficult to set a simple firm number for such admissions, although the number of such vacancies arising annually is surely at least several hundred thousand. The experimental, or *tatonnement*, approach—trying different numbers from one year to the next, and checking the results against apparent shortages or excesses of these workers—is a feasible device offered by the LVFW procedure; but it would be difficult to operate under EIQ, because the quotas must be announced in advance and held steady in the face of large numbers of applicants, who must then go onto a waiting-list with several years' lag.

Second, the admission of immigrant workers entails their right to bring in their dependents over the succeeding years. The actual record indicates that for every 100 immigrants who declared their occupation, about 90–110 dependents followed them in subsequent years. We must therefore anticipate a total inflow of alien population of approximately double the number to be authorized for filling our job vacancies.

Third, as these persons become permanent additions to the U.S. population, there will be no means of adapting their numbers to changing needs of the U.S. economy, such as might result from seasonal changes, cyclical recession, or longer-run technologic shifts, inter-industry shifts, etc. In contrast, the LVFWs will come for one to three years, their scheduled returns are a source of flexibility, and their entry numbers too can be varied.

Fourth, the employers of the permanent immigrant workers would lose the 9-percent payroll advantage they now get from the employment of illegals, namely the omission of Social Security taxes and unemployment fund taxes, as well as the wage discount that some employers enjoy when they have illegal workers. To be sure, several studies have found that these omissions and differentials are neither universal nor very large; yet they would lead some employers to go on preferring illegal aliens. That is, the EIQs would not be as effective as LVFWs in preempting the jobs now going to illegals.

Fifth, the applicability of the quota enlargement raises political issues about invidious treatment. If the enlargement is directed solely at Mexicans, who are the great bulk of the present illegal entrants, then we must explain to other countries why they are not given parity treatment, and indeed why the United States is rewarding the largest group of alien lawbreakers with a legitimization of their behavior. To be sure, somewhat similar arguments could be used against the LVFW program, but the latter does not offer permanent U.S. residence along with the possibility of obtaining U.S. citizenship. Furthermore, while other countries might protest the concentration of the immigration-enlargement program on Mexicans alone, the Mexican government might well protest and resent the numbers to be admitted under this program as being no adequate substitute for the hundreds of thousands of Mexicans currently streaming across the border. That is, whereas the LVFW program can offer large numbers of admissions over the next few years, precisely because it is a *temporary* worker program, the EIQ program would almost certainly set much smaller numbers because of the *dependents* issue, the *permanence* feature, and the *inflexibility of the quotas.*

On balance of all these considerations, we find that an LVFW program is preferable to an EIQ program, in terms of flexibly meeting the variable needs of our labor market, supplanting illegal inflows as far as possible, and limiting total alien inflows to the absorptive capacity of our economy within acceptable social standards, while continuing a relatively large and cooperative avenue of opportunity for the surplus labor of foreign countries.

Notes

1. The estimates of foreign workers given in this paper are drawn, with some revisions and updating, from flow calculations set forth in E. P. Reubens, "Aliens, Jobs and Immigration Policy," *The Public Interest* 51 (Spring 1978): 116–17. The resulting figures are consistent with the best-informed current estimates, as indicated below.

Our estimate for the current net inflow of foreign workers, at close to 1 million annually, is derived from INS reports covering the years 1977–1979 on the actual numbers of: (a) admissions of authorized permanent and temporary aliens and (b) apprehensions of illegal entrants at the border and elsewhere. To these data we have applied estimated ratios of duplications among persons apprehended in each year, and evading entrants in proportion to apprehended persons, and estimated short stays and return flows, and labor-force participation rates.

The reported admissions of authorized permanent settlers, at approximately 400,000 a year, reduced by a 25 percent return rate (based on inter-censal data), and further reduced in terms of a 60 percent labor-participation rate (derived from White House, Domestic Council, "Preliminary Report of the Domestic Council Committee on Illegal Immigrants," December 1976), yield a figure of 180,000 net annual inflow of these foreign workers. In addition, the present special program of admissions of refugees (mostly from Vietnam and from Cuba), at approximately 200,000 a year, reduced by an assumed 50 percent labor-participation rate (in view of large proportions of nonworking dependents), and assuming virtually zero returns for the present, yields a figure of 100,000 net annual inflow of these foreign workers. In further addition, the various programs admitting temporary foreign workers (mostly on H-1, H-2 and Exchange Visitors visas), at approximately 100,000 a year (assuming that entrants for a few months balance those staying more than a year, to give an average of one-year stay), and accordingly assuming an annually revolving stock with 100 percent labor participation (their dependents are not counted here), yield a current revolving figure of 100,000 full-time equivalent foreign workers of this type.

To the foregoing legal admissions of foreign workers, we add our estimate of the current net illegal inflow. Beginning with the reported apprehensions, at approximately 1 million a year, we reduce this figure to 600,000 on account of estimated duplications of apprehended persons during the year, and then double it to represent the number of successful evaders in estimated proportion to those who were apprehended and deported. Both of these estimated ratios were obtained from experienced INS agents in five of the District Offices dealing with the largest inflows of illegals. We apply to the figure of

1,200,000 annual illegal entrants a labor-participation rate of 80 percent (in view of the predominance of young, able-bodied adults in this inflow), and then deduct as much as 40 percent for short stays and return flows. Compare the much better measured movements of guestworkers in Western Europe, where the most relevant groups—Turks and Yugoslavs—during the most relevant period—1969–1973—showed an annual return rate of 21 percent and 43 percent, respectively; and note that short-stay inflows of Mexican "wetbacks" into the United States for seasonal agricultural work are now a small proportion of the total inflow. For these and other data on the European experience, see W. R. Böhning, Chapter 4, this volume. These calculations yield a figure of 600,000 net current inflow of illegal foreign workers (full-year-equivalent workers who stay on here). The sum of all the foregoing classes yields an aggregate annual figure of close to 1 million current net inflow of foreign workers of all these kinds.

2. Our estimate for the 1979 stock of foreign workers of all kinds is primarily a net accumulation (gross inflows reduced for return flows and inactivity) over the span of the previous eight years (1972–1979, inclusive).

For the authorized permanent settlers, at the annual figure from note 1 of 180,000 net inflow, sustained rather closely over these years, the accumulation comes to 1,440,000 workers. For the refugees, whose numbers were relatively small between 1973 and 1979, an accumulation of 120,000 workers is adopted. The temporary foreign workers, treated as a revolving stock, constitute just 100,000 workers. Finally, for the illegals—whose numbers have been rising strongly during the 1970s, so far as the entry trend may be measured by the reported apprehensions—we adopt an average of 480,000 annual net inflow, and multiply by eight years, to yield an accumulation of 3,840,000 illegal workers over these years. The sum of all the foregoing classes yields an accumulated stock of 5.5 million foreign workers of all these kinds.

The above figures are in fairly close accord with some analytic estimates for the most debatable class, the illegal alien workers. The calculation by Lancaster and Scheuren in 1978, by matching the 1973 Current Population Survey with IRS income tax records and Social Security earnings and benefits records, yielded a figure of 3.9 million illegal residents aged 18–44 in 1973; almost all of these would have been in the labor force, and subsequent net inflows would almost certainly have raised this number well above our estimate of 3.84 million illegal workers as of 1979. See Clarise Lancaster and Frederick J. Scheuren, "Counting the Uncountable Illegals: Some Initial Statistical Speculations Employing Capture-Recapture Techniques," in *Proceedings of the Social Statistical Section, American Statistical Association*, 1977. The Lancaster and Scheuren estimates, along with several other "analytic" estimates and with the "survey" methods used by the INS and by the Mexican agency CENIET, have all been severely criticized in a paper by specialists of the U.S. Census Bureau (see note 6, below) from methodological standpoints, yet those specialists themselves settle upon 3.5–5.0 million as the most likely range of estimates for all the illegal residents; and an 80 percent participation rate brings the number of illegal workers to an upper limit exceeding our estimate of 3.84 million above.

Our estimate of the accumulated stock of illegal workers is not inconsistent with the North and Houstoun data showing that the average stay of illegals apprehended by INS is between 18 and 24 months in length. See David S. North and Marion F. Houstoun, *Characteristics and Role of Illegal Aliens in the U.S. Labor Market* (Washington, D.C.: U.S. Dept. of Labor, March 1976). Many of those respondents evidently were referring to their most recent stay since their last entry into the United States, rather than their whole stay interrupted by various voluntary returns home and reentry into the US; such movements are covered in our deduction of "40 percent for short stays and return flows." Contrarily, our estimate is not consistent with the frequent assertion that most or all Mexican illegals come into the US for a short stay averaging only six months in length; that belief implies that the stock at any moment is only one-half of the gross annual inflow; and it further implies that there is no accumulation of these persons over the years, contrary to much evidence.

3. According to official reports of the U.S. Department of Labor, unemployment rates

for recent years in New York City, Buffalo, Jersey City, Philadelphia, etc., are almost double those for Austin, Dallas, Houston, Denver/Boulder, and about 50 percent higher than in Phoenix and Albuquerque, although the northern rates are matched in a few southwestern border communities where the Mexican illegals first congregate; and unemployment rates in California are relatively closer to the northeastern rates. See *Unemployment and Training Report of the President* 1979, Table D-8.

4. The Mexican net inflow of workers is comprised of (a) about 33,000 from net legal admissions for settlement (quota and nonquota admissions reduced for returns and inactivity); plus (b) small numbers of legal temporary admissions of Mexican workers; plus (c) perhaps 450,000 net illegal entries of Mexican workers (derived from our estimate of the total net illegal inflow of 600,000 a year, reduced for the Mexican share— taken as 80 percent by adjustment from the 90 percent of total apprehensions shown in INS *Annual Reports*, Table 30—and further reduced for a lower rate of stay-on by Mexicans than by some other illegal groups).

The Mexican share in the recently accumulated total stock of alien workers is comprised of (a) about 260,000 from eight years of net legal admissions for settlement (at a rather steady rate of admissions); plus (b) small numbers of legal temporary revolving stock; plus (c) perhaps 2,500,000 workers of originally illegal entry (taking 65 percent of the whole accumulated stock of illegal workers); and confirmed by the eight-year accumulation of 300,000 a year on average of the 1970s for net illegal entries of Mexican workers; and also fairly close to the upper limit of the Census Bureau specialists' suggestion (note 6) of 3 million for the Mexican illegally resident population, when adjusted for labor-force participation).

5. The CENIET claim appears in Carlos Zazueta and Rodolfo Corona, *Los Trabajadores Mexicanos en los Estados Unidos* (Mexico: CENIET, December 1979). Compare Alfred Stepan, "The United States and Latin America," *Foreign Affairs* 58, no. 3 (America and the World 1979): 668–69.

6. See Jacob S. Siegal, Jeffrey S. Passel, and J. Gregory Robinson, "Preliminary Review of Existing Studies of the Number of Illegal Residents in the United States," Paper commissioned by the Research Staff of the Select Commission on Immigration and Refugee Policy, January 1980. The authors are staff members of the Census Bureau, but this paper is not an official publication of the Census Bureau.

7. Ibid.

8. In neo-classical theory, "surplus labor" is defined as that portion of the labor supply which remains unemployed beyond the point where the marginal product of labor comes down to the "prevailing wage"; or still more exigently—assuming wages to be flexible all the way down to zero—surplus labor is indicated beyond the point where the marginal product of labor reaches zero.

9. " 'Little Detroits' Boom in Mexico," *New York Times*, March 3, 1980, pp. D1 and D5. On the whole economic context of labor supplies exceeding demands in Mexico, see E. P. Reubens, "Surplus Labor, Emigration and Public Policies in Mexico," in *U.S.–Mexico Economic Relations*, edited by B. W. Poulson and T. N. Osborn (Boulder, Colo.: Westview Press, 1979).

10. Vernon M. Briggs, Jr., Chapter 8, this volume, p. 235.

11. See Harold Wool and Bruce Phillips, *The Labor Supply for Lower-Level Occupations* (Washington, D.C.: National Planning Assn., 1975); also Michael Piore, "Illegal Immigration in the United States," in *Illegal Aliens: An Assessment of the Issues*, National Council on Employment Policy (Washington, D.C.: G PO, October 1976). These projections are consistent with labor market analyses by the Bureau of Labor Statistics. See also Michael Wachter, *The Labor Market and Immigration: Outlook for 1980s* (University of Pennsylvania, Center on Organizational Innovation, February 1979) mimeographed.

12. Briggs, Chapter 8, p. 237.

13. Ibid., p. 238.

14. See Department of Health, Education and Welfare, *A Report to the President and Congress on the Status of Health Professions Personnel in the United States, 1980*

(Washington, D.C.: G PO, April 1980); and U.S. Congress, Office of Technology Assessment, *Forecasts of Physician Supply and Requirements* (Washington, D.C.: G PO, April 1980). These two reports, issued less than a week apart, agree on the predicted supply of physicians in the United States at about 600,000 in 1990 (a figure reached by adding an annual increment of 15,000 to the present stock, which is 450,000 according to the second report but only 409,000 according to statements in the first report; both reports are unclear as to allowances for attrition in the stocks). There is substantial disagreement between the two reports on the prospective "need" or "requirement" for physicians. The first report anticipated need rising by 1990 to a range of 553,000–596,000. The second report, which explicitly assumed no long-term increase in the per capita use of physicians, came to only 415,000 needed in 1990, *less* than its estimated *present* stock of 450,000.

15. The projections of "need" or "requirement" for physicians by 1990 depend on projected population growth, per capita income growth, the income-elasticity of demand for medical services, and on the supply-side changing productivity of doctors. Adopting reasonable values for these variables, there would have to be an unheard-of rise in doctors' productivity to produce the stationary or actually reduced figure for needed doctors as put forward by the Office of Technology Assessment. Indeed, the more likely prospect is a need for at least 600,000 doctors in 1990 as forecast by the HEW report at its upper range, probably still more, and certainly at or above the prospective supply.

16. J. N. Bhagwati and A. Partington, eds., *The Brain Drain and Taxation*, 2 vols. (Amsterdam: North Holland Publishers, 1976).

17. See E. P. Reubens, "Temporary Admission of Foreign Workers: Dimensions and Policies," Special Report no. 34, National Commission for Manpower Policy (March 1979), pp. 40–41, based on data of U.S. Agriculture and Labor departments.

18. Cited in previous note.

19. Briggs, Chapter 8, p. 233.

20. See Mark J. Miller and David J. Yeres, "A Massive Temporary Worker Programme for the U.S.: Solution or Mirage?" World Employment Programme Research Working Papers WP 44 (Geneva: International Labour Office, November 1979; mimeo.). See especially p. 26 and Appendix (a).

21. See a *New York Times* dispatch by Alan Riding, published February 19, 1979, covering President Carter's visit to Mexico City: "In private conversations with Mr. Carter, the Mexican leader proposed that Washington give the legal status of 'guest migrant worker'—similar to that of Turkish workers in West Germany—to 750,000 Mexicans a year, as well as increase the annual quota of permanent immigrants. He also suggested some form of amnesty for undocumented Mexicans who are already in the United States in order to avoid mass deportations. In exchange, Mexico would study ways of tightening its own borders against illegal migrants."

22. For a brief overview of the range of opinion, see "Mexican Migrants and U.S. Responsibility: Visas for Temporary Workers?—An Initial Survey of the Issues" (College Park, Md.: Center for Philosophy and Public Policy, 1979), photocopy.

23. Evidence that legal temporary worker programs can preempt the market for illegals, without severely damaging the market for native workers, can be drawn from both the U.S./Mexico bracero program of 1942–1964 and the Western European guestworker programs since the 1950s.

For indications that the bracero program in the US had little if any depressing effect on local wages, actually impacted few American workers, and mainly displaced illegal entries from Mexico, see Larry C. Morgan and Bruce L. Gardner, "Lessons from the Braceros," Paper read at the University of Illinois Conference on Immigration Issues and Policies, April 1980; later published in *The Gateway: U.S. Immigration Issues and Policies*, edited by B. Chiswick (Washington, D.C.: American Enterprise Institute, 1981). That paper is supported by data of the U.S. Agriculture Department, in its quarterly *Farm Labor*, which show that over the period 1957–1977—which includes the bracero era, its termination, and the emergence of massive illegal entries—farm wage rates rose steadily and strongly, outrunning inflation of the cost of living, and closely paralleling and sometimes outrunning the rise of nonfarm wage rates (see Reubens, "Temporary Admission of Foreign Workers"). Those findings rebut the often-heard claim that the inflow of Mexican workers undermined the position of U.S. farm workers.

In the case of the Western European countries, which employed about 6 million foreign workers in the early 1970s, mostly at jobs rejected by native workers, it is estimated that only about 10 percent were illegals (W. R. Böhning, "International Migration in Western Europe: Reflections on the Past Five Years," *International Labor Review* 118, no. 4 [July–August 1979]: 402). Since about 1975, however, when most of the receiving countries began to curtail official recruitment and to press for repatriation, there have been journalistic reports of rising illegal entries.

24. Briggs, Chapter 8, p. 240.

8

Foreign Labor Programs as an Alternative to Illegal Immigration: A Dissenting View

VERNON M. BRIGGS, JR.

Introduction

Illegal immigration into the United States has existed as an issue since attempts to regulate entry were initiated in the 1880s. It has, however, become a prominent national issue only since the 1960s. With the annual number of apprehended illegal immigrants now totaling more than a million persons; with the number of nonapprehended illegal immigrants even greater; and with the accumulated stock of illegal immigrants estimated to be anywhere from 3 to 12 million persons (the 6 to 8 million figure being the most commonly agreed upon), it is obvious that the existing immigration policy of the nation is in a shambles.[1] The mounting numbers of persons who enter illegally, however, are not the only reason that the issue has come to the forefront. There is also concern over the short-term adverse impact of illegal immigrants on employment and income opportunities for certain groups of citizen workers with whom they compete (most notably minorities, women, and youth) and, over the long run, with the possible creation and institutionalization of a permanent subclass of rightless persons within American society.

During the late 1960s and early 1970s numerous commission reports, congressional hearings, and academic writings detailed both the rising number of illegal immigrants and the insidious nature of the illegal immigration process for all parties. These efforts contributed momentum to the movement for reform of the existing immigration system. In August 1977, the Carter administration announced a set of reform proposals and forwarded them to Congress. But despite the urgency of the president's request, the only congressional response was the establishment of a study commission in 1978. Subsequently, in early 1981, the Select Commission on Immigration and Refugee Policy issued its comprehensive report, which concluded that the nation's "immigration policy is out of control."[2]

The appointment of a commission to study the issue was, of course, a standard political ploy to buy time. It gave the appearance of action when, in fact, little of substance was occurring except talk. In general, politicians create such commissions in the hope that by the time the commissions finish their work, the issue will have faded in importance and no action will be needed. But in this case, no one believed that illegal immigration would have receded as a domestic issue by the time the Select Commission issued its final report. Hence, the essential rationale for the Select Commission's existence was to allow more time for dialogue over appropriate policy alternatives. The politicians were simply not yet ready to act on President Carter's proposals in 1977, and they had nothing better to suggest themselves. More important, most of the usual political coalitions were split over the appropriate remedies to be applied (if any).[3] For example, even within the Chicano community and the Catholic Church there were deep internal divisions.[4] This issue has divided both liberals and conservatives; time was required for new coalitions to develop and for a consensus to be formed as to the appropriate remedies to be applied.

Among the various policy alternatives that have been discussed as remedies for the problem of illegal immigration have been proposals for some type of foreign worker program for the United States. The exact format of each proposal differs. Some call for expansion of the limited labor importation programs that are currently in existence. Others argue for new programs similar to those introduced in Europe following World War II but which, since the mid-1970s, have either been terminated or are being phased out.[5]

In passing, it should be noted that the immigration reforms presented by the Carter administration did not include any recommendation for a foreign worker program within its comprehensive package. Likewise, the Select Commission specifically recommended against including a foreign worker program among its multiple suggestions for reforms.[6] Shortly after taking office, however, the Reagan administration disregarded this advice. In July 1981, the administration recommended to Congress as part of its immigration reform proposals that an experimental foreign worker program with Mexico for 50,000 persons be established.[7]

The objective of this chapter is to review the experience of the United States with various past and present foreign worker programs, to outline some of the proposals for new foreign worker programs, and to make known why foreign worker programs are a wrong prescription to the nation's problem of illegal immigration.

Past Foreign Worker Programs in the United States

Foreign labor programs are not new to the United States. There have been several such programs in the past, and there are several ongoing at the present.

Thus, if experience is a form of education, lessons can be learned from looking at both the past and the present before any evaluation is offered concerning the merits and demerits of similar undertakings for the future.

THE FIRST BRACERO PROGRAM

It is ironic that, only months after the United States enacted the most restrictive immigration legislation in its history—the Immigration Act of 1917—the first foreign labor program was initiated.[8] In response to strong pressure from the large agricultural employers of the Southwest, Congress included in this very restrictive legislation a provision that would allow entry of "temporary" workers who were "otherwise inadmissible."[9] The statute allowed the Secretary of Labor to exempt such persons (Mexicans in this instance) from the head tax required of each immigrant and from the ban on any immigrants over age 16 who could not read. In May 1917, such an order was issued for the creation of a "temporary" farm worker program. Later it was expanded to allow some Mexican workers to be employed in nonfarm work. When the program was announced, so were a number of governing rules and regulations. Ostensibly, these rules were designed to protect both citizen workers and Mexican workers, as well as to ensure that the Mexicans returned to Mexico after their work was completed. But, as has been the historic pattern, "these elaborate rules were unenforced."[10]

The "temporary" worker program was enacted during the period of World War I. It was partly justified as being in the national defense. This program, which Kiser and Kiser refer to as "the first bracero program," was extended until 1922, well after the war had ended in 1918.[11] It was terminated because its rationale as a national defense policy could no longer be maintained; because organized labor contended that the program undermined the economic welfare of citizen workers; and because many people believed that there were no labor shortages but only greedy employers who wished to secure economic gains from being able to secure cheap and compliant workers. During its lifespan, 76,862 Mexican workers were admitted to the United States, of which only 34,922 returned to Mexico.[12]

THE SECOND BRACERO PROGRAM

With the advent of World War II, the military requirements of the United States and its related manufacturing needs led to assertions that another labor shortage existed in the agricultural sector. The growers of the Southwest had foreseen these developments before the Pearl Harbor attack in 1941. They made two fateful decisions: first, the pool of cheap labor in Mexico was to be tapped to fill the labor deficit; second, the federal government was again to be the vehicle of deliverance.[13]

The initial requests of U.S. growers for the establishment of a contract labor program were denied by the federal government in 1941. By mid-1942, however, the U.S. government had come to favor the program, but the government of Mexico balked at the prospect of a formal intergovernment agreement. The unregulated hiring of Mexican citizens by foreign nations is prohibited by Article 123 of the Mexican Constitution of 1917. Moreover, in the 1940s the Mexican economy was flourishing; Mexican workers justifiably feared that they would be drafted; there were bitter memories of the "repatriation drive" of the 1930s; and there was knowledge of the discriminatory treatment accorded people of Mexican ancestry throughout the Southwest at the time.

Negotiations between the two governments, however, resulted in a formal agreement in August 1942. The Mexican Labor Program, better known as the bracero program, was launched. Mexican workers were to be afforded numerous protections with respect to housing, transportation, food, medical needs, and wage rates. Initiated through appropriations for Public Law 45, the program was extended by subsequent enactment until 1947. Braceros were limited exclusively to agricultural work; any bracero who was found holding a job in any other industry was subject to immediate deportation. When the agreement ended December 31, 1947, the program was continued informally and without regulation until 1951. In that year, under the guise of another war-related labor shortage, the bracero program was revived by Public Law 78. This program continued to function until it was unilaterally terminated by the United States on December 31, 1964.

The bracero program demonstrated precisely how border policies can adversely affect citizen workers in the United States—especially, in this case, the Chicanos who composed the bulk of the Southwestern agricultural labor force. Agricultural employment in the Southwest was removed from competition with the nonagricultural sector. At the program's peak, almost one-half million braceros were working in the agricultural labor market of the Southwest. The availability of Mexican workers significantly depressed existing wage levels in some regions, modulated wage increases that would have occurred in their absence in all other regions, and sharply compressed the duration of the employment many citizen farm workers could find.[14] Citizen farm workers simply could not compete with braceros. The fact that braceros were captive workers who were totally subject to the unilateral demands of employers made them especially appealing to many employers. The bracero program was a significant factor in the rapid exodus of rural Chicanos between 1950 and 1970 to urban labor markets, where they were poorly prepared to find employment and housing.[15]

A lasting effect of the second bracero program was its exposure of hundreds of thousands of penniless Mexican workers to the wide array of economic opportunities, as well as the higher wages and benefits, that were available in the United States economy. It is not surprising that both paralleling the bracero years and immediately following the program's termination of 1964 there has been an accelerated growth in the number of illegal immigrants.[16] Many thousands of these illegal aliens were former braceros, who had been attracted to the Mexican border towns from the rural interior of central and northern Mexico by the existence of the contract-labor program. To this degree, there is an element of truth to the proposition that the United States itself has created the illegal alien problem. By the same token, however, it is grossly simplistic to conclude that the problem would not eventually have surfaced in the absence of the bracero program. The vast economic differences between the two national economies are simply too great.

Present Foreign Worker Programs in the United States

As the bracero programs are no longer operational, it is instructive to review some of the prevailing policies that permit workers who live in other countries to be employed in the United States. From these experiences it is possible to deduce some of the effects of the new proposals for foreign worker programs.

BORDER COMMUTERS

Border commuters are a subgroup of a larger immigration classification known as resident aliens. Resident aliens are foreign-born nationals who apply for permission to live and to work in the United States on a permanent basis. They can retain their own original foreign citizenship. After a period of five years, they may apply at will to become citizens, or they may remain resident aliens indefinitely. A substantial number of resident aliens never elect to become naturalized citizens.

All resident aliens are issued a card from the INS that is officially known as an I-151 card. In 1977, there were 4.5 million resident aliens registered with the INS.[17] Nearly 75 percent of them reside in six states, with California, New York, and Texas accounting for 53 percent of the total. Persons from Mexico are by far the most numerous of this group, numbering 938,972 (or 20 percent) of the total in 1977. More than 75 percent of all resident aliens from Mexico reside in California and Texas. Many live along the border region.

There are two types of resident aliens. The larger group are resident aliens who live and work on a permanent basis in the United States. Members of the other resident alien group work regularly in the United States but reside permanently in either Mexico or Canada. This latter group are called "commuters" or, more commonly, "green carders" (so named because each time they cross the border they must show their I-151 card, which was originally green in color; it is now blue). Thus, the important distinction is this: all commuters are green carders, but most green carders are not commuters.

At the risk of becoming confusing, it should be noted that there are also two types of commuting green carders. One is the commuter who crosses the border on a daily basis; the other works in the U.S. on a seasonal basis. Generally speaking, the daily commuter is the one whose presence is felt in the border economy of the United States—especially the southern border. The seasonal commuter generally moves much further inland and returns to his or her home in Mexico only during the off-season of the industry in which he or she is employed. The impact of the seasonal commuters—who may be employed in construction, farming, or a tourist industry—is diluted by their being employed in jobs scattered all over the nation. The daily commuters, on the other hand, are much more concentrated. Accordingly, they are highly significant in their local labor-market impact. David North has aptly observed that the daily "commuter is this generation's bracero."[18]

Because of the extreme differences in economic development between Mexico and the United States, commuters from Mexico are often willing to work for wages and under other employment conditions that are impossible for a person who must confront the daily cost of living in the United States on a permanent basis. The commuter has a real income advantage. Also, commuters often act as strike-breakers in labor disputes along the border and, accordingly, are one factor that explains the scarcity of unions in the region. A study in 1970 placed the number of daily commuters from Mexico at 70,000.[19] This would mean that roughly one out of every eleven persons employed in 1970 in the U.S. counties along the border was a commuter. Obviously, a work force of this magnitude exerts a tremendous impact on these U.S. border communities. Unofficial estimates (there are no official estimates) from INS of the number of daily border commuters in 1978 placed the figure at about 100,000.[20]

As a result of the unfair real income advantage that the commuting worker has over the resident U.S. worker in the competition for jobs, the legitimacy of their status has been a continuing source of dispute. To understand the nature of this long controversy, it is necessary to understand the evolution of the commuter phenomenon.

Prior to 1917, there were virtually no restrictions placed on immigrants (except those from Asia) who wished to work in the United States. In 1917 and 1921, temporary restrictions were imposed on immigration and, shortly afterwards, the Immigration Act of 1924 established the first permanent numerical restrictions on immigration. Persons from the Western Hemisphere, however, were not included in the quotas established by the act. But all people entering the United States were required by this act to be classified as either "immigrants" or "nonimmigrants." "Immigrants" were defined as all entrants except those designated as "nonimmigrants who are visiting the country temporarily for business or pleasure." For a short interval, workers who lived in Mexico but commuted to jobs in the United States were classified as "nonimmigrant visitors" who were free to cross the border "for business." By arbitrary administrative decision of the INS in 1927, however, the status of these people was changed to "immigrants." Subsequently, in 1929, the U.S. Supreme Court upheld the INS decision, with the famous ruling that "employment equals residence" (thereby neatly avoiding the permanent residency requirement of the immigration statutes).[21]

There are, however, several differences between a green carder and other permanent resident immigrants. Green carders may not be unemployed for more than six months without losing their immigration classification; they may not serve as strikebreakers; and they cannot count the time they live outside the United States toward the five years needed to be eligible to apply for permanent citizenship. In reality, these differences are of absolutely no consequence. The unemployment restriction is not enforced; the anti-strikebreaker rule is so easily circumvented that it is essentially meaningless; and many green carders have absolutely no interest in becoming American citizens.

Surprisingly, the question whether or not a green carder must reside in the United States has been the subject of extensive controversy, and over the years, the immigration statutes have changed considerably. Since the Immigration Act of 1965 was passed, it has been charged that the prevailing law actually forbids the practice of commuting since the reentry rights of a resident alien are limited to a person who is "returning to an unrelinquished lawful permanent address."[22] Before 1965, the INS reasoned that any commuter who had been accorded the "privilege of residing permanently" was always entitled to enter the country. The Immigration Act of 1965, however, altered the previous statutory language. The amended language restricted informal entry to "an immigrant lawfully admitted for permanent residence who is returning from a temporary visit abroad."

Accordingly, one legal scholar has concluded: "No distortion of the English language could result in a finding that the commuter was entering the United States after a temporary visit abroad to return to his principal, actual dwelling place. Rather, the commuter was simply leaving his foreign home and entering the United States to work."[23] He argued that since 1965 the status of border commuters is "not merely lacking in statutory authority" but that the practice is "actually prohibited."

In November 1974, however, the U.S. Supreme Court rejected this logic by upholding the INS position that daily and seasonal commuters are lawful permanent residents returning from temporary absences abroad.[24] Essentially, the Court said that it was not going to overthrow 50 years of administrative practices by judicial decree. If the Congress wished to outlaw the practice of border commuting, it would have to act in a more specific legislative manner.

It is worthy of note that the U.S. Department of State has consistently contended that any interruption in the commuter program would seriously harm relations between Mexico and the United States. Former Secretary of State Dean Rusk testified before Congress that the border towns of the two nations "have grown into single economic communities" and that "a disruption in the life of these communities would do real harm to good neighbor relations in the area."[25] Nevertheless, the sanction given to commuters means that the citizen workers of the border region must compete directly with these commuters. As one noted labor market analyst has observed:

> The United States worker who competes with the traffic of workers from Mexico is caught in a situation where he pays a substantial part of what the Secretary of State regards as a form of foreign aid to a neighboring nation.[26]

It is true, of course, that these resident aliens who commute could simply move across the border and live in the United States at will. In this sense, they are not truly foreign workers as the term is usually applied. But as long as they do not reside in the United States, they function in a capacity that is identical to being foreign workers. They enjoy the real income benefits of earning higher wages in the United States while paying the lower living costs of Mexico. This gives them an advantage over citizen workers who must compete with them for the identical job opportunities. In reality, most commuters have no intention at all of becoming U.S. citizens. They are only availing themselves of a loophole in the U.S. immigration policy that adversely affects citizen workers.

"VISITOR WORKERS"

There is another, more pernicious group of commuting foreign workers whose status, unlike that of commuting green carders, is not debatable. It is simply illegal. Nonetheless, they pass through the legal checkpoints by the thousands each day to jobs in border towns of the United States. They are not citizens of the United States nor have they any claim to citizenship. For lack of a better name, they can be called "visitor workers." They do constitute a foreign worker program, although they are never discussed as such.

The phenomenon of visitor workers arises because citizens of Mexico who live permanently in Mexican border towns are accorded special passage privileges to enter the United States at will. The only travel restriction is that they must remain within a prescribed distance of the border. These Mexican citizens request an I-186 card from the INS. These cards are white and, as one can imagine, the bearers are known as "white carders." The I-186 card is for persons known as "legal visitors" or "border crossers." Technically, the bearer of the card can remain in the United States for up to 72 hours on any single visit and is restricted to a radius of 25 miles of the border. The holder of an I-186 card, however, is specifically forbidden from seeking employment or being employed anywhere in the United States.

In fact, however, there is little to stop a white carder from working, and many do. Prior to January 1, 1969, a white card was valid for only four years. Since that time, however, the cards are no longer dated. As a result, no expiration appears on the card. The INS claimed that the renewal procedures were too time-consuming and costly. As can be imagined, the result is that many Mexican citizens regularly cross the border to work within the border perimeter.[27] Given the immense number of people who cross the border check points each day as well as the pressure to expedite the flow, little can be done by INS officials to police the prohibition against working that is supposedly a condition for receipt of the I-186 card.

Although visitor workers are a well-known factor to all familiar with the border region, they are the least mentioned and the least studied. Typically, these persons are day workers or live-in workers in casual occupations. It is not uncommon for lower-middle income families to have maids in many border cities.[28] As visitor workers are illegally employed, they seldom complain about the wages and working conditions. Since most of these persons are women with families on the Mexican side of the border, they are greatly restricted in the geographical area in which they work.

The women crowd into occupations that are already in surplus in the local labor market. Although visitor workers are a small component of the daily number of persons who cross the border, it is likely that they still constitute a significant number of persons in the occupations in which they work.

Exactly how many white carders there are is a mystery. The INS reports that over 2.2 million cards were issued in the Southwest between 1960 and 1969.[29] There is no estimate of how many have been issued since then, except that the number each year is in the "tens of thousands." How many of these white carders have abused their visiting privileges by seeking employment is unknown. The fact that the statistics of green and white carders are either vague or completely unknown was labeled "astonishing" by the comprehensive UCLA Mexican-American Study Project conducted in 1970.[30]

In passing, it should also be noted that the white card is also a popular device for illegal immigrants to use to cross the border. Having entered the United States, the card is often simply mailed back to Mexico and the person then moves farther north outside the 25-mile zone. This avoids the possibility that the card might be confiscated if the bearer were apprehended. In this event, the person simply indicates that he or she is an illegal immigrant and wishes a voluntary departure back to Mexico. There the original white card is waiting for use again.

H-2 WORKERS

In 1952, the enactment of the Immigration and Nationality Act authorized the Attorney General of the United States, acting through the Immigration and Naturalization Service of the U.S. Department of Justice, to admit nonimmigrant persons for temporary jobs "if unemployed persons capable of performing such service or labor cannot be found in this country,"[31] This was section H-2 of the act and, accordingly, the program itself is popularly referred to as the "H-2 program." The U.S. Department of Labor (DOL) has the responsibility for the decision as to whether citizen workers are actually available. In making its determination, DOL has devised a system of adverse wage rates and working conditions. These wage rates and working conditions must be provided by any employer who seeks to hire foreign workers under the H-2 program. The purpose of the requirements is supposedly to prevent the possibility that the program will depress existing work standards. The final entry decision, however, resides with the Department of Justice. Hence, it does happen on occasion that the Department of Labor is overruled. The size of the H-2 program has fluctuated widely: from a high of 69,000 in 1970, it has declined to about 23,000 in 1978.

As of the period 1978–1979, four rural industries have been the primary users of H-2 workers.[32] These are the sugarcane industry in Florida (using Jamaicans); the apple industry in a number of eastern states (using Jamaicans); the woodcutting industry in Maine (using Canadians); and sheepherding (using Peruvians and Mexicans). In several minor programs involving row crop harvesting in recent years Mexican workers have been admitted as H-2 workers. Although all of these users of H-2 workers may seem to be rather minor industries, they all have very powerful and influential political lobbies, as the Department of Labor has regularly found out to its misfortune.[33]

The H-2 program incorporates all of the undesirable features of the aforementioned bracero program. The workers are totally dependent upon the employers; eligibility to be chosen for the program depends upon one's contacts with certain officials of one's government; it is often considered a privilege to be selected. If chosen, the worker can be assured of the opportunity to return again only if his work and attitude please the American employer. This is because the employer may "request by name" a set proportion (usually 50 percent) of the current year's H-2 workers to return the following year. In effect, this means that the workers must compete with one another on terms that are very favorable to the employer. If any part of the worker's demeanor or work is unsatisfactory to the employer, the worker may be deported at any time without an appeal. Given this system, Martin and North conclude, "It is little wonder that H-2 aliens are 'hard working and diligent.' "[34]

Proposals for New Foreign Worker Programs for the United States

In addition to the previously discussed forms of foreign worker programs, there are, of course, the millions of illegal immigrants who work in the United States. They do constitute a foreign labor program, albeit totally unregulated. Officially, of course, illegal immigrants are unsanctioned, but because the immigration policy of the United States is so blatantly tolerant of their presence, it can be argued that they are unofficially condoned by the government and welcomed by many employers. Certainly, a nation which levies no penalties on employers for hiring illegal immigrants, gives voluntary departures back to their homelands to 95 percent of those who are apprehended, and has an immigration enforcement agency that is chronically underfunded and understaffed can hardly be taken seriously in its claims to oppose illegal entry.

But because of the mounting number of persons involved and because of the inherent danger both to the illegal immigrants themselves and to the nation as a whole with such an assemblage of rightless persons in its midst, comprehensive immigration reforms have been offered by the Carter and Reagan administrations, the Select Commission on Immigration and Refugee Policy, and others. Although neither the Carter proposals nor the Select Commission's report included any recommendations for a foreign worker program as a potential remedy to this problem, a number of such proposals have been offered by others, including the current administration. It is useful to review a sampling of these proposals.

One proposal, an attempt to draw from Western Europe's years of experience with foreign worker programs, has been suggested by W. R. Böhning. Addressing *only* illegal immigrants from Mexico, he says that the United States has a demand for unskilled workers because they are "cheap and industrious."[35] He argues that illegal immigrants are "not a marginal element of the United States labor market" but that "they are necessary for the smooth functioning of the economy as it exists today."[36] In fact, he alleges that there is a "genuine demand" for their work.

Under the Böhning Plan, a Mexican worker—called an *undocumentado*—could get a visa to cross the border and look for a job anywhere, just as if he or she were a citizen worker. The worker would have three months to find a seasonal or nonseasonal job. If a nonseasonal job were found, the worker would request a contract for up to twelve months. At the end of the period, the contract could be renewed "on the spot." If the undocumentado could find only seasonal contract work, he or she would have to return to Mexico but could be requested by name the following year. If a Mexican could not find work after three months or for a full season, he or she would have to return to Mexico or be subject to deportation. After returning to Mexico, they would then compete with all other Mexican workers to get back on the list of visa eligibles. Essentially, the program would work like a union hiring hall similar to that used in the construction and longshoring industries, where casual employment is a key employment feature. No indication is given as to how a person would be selected to become an undocumentado.

While in the country, the undocumentados would be accorded all economic and social rights. Nonseasonal workers would be entitled to be joined by their wives and children not later than at the renewal of their first contract, while for seasonal workers family reunification would be possible, at the latest, after two consecutive seasons in the United States. After five years of continuous residence, the undocumentado could apply for permanent resident alien status. Stiff penalties would be placed on employers who hire illegal immigrants as well as on illegal immigrants who were apprehended, but no further changes would be made in the existing immigration system.

Another proposal for "a temporary labor program" has been made by Charles Keely. His program would permit foreign workers to be employed "in regions and sections" identified by the U.S. Department of Labor "as in need of labor."[37] The decision would be made after consultation with both employers and labor unions. Temporary workers could be granted immigrant status (i.e., become resident aliens) if they could find work for some set period of time (he suggests a work duration of from 15 to 25 consecutive months). The basis of the plan is that "if a worker worked here, he could build up some rights to settle."[38] Family members would be able to accompany the temporary immigrants and would be entitled to all social programs available to citizen workers. Keely does condition his proposal with additional recommendations for enforcement of existing labor laws and sanctions against employers of illegal immigrants.

A third proposal pertains to the existing H-2 program and is associated with work done by Edwin Reubens.[39] He sets forth two possible new variants of an expanded foreign worker program: "a new H-2 program" and "an improved H-2 program." With regard to the "new" H-2 program, he suggests the possibility of enlarging the existing program "in certain jobs" for periods of one year with renewals of up to three years. After this period the H-2 holder would have to leave the country and join the pool of job seekers back in his or her country. The next cohort of job seekers would not be admitted until the preceding group had departed as scheduled. The three-year period is designed to overcome the objection of labor unions that short-term workers are hard to unionize. The prolonged stay is intended to encourage the foreign workers to develop a commitment to the job as well as to join unions.

Reubens also suggests that the new H-2 program be limited to the expansion of "those jobs of low skill, low paid work which currently are often filled by undocumented aliens and are not very attractive to American unemployed workers."[40] He argues that this has been the focus of the guestworker programs of Western Europe. He states that the complaints about these guestworker programs in Europe have been more related "to local social pressures and disparities than to any undercutting of wages or working conditions"; hence, it would be wise to avoid the social pressures by excluding all dependents of the foreign workers. This requirement, he suggests, should be made clear to all applicants for H-2 permits and those who cannot accept this deprivation "should not volunteer for the program." Furthermore, he suggests that the U.S. Department of Labor should "conduct an outreach program in the source countries" to "ensure that appropriate types and numbers of persons are recruited" that will "meet the actual needs of U.S. labor markets." The wage rates would be set by the U.S. Department of Labor to be at "comparative wage minimums" to those paid to domestic workers. As such, these established rates could be used to "sustain present labor standards," and they could be raised gradually in order to be attractive to more citizen workers.

Reubens does state that, if this proposal is intended to absorb the jobs currently held by undocumented aliens, it would have to enroll "hundreds of thousands" of H-2 holders a year.[41] This, he notes, could easily overburden the existing administrative capability of the appropriate government agencies if any sizable number of persons elected not to leave as scheduled. The thrust of his proposal is designed for workers from Mexico, although he does not explicitly restrict it to them.

A second option offered by Reubens is simply to improve the existing program. This proposal would keep the program to its present small level of magnitude but improve the existing procedures for recruiting citizen workers before relying upon H-2 workers (by establishing better job information channels, upgrading existing jobs, enhancing mobility, and providing more training), and would tighten the existing certification processes for occupations and industries in need of H-2 workers. (It should also be noted that Reubens adds that along the Mexican–U.S. border, "the need for low-level workers at certain times of the year" could be more easily met by simply making it easier to secure green cards for daily crossers.[42] But a green card holder is a resident alien. As discussed earlier, when such a card is issued, the bearer is entitled to hold the card forever and even to become a citizen after five years. It certainly is an error to talk about green cards as a means of meeting seasonal labor needs.)

The Reubens proposal was prepared for the National Commission for Manpower Policy. After considering the proposal, the chairman of this commission, Professor Eli Ginzburg, wrote to the Secretary of Labor that he advised "strongly against" any expanded H-2 program.[43] Included within the Select Commission's final report in 1981 was a similar warning against an expanded H-2 program. Acknowledging that the H-2 program has been a source of criticism, the Commission still concluded that "a continuation of the program is necessary and preferable to the institution of a new one."[44] Several suggestions were made to "streamline" the administration of the program. It recommended that employers be required to pay both Social Security and unemployment compensation payroll taxes on all H-2 workers in order to remove "inducements to hire H-2 workers over U.S. workers."[45] It was also a major conclusion of the Commission that there should not be any new temporary worker program as part of any strategy to combat illegal immigration.[46]

By the time the Commission issued its report, the Carter administration was no longer in office. It fell upon the Reagan administration to respond. It did so by forming a review committee called the Task Force on Immigration and Refugee Policy, chaired by the Attorney General. The Task Force released its response on July 30, 1981. In its report, no mention was made of the H-2 program, but an "experimental temporary worker program for Mexican nationals" was proposed.[47] The new program would be for a two-year trial period and would be limited to 50,000 workers in any given year. The details are sketchy, but the program's outline stated that the workers would be in the United States from nine to twelve months at a time. Geographic and occupational restrictions might be imposed but, subject to these restraints, workers would be free to change employers at will. They would not be bound to any single employer. Also, employers would be required to pay the same payroll taxes applicable to citizen workers. The workers could not bring their families with them and they would be ineligible for most social programs (i.e., food stamps, unemployment compensation, or welfare assistance).

Criticisms of New Foreign Worker Proposals

By common agreement of all of the literature, the effect of the presence of illegal immigrants is disproportionately felt in the low-wage labor markets of the United States. Most of the illegal immigrants—especially those from Mexico and the Caribbean area—are themselves poorly skilled, poorly educated, and have language limitations. Even those persons without these characteristics are often downgraded into the same labor market due to their fear of exposure or their inability to produce proper credentials.

It is not necessary to nitpick the deficiencies of proposals for a new foreign labor program. Obviously all of them are simply conceptual sketches. None has scratched the surface of such critical issues as how the workers are recruited, what are their job entitlements, what are the limitations to be placed on employer prerogatives to limit exploitation, what means are to be used to test for job certification, and what protections are to be included for citizen workers and for unions to assure that prevailing standards are not undermined. Moreover, none of them even considers the fact that the INS is in a current state of total administrative chaos.[48] The INS cannot handle the paperwork associated with the legal immigration system, let alone the illegal immigrants. It is inconceivable that INS could administer a new foreign worker program. All of these matters must, of course, be settled before such a foreign worker program is initiated. But anyone familiar with the history of regulatory efforts associated with the H-2 programs, the bracero programs, and the various border commuter systems knows that the task will be—to put it mildy—formidable.

Aside from these administrative matters, the major criticisms of foreign worker programs are their conceptual design, their impact, and their magnitude. All of these considerations are sufficiently serious to counter any alleged merits they might have.

The rationale for proposals for new foreign worker programs is the existence of illegal entry on a massive scale. It is not based on the existence of a demonstrated need in the labor market. Unemployment rates in the United States are among the highest of any of the Western industrialized nations. Moreover, the unemployment rates among Hispanics, blacks, women, and youth far exceed the national aggregate unemployment rates. All of the proposals (as well as the existing foreign worker programs) are designed exclusively for recruiting more workers for the unskilled and semiskilled occupations in primarily low-wage industries. These are precisely the same secondary labor-market jobs in which those citizen workers with the highest unemployment rates are already found. No one is suggesting that there be a foreign worker program to supply more doctors, professors, lawyers, or business executives. Not only would such proposals lead to charges of a "brain drain" from emerging nations, but also the domestic opposition of these privileged and protected workers in the primary labor market could be counted upon to kill any such idea at the moment of its conception. Rather, it is because it is a program that may benefit the privileged but will adversely affect opportunities for the less fortunate and the least politically organized groups in American society that such proposals are put forth. The proposal for a foreign worker program is clearly class-biased.

There is no evidence at all that citizen workers will not do the work illegal immigrants now do. This fundamental point is asserted—without one shred of empirical evidence to support it—in the works of Piore, Cornelius, and Böhning, to mention only a few.[49] But none of these works cites a single occupation or industry in which they can deny that the vast majority of workers are U.S. citizens. Hence, it cannot be the *type* of work that makes illegal immigrants attractive. Rather, it is the prevailing wage rates and working conditions that determine worker availability. Each year thousands of persons apply for the privilege of collecting garbage in San Francisco and New York City, but they do not do so in many other communities. Why? Because garbage collectors in these two cities are very highly paid, they are unionized, and they enjoy liberal fringe benefit packages. The same can be said of applicants for apprenticeship positions in the building, machinist, and printing trades, where supply always exceeds demand, although the jobs are often dirty, dangerous, and physically demanding. Again, it is *not* the *type* of job, but rather the fact that the associated economic benefits are good that explains why applicants seek such jobs in such great numbers. For the contentions of Piore, Cornelius, and Böhning to be valid they must be willing to argue that, no matter what the wages or benefits associated with certain occupations in the American economy, there will be few people who will want to do the work. Certainly no one can seriously argue this point when it is regularly refuted by everyday practice.

Some studies can show selected labor markets in which illegal immigrants have made a collective impact on certain occupations and certain industries.

They can find employers who hire illegal immigrants and who contend that U.S. citizens are increasingly difficult to find. But it is just as valid as a counter-argument to say that it is precisely because of the presence of sizable numbers of illegal immigrants that citizen workers are more difficult to recruit. In other words, these employer arguments are a self-fulfilling prophecy. It is because illegal immigrants crowd into certain industries that many low-income citizen workers are forced to withdraw. Few citizen workers can satisfactorily compete with illegal immigrants when the ground rules favor whoever will work for the least pay and under the most arbitrary terms. Yet it is for exactly these same low-wage occupations and industries that foreign worker programs would be designed to supply additional workers.

Data on employment patterns of illegal immigrants are limited. Only two studies have made serious efforts to discern this information with any sem-blance of scientific reliability. One was a nationwide study made of appre-hended illegal immigrants by David North and Marion Houstoun in 1976.[50] The second was a study made of unapprehended illegal immigrants in Los Angeles in 1978 by a research team from the University of California at Los Angeles (UCLA).[51] Both studies were funded by the U.S. Department of Labor and both have their limitations, but the conceptual weaknesses of the two tend to be offsetting. The North and Houstoun study was composed entirely of appre-hended illegal immigrants. Because a disproportionate number of appre-hended Mexican illegal immigrants are employed in agriculture, the North and Houstoun study has a bias in the number of farm workers. Conversely, the UCLA study was done entirely within the urban center of Los Angeles. As a result, it disproportionately underestimates the employment of Mexican illegal immigrants in agriculture.

Table 8.1 contains an occupational break-down of the employment patterns from both of these studies. Clearly, the illegal immigrants are concentrated in the unskilled occupations of farm workers, service workers, and nonfarm laborers, as well as the semiskilled occupations of operatives. A significant number are also in the skilled blue collar occupation of craft workers.

In comparison, Table 8.2 shows a distribution of the occupational patterns in the United States of *all* workers; of all Hispanic workers (i.e., Mexicans, Cubans, Puerto Ricans, and others of Spanish origin); all workers of Mexican origin; and all black workers for 1977. The match between the data contained in Table 8.1 and that in Table 8.2 is almost perfect. With respect to Chicanos (i.e., those persons of Mexican origin who are citizen workers), it is obvious that they are employed disproportionately in exactly the same occupations as most illegal immigrants. The employment pattern of Chicanos, in fact, far more closely resembles the pattern of illegal immigrants than it does the distribution pattern of all U.S. workers. The fact that both Chicano workers and illegal immigrants are geographically highly concentrated in the same selected urban and rural labor markets of the five states of the Southwest makes it certain that the two groups are highly competitive in the same labor markets. These figures should dispel the myth that somehow illegal immigrants take only the jobs that U.S. citizens shun.

The data on blacks in Table 8.2 is given only to document the millions of

Table 8.1   Distribution among Occupations by Percentage of Illegal Immigrants, from Two Research Studies Prepared for the U.S. Department of Labor

	Detention site study 1974–75[a] all apprehended aliens	Los Angeles Community Study 1972–1975[b]		
		Total	Previously apprehended aliens	Never apprehended aliens
White collar	5.4	10.5	6.6	12.1
Professional and technical	1.6	4.3	2.7	5.0
Managers and administrators	1.3	0.7	.8	.7
Salesworkers	1.1	1.9	.8	2.3
Clerical	1.4	3.6	2.3	4.1
Blue collar	55.2	73.0	79.0	70.4
Craft workers	15.3	28.8	32.8	27.1
Operatives	25.1	31.8	31.1	32.1
Nonfarm laborers	14.8	12.4	15.1	11.2
Service workers	20.6	16.1	14.2	16.9
Farm workers	18.8	.4	.2	.5
Total percent	100.0	100.0	100.0	100.0

Source: [a]David S. North and Marion F. Houstoun, *The Characteristics and Role of Illegal Aliens in the U.S. Labor Market: An Exploratory Study* (Washington, D.C.: Linton & Company, 1976), p. 104.

[b]Maurice D. Van Arsdol Jr., Joan Moore, David Heer, Susan P. Haynie, *Non-Apprehended and Apprehended Undocumented Residents in the Los Angeles Labor Market.* Final Draft submitted to the U.S. Department of Labor under Research Contract No. 20-06-77-16 (October 1978), p. 95.

citizen workers who are employed in the same occupations as illegal immigrants. Black workers, of course, are not geographically concentrated in the same labor markets as Chicanos or Mexican illegal immigrants. But nonetheless, in a number of specific labor markets (e.g., in Los Angeles, San Antonio, and Houston) they do compete. Likewise, it is increasingly the case that black workers in labor markets in the East and in the north-central states are feeling the adverse effects of competition from illegal immigrants from nations other than Mexico.[52]

As every economist knows, it is impossible to separate the employment effects from the wage effects whenever there is a change in the supply of labor.[53] Hence, the presence of foreign workers would not only affect job opportunities

Table 8.2   Distribution among Occupations by Percentage of All Employed Persons in the United States: All Employed Hispanic Persons, All Employed Mexican Origin Persons, and All Employed Black Persons, 1977

	All U.S. workers		All hispanics		Mexican origin		Black workers	
Total employed	90,546,000		3,938,000		2,335,000		9,812,000	
Percentage	100.0		100.0		100.0		100.0	
White collar	49.9		31.7		27.2		35.3	
Professional and technical		15.1		7.4		5.6		11.8
Managers and administrators		10.7		5.6		4.9		4.8
Salesworkers		6.3		3.7		3.0		2.6
Clerical		17.8		15.0		13.7		16.1
Blue collar	33.3		46.6		49.3		37.6	
Craft workers		13.1		13.7		15.0		9.0
Operatives		11.4		20.9		20.4		15.1
Transport operatives		3.8		4.1		4.6		5.2
Nonfarm laborers		5.0		7.9		9.3		8.3
Service workers	13.7		17.1		16.5		25.0	
Farm workers	3.0		4.4.		6.9		2.2	

Source: Morris Newman, "A Profile of Hispanics in the U.S. Work Force," *Monthly Labor Review* (December 1978), pp. 3–13; and *Employment and Training Report of the President, 1979* (Washington: U.S. Government Printing Office, 1979), pp. 262–63.

but also affect wage levels in any given labor market. The wage effects are part of the attractiveness of illegal immigrants to American employers. These employers are able to obtain workers at less cost than would be the case in their absence. This does *not* mean that most employers exploit these workers by paying wages below the federal minimum wage. Obviously, some malevolent employers do pay lower than legal wages, but this is clearly the exception in the present era. Available research shows that most illegal immigrants do receive at least the federal minimum wage, and many receive much more.[54] A foreign worker program, therefore, would not serve as a means of raising wages to the established federal wage floor, since most illegal immigrants are already at that level or beyond. Rather, its presence would modulate against pressures for wages to increase in the low-wage labor market over time.

Most of the wage exploitation that occurs at present is simply the result of the fact that illegal immigrants are available at wage rates that are lower than they would be if the same employers had to hire only citizen workers. This situation, of course, can only be exacerbated by the additional supply of foreign workers. This is exactly the impact that the braceros had in the past. The thorough report on the bracero program by the President's Commission on Migratory Labor found, with respect to wage levels for agricultural workers, "that wages by states were inversely related to the supply of alien labor."[55] Likewise, North's comprehensive study of the commuters found that the minimum wage was essentially the prevailing wage for most commuters.[56] From the fact that the border region contains the three poorest standard metropolitan statistical areas in the country (Brownsville, McAllen, and El Paso), plus the facts that the unemployment rates all along the border are consistently above national rates (frequently they are in double digits) and the labor force participation rates (especially among women) are among the lowest in the nation, it is obvious what the employment and wage effects of a foreign worker program will be upon citizen workers in the secondary labor market.

But the real cause for exploitation is that foreign workers can be expected to be docile workers. Citizen workers know that they have job entitlements, which include minimum wage protection and also extend into a number of other areas, such as overtime pay provisions, safety requirements, equal employment opportunity protection, and collective bargaining rights. It is these additional employee entitlements that an employer can often escape if foreign workers are available. For even though foreign workers (and illegal immigrants too, for that matter) may technically be covered by these work standards, their presence creates a situation in which these safeguards cannot be guaranteed in practice; since enforcement mechanisms for most of these laws are based largely upon employee complaints or actions. It is highly unlikely that foreign workers will know their rights. Even if they are so knowledgeable, they will probably be reluctant to do anything about abuses for fear of losing their jobs. In fact, given the job alternatives available in their native lands, they may not even perceive the violations are being exploitative.

As for unionization, the occupations in which illegal immigrants and commuters are concentrated are rarely unionized at present. The availability of foreign workers will virtually guarantee that unionization will not occur in these labor markets. Hence, a foreign worker program would definitely function as an antiunion device.

Even if the wage rates that an employer must pay are identical for foreign workers and for citizen workers, the foreign workers will be preferred. The probability that foreign workers will be less likely to make demands for job rights or to join unions will make them highly prized. Thus, these will be the critical considerations that will provide, as they now do, the crucial advantages for employers in hiring illegal immigrants.

Another flaw in these proposals is their intended magnitude. A foreign worker program cannot do anything to reduce illegal immigration unless the program is significant in size (at least in the 500,000- to 750,000-person range). But the larger the program, the greater the certainty of adverse impact on citizens. On the other hand, if the scale of the program is small, where will be the deterrence to illegal entry? There must be some limitation on the size of the program and, if there is, what will prevent others, who are not selected, from coming, or others, whose period of work has expired but who wish to remain, from staying? All of the unresolved features of the present system (i.e., employer sanctions, the identification question, amnesty, the use of the voluntary departure system, and the budget and personnel deficiencies of the INS) would remain. A foreign worker program does not resolve any of the current policy problems, but it certainly adds a host of new ones. Certainly, no move should be made even to consider a foreign worker program until all of the ancillary questions are settled.

Moreover, most of the discussions of the foreign worker option assume, implicitly or explicitly, that the program would be a bilateral arrangement with Mexico. This has certainly been true of past experience. But times have changed in both Mexico and the United States. Indeed, it is no accident that the momentum for immigration reform began in the 1960s and 1970s when there was heightened domestic interest in civil rights and the eradication of poverty.[57] The point is that illegal immigrants are streaming into the United States from almost every country in the world. President Carter's message accompanying his immigration proposals stated that 60 countries are "regular" sources of illegal immigration.[58] Fifteen countries have been identified as the major source countries of illegal immigrants.[59] Although about 90 percent of the illegal immigrants apprehended annually are from Mexico, this is merely the result of the concentration of INS apprehension techniques on undocumented entrants in the Southwest. It is doubtful if Mexicans compose as much as 60 percent of the total stock of illegal immigrants in the United States. There are millions of other illegal immigrants who are not Mexicans. Generally, they enter the country with proper documents but overstay their visas. Many face situations of economic deprivation and political persecution at home that are worse than those conditions confronting Mexicans. In fact, compared to many other countries in the Caribbean, Central America, and South America, economic life in Mexico is considerably better.[60] Many of these other countries in the Caribbean—such as Haiti, the Dominican Republic, Jamaica, Barbados, and Trinidad—have large black populations; all of them (and others) are regular sources of "visa abusers." In many instances, the question is not why so many of them seek entry into the United States but, rather, why any of them stay behind, given the bleak futures that confront them. The same can be said of many Asians from Hong Kong, Korea, the Philippines, and Singapore, which are also major sources of illegal immigration. Hence, it is very unlikely that any foreign worker program could be or should be restricted to workers from Mexico. If it were, it would be a racist proposal and it would have nothing to offer as a solution to illegal entry from other nations of the world.

In addition, the proposals for a foreign worker program completely neglect all of the experience that the United States has had (as well as many cases in Europe) with foreign worker programs.[61] Specifically, when workers come from economically less-developed countries to a country such as the United States, they are made aware of opportunities often beyond their wildest imagination. The relatively higher wages and the broader array of job opportunities will create, as they have in the past, a tendency for many to remain. A situation is also set up in which children are born and marriages occur. Both of these actions involve potential claims for citizenship. In the United States, with its multiracial and multiethnic groups, it is far more likely that these pressures will occur than would ever be the case in Europe. Rather than reduce the costs of uncontrolled immigration to American society, a foreign worker program will only add to the problem.

Concluding Observations

H. L. Mencken once quipped that "For every complex problem there is always a simple answer—and it is always wrong." A foreign worker program is no answer to the complex problem of illegal immigration. To be effective, it would have to be substantial in size; but if it were substantial in size, it would clearly have an adverse impact on certain segments of the domestic labor force. Furthermore, even if it were conceptually feasible, the INS, as now staffed and budgeted, is totally incapable of administering such a program without its becoming a fiasco. Likewise, it is also very doubtful that the Department of Labor could handle such a program.

A foreign worker program would certainly increase illegal immigration by exposing more foreign workers to the economic attractions of the American labor market. It would also adversely affect job and income opportunities for many of the persons in the American economy who are the least able to defend themselves from competition. It is not surprising, therefore, that a 1979 conference on "Jobs for Hispanics"—sponsored by the Labor Council for Latin American Advancement and attended by both Hispanic trade unionist and many nonunionists from Hispanic community groups across the country—took a strong and unanimous stand against a foreign worker program. In their conference manifesto, called the "Declaration of Albuquerque," they called for a number of policy changes that would be beneficial for and protective of illegal immigrants. But with respect to the idea of a "guestworker" program, they emphatically stated: "The federal government should *not* include any type of 'Bracero' program or foreign labor importation, as a solution to the current problem of undocumented workers."[62]

Foreign worker programs are of interest to employers only as a means of reducing their costs of production or enhancing their control over their workers, who are completely dependent upon their employers.[63] Citizen workers who compete with foreign workers will find, as in the past, that their existing work conditions usually become frozen or decline. Under few circumstances will they improve. Efforts to establish unions are thwarted or, at a minimum, made more difficult. These callous motivations should not be rewarded.

A foreign worker program will in no way diminish the need to reform the existing immigration system of the United States. Until the system is made capable of accomplishing its stated goals of effectively regulating the flow of immigrants into the United States, illegal immigration will flourish regardless of the existence of a foreign worker program. But if such a program were enacted, it might deceive some people into thinking that an answer had been provided. Indeed, a foreign worker program has great political attractiveness *because* it gives the appearance of being a remedy while avoiding the necessity of taking the actions that are mandatory for the achievement of an end to illegal immigration.

In 1980, the United States admitted over 808,000 legal immigrants and refugees. This is a commendable attribute of American society, for not only did the number exceed the total legal immigrants admitted by all the remaining nations of the world combined, but the admissions were essentially on a nondiscriminatory basis. This accomplishment should not be allowed to be tarnished by the continued flow of millions of others who have flouted the legal system by illegal entry. The proposals for a foreign worker program must be recognized as being simply a placebo: they offer an immaginary remedy to a real problem. Such an idea is not neutral in its long-term effects, since it can only make an already bad situation much worse. What is offered as a tonic is actually toxic.

Notes

1. By its very nature as an illegal activity, the stock of illegal immigrants in the United States at any one time cannot be measured accurately. Especially with respect to Mexico, there is the problem of flow: some illegal immigrants come and go all the time. Precise figures, therefore, are nonexistent. The range of figures cited in the text is drawn from the following partial list of relevant studies of the issue of illegal immigration: Wayne Cornelius, *Mexican Migration to the United States: Causes, Consequences, and U.S. Responses* (Cambridge: Center for International Studies, Massachusetts Institute of Technology, 1978); Walter Fogel, *Mexican Illegal Alien Workers in the United States* (Los Angeles: Institute of Industrial Relations, University of California, 1978); Immigration and Naturalization Service, *Annual Report 1974* (Washington, D.C.: U.S. Government Printing Office, 1974); Lesko Associates, "Final Report: Basic Data and Guidance Required to Implement a Major Illegal Alien Study During Fiscal Year 1976,"mimeographed (Washington, D.C.: Lesko Associates, 1975); David S. North and Marion F. Houstoun, *The Characteristics and Role of Illegal Aliens in the U.S. Labor Market: An Exploratory Study* (Washington, D.C.: Linton and Company, 1975); Jacob S. Siegal et al., "Preliminary Review of Existing Studies of the Number of Illegal Residents in the United States," mimeographed report prepared by the U.S. Bureau of the Census, January 1980.

2. Select Commission on Immigration and Refugee Policy, *U.S. Immigration Policy and the National Interest* (Washington, D.C.: U.S. Government Printing Office, 1981), p. 5.

3. Gilbert Merkx, "A Review of the Issues and Groups Involved in Undocumented Immigration to the United States," in *The Problem of the Undocumented Worker*, edited by Robert S. Landmann (Albuquerque: University of New Mexico Press, 1979).

4. Vernon M. Briggs, Jr., "La Confrontacion Del Chicano Con El Immigrante Mexicano," *Foro Internacional* 18, no. 3 (1978): 514–21.

5. Philip L. Martin, *Guestworker Programs: Lessons from Europe*, Monograph no. 5 (Washington, D.C.: Bureau of International Labor Affairs, U.S. Department of Labor, 1980).

6. Select Commission, *U.S. Immigration Policy*, p. 45.

7. U.S. Department of Justice, "U.S. Immigration and Refugee Policy" (July 30, 1981), p. 5 (mimeographed materials). See also Robert Pear, "Reagan Aides Draft a Plan to Let Mexicans Work in U.S. as Guests," *The New York Times*, May 11, 1981, p. A-1.

8. George C. Kiser and Martha Woody Kiser, *Mexican Workers in the United States: Historical and Political Perspectives* (Albuquerque: The University of New Mexico Press, 1979), chap. 1.

9. *U.S. Statutes at Large* 34, part 1, pp. 874–98.

10. Kiser and Kiser, *Mexican Workers in the United States*, p. 10.

11. The term *bracero* is a corruption of the Spanish word *abrazo* which means "arm." Literally, the term means "one who works with his arms."

12. Henry C. Kiser, "Mexican American Labor Before World War II," *Journal of Mexican American History* 2 (1972): 130.

13. Ernesto Galarza, *Merchants of Labor: The Mexican Bracero Story* (Charlotte, N.C.: McNally and Loftin, 1964); Richard Craig, *The Bracero Program: Interest Groups and Foreign Policy* (Austin: University of Texas Press, 1971); and Carey McWilliams, *North From Mexico* (New York: Greenwood Press, 1968), pp. 265–67.

14. President's Commission on Migratory Labor, *Migratory Labor in American Agriculture: Report* (Washington, D.C.: U.S. Government Printing Office, 1951), pp. 56–59; also H. N. Delton, "Foreign Agricultural Workers and the Prevention of Adverse Effect," *Labor Law Journal* (December 1966): 739–48; and Donald Wise, "The Effect of the Bracero on Agricultural Production in California," *Economic Inquiry* (December 1974): 547–55.

15. Vernon M. Briggs, Jr., *Chicanos and Rural Poverty* (Baltimore: Johns Hopkins University Press, 1973), p. 29.

16. See Vernon M. Briggs, Jr., *The Mexican-United States Border: Public Policy and Chicano Economic Welfare Studies*, Human Resource Development No. 2 (Austin: Bureau of Business Research, 1974), pp. 6–9; David S. North, "A Preliminary Analysis of INS Apprehension Data, 1970–78," mimeographed (Washington, D.C.: Trans-Century Corporation, 1979); and the projections to 1991 in "Illegal Aliens: Estimating Their Impact on the United States," in *Report of Comptroller General to the U.S. Congress* (Washington, D.C.: U.S. General Accounting Office, 1980), pp. 82–83.

17. *Annual Report: Immigration and Naturalization Service: 1977* (Washington, D.C.: U.S. Government Printing Office, 1978), p. 21.

18. David S. North, *The Border Crossers: People Who Live in Mexico and Work in the United States* (Washington, D.C.: Trans-Century Corporation, 1970), p. 72.

19. Anna-Stina Ericson, "The Impact of Commuters on the Mexican-American Border Area," *Monthly Labor Review* (August 1979): 18.

20. This estimate (or guesstimate) was provided to the author by officials of the San Antonio district office of the Immigration and Naturalization Service in 1978.

21. *Karnuth v. Albro*, 279 U.S. 231 (1929).

22. Sheldon L. Greene, "Public Agency Distortion of Congressional Will: Federal Policy Toward Non-Resident Alien Labor," *George Washington Law Review* (March 1972): 442, citing 8 C.F.R. 211.1 (b) (1) 1971.

23. Ibid., p. 443, citing 8 U.S. 65 (1974).

24. *Saxbe v. Bustos*, 419 U.S. 65 (1974).

25. U.S. Congress, House of Representatives, Committee on the Judiciary, Subcommittee No. 1, *Study of Population and Immigration Problems* No. 11 (1963), p. 62.

26. Fred H. Schmidt, *Spanish Surnamed American Employment in the Southwest* (Washington, D.C.: U.S. Equal Employment Opportunity Commission, 1970), p. 62.

27. E.g., see discussion in Gilberto Cardenas, "Manpower Impact and Problems of Mexican Illegal Aliens in an Urban Labor Market" (Ph.D. dissertation, University of Illinois, 1976), p. 31.

28. E.g., see "Violence, Often Unchecked, Pervades U.S. Border Patrol," *New York Times*, January 14, 1980, p. D-8.

29. U.S. Congress, Senate Committee on Labor and Public Welfare, Subcommittee on Migratory Labor, *Hearings on Migrant and Seasonal Farmworker Powerlessness*, 91st and 2nd sessions, pt. 5-A, p. 2145.

30. Leo Grebler, Joan W. Moore, and Ralph Guzman, *The Mexican American People* (New York: Free Press, 1970), p. 73.

31. 8 U.S.C. Section 1101 (a) (15) (H) (ii).

32. Philip Martin and David North, "Nonimmigrant Aliens in American Agriculture," Paper presented at the Conference on Seasonal Agricultural Labor Markets in the United States, Washington, D.C., January 10, 1980, p. 9.

33. Ibid., pp.12–13.
34. Ibid., p. 20.
35. W. R. Böhning, "Regularizing Undocumentados," World Employment Programme, Working Paper no. 36 (Geneva: International Labour Organization, 1979), p. 7.
36. Ibid., p. 11.
37. Charles B. Keely, *U.S. Immigration: A Policy Analysis* (New York: The Population Council, 1979), p. 60.
38. Ibid., p. 61.
39. Edwin Reubens, *Temporary Admission of Foreign Workers: Dimensions and Policies*, Special Report no. 34 of the National Commission for Manpower Policy (Washington, D.C.: U.S. Government Printing Office, 1979).
40. Ibid., p. 59.
41. Ibid., p. 60.
42. Ibid., p. 69.
43. Letter to Secretary of Labor Ray Marshall from Eli Ginzberg, chairman of the National Commission for Manpower Policy, dated May 1, 1979, p. 2.
44. Select Commission, *U.S. Immigration Policy*, p. 227.
45. Ibid., p. 228.
46. Ibid., p. 45.
47. U.S. Department of Justice, "U.S. Immigration and Refugee Policy," p. 5.
48. See the five-part series "The Tarnished Door: Crisis in Immigration" in the *New York Times*, January 13 through January 17, 1980.
49. Michael J. Piore, *Birds of Passage: Migrant Labor and Industrial Societies* (New York: Cambridge University Press, 1979), chap. 2; Cornelius, *Mexican Migration to the United States*; and Böhning, "Regularizing Undocumentados."
50. North and Houstoun, *Characteristics and Role of Illegal Aliens*, p. 104.
51. Maurice D. Van Arsdol Jr., Joan Moore, David Heer, and Susan Haynie, *Non-Apprehended and Apprehended Undocumented Residents in the Los Angeles Labor Market* (Final draft submitted to the U.S. Department of Labor under Research Contract No. 20-06-77-16, October 1978), p. 95.
52. Jacquelyn J. Jackson, "Illegal Aliens: Big Threat to Black Workers," *Ebony*, April 1979, pp. 33–40.
53. Fogel, *Mexican Illegal Alien Workers*, chaps. 6 and 7.
54. North and Houstoun, *Characteristics and Role of Illegal Aliens*, pp. 128–30. This does not mean that the problem of payment below the minimum wage is unimportant. It is a serious problem, but it merely is not the general case.
55. President's Commission on Migratory Labor, p. 59.
56. North, *The Border Crossers*, pp. 110–21.
57. Vernon M. Briggs, Jr., "Migration as a Socio-Political Phenomenon," Paper presented at the International Conference on Border Relations, La Paz, Baja California, Mexico, February 28, 1980.
58. Office of the White House Press Secretary, "Message of the President to Congress on Illegal Immigration," mimeographed (Washington, D.C., August 4, 1977), p. 7.
59. Domestic Council of the White House, "Preliminary Report of the Domestic Council Committee on Illegal Immigrants" (Washington, D.C.: Domestic Council, December 1976), p. 39. (This report was subsequently made the final report of the Committee.)
60. Calvin P. Blair, "Mexico: Some Recent Developments," *Texas Business Review* (May 1977): 98–103.
61. E.g., see Ray C. Rist, "Migration and Marginality: Guestworkers in Germany and France," *Daedalus*, Spring 1979, pp. 95–108.
62. Labor Council for Latin American Advancement, "Declaration of Albuquerque and Employment Action Program," Conference Report of the National Conference on Jobs for Hispanics, August 1979, p. 10. (Emphasis is in the original.)
63. David North and Allen LeBel, *Manpower and Immigration Policies in the United States*, Special Report no. 20 of the National Commission for Manpower Policy (Washington, D.C.: U.S. Government Printing Office, 1978), p. 215.

Index

Abuses, of Mexican workers in U.S., 54, 60–61, 75, 78, 80. See also Discrimination; Exploitation

Adverse effects on domestic labor: of alien workers, 15–16, 19, 25, 223, 235–38, 242; of bracero program, 65, 73–75, 225–26, 240; of commuters, 230; denied, 74, 198–99; of H-2 program, 198, 207–8, 231–32

"Adverse effect" wage rates, 207, 231

Agrarian reform. See Land reform

Agreements: bilateral (see Bilateral agreements); as source of obligation, 20, 34–35, 37

Agriculture, Department of, 56

Agriculture, Mexican: adverse effects of migration on, 59, 63, 67, 71, 89n.56; attitude toward, 174; crisis of, 168, 178–79, 180; development in, 141–43, 148, 149, 150–52, 156, 165–67, 180; productivity in, 141, 142–43, 149–50, 152–53, 156; surplus labor in, 23, 163, 164, 193. See also Irrigation; Rainfed agriculture

Agriculture, U.S.: adverse effects of migration in, 73–75, 207–8, 226; lobby, 70, 73; migrant labor in, 51, 56, 76, 191, 195, 196, 197, 207, 225, 226; perceived shortages in, 49, 57, 61, 197, 207–8

Aleman, Miguel, 166

Aliens, numbers of, 188–91, 218–20n.1–4

Aliens, rights of, 25, 33, 132–33, 214; obligations to respect, 35–36, 93; obligations to uphold, 36–37, 40–41, 43; restrictions on, 31, 33, 34–35, 37–38, 38–41, 100; undocumented, 41–43

American Convention on Human Rights, 33

American Farm Bureau, 60

Amnesty, for undocumented workers, 31, 43, 103, 200, 206, 241

Anderson, Clinton P., 64

Arizpe, Lourdes, 23

Article 123, 54, 226

Asylum: duty to grant, 42; right to, 33

Austria, migration in, 101, 123

Autonomy: of persons, 32, 34, 37, 40; of states, 35, 36

Bargaining position, Mexican: 57, 60, 62, 67–70

Basic rights, 19, 28n.11. See also Fundamental rights

Baučić, I., 118

Beans, 142, 148; self-sufficiency in, 149, 152–53

Belgium, migration in, 101, 103, 123

Benefits, of migration: to consumers, 17, 19, 25, 200; to employers (see Employers, benefits of migration to); to Mexico, 25–26, 212 (see also Escape valve; Safety valve); to migrants, 26, 193, 203; to U.S., 53, 181, 196–200

Bentham, Jeremy, 17

Bhagwati, J. N., and A. Partington, 206

Bilateral agreements, 49, 54, 55–56, 59–60, 65, 69, 70, 71, 241

Bi-modal development, 141, 142–43, 155–56, 166–167. See also Economic dualism

Birth control, 192

Blacklisting, by Mexican government of U.S. areas and growers, 60, 61, 67, 68

Blacks, employment of, 57, 236, 237–39, 241. See also Minorities

Böhning, W. R., 232–33, 236

Böhning Plan, 232–33

Border communities: commuters in, 227–29, 230; effects of migration on, 62, 212, 226; Maquiladora program in, 77, 193

Border commuters, 227–30

Border industrialization program. See Maquiladora program

Border Patrol, 54, 64, 65, 71, 92n.97

Boundaries, moral significance of, 21–22, 35, 40, 213–14

Bracero program, 171, 178, 191, 225–27; adverse effects of, 65, 73–75, 225–26, 240; chronology of, 81–84; exploitation under, 70, 80, 209, 231–32; first, 54, 225; 1942–1946, 55–62; 1947–54, 62–73; 1955–1964, 73–76; as stimulating illegal immigration, 67, 80, 226–27; as substitute for illegal immigration, 65, 66, 76, 77, 78, 80, 191; and U.S. responsibility, 23, 24, 226–27

Braun, R., 118, 119

Briggs, Vernon, 197, 198, 199, 210, 216

Brownell, Herbert, 65

Bureau of Employment Security, 73

Bureau of Immigration, 53, 54

Bustamante, Jorge, 78, 162, 178

California, 57, 59, 62, 65, 74–75, 199, 227

Capital-intensity, 168, 169, 192–94

Capitalism, and migration, 106, 107, 164, 165, 180

Cárdenas, Lázaro, 53, 141, 151, 156, 165

Carter, Jimmy, 212, 224, 241

Carter administration, 31, 223, 232, 235

Cash-crops, 168–69, 171, 172, 173, 176

Castillo, INS Commissioner, 113

CENIET study, 178, 190

Census Bureau, U.S., 190–91, 195

Chicanos, 224, 226; employment patterns of, 237–39

Choice of employment: in European guestworker programs, 101, 104, 133, 209; in proposed programs, 208, 209, 232–33; right to, 134, 213

Citizenship: eligibility for, 31, 206, 217, 227, 228, 229, 230; and human rights, 36, 37, 42

Civil rights, 17, 33, 38, 215; of aliens, 37–38, 200, 209

Comité Nacional de Repatriación, 52

Commission de Rio Balsas, 143

Common Nordic Labour Market, 101, 133

Compensation, 21; to Mexico, 22, 214–15; to source countries, 205–6, 213

Competition: of border commuters with native workers, 228, 229–30; of braceros with native workers, 74–75, 226; of foreign workers with na-

The Editors and Contributors

Peter G. Brown is Associate Dean of the School of Public Affairs of the University of Maryland at College Park and was founding director of the Center for Philosophy and Public Policy. He is coeditor (with Henry Shue) of *Boundaries: National Autonomy and Its Limits* and *Food Policy: The Responsibility of the United States in the Life and Death Choices;* and of *Human Rights and U.S. Foreign Policy.*

Henry Shue is Acting Director of the Center for Philosophy and Public Policy of the University of Maryland at College Park. His work includes *Basic Rights: Subsistence, Affluence, and U.S. Foreign Policy;* and *Food Policy: The Responsibility of the United States in the Life and Death Choices* and *Boundaries: National Autonomy and Its Limits,* both of which he coedited with Peter G. Brown.

Lourdes Arizpe is a Guggenheim Fellow at the Institute for Development Studies, University of Sussex, and a member of the faculty of El Colegio de México. She is the author of *Migración, Etnicismo y Cambio, Indigenas en la Ciudad: El Caso de las 'Mariaso' Sep-Setentas,* and *Parentesco y Economia en una Sociedad Nahua.*

Roger Böhning is a staff member of the International Labour Office, Geneva, with special responsibility for questions of international migration. His books include *The Migration of Workers in the United Kingdom and the European Community* and *Towards a System of Recompense for International Labour Migration.*

Vernon M. Briggs, Jr., is Professor of Labor Economics and Human Resource Studies at Cornell University and a member of the National Council on Employment Policy. He is coauthor of *Chicanos and Rural Poverty: The Chicano Worker, Employment, Income, and Welfare in the Rural South,* and *Labor Economics: Wages, Employment, and Trade Unionism.*

Manuel García y Griego is the author of *El volumen de la Migración de Mexicanos No Documentados a los Estados Unidos (Neuvas Hipótesis).* He is a member of the faculty of El Colegio de México, and coeditor of *Mexican–U.S. Relations: Toward Conflict or Convergence?* (forthcoming).

Judith Lichtenberg is a Visiting Research Associate at the Center for Philosophy and Public Policy of the University of Maryland at College Park. She has contributed a chapter to *Boundaries: National Autonomy and Its Limits* and is the author of "The Moral Equivalence of Action and Omission," *Canadian Journal of Philosophy,* Supplementary Volume 8, *New Essays in Ethics and Public Policy,* (forthcoming).

James W. Nickel is Visiting Professor in the Jurisprudence and Social Policy Program of the University of California at Berkeley Law School and Professor of Philosophy at Wichita State University. He has written a number of influential articles on human rights and questions of racial justice in such journals as the

Columbia Law Review, American Philosophical Quarterly, and *Philosophical Forum.*

Edwin P. Reubens is Professor of Economics at the City College of the City University of New York. He has been a consultant on labor, migration, and development to the United Nations, the U.S. Agency for International Development, the Select Commission on Immigration and Refugee Policy, and the National Commission for Employment Policy, for which he wrote Report No. 34. He is a contributor to *U.S.-Mexican Economic Relations* and to *The Challenge of the New International Economic Order,* edited by Edwin P. Reubens.

August Schumacher is Senior Rural Development Economist with the World Bank. His chapter was developed during a year as visiting scholar at the Harvard Business School. The analysis derives from field work on Mexican agriculture and rural development undertaken from 1972–1980 as part of the World Bank's lending operations in that country.